The Community of Lenin; Memorial Book (Lenin, Belarus)

Translation of
Kehilat Lenin; Sefer Zikaron

Original Book Edited by: M. Tamari

Originally published in Tel Aviv, 1957

JewishGen
מרכז עולמי לגנאלוגיה יהודית
The Global Home for Jewish Genealogy

A Publication of JewishGen
Edmond J. Safra Plaza, 36 Battery Place, New York, NY 10280
646.494.2972 | info@JewishGen.org | www.jewishgen.org

MUSEUM OF JEWISH HERITAGE
A LIVING MEMORIAL TO THE HOLOCAUST

The Community of Lenin; Memorial Book (Lenin, Belarus)
Translation of *Kehilat Lenin; Sefer Zikaron*

Copyright © 2025 by JewishGen. All rights reserved.
First Printing: September 2025, Elul, 5785
Original Yizkor Book Edited By: M. Tamari
Project Coordinator: Sanford A. Kaplan z"l
Cover Design: Irv Osterer
Layout, formatting and indexing: Jonathan Wind

JewishGen Press is not responsible for inaccuracies or omissions in the original work and makes no representations regarding the accuracy of this translation. Digital images of the original book's contents can be seen online at the New York Public Library website or the Yiddish Book Center website.

Library of Congress Control Number (LCCN): 2025935603

ISBN: 978-1-962054-28-7 (hard cover: 430 pages, alk. paper)

About JewishGen.org

JewishGen, is a Genealogical Research Division of the Museum of Jewish Heritage - A Living Memorial to the Holocaust, serves as the global home for Jewish genealogy.

Featuring unparalleled access to 30+ million records, it offers unique search tools, along with opportunities for researchers to connect with others who share similar interests. Award winning resources such as the Family Finder, Discussion Groups, and ViewMate, are relied upon by thousands each day.

In addition, JewishGen's extensive informational, educational and historical offerings, such as the Jewish Communities Database, Yizkor Book translations, InfoFiles, Family Tree of the Jewish People, and KehilaLinks, provide critical insights, first-hand accounts, and context about Jewish communal and familial life throughout the world.

Offered as a free resource, JewishGen.org has facilitated thousands of family connections and success stories, and is currently engaged in an intensive expansion effort that will bring many more records, tools, and resources to its collections.

Please visit https://www.jewishgen.org/ to learn more.

Dr. Paul Radensky

About the JewishGen Yizkor Book Project

Yizkor Books (Memorial Books) were traditionally written to memorialize the names of departed family and martyrs during holiday services in the synagogue (a practice that still exists in many synagogues today).

Over the centuries, as a result of countless persecutions and horrific atrocities committed against the Jews, Yizkor Books (Sefer Zikaron in Hebrew) were expanded to include more historical information, such as biographical sketches of famous personalities and descriptions of daily town life.

Following the Holocaust, the idea of remembrance and learning took on an urgent and crucial importance. Survivors of the Holocaust sought out other surviving residents of their former towns to memorialize and document the names and way of life of those who were ruthlessly murdered by the Nazis. These remembrances were documented in Yizkor Books, hundreds of which were published in the first decades after the Holocaust.

Most of these books were published privately, or through *Landsmanshaftn* (social organizations comprised of members originating from the same European town or region) that still existed, and were often distributed free of charge. The languages used to document these crucial histories and links to our past were mostly Yiddish and Hebrew. JewishGen has undertaken the sacred responsibility of translating these books into English so that the culture and way of life of these communities will be preserved and transmitted to future generations.

In 1986, a group of farsighted JewishGenners started a project to pool their efforts together in groups based upon their ancestors' towns and donate funds to translate the Yizkor books of their ancestral towns into English. As the translated material became available, it was made accessible for free at https://www.JewishGen.org/Yizkor . Hardcover copies can be purchased by visiting https://www.jewishgen.org/Yizkor/ybip.html (see section below).

It is our hope that the translation of these books into English (and other languages) will assist the countless Jewish family researchers who are so desperately seeking to forge a connection with their heritage.

Director of JewishGen Yizkor Book Project: Lance Ackerfeld

About JewishGen Press

JewishGen Press (formerly the Yizkor Books-in-Print Project) is the publishing division of JewishGen.org, and provides a venue for the publication of non-fiction books pertaining to Jewish genealogy, history, culture, and heritage.

In addition to the Yizkor Book category, publications in the Other Non-Fiction category include Shoah memoirs and research, genealogical research, collections of genealogical and historical materials, biographies, diaries and letters, studies of Jewish experience and cultural life in the past, academic theses, and other books of interest to the Jewish community.

Please visit https://www.jewishgen.org/Yizkor/ybip.html to learn more.

Director of JewishGen Press: Joel Alpert
Managing Editor – Peter Harris
Publications Manager - Susan Rosin

Notes to the Reader

The images in the original book were reproduced from photographs from the time of the first edition. These reproductions were already of poor quality, most being pre-war and others at least 60 or more years old. As a result, the images in the book are the best achievable.
A reader can view the original scans of the book on the websites listed below.

The original book can be seen online at the Yiddish Book Center website:

https://www.yiddishbookcenter.org/collections/yizkor-books/yzk-nybc313851/tamari-moshe-kehilat-lenin-sefer-zikaron

OR

at the New York Public Library Digital Collections website:

https://digitalcollections.nypl.org/items/dc6bfb50-096e-0133-6ce8-58d385a7b928?canvasIndex=0

To obtain a list of Shoah victims from **Lenin (Belarus),** the reader should access the Yad Vashem web site listed below; one can also search for specific family names using family name option. These lists are continually updated by Yad Vashem, so it is worthwhile to periodically search them.

There is more valuable information (including the Pages of Testimony, etc.) available on this website: https://yvng.yadvashem.org/

A list of all books available from JewishGen Press along with prices is available at: https://www.jewishgen.org/Yizkor/ybip.html

Cover Photo Credits

Cover Design: Irv Osterer

Front Cover:

The Tarbut School, 1928   [Page 139]

In the top row:
Shimon Shusterman, from Moritz in Argentina, Yitzhak Yulevich son of
Alter. Moshe Boktzin(in Israel), Yitzhak son of Assana, Avraham Lilenberg (in Israel).
Second row from top:
Leah Margolin daughter of Libbe, Babel Chinitz daughter of the
Cantor (in Israel), Hannah Chinitz daughter of Shmuel, Hannah Zaretzki daughter of
Reba, Batya Zaichik daughter of Aharon-Leib, Sarah Zaichik daughter of Shaindel.
The third row, the teachers:
 Yehuda Rubenstein, Pepperberg Morsha. Meir Boktzin (in Israel), Aharon-Lev Zaichik.
Bottom row: Shmuel Mishelov, Tcharna Vacharbin (in Israel), Zema Schneidman.

Back Cover:

The First School in Lenin, 1913 [Page 138]

In the center of the bottom row, the teachers:
Aharon-Leib Zaichik (killed by the Nazis), Haim Shalev (Nakritz) (in Israel), Yoshke Boktzin (in America).
In the top row:
Second from the right: Asher Tcherin (son of Avraham Yitzhak), the tenth - Mishal Schmelkin son of
Zashama (died in Israel), the fourteenth – Yaakov Yulevich (son of Nahum Natan), the fifteenth - Dov
Migdalovich (son of Moshe Nisan), the nineteenth - Menashe Yulevich (son of Yisrael), the third from the
left – Elka Kolpanitsky (daughter of Bezalel).
Second row:
Eirst on the right: Haim Slutsky (son of Yisrael), fourth - Eliyahu Nakritz, fifth - Nahum Nakritz (sons of
Isser),
sixth - Dov Zaichik, seventh - Mordechai Zaichik (sons of Aharon Leib), eighth - David Golob-Yonai (son of
Hunia), thirteenth – Masha Azier (daughter of Yitzhak).
Bottom row:
First on the right: Menashe Latocha (son of Moshe), thirteenth – Pinhas Zaretzki (son of Moshe Reuven),
sixteenth - Tzvi (Hirshl) Grib (son of Arye), second from left - Sonia Rubenstein (daughter of Shayma).
All are in Israel.

Geopolitical Information

ESTONIA

2012 Border — ·········· **1940 Border**

BELARUS

0 25 50 75 km

0 25 50 75 miles

Riga

LATVIA

RUSSIA

LITHUANIA

Vilnius

Kaliningrad

BELARUS

Minsk

POLAND

Warsaw

Lenin

UKRAINE

Kyiv

Lviv

Map of Belarus showing the location of **Lenin**

Lenin

Lenin, Belarus is located at 52°20' N 27°29' E 108 miles S of Minsk

	Town	District	Province	Country
Before WWI (c. 1900):	Lenin	Mozyr	Minsk	Russian Empire
Between the wars (c. 1930):	Lenin	Łuniniec	Polesie	Poland
After WWII (c. 1950):	Lenin			Soviet Union
Today (c. 2000):	Lenin			Belarus

Alternate Names for the Town:

Lenin [Rus, Bel, Yid, Pol], Lenino

Nearby Jewish Communities:

Mikashevichi 8 miles S
Zhytkavichy 18 miles ESE
Lakhva 18 miles WSW
Skavshin 20 miles NE
Remel 21 miles SSW
Turov 21 miles SSE
Kazhan-Haradok 21 miles WSW
Davyd-Haradok 23 miles SSW
Starobin 28 miles N
Luninyets 29 miles WSW

Jewish Population: 753 (in 1897), 928 (in 1921)

Table of Contents

Yiddish

The Community of Lenin; Memorial Book (Lenin, Belarus)

52°20' / 27°29'

Translation of
Kehilat Lenin; Sefer Zikaron

Edited by: M. Tamari

Published in Tel Aviv, 1957

Acknowledgments

Project Coordinator:

Sanford A. Kaplan z"l

**Our sincere appreciation to Zvi Isers, of Holon, Israel,
for permission to put this material on the JewishGen web site.**

This is a translation of: *Kehilat Lenin; Sefer Zikaron* (The Community of Lenin; Memorial
Book),
Editors: M. Tamari, Tel Aviv, Former Residents of Lenin in Israel and in the USA, 1957 (H,Y,
407 pages).

Note: The original book can be seen online at the NY Public Library site: Lenin

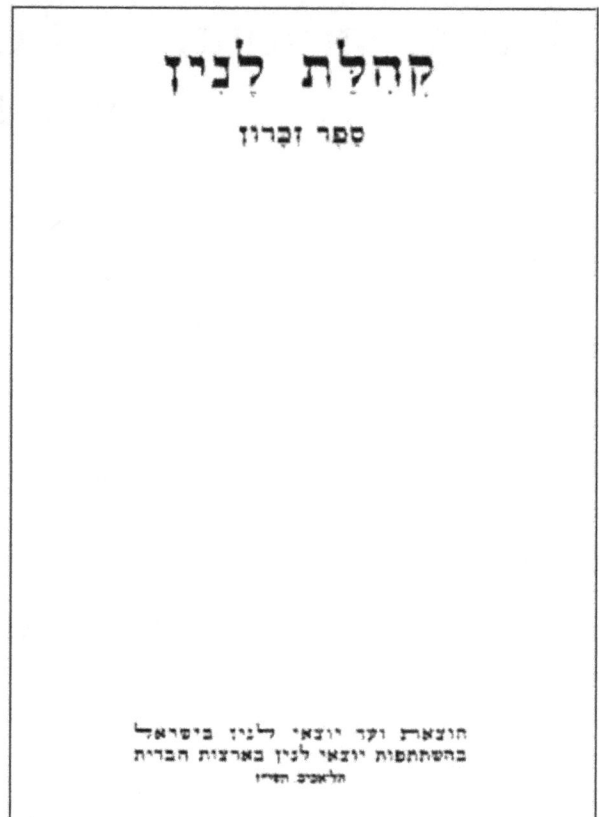

קְהִלַת לֶנִיז

סֵפֶר זִכָּרוֹן

הוצאת ועד יוצאי לעניז בישראל
בהשתתפות יוצאי לעניז בארצות הברית
תל־אביב, תשי"ז

Hebrew

The Story of Lenin

[Page 11]

The Beginnings of Lenin

by Engineer Mordechai Zaichik and Yitzchak Slutsky

(Adapted by Ben-Zion Forman, Tel Aviv)

Translated by Jerrold Landau

A.

We are unable to determine with precision the time of the founding of our town, and we cannot even provide exact statistics about its growth and development during its early days. We do not possess historical documents, for nobody thought of recording all of its annals and the details of what took place with its inhabitants.

From the inscriptions that are engraved on the tombstones in the old cemetery, from looking in the ledgers of the Chevra Kadisha (burial society) and from discussions with elders of the town who heard traditions from their fathers and father's fathers – we can estimate that Lenin was the youngest of its neighbors: Lachwa, Dawid Grodek, Turow, Starobin and others.

What we do know is that at the beginning, the town as a small farming village whose residents were White Russians. Jews began to settle in that region only approximately 250 years ago, at the beginning of the 18th century. When the number of the residents of the village increased, it became a town.

The following are the proofs:

    1.   In the Ledger of the Council of the Four Lands, in the place where it talks about the city of Pinsk and its environs, many towns in "Pulsia" are mentioned, including all the neighbors of our town – Lachwa, Dawid Grodek, Kozhan Grodek, Turow, and others. However, the name of Lenin was not mentioned among them; that is to say, it did not exist in those days.

    2.   In all of the aforementioned towns, all of the residents, Jews and gentiles, were considered as and registered as burghers (Meshchani). Not so in our town – only the Jews were registered as burghers. The Christian residents were considered – until the latter days – as village farmers (Krastiani).

    3.   The elders of the community relate that they heard from their fathers that 200 years ago, the Jewish residents of the town would bring their dead to be buried in the towns of Lachwa, Turow and Starobin. From this it can be deduced that in those days, Lenin had not yet been recognized as a town by the authorities, so the Jewish residents did not have the right to set aside a parcel of land as a cemetery.

Two elders who lived with us here in Israel – Reb Mordechai Yulevich of blessed memory, and, may he live, Reb Avner Yonai (Golob), relate that when they were approximately 40 years old, that is approximately 50 years ago,

[Page 12]

a wooden monument that was rotted at the bottom section was found in the cemetery, tottering and falling over one of the graves. Upon it was engraved the name of a person who was brought to burial approximately 40 years before the weakening of the monument. They were sure that this was the oldest monument in the cemetery. In their opinion, there was no Jewish cemetery in the city until the end of the first half of the 18th century. Only dead babies were buried in a small field in the center of town which was set aside for that purpose, apparently discretely and without the knowledge of the authorities. That is the almost square plot, approximately 10 meters by 8 meters, between the houses of Reb Eliahu Dolgin and Reb Mordechai Steinbok of blessed memory. That plot remained desolate until our day, for the townsfolk were careful not to step upon it or to do any work on it.

From all this, we can state with certainty that our town is at most 250 years old, and that prior to that, a small farming village named Lenin stood on the place.

B.

There are those that claim that the village was called its name after the word for flax, "lion" in Russian, which the farmers would grow in the bogs around the village. Others say that it was called thus after the name of a countess named Lena, the daughter or wife of the estate owner. The name was corrupted by the residents, who would call our town Liolin.

The estate of Lenin was large, approximately 40,000 square kilometers. It was situated between large regions on three sides –Slutsk, Mozir and Pinsk. These large areas were mainly covered by forests and waters – natural marshes, rivers and ponds.

The estate is situation mainly in the areas of Russia known as the Pinsk Marshes or the Pulsia Marshes.

Our town lies modestly in the forests, up to the boundary of this marsh region, as it seems to me. The route that leads northward from the town to the town of Starobin and from there to the regional center of Slutsk approximately 100 kilometers long, passes by forests, fields and meadows – dry areas. This is not the case with the routes that go southward and westward from the town – to the train station of Mikaszewicze and the towns of Luchow and Turow: the forests, fields and meadows are surrounded by marshes and ponds on both sides. The Sluch River that begins near the city of Slutsk and upon whose banks our town is situated flows into the Pripet waterway 20 kilometers away, which cuts through the Pinsk Marshes in the center. During the rainy autumn days, and even more so during the melting of the snow in the spring, the Pripet River floods over very wide areas and cuts off the connection between the near and far settlements in these regions.

What was the merit of the village of Lenin, and what was its force to attract Jews who gathered to it from far off and nearby cities, both large and small, settled in it, and turned it into a town?

It seems that this was caused by its geographic situation. The Sluch River, the highway that runs through its entire length, and the location of the village at the gateway to the marshes and the forests – these factors helped

[Page 13]

to make this village as the center for the forestry trade and industry. The forest grew on its own from the soil of the marshes. Its treetops reached the heavens and its cuttings were thick. There were tall pine trees alongside solid, wide-branched oaks. Some distance away there was a grove of white birch trees, as if separate from the community of trees. Below these giants of the forest, sheltered in their shade, there grew fruit-bearing and non fruit-bearing bushes, broad ferns, and an abundance of all sorts of truffles and mushrooms.

At times, one of the old trees no longer had the strength to stand on its roots – it would buckle and fall down at an unusually strong wind and remain in the marsh at its full height. There were no small number of trees that fell in the marsh soil. The foliage of one such tree would almost touch the roots of the fallen tree in front of it – and this would serve as a form of a bridge over the natural marshes for the forest animals and also for humans, the local children who were expert in walking over these partial planks. (During the Second World War, these also served the partisans who spread out through the Pulsian Forests.)

The large estate was originally owned by German noblemen. The elders know the name of the last German estate owner, Count Wittgenstein. He had no children and left the estate to his wife who sold it to a Russian man named Ogrokov.

The German estate owners partitioned small plots to those who came to settle in the town in order to build residential homes. These were in the valley that was between the pond and the banks of the Sluch River. At the beginning, these houses were small, poor, and crowded one against the other, since the entire length of this valley was not greater than 300 meters. The plots and their boundaries are listed in the ledgers of the estate on a very well crafted map. The residents had to pay modest lease fees, and they also had to pay a special payment for the right to obtain heating wood from the forests of the estate. It is obvious that this payment was collected according to the number of ovens in the building. Each resident who owned cows had to pay for a permit for each cow to allow it to graze. Summer was the time of harvesting blackberries, truffles and mushrooms. Each harvester had to pay a set fee for each measure. The guardians of the forest would confiscate the utensils and the harvested produce from anyone who was caught harvesting without a proper permit.

C.

During the time of the first owners of the estate – the German noblemen – the lumber business was concentrated in the hands of Jewish forest traders. As well, the production and supply of tar and turpentine was in the hands of Jewish manufacturers.

Until this day, every native of our town remembers positively the name of the forestry merchant Ben-Zion Tziglig. He was a wealthy and honorable man, and he did not hesitate to support his wide-branched family. He would travel abroad annually to deal with his forestry products that were floated on barges during the springtime.

[Page 14]

Mordechai Tziglig, the father of the aforementioned Ben-Zion, built a large house with many rooms in the center of town. It was surrounded by a large yard. All of the lumber and forestry merchants would come to his house.

From among the Jews who came to Lenin on account of their business and work, there were some who settled there permanently. With the passage of time, the families consolidated according to their places of origin. It was possible to accurately ascertain the place of origin of every family.

The following families came from Slutsk: Slutsky, Gryov, Dolgin, and Rubenstein. The following families came from Starobin: Starobinski and Chinitch. The Tzigligs came from the town of Lachwa, and until our day were registered officially as residents of Lachwa. The Horodichkys came to us, of course, from Dawid Grodek.

All of these contributed to the unique character of our town, which was different from the character of other Jewish town. Aharon Singalovski described this in brief: "A town without a market place, without the stalls and booths of peddlers, and whose small number of shopkeepers were not shopkeepers but rather scholars, intelligentsia, and honorable citizens."

Chaim, the father of Herzl Paperna, and his wife Charna Chana, who came to our town from the city of Bobruisk, were the first shopkeepers. It is said that he traveled to the city of Volozhin and asked the Rosh yeshiva to choose a groom for his granddaughter Sara Leah the daughter of Herzl Paperna. The Rosh Yeshiva selected a diligent student, Reb Zalman Schmelkin, a native of Slutsk. He was called Zhama by our townsfolk. With the passage of time, he acquired a vast amount of erudition. At times, he would say jokingly: The elder Reb Chaim Paperna, the father of his father-in-law Herzl, was appointed over the Hamelitz newspaper. He read it from Alef to Tav and did not skip over even one dot or punctuation mark. He would explicate the newspaper and read it with great devotion, starting from the word "Hamelitz" and ending with the last word and last dot in the last article: "London 15.10 the fifteenth of the tenth month, two stripes"[1]

The old woman Chana, the widow of Reb Isser Nakritz, who died on the 21 of Cheshvan 5714 (1953) at the age of 84, told us that she heard from her grandmother of the Braker family, that when they arrived in the town from Slutsk and she went out on the street for the first time on the day after she arrived, she returned to her home perplexed and said, "What is this?! A terrible plague has apparently taken its victims here. Go out and see that all the townsfolk that I have seen go around without shoes on their feet. They walk around in socks like mourners."

Indeed, according to the stories of the elders, many of the poorer residents of the town would trod through the mud in the street in those days barefoot in the summer, and in the winter with a type of reed shoe made from wooden wicker fibers upon their feet that were covered with rags, in the manner of the village farmers of Pulsia to this day. As was customary, towns used to ascribe nicknames to their neighbors, as a form of recognition. Perhaps it was for this reason that the residents of our town were nicknamed Leniner Lapties". ("Lapti is a reed shoe in Byelorussian).

[Page 15]

D.

Until the 1870s, the fate of all Jewish towns in the Pale of Settlement of Russia was similar to the fate of our town. Aside from a small number of well-to-do people and one or two how almost became wealthy, poverty and backwardness pervaded in the town. Epidemics broke out on occasion and felled many victims. There was no physician in town, and not even an experienced medic.

The few elders of our town still recall the cholera epidemic that broke out in our town 80 years ago. They related that as the disease spread throughout the town, and there was no house where there was not a death, they began – as was the custom in those days – to examine the deeds of their friends, to try to figure out whose sins had caused this great disaster. They searched and found – and hatred, dispute and slander pervaded in town. Despite this, they found wise people who advised that rather than investigating sins and sinners, it would be better to investigate the sanitary state of their bodies, homes and yards. Many listened to their advice. The elders state that before eating, many people did not suffice themselves with washing their hands according to the laws of the Code of Jewish Law, but rather washed their hands with alcohol.

As in all Jewish towns in those days, fires broke out on occasion. Since there were no fire extinguishers, the fire spread quickly to the straw roofs, and consumed house after house within moments.

However, the residents slowly overcame the afflictions that came upon them. After every fire, the town was rebuilt and even improved somewhat. New wooden houses were built. The straw roofs gradually diminished until they disappeared completely and were no longer found atop Jewish homes. In our days, the roofs were already made out of wooden shingles.

In 1891, something occurred that brought an economic improvement and general progress to the town. The large estate that was, as had been stated, in the hands of the German dukes and barons, was sold to a Russian man named Stefan Feodorovitch Ogrokov.

Thus did a new era begin in the annals of Lenin.

The Estate

by Yehuda Greenberg of Argentina

Translated by Jerrold Landau

As I recall my dear town of Lenin – which was called Liolin by the Jews – and its good hearted citizens, my heart rejoices that I too was numbered among its residents. The Jewish community consisted of approximately 120 families, which is 700-800 souls. The earned their livelihoods as merchants, shopkeepers, artisans, craftsmen and porters.

Until 1891, the town and its environs were owed by Princess Hohnloha, scion of German royalty. However, the Russian government passed a law in 1890 stating that only Russian citizens have the right to own real estate in that land, and that all land owners are required to obtain Russian citizenship. This was not pleasing in the eyes of the German princess, so she sold her large estate

[Page 16]

which was upward of 35,000 square kilometers, to the Russian citizen Stefan Feodorovitch Ogrokov.

That year, a new landowner came to the town along with his workers and officials, who were headed by two Jews, Semion Perelovitch and Greenberg. When they arrived, the previous residents had not yet vacated their residents, so Ogrokov and his men lived in the house of Ben-Zion Tziglig for a year and a quarter. In the interim, the buildings were vacated and renovated according to the tastes of Ogrokov and his people.

The estate of Ogrokov extended for very wide areas in the three directions of Mozir, Sluts and Pinsk. Its forests were the largest of the forests in the region of Minsk. New orders were established in the estate, and it was divided into three administrative areas: Lenin (the central administration) Chuchovitch and Dyakovich. Ogrokov purchased the estate for 1,100,000 rubles. He only paid a portion of this in cash, and he owed the rest through contracts payable at specified times. Within a brief period, he was not able to meet his debt, and officials of the executive office often came and seized large portions of his property.

They began to search for sources to cover the debts. Semion Perelovitch, the Jewish manager, brought his brother Yaakov Perelovitch, a well-known merchant, for this purpose. He organized a sort of partnership of forestry merchants, which included Yaakov Rogovin of Minsk, Moshe Leb and Pinchas Kaplan of Lachwa, and others. They began to cut down trees in the forest, and in exchange, they paid Ogrokov's debts.

Thus did our town develop economically in the realm of practical work. Porters were employed and paid well. When they could not do all the work, wagon drivers came from nearby towns. With the passage of time, some of them settled in Lenin. The few shopkeepers who were always short of customers slowly strengthened and began to earn more income.

An era of economic success came to the town, to the point where it aroused the jealousy of nearby towns. The porters of the town were from three families.

a) The Baruch family, consisting of five brothers – Mordechai Leib, Isser, Yehoshua, Zelig and Yaakov, all of blessed memory. Each one of them was married, had children, and was an honorable householder in the town. The family ties among the brothers were strong. Some of them maintained the transportation link between the town and the Mikaszewicze train station. They were men of culture and politeness and knew how to conduct pleasant conversation with the travelers during the journeys that were fraught with obstacles. Some descendents of these families are living in Israel.

b) The family of Yechiel Hacohen Temkin, which also consisted of five brothers. One of them, Zecharia, lived in Malakhovitch. The brothers Moshe, Hershel, Chaim and Yehuda, as well as the daughters Bluma, Mina and Leah lived in Lenin. Their father excelled at hosting guests. The doors of his home were opened wide to any passer-by and to anyone who was hungry or thirsty. Descendents of this family also live in Israel.

c) The family of Yechiel Zaichik.

On a summer's day in 1897, Mordechai Tziglig came from the "office" where the only official

[Page 17]

of the Jewish residents of Lenin worked and spread the news of the death of Ogrokov. He said that the "office" would be closed for a month in observance of a period of mourning for the death of the owner of the estate. The elder Ogrokov left behind a son, and the estate of Dyakovich was divided among his three daughters. At the conclusion of the mourning period, Ogrokov's son came to the office, accompanied by a group of workers and officials, and he appointed Pangalos as the manager of the office. This manager began to institute new orders in the conducting of the forestry business. His first deed was to distance the Jewish merchants and to cut off business links with them. He felt that the "office" itself and its administrators were able to conduct the forestry business, the flotation along the river and the business outside the country. However, it did not work out as he planned. He failed. The management of the office and its business was transferred to the hands of a manger named Chruschtschow, the brother of Ogrokov's brother-in-law. However, he had no more success than his predecessor. In the wake of these definitive failures, the younger Ogrokov came and appointed a Jew, Lazer Pavelovitch Levin as the office manager. At this time, well-known forestry merchants came and established contact with the "office" These merchants included Mr. Lobzinski, the brother-in-law of Chaim Weizmann[2], and the well-known merchant Gur from the city of Kremenchug. Thus did a period of success return to the town.

Levin was a Jew in heart and soul. He would attend the synagogue and attempt to draw the Jews of the town near. He lived for a long time in the home of Ben-Zion Tziglig. Later, he moved his family to the town and lived in one of the buildings of the "office".

Proper protocols were maintained in the estate during the time of the management of Lazer Levin. Experienced workers from different nationalities were invited – Germans, Frenchman, Jews and also Latvians, who new the business of cutting trees. The estate was divided into quarters. He began to dry the marshes of the estate. This work employed many workers who dug many conduits so that the water that covered the marshes could drain away.

He managed the office in a liberal spirit. He sent Avraham, the son of the cantor and shochet Yisrael, to study music in a conservatory. Along with him, he sent a young, talented Russian to study agriculture. Both of them had their tuition paid by the "office". The management of Levin set a tradition that pervaded even under the Russian administrators that followed him – where someone with a Russian name was not shown any favoritism over someone of a different nationality.

Later, he brought a new official to the "office", Zelig Singalovski, who lived with his family in the town for several years. During his tenure, he spread his spirit upon Lenin, he influenced it only positively, and contributed greatly to the raising of its cultural level. The Singalovski children (the only daughter Sara and five sons Yehoshua, Yaakov Nachum, Shachna and Aharon[3] studied in high schools in large cities throughout the year, but they would return home for festivals and holidays and bring the spirit "of the wide world" with them. The youth would awaken when they would come, and many of them would come to hear news from them. Indeed, they had what to tell.

[Page 18]

Sources of Livelihood and Economic Existence

by Mordechai Zaichik

Translated by Jerrold Landau

Shortly after the end of the First World War, during the years 1922-1926, many stores opened in our town. They literally sprouted like mushrooms after a rain… A store was opened in every home, in every entranceway or hallway – whether for linens, haberdashery, groceries or fruit (a few apples or pears – this was also a store!). For the most part, these stores were general stores so to speak, which sold good of all types: starting from needles, salted fish, to linens and shoes.

However, the situation did not last for a long time. Simply, there were not a sufficient number of purchases in our town for these stores. They closed one after the other. Those that remained continued on until the last day of our community.

Aside from commerce, the residents of our town were involved in other trades such as: carpentry, building, tailoring, shoemaking, blacksmithing, teaching, peddling in the villages, etc. Of course there were also those who were unemployed.

On account of the forests that were found in the area around our town, there were those who were involved in the forest trade and everything related to it. A plywood factory was opened in the neighboring town of Mikaszewicze which also employed many Jews of Lenin.

The Breakdown of the Jewish Population by Profession in the 20 Years Following the First World War.

Profession or Trade	Number of families earning their livelihood
Merchants and shopkeepers	140
Builders and carpenters	115
Tailors and hatmakers	90
Blacksmiths, tinsmiths, watchmakers and mechanics	95
Shoemakers and sewers	85
Forest workers and supervisors	70
Physicians, pharmacists, lawyers, teachers and clergymen	85
Plasterers, painters, simple workers	65
Wagon drivers	85
Butchers	50
Temporary workers, unemployed, those supported from America	190
Total	**1,070**

As this table demonstrates, 81% of the population earns its livelihood from all types of trades. The rest live from unsteady work or support from family in America.

[Page 19]

Until the First World War

[Page 21]

The Appearance of the Town Until the Year 1910

by Mordechai Zaichik

Translated by Jerrold Landau

The main street passed by the area between the Sluch River and the pond that is adjacent to it, which was the most populous part of the town. It was completely populated by Jews. The old synagogue stood in the area of the center of town. The homes of the rabbi and other members of the clergy spread out around it, and next to them were the bathhouse and the mikva (ritual bath).

For some reason, this center was located in a muddy area, and all of the sand wagons that stumbled in it were not able to manage. Even during the summer, when the land had dried up around it, the mud reached to the knees. In the fall, one could only traverse the alleys in this center of town with tall rubber boots. On the main street, opposite the synagogue, a walkway make of thick wooden planks was constructed leading from one end of the street to the other, and ditches were dug on both sides – but the mud stood in its place.

It should come as no surprise that our town was not noted for its cleanliness. Pigs and goats wandered through the street, going wherever they wanted to. Goat dung would sully the few sidewalks, the porches and the corridors. The estate owner Milinritz only changed his mind and forbade the raising of goats in the town about 40 years ago.

Behind the main street and parallel to it was the Street of the Gentiles. It was according to its name: White Russians lived in it, and only at the end of the street, at the shore of the pond, live the Tziglig brothers who were nicknamed the "Bruches" after Baruch the son of David Tziglig. There was a lot of deep mud on this road as well. The end of the street facing the pond, where the brothers, the sons of Baruch lived – was better than this, for it was dry during the summer.

Podlifia Street in the spring, at the time of the melting of the snow

[Page 22]

The third street in the town, Podlifia Street, was located parallel to the pond, starting next to the bridge of the pond. Jews lived on about half of the street, starting from the end near the bridge. Christians lived from the middle until its other end. The new synagogue stood on that street, not far from the main street. At the beginning of the spring, when the snow and ice melted, the corner of this street was covered with water. At times, the only access to the synagogue was with a raft or barge.

The inn of Zalman Schmelkin stood on the other side of the bridge, next to it. After it was the poorhouse, which later became the fire hall, which housed small fire engines and 2 or 3 small barrels. This hall and the firefighting utensils which were located there were under the command of Chaim Shuster, who organized the fire brigade. He was fully involved in this, and regarded this activity as his life's work.

From that point onward, there was a non-built-up section on both sides of the road until the town hall (Volost) and the home of Dov-Ber Baruchin which was opposite the town hall. At this point, the road leading to the Mikaszewicze Train Station branched out southward. There, there stood a lone house with a smithy next to it – the home and workplace of Reb Yisrael Gelanson the smith. Further on there were about two more lone houses. There were other smithies at the edge of the city, farther on from the town hall and the home of Dov-Ber Baruchin.

After the First World War, the city spread out from its narrow bounds between the pond and the river. New, large wooden houses were built across the bridge, as a continuation of the main street. As well, residential houses were built on both sides of the road to Mikaszewicze. Lachwa Street took on the form of a veritable street.

The built up area over the bridge was better than the area between the pond and the river. The streets were cleaner, and there was no mud on them.

In "Ruska Yevreiska Encyclopedia" (The Russian Jewish Encyclopedia) we find that the town of Lenin, in the region of Mozir, province of Minsk, had a population of 1,173 people in 1873. 753 of them were Jews, comprising 64.2% of the population.

[Page 22]

During the Years of the First World War

by Mordechai Zaichik

Translated by Jerrold Landau

The outbreak of the First World War did not have a special impact upon the population of the town. Many of the youth of our town were drafted to the army. During the war, older men were also called up, but not in great numbers. The town itself did not suffer at all from military action. The front was far enough away from the town. Only when the regime changed from time to time – to the Russians, the Germans or the Poles – were lone shots heard. Quiet pervaded immediately. The population lived without fear of the Poles and Germans, even though they were strange in their language and customs.

At first the Russian army, headed Commandant Kozachinski, rules our town.

This commandant was handsome, but very exacting and strict. He was prepared to administer beatings for any small matter. Therefore, when he was even seen in the street, coming out of his residence in the home of Avraham Yitzchak Chinitch, people

[Page 23]

would flee and hide from his face. During the time of his rule, the boulevard was removed from the main street, but the trees were not uprooted. Commandant Pashkovski came at the conclusion of his rule. Like his predecessor, he had a wonderful temperament[4]. Once during a service that was conducted in his presence in the Old Synagogue, he was presented with the gift of a cake…

Commandant Pashkovski remained in the town even after the war.

The Germans did not remain in town for a long time. They caused no troubles and unpleasantness, and the population got accustomed to them. To the population, it made no difference who was ruling the city. The main thing was that they would not be cruel. The wish of everyone was that the war should end quickly, and the draftees should return to their homes.

The entrance of the Poles left a harsh impression upon the townsfolk. They prepared for their arrival for several days. Everyone hid in the cellars – at times several families in one cellar. In the interim, they would spend time together and tell each other various stories.

In the morning, when we peeked outside, we saw the Poles entering the town, shooting with their guns and running along the length of the street next to the houses. At that time, the Russians retreated to the other bank of the Sluch River.

The Polish army set up their field kitchen next to the well that was adjacent to the Old Synagogue. The soldiers knocked on the doors of the homes requesting milk, eggs, etc. Nobody could understand their language, except for the wife of Shlomo (Tatel) Aka.

They were busy most of the time with cleaning their quarters, smoking and even playing cards. They would be very noisy when they talked among themselves – or perhaps it only seemed that way to us, for we did not understand their language.

As is known, the Polish army ruled over our city twice. After the first conquest, they were thrown out by the Bolsheviks who pursued them to Warsaw. After the "Miracle on the Wisla River", the Poles pursued the Bolsheviks to Kiev.

Every situation of change was generally unpleasant. There were exchanges of bullets, and it was necessary to guard the horses and cows from confiscation by the army. Therefore, people would bring their animals together in the forest under the protection of the shepherd in the forest, and the women would go out twice a day to milk them. At night, a group of men would go out to the forest to guard them. They would light a bonfire there and sit and talk by the light of the fire. On such nights, the sounds of machine guns could be heard from the bridge over the Sluch River.

As in all places in the country, two revolutions passed over our town in 1917.

Even we students marched in the parade with revolutionary songs in our mouths and various placards in our hands. We had barely absorbed what had taken place, but we were very impressed by the bands that appeared in our town for the first time, and the singing of the "International" from the porch of the only two story house in our town.

At the end of the war, the Lan River next to Shiankievitz, approximately 20 kilometers west of our town, as established as the provisional border between Russia and Poland. Our town was provisionally within the borders of Russia.

[Page 24]

Rumors spread that the border would be set in the center of our town, which would divide the pond into two: one portion would be for Russia and the other portion for Poland. The people of the town were uncertain on which side to remain, and did not know which would be better.

During that era, there was not yet a serious guard at the border, and many families from the Russian side (including families from Lenin) crossed the Lan River and immigrated to America.

After the peace treaty was signed in Riga, the Sluch River was designated as the border, and as a result, Lenin remained within the borders of Poland. Border guards were placed on both sides of the bridge: Russian guards on one side and Polish guards on the other.

During the first years, the guards were not very strict. Many people took advantage of this and stealthily crossed the border back and forth. Later, they became stricter.

Public schools as well as evening schools for adults were opened in our town, for the government was interested in teaching the Polish language to the population. Even so, most people continued to speak Russian. Even in the Gmyna (local council) the officials were forced to speak Russian with the farmers who came to arrange their affairs.

During the first years after the war, bands of robbers wandered through the routes in our vicinity, as in other vicinities. They attacked stores and pillaged them, especially in the village.

In the first years following the war, many Jews who were residents of the villages of the region, such as Zalytycze, Hryczynowicze, Grabow, and others, moved to our town. This was because of the attacks of the robbers who threatened the security of their lives and property, for they were isolated from the gentiles in the village. Aside from this, there was an additional benefit with the town, in that they could live among Jews. There were synagogues, a rabbi, and the rest of the clergy that was necessary to live a Jewish life.

At the beginning of 1939, the population of Lenin was comprised of the following:

Jews	1,070
Byelorussians and Russians	900
Poles	40
Others	30
Total	**2,040**

The Christian population grew through natural increase, for almost nobody of them immigrated to other countries. However, the Jewish population also grew through natural increased as well as the families who moved to our town from the villages.

[Page 25]

Between the Two Wars

[Page 27]

The Influence of the Border on Life in the Town

by Mordechai Zaichik

Translated by Jerrold Landau

The geographic situation of our town, located on the Sluch River which served as the boundary between Russia and Poland from the end of the First World War until 1939, greatly influenced its development.

First of all, there was a constant curfew imposed on the town, restricting anyone from being on the streets from the early hours of the evening until the morning. People who lived outside of our town had to obtain a special permit from the regional authorities in Luniniec, so that they would be able to enter the town. This law applied to merchants as well as relatives of the residents who wished to remain in the town for some time. The permit was only given for a restricted period. Of course, this situation had an influence in the economic development of the town.

There were great difficulties when the youth wished to put on a performance. The play had to be translated into Polish and presented to the censor for authorization before a permit would be granted, despite the fact that the same play had been performed elsewhere in the country without any restrictions. This was the situation as well with presentations from independent powers or speakers from outside.

Despite the fact that the border guard was sufficiently strong, there were incidents where people crossed back and forth over the border.

From time to time, there were incidents where a horse or some geese crossed to the other side of the border. Telephone negotiations took place between the two sides, and a special delegation arrived that was permitted to return the lost animals to their homes.

On the great Christian festival (Kraszciania)[5] that took place on January 19 according to the new calendar, farmers from the entire region went out to the Sluch River to collect holy water in bottles. Farmers would also gather together on the Russian side, and thereby families and relatives who were separated by the border would meet. However, with the passage of time, the authorities on both sides forbade this. After some time, a definitive ban was issued on bathing in the river, which at first was restricted to a specific place. Indeed, individuals were able to obtain permits for bathing, but it was especially difficult for Jews to obtain such permits.

[Page 27]

Border Changes at the End of the First World War

by Anonymous

Translated by Jerrold Landau

Until the First World War, nobody from our place had heard of incidents of murder – and if anyone would have heard they did not believe such. The Christians of our place, White Russian farmers, were people of peace and toil. Understanding relations prevailed between them and their Jewish neighbors. The Jewish residents did not complain about the relationship of the Christian residents to them. Nobody hesitated to go out alone on a journey or to traverse the thick forests by wagon or by foot.

[Page 28]

Nobody thought that danger awaited them from his fellow. On the contrary, if one encountered someone on his journey, they would be happy to meet and enjoy the opportunity for conversation.

However, things changed after the First World War. Freed soldiers returned home after the First World War. Their hands were sullied with the blood of the enemy and their feet had trodden on the corpses of the fallen. The blood of man had become cheap.

Nevertheless, it was not people from our town who started the deeds of murder and the spilling of innocent blood. Rather, the Poles who came to us through their conquest started this. During their first retreat, when they were being pursued to the neck by the Bodyuni Army, they left a trail of blood in their wake: they pillaged, set cities and villages on fire, tortured, cut off and plucked out beards of the elderly, and spilled blood. They murdered Aharon Slutsky from the village of Puzicze with great torture. They tied him by his hands to the shaft of a wagon, to which was hitched a yoke of galloping horses. The man was dragged and rolled for several kilometers along the road until he died. He was found crushed and maimed after a few days and brought to a Jewish burial. They did not merely cut off with scissors the beard of Avraham Rubenstein, an upright and righteous man, but rather literally plucked it out with a dull sword… When the Jewish residents of the town saw that evil was befalling them, and that death was awaiting them at the hands of the cruel murderers, they fled for their lives along with their children to the forests. They wandered around for seven days and seven nights, frozen with the cold and ice, hungry and thirsty, until they found out by chance that the Polish army had retreated and also burned the wooden bridge behind them. Only then did they return to their homes, which they found empty. The pillagers did not leave any food behind, not even a spoon or a knife. The ovens were dismantled, and the books were torn, with their pages scattered on the floor.

The Bolsheviks chased after the Poles and arrived to the suburbs of Warsaw. Then a sudden turning point took place – the Poles called this historical event the "Miracle on the Wisla River". The Bolsheviks began a panicked retreat, and the Poles, drunk with victory, chased after them and returned to us. The fear of death overtook the Jewish settlement, for we had heard about the atrocities of the Polish brave men[6]. 37 notable men of Pinsk were stood up against a wall and shot for no reason. Indeed, it was not for naught that we were afraid: the evil reached us as well. In the village in Czimszwice, approximately 8 kilometers from our town, the Poles found a "Bolshevik spy", who was a resident of that village, the Jew Orihyu, 60 years old with a long beard, a righteous and upright man. He was taken from his home along with a Jewish youth. They were brought through the town, before the eyes of the residents who were weeping for him in the privacy of their hearts (so as not to bring suspicion onto themselves, Heaven forbid, of supporting a "Communist"). He was brought to the Mikaszewicze train station and shot to death. Nobody knew the reason for this. To add to the fear, news arrived about the murderous partners of the Poles, the "Balchow" gangs who came along with the Polish army or in its wake and perpetrated mass murder upon the Jewish resident with such cruelty and wickedness that anyone hearing about this would have his hair stand on end and blood freeze in the veins.

Deep sorrow and heavy mourning enveloped our town when the news arrived of the murder of 18 young people who went out of the city of Turow to cross over to the Zytkowiczei train station. They included two sons of the Lenin resident Mr. Eisenstat, and Eliezer Kolpanitsky. A few days before this, Eliezer left his home and traveled to Kiev to continue his medical studies at university. On the way he heard about the Balchow gangs that were approaching our town. Apparently, his conscience did not permit him to leave the town, his parents, family members and all the residents of the town

[Page 29]

during the time that the danger of death was hovering over them. Eisenstat's two sons and 15 other young people from nearby towns did the same. When the rabbi of the city of Turow found out about the plans of these youths, he summoned them to visit him and begged them not to go out on the journey, for death would be stalking them with every step. However, the youths could not be convinced. They were afraid about what was taking place in their homes. They went out on the journey and fell into the hands of the Poles who accused them of espionage (in their manner of that time to accuse of espionage any Jew who was found outside his area of residence). All 18 were taken to be shot.

Many of the Christian youth of our area joined the Balchow gangs of murderers. Most of them were liberated soldiers who returned home after the war and were unable to or did not want to return to the pattern of their former lives from the time of peace. After the Balchow gangs were dispersed, these youths returned to their villages, with the desire for robbery and murder in their hearts. Then difficult times came upon the residents of our town, and sevenfold difficulties for the Jewish residents of the nearby villages.

The family of Aharon Migdalovich waited anxiously for the return of their son Yitzchak after he had been absent from the house for a long time – but in vain. A shepherd came after several months and informed them that he saw the remains of a human skeleton lying in the forest. His parents immediately went out along with many other residents of Lenin to the place which the shepherd mentioned. That day, we saw a vision that was terrifying to the heart and soul. The people returned from the forest with lowered heads as they accompanied the father and mother who were carrying the remains of their son Yitzchak in an apron.

During those days, the Red Army and the Polish Army reached a ceasefire agreement, and the sat down in the city of Riga to negotiate the conditions of peace and the establishment of boundaries. They negotiated there for approximately a half a year. In the interim, a provisional border was established on the Lan River about 20 kilometers west of the town. A 15 kilometer wide strip on both sides of the border was established as a neutral area. Many of the villages that were connected with our town, including the village in which we were born, became part of that lawless area. Who can describe he suffering and tribulations of the residents of that area – especially of the Jewish residents?! Divisions of he Polish Army or bands from the White Army under Polish protection entered and inquired about who had offered assistance to the Red Army, or who was suspected of this – and the people were taken out to be killed with cruel deaths. After some time, these bands fled for their lives, and divisions of the Red Army came in their place – they demanded that the tables be placed near the window so that they could set up machine guns. They would open fire for no particular reason and investigated if there were any counter revolutionaries in the village.

This division would leave in the middle of the night, and toward morning, another gang would come, and so on…

There were farmers who found it appropriate to offer assistance to the handful of Jews in their village. They dressed them in farmers' clothes, brought them into their homes, and kept them together with their family members. They did this discretely and secretly so that this would not be known to the bloodthirsty youths.

Finally, the two sides signed a peace treaty in the city of Riga, and the border was moved from the Lan River to our Sluch River. We remained in the bounds of Poland. We were cut off from the city of Starobin and other nearby cities that were close to us, and many of whose residents were our relatives. However, this also worked out for the best. We awaited the worst. Rumors spread that the border would pass through the pond, and that the city would be split

[Page 30]

through the middle. There were those of us who took these rumors seriously and debated, while there was still time, which side of the border it would be best to live on.

After the border had been established according the Riga peace treaty, it seemed that peace and quiet prevailed in the land. The Polish government began to impose order in the country. The activities of the government were noticeable in our town as well. A public school was opened whose purpose was the imparting of the Polish language to the border town.

Nevertheless, the desire for robbery and murder by the young villagers who were remnants of the Balchow gangs of murderers were expressed discretely and secretly. An anonymous force organized these beings into gangs whose purpose was to carry out deeds of terror in the border towns within the Russian boundaries. Storehouses of arms, weapons and military equipment were prepared in several villages along the Polish border. The murderers gathered together in the darkness of the night, received their weapons, crossed the border and paraded around at night under the protection of their friends and acquaintances in the villages within the Russian boundary. In the morning they would launch a surprise attack upon the town in which they arrived. They would slaughter men, women, and children. After perpetrating these acts, they would flee to the place from whence they came, return their weapons to the secret storehouse, and return to their villages and homes with their booty. We heard about the slaughter that these murderers carried out in the towns of Lyuban, Starobin, Piotrkov, and others.

The pure and righteous man Yaakov Eliahu Kolpanitsky and his comrade on the journey Eliahu the son of Herzl Chinitch were killed by these murderers in one of the villages within the Polish boundary. Apparently a command was issued to these gangs not to murder anyone within Poland, but they apparently ran into a gang that was returning from its activities across the border, and there were some people among this gang whom these two Jews recognized. These people murdered these two Jews so that there would be no eyewitness to their deeds.

Translator's Footnotes:

1. I am not sure of the exact translation. It seems to be some sort of technical publication term, not meant to be read by the readers.
2. Chaim Weizmann was the first president of the State of Israel.

3.   There is a footnote in the text here: "See the article on Aharon Singalovski" in the section on Personalities.
4.   This seems like sarcasm.
5.   Epiphany.
6.   It seems that this was meant as sarcasm.

[Page 30]

My Visit to Lenin in 1936

by Sara Fogelman (Kolpanitsky)

Translated by Rachel Ben-Chaim (Rochelle Moss Kaplan)

**In memory of my parents
Dina and Betzalel Kolpanitsky,
murdered by the Nazis**

It was almost as if my heart had a premonition that a big tragedy was about to happen, one that would forever separate me from my family. After ten years of living in the Land of Israel I decided to visit my family in Lenin, where I was born. After I completed all my preparations for the trip, the terrible riots of 1936 broke out all over the country, just a few days before I was supposed to leave. I had to make a very difficult decision, whether to stay home or to go ahead with my plans. But, after making the initial decision to visit my family, I set out.

My first impression, upon arriving in Poland, was very gloomy. Passing through Brisk I noticed broken windows and closed shutters. These were the days of the infamous "Przytyk" pogroms and the terror of the "Endeks" in Poland, that even Brisk suffered damages. On the way I met with Jews, spoke to them and even offered them cigarettes from the Holy Land, that I had brought with me. An old Jew, took the cigarette, stared at the Hebrew letters on it and with shaking hands divided the cigarette into two. One half he put into his pocket and other half he smoked. I watched him as he trembled and asked him why he did what he did. His answer was: "In another few days we will be celebrating the Feast of Pentecost and I will want to smoke the cigarette from the Holy Land". I was so moved by that I couldn't hold back my tears. I saw how much the Jews are attached to our Land, to our country.

I arrived at my parents' home towards evening. I was greeted not only by my immediate family and close friends, but most of the town's residents came out to welcome me as well. Because Lenin was close to the border, traffic was forbidden after darkness. If a youngster was late in returning from his girlfriend's house on Friday night, he would have to spend the rest of the night in jail. That is why the town folk rushed back to their homes, leaving me with my family and closest relatives, who remained with me until morning.

I did not like the change that I found in my parents. Ten years had left a noticeable mark on them. In contrast, I found a blessed change in the children, who developed into handsome youngsters.

I spent a few months with my family, and the journeys around the village where I spent my childhood, brought back many memories. There is the Heder where the teacher, Aharon-Leib, of blessed memory, taught me reading and writing. At the time, it was a full day of learning and in the winter we would return home when it was already dark. Each child carried a small lantern which would light up the way through the yard of the infirmary, the local hospital. I remember the fear that gripped us when we passed the gentile patients, wandering around the yard. At that point we started to run, until we were out of breath. The running put out the fires in our lanterns, and that made us run even faster. By the time that we reached our homes, we were out of breath and covered with sweat.

There is the old Synagogue where the children would run to see the wedding ceremonies that took place in the yard, with the old mothers dancing in front of the bride and groom, waving big braided challahs. And there is the Pozharna Hall, where the tremendous red barrels that belonged to the fire department stood. This hall also served as the local theatre and was the venue for their performances. When I passed it I remembered, as a child, how I would recognize furniture, props or clothing that belonged to my parents and was now part of the performance on stage. Once, during a performance, I yelled "mamma, that's ours". All that was necessary was to collect various items from each household. That way, everyone took part in the production.

When I walked past the Rabbi's house, I remembered how my mother, of blessed memory, would send me there to buy candles and yeast for Shabbos. Not far from the Rabbi's house was the bath house, covered with moss and its' collapsing roof.

And so I continued until I reached Podlipya Street, where I stood next to the new Synagogue, where my family prayed. The sexton, Reb Chaim, saw me and invited me to enter the Shul. We stood in front of the magnificent Ark that instilled its holiness upon us. And there, to the right of the Holy Ark, in the third row, was my father's seat. No one could ever compare to me, standing next to my father, holding a flag, waiting for the Simchas Tora procession to begin. Upstairs, in the women's section, I sat next to my mother, waiting to hear the Shofar blowing on Rosh Hashana. From there I would also listen to the sermons of the emissaries.

And then I reached Reb Asher's house, where the matzoh bakery, the Gordich, stood. There we would bake the matzos for Passover. Even now I could almost smell the fresh odor of spring blended with the smell of freshly baked matzos. There was a custom in our town that between Purim and Passover, the teenage girls would roll and imprint the holes on the matzos for the needy families that could not afford this addition. For us it was an exciting experience.

Lenin was small, but beautiful. Few were wealthy, the majority were simple laborers – modest and honest Jews. In Lenin we had no thieves, snitches or murderers. A happy event in Lenin was celebrated by all, and, if there was a tragedy, it was everyone's tragedy.

During my visit in Lenin a young girl became very ill and had to be rushed to the hospital in Brisk, where she was to undergo surgery. Her parents did not have the money and could not afford such an expense. Word spread throughout Lenin, money was collected and within hours the girl was on her way to Brisk. And that was not the only case of helping one another in times of distress.

Everyone in Lenin, the youngsters as well as the elderly, smothered me with love. They listened with great interest to my stories about life and work in the land of Israel, about the pioneers in the Galilee and the Emek. Their eyes lit up with enthusiasm and it seemed as if they were all prepared to leave on the next boat to Palestine.

The youth were committed and loyal to the Hebrew language. Even the young children babbled a bit in Hebrew. One day I came to the local grocery store when a young girl entered and asked, in Hebrew, for a herring. The shopkeeper did not understand what the girl was asking for and asked her what she wants. Again, the girl answered "herring" This time I translated what the little girl said and then, asked the girl why she was talking Hebrew. Her answer was "we pledged that we were not going to speak any other language but Hebrew and if they don't understand us, let them learn!" I was very impressed by that answer and kissed the girl on her forehead. I had a similar experience in my parents' home. My ten year old niece taught her grandmother Hebrew. It was agreed upon that the old lady would donate the tuition fee to the Jewish National Fund. After a few lessons, when the debt mounted up, her granddaughter threatened that she would be forced to confiscate her furniture – just as the government would do in those days.

The desire of all of the Jewish inhabitants of Lenin to emigrate to the Land of Israel was so strong, despite the headlines at that time about the blood riots that were raging throughout the country.

When the time came for me to return to Palestine the mood in my parents' house became very gloomy, because my sister was also leaving with me. All of Lenin came to bid us farewell and the parting from my elderly parents was extremely difficult. It was as if we had the feeling that we are separating forever, not only from my parents but from all of the Jews of Lenin…

[Page 33]

The External View of the Town Before the Holocaust

by Mordechai Zaichik

Translated by Jerrold Landau

After the First World War ended and the Sluch River was established as the border between Russia and Poland, the town developed in a significant manner from all perspectives.

First of all, they began to build new houses, of course made out of wood. After all of the lots on the old streets were built up, the construction spread to the other side of the pond, on both sides of the bridge ("Greblia") until the public school which was at the beginning of the Lachwa Road. Aside from this, a new road was built in the direction of the smithies, on the route that led to the village of Ioviche. This street, which was actually a continuation of the former main road between the pond and the river, then became the main artery of the town, running a length of 1 ½ kilometers. Thus did it happen that the Russian cemetery, which used to be outside of the bounds of the town, was now incorporated into the town between the houses that had been built.

The little bridge

At the end of that street, to the right, a Catholic church and a "mayak" (watchtower) were built. In the latter years, a large building was built in which the Soviet "Rayasfolkom" was located. This street was called "The large one", but it also had a nickname "Zladiewka".

Lachwa Street also developed during the first decade after the First World War and was filled with new houses.

[Page 34]

A large assembly hall was built in the town ("Dom Ludowi") with a hall for theatrical performances, cinema, and a club. There was a sports field adjacent to it. At the end of the street that joined with Makowice Street, a flourmill was built, as well as a millet mill, and a wool processing plant which produced felt for farmer's coats, slippers and the like.

An electric power generator was also built there which provided light for the entire town and the area.

The appearance of the town improved because all of the streets were raised by packing them with earth. Thereby, the constant plague of mud was solved definitively. This situation also improved Podlifia Street, which was always the lowest and was covered by water every spring to the point that it was only possible to reach the houses and the new synagogue with the help of barges and rafts, literally like in Venice!

The street in which the "Volost" was formerly located was paved with stones, as in large cities. Every wagon with iron wheels that passed by would raise a deafening racket.

On the other hand, the new street that was called "Zladiewka" was wide and always dry. At its widest point, at the end, a small, lovely garden was planted, surrounded by a green fence.

An order was issued to widen the sidewalks to a width of one meter and to strengthen them, as well as to set up the fences near the houses in a straight line and paint them with a uniform color.

Trees were planted on the sides of the streets, which took well and flourished with the passage of the years.

The name of the town, "Lenin" was a cause for astonishment for everyone. Nobody could understand how a Polish town could be called thus! They began to ad an "o' to its name, that is – "Lenino". Only in 1939, approximately six weeks before the outbreak of the war, did the Polish government decide to change the name of the city to Sosnkowica, after the Polish general Sosnkowski.

However, with the conquest of the town by the Soviets on September 17, 1939, it reverted to its old name of Lenin.

[Page 37]

Immigration to Israel

My Immigration (Aliyah) to the Land of Israel

Yehoshua Greenberg

Translated by Janine Sherr

It was a tradition among the young people of our town to celebrate Simchat Torah in our own homes. We would bring the Sefer Torah (Torah Scroll) from the Old Synagogue and would take turns being called up to the Torah. Following the Torah reading, Avram'ke, the son of R' Yisrael, would lead the congregation in the Musaf Prayer. My mother, ever the diligent housewife, would prepare cakes and other treats for the feast. Much wine and liquor would be consumed by the guests, and the dancing and celebrating would continue late into the night.

On Simchat Torah of 1903, while we were all dancing to the tune of "Next Year in Jerusalem", I was suddenly overwhelmed by a great feeling of excitement and I passionately declared: "You shall all see: by this time next year I will be living in the Land of Israel!"

I kept my promise.

On the day of my departure, all of the town's people gathered to bid me farewell. I traveled via Kiev. Dr. Mandelstam and Hillel Zlatapolski provided me with a letter of reference for Mr. Ussishkin, in which they requested that he do everything in his power to help me reach Jaffa. Unfortunately for me, I found Mr. Ussishkin in particularly bad spirits , since he was in the midst of a bitter dispute with Mr. Herzl regarding the Uganda question, and consequently, he refused to meet with me.

I traveled from Kiev to Odessa where I met a dear and kind-hearted gentleman, R. Mordcha-le Tzemerinski, who arranged for my illegal immigration to the Land of Israel.

I arrived in Israel and I wandered to and fro for approximately two months , but I never felt settled. So, I began to make my way back to Lenin. I endured many hardships and tribulation en route: the Russian-Japanese War erupted and my journey from Constantinople to Kiev took six months. I was caught without a passport by the Russian police, and then, as the law required in those times, I was forced to continue on my way escorted by an entourage of policemen from village to village, and from city to city, until, at last, completely exhausted, I arrived back in Lenin.

Our Immigration (Aliyah) to the Land of Israel

Chaim Shalev

Translated by Janine Sherr

Wherever I go, I am always going to the Land of Israel.

(R. Nachman of Braslav)

Love of the Land of Israel, and the desire to build and settle the land, were feelings that were deeply entrenched in the hearts of the majority of the Jews of Lenin. With the exception of a very small group of elders (fewer than ten in number), most of the Jews of Lenin were devoted Zionists. In 1912, there were already Jews who dreamed of immigrating to Israel. Among those who sought to immigrate was Eisel Reinless Borstein, sister of the well-known teacher and Hebrew linguist, Yehuda Leib Grodzinski (Gur), who had lived in Israel since 1887. He was the author of the "Dictionary of the Hebrew Language", and was famous for having composed the pocket Hebrew-Hebrew dictionary, in collaboration with Y. Klausner.

[Page 38]

In response to our letter to him (to Gur) in which we expressed our wish to immigrate to Israel, he wrote:

"My dear young people, you who are strong in body and brave in spirit, whose hearts are as strong as the heart of a lion, you shall surely be successful in settling here."

Needless to say, this response was not one that our parents wished to hear, and they absolutely refused to allow us to go. Since we were dependent upon our parents to finance our journey, the matter was put off, but not forgotten. In the meantime, World War I broke out, and we were all drafted into the army and sent to the front lines. Some of us were killed; others were injured or taken captive by the enemy. When we returned to the town in 1920, physically and emotionally exhausted, we turned our attention once more to our goal of immigrating to Israel.

One day, after the Poles had retreated past Warsaw to avoid the advancement of the Bolshevik troops, my cousin Ephraim Zaretzki and I, along with Pesach Ben Mones Zavin (who lives today in the United States) and Menashe Borstein, decided to set out on the journey to Israel. This is the story of that journey.

In the house of Teitel Oko, where my parents lived, the chief officers of the Polish army set up their base. Being in close proximity to these officers allowed me to befriend some of them, although I found that many of these officers were wicked and corrupt. In fact, many of these soldiers would hound us for bribes, and would follow our every move. On the day of the great retreat of the Polish troops, when these officers were feeling discouraged and despondent, I seized upon that moment to inform them that some of my friends and I, all of us Polish patriots and enemies of the Bolsheviks, desired to accompany them when they left the area. The officers were pleased by this idea and agreed to allow us to come with them. They even confiscated a wagon from one of the gentile neighbors to aid us in our travel.

With a heavy heart, we left our town on the 17th day of Tammuz (an inauspicious date on the Jewish calendar) at noon, leaving behind our dear families to bear the yoke of a cruel and tyrannical regime. At midnight, we reached the forest. The Polish army halted its march and stopped to rest. There I was among a sea of wolves, avowed enemies of the Jewish people, who were ready to attack any Jew just for being a

Jew. It is not difficult to imagine how frightened we all were, young Jews, trapped in the midst of the enemy. Nonetheless, we did not despair – the light of Zion cast its light upon us from afar, infusing us with hope and faith and the courage to carry on.

After several days of wanderings and hardships, we arrived in Luninietz. At this point, several officers asked us where we were heading. Somehow, we mustered our courage and informed them that we intended to travel to Palestine. When they heard what we had said, they burst out laughing and began to taunt us: "You poor fools! Are you really going to go to a desolate and forsaken land? Surely you will die there of starvation!" While speaking to them, we discovered that there were some Jewish men among the ranks of these top officers. This discovery raised our spirits. Moreover, it is only thanks to these Jewish officers that we were saved from a bitter fate. The Polish officers wanted to punish us with hard labor, but these Jewish officers came to our defense, claiming that we were not criminals but loyal citizens who were escaping from the Bolsheviks, and therefore, we should be treated with courtesy. The Polish officers heeded their words.

As we continued on our journey, we witnessed death and destruction everywhere. Cities and villages were mercilessly pillaged and set ablaze. Jews were hiding like mice in small holes. Stark images from Bialik's famous poem, "In the City of the Slaughter" appeared before our eyes, as cruelty and suffering surrounded us. We keenly felt the pain of our brothers and we were determined to leave behind this blood-soaked land.

[Page 39]

After further wanderings and tribulations, we finally arrived in Pinsk. We left the Polish officers and rented a room in a hotel. Immediately, even before we had a chance to rest from our journey, we began to plan how we could continue on our way to Palestine. At this point, I would like to acknowledge the courage and quick thinking of our friend, Pesach Zavin, who was always practical and intelligent, determined to succeed and to reach his goals, regardless of how trying the circumstances. He tended to be very talkative and to express his opinions and thoughts in a direct manner. He apparently did not believe in the teaching of our sages: "There is a time to speak at length and there is a time to be quiet"!

In those days, a law was decreed that one was not allowed to travel from place to place without a travel document, issued by the commander-in-chief of the army. Pesach was not deterred by this obstacle, and he did not rest until he managed to secure for us, with the help of a Jew called Buchman, the required travel documents. And then, we had another hurdle to overcome, one even more daunting than the first. All of the points of entry to and from the city were closed; no one was allowed to enter or to leave, and the one available vehicle of transportation, the train, was packed with soldiers and other people of rank and distinction who had special privileges. Thus, we were now in the midst of a great dilemma, and our anxiety increased from day to day. Yet, Pesach did not give up. He searched relentlessly in every corner, he even formulated a special phrase that he would recite, (in Polish) "Koneyachno Povlagadarim", which translated means: "There is no doubt that you shall be thanked (rewarded)". In other words, he would say to those to whom we turned for assistance: if you wish, we can simply thank you for your efforts on our behalf; however, if you reflect more deeply upon the meaning of our words than perhaps you shall understand that we are willing to pay you in other ways for your services. Ultimately, most people understood what he was telling them, and soon all doors were open before us.

Pesach searched all over until he found an elderly conductor of a train, whose cars were mostly crammed with the belongings of an army general, but included one car which was filled with sacs of mail. After extensive negotiations with the conductor, in which Pesach emphasized our particular circumstances and our lofty goals, as well as his usual hints of more lucrative remuneration, the conductor finally relented. For a sum of 3000 Polish marks, which he requested to collect from us up front, the conductor agreed to hide us in the "mail car" until the train would reach Brest-Litovsk. Pesach quickly came to tell us the good news and explained in detail what had transpired. Once again , we were taken aback by his diligence, determination, and resourcefulness. However, it seemed to us that this idea was very far-fetched and unrealistic. For who could guarantee us that this elderly man was not simply taking advantage of a group of young, impressionable, and vulnerable Jewish boys, who were seeking a way to get to Palestine through money and their own wits? What would happen, indeed, if after he took our money, he would abandon us to our own devices and we would be left bereft of everything? These doubts tormented us endlessly and prevented us from arriving at a final decision. Pesach noticed that we were vacillating and avoiding making a decision, so he said to us:

"Hand me a written referral and I will go ahead without you. "At this point, I must add that I had been the head of the "Young Zionists" of our town and I held the official stamp of the organization. I immediately gave him my approval, took a piece of paper, and wrote a letter of reference for him. I wrote: "I affirm herein that Pesach Zavin is an upstanding and honest man, a loyal Zionist, and worthy of all support, etc." In our naivete, we actually believed that such a document would suffice to open doors for him when he would finally arrive in Israel (almost like his "magical" Polish phrase!)

The letter of referral stated as follows:

[Page 40]

Young Zionist Council of Lenin

(No. 49)

A Document

We, members of the Young Zionists Council of Lenin, hereby affirm that Zelig _____ has been a bona fide member of our organization for many years. He has always been an active and productive member of our society. We know that his deepest desire and aspiration has always been to live in the Land of Israel. We, therefore, request that the Zionist Council make every effort to be of assistance to our dear friend.

> With Warm Greetings to Zion.
> Respectfully Yours,
> Chairman Eliyahu _____
> Secretary _____

18th of Elul, 5681
(September, 1920)

As I was finishing writing my letter for him, while struggling inwardly with my doubts regarding this situation, my friends and I discussed the matter again and agreed to join Pesach in his journey. We took our bundles and headed towards the train station. To our great surprise, we found the old conductor there, and after a brief negotiation with him, we entered into a dark and narrow boxcar, and each one of us, in our own corner, whispered a silent and fervent prayer to the Almighty to protect us during our upcoming perilous journey.

For twelve straight hours we sat stooped over, in a painful and tight position, literally holding our breath, in a narrow and stifling boxcar, without letting out a noise from our mouths in fear of the soldiers who surrounded us, just waiting for an opportunity to give vent to their fury and frustration. At midnight, the train started to move and we could finally breathe freely. Due to the clatter of the wheels of the train, we were able to exchange some words amongst ourselves aloud without outside interference. The amount of food that we had packed with us was enough to satisfy our needs; however, our thirst soon became overwhelming. But, lo and behold, at one station along the journey, the door to our car opened briefly and the old conductor handed us a can of water, which helped to revive our bodies as well as our spirits.

The train ride lasted for three days, and on Shabbat afternoon, which that year came out on Erev Tisha B'Av, we arrived in Brest-Litovsk in Lithuania (also known as Brisk). It was an oppressively hot and stifling day. Our train stopped at a distance from the station; from there we were forced to drag our weary bodies and our meager belongings for quite a distance until we reached a hotel. As we entered the hotel, we were informed that we needed to acquire travel documents if we intended to continue on our journey. We overlooked our feelings of exhaustion and almost forgot about all that we had experienced. We quickly hurried to the officer in charge of the city, and to our great joy, we were able to obtain the required documents without much trouble. When this occurred, we could clearly perceive the "hand of God" easing our path. While were away from the hotel, a group of soldiers came by to draft men into forced labor. Fortunately, the owner of the hotel was a physically intimidating man, and was able to stop them, by virtue of his physical strength, persuasive words, and offers of money. The soldiers were turned away and never returned to harass us.

[Page 41]

After Shabbat, we gathered in the hotel some minyanim (groups) of Jewish men, both from the local community and from groups of refugees (like ourselves), for a reading of the Megillah of Eicha. It seemed to me that this was the first time in my life that I actually understood the profound meaning of the Megillah and was personally moved to tears by this ancient scroll. The Megillah's message was very relevant to us in our present circumstances. Each verse and word struck a deep cord in my heart, and seemed to emerge from the depths of the pain and agony of my fellow Jews. And when we reached its concluding verse: "Why do You forever forsake us…..return to us, God, and we shall return to You, renew our days as days of Old", we each felt like abandoned and forgotten children who had been cast away by their father.

Despite our weariness from our travels, and the fears that we had experienced over the past few weeks, we still experienced a restless night filled with thoughts about our past and worries about our uncertain future. The following day at daybreak, we hurried towards the train station. For an entire day, we circled around the station until towards evening we managed to push ourselves into an overcrowded train car. The crowding and suffocation were intolerable, but with great effort we found a little corner for ourselves and our belongings. The train had just passed the twenty-third stop from Brest-Litovsk, when suddenly a group of soldiers from the Helerchikas brigade burst into our car. This particular brigade was infamous for its cruelty towards Jews. As they entered the car, they began with their cursing and started to abuse the Jews in the car; they cut off the sides of the "kapote" of one Jew, and they cut the beard of another and continued to perpetrate other humiliating and hateful acts. Witnessing such acts of brutality, we were extremely frightened, and could see before our eyes the words from Megillat Eichah: "We were a disgrace before our enemies, a mockery to our neighbors…" We realized that we were in a dangerous situation; but then, to our surprise, we were saved from this terror by a compassionate and beautiful nun, who wore a red cross. She began to tell frightening but fascinating war stories, about how she herself had witnessed miracles occurring to brave soldiers. She also recounted a terrifying story about her brothers who had met a valiant death in the battlefield.

With the strength and conviction of her voice, she managed to stir the passions and to captivate the souls of these savage men, who were calmed and quieted by her words. Suddenly, she turned to our group, winked her eye, and whispered in our ears in Yiddish: "They will always live this way, mark my words." When we heard her words, we felt revitalized. Thus, we were rescued through the ingenuity and bravery of a woman, who saved us from the hands of a band of wicked men, and we were able to reach Warsaw in peace.

In Warsaw, we took up lodgings for one month in the buildings for Olim that were under the auspices of the Aliyah Council. Here, they welcomed us with open arms. They investigated our individual histories, and were particularly interested in finding out which occupations we intended to choose for ourselves once we arrived in Israel. Overnight, we all became farmers- workers from birth.

[Page 42]

From Warsaw we travelled to Krakow. In Krakow, we handed our passports to the Palestine office so that they could be stamped, which would ensure our legal entry into the country. The next day, we sent Pesach, our loyal and energetic messenger, to collect the passports. Then we discovered that a new problem had befallen us: Pesach was told that our passports had been lost. Pesach began to plead, beg, and bargain with the authorities in all the languages that he knew, all to no avail. He ran from one clerk to the next and accosted them with innumerable questions, recounting our tragic story again and again. They could truly empathize with our difficult situation, for who more than Polish and Russian Jews could understand the saying that was popular at that time: "A Jew means a body and a passport"! In other words, if you take away a passport from a Jew, it is as if you removed part of his soul.

For over two weeks, we suffered terrible anguish and we wandered lost and helpless around Krakow, until, at last, we were informed that our passports had been found. I would be remiss if I did not acknowledge with gratitude the support of the director of the Palestine office, the daughter of Dr. Y. Tahon. When she heard from Pesach about our tragic situation, this generous woman sustained us with a gift of several hundred Polish marks.

Many years after that horrible incident involving our passport, we were able to solve the mystery of what had really transpired. Other Jews, probably war refugees like ourselves, took our passports, removed the photos, and used them to cross the border into Palestine. Many years ago, I met a milkman in Tel Aviv who smiled at me and said: "Mr. Nakritz (this was my former name), we both have the same name!"

"How is that possible?" I asked with astonishment.

"Well, you see, thanks to your passport in Krakow that disappeared…I was able to come here!"

From Krakow, we travelled to Pressburg (Bratislava) in Czechoslovakia, which was the city of R' Yom Tov Lipman Heller and R' Akiva Eiger. On the way, we were joined by a young man from Lelchich, named Berel Shapira, and from that day on we called our group, which now had five members, "The Lenin Group". For political reasons, we were forced to stay in Pressburg for one month's time, but this time we were not worried. We were village boys who were living in the big city for the first time, and we were captivated by the beauty and wonders of the city. Our only concern was that by this time our money supply had considerably diminished, and Menashe Borstein was left without a single penny! We managed to find ourselves temporary employment and thus we were able to save some money. Since we were all members of "The Lenin Group", we pooled our resources and shared our food; we lived frugally and were satisfied with our lot. And even though we had already experienced our share of miracles, something occurred that in our particular situation could only be considered divine intervention! One day, Menashe Borstein went downtown to a place where thousands of people pass by each day, and there he found a treasure- a bundle that contained one hundred eighty Czech crowns! We were all delighted by his wondrous find.

[Page 43]

From Pressburg we continued on to Vienna, where we spent more than a month. We thoroughly enjoyed our stay in the Austrian capital, one of the world's largest cities, famous for its beautiful buildings and castles, as well as its magnificent institutions of art and culture. We toured the city and were thrilled by everything that we saw there. Every day we discovered new and exciting sites. Here we also had the opportunity of hearing lectures from Eliezer Kaplan, Berel Katznelson, Lipman Levinson, Lozinski, and others, who spoke at great length about the Land of Israel and sought to explain the principals of the United Labor Party, which was then in its infancy (it had just recently been founded). Our hearts, however, were more drawn to the "Poel HaTzair" (Young Labor)party, though the truth is that we did not really grasp the differences between these two groups.

From Vienna, we travelled to Trieste, and from there we set sail for Israel on the freighter ship "Bukovina", that was carrying a transport of mortar and charcoal and docked for several days at every port. This journey, that would usually take a passenger ship less than a week to complete, took us twenty four days, under very precarious conditions. Nonetheless, the journey was not difficult for us and did not dampen our spirits. Pesach, a tailor by trade, befriended the sailors and won them over through his expertise in tailoring , by mending their tattered shirts. They rewarded him for his services by offering us more food.

On the twenty fifth of Cheshvan 5681, November 5, 1920, we reached the shores of Israel. On Shabbat morning, the ship docked in Jaffa, and in the afternoon we were already strolling around Tel Aviv, on Sderot Rothschild (Street), that stretched in those days until Nachalat Binyamin Street. We were alone and poor, without homes, without families, and without much hope for employment. Nonetheless, we suddenly found ourselves walking erect and proud. All of the suffering, trials and tribulations that we had experienced in order to come here, completely disappeared, as if they had never happened. Our dark and sorrowful outward appearances now shone with light. For a great and everlasting joy now brightened our countenances. It could only be the immeasurable joy of "sons returning to their borders" (Jeremiah 31:17)

The Holocaust

[Page 47]

A. The Town of Lenin 1939 – 1941

by Mordechai Zaichik

Translated by Amy Samin

On Friday, the first of September 1939 at dawn, Hitler and his Nazi army surrounded Poland, and after about 14 – 15 days had passed, they had occupied the entire country, except for isolated spots where the remnants of the Polish army continued to courageously defend itself.

Then the Red Army crossed the western border and occupied the Ukraine and White Russia. The town of Lenin, near the border, passed into the control of the Soviet Union; thanks to which the Jewish population of the place was able to live a normal life for almost two more years. In that regard their fate was much better than that of the residents on the other side of the Bug River, who immediately fell into the hands of the Nazis with their occupation of Poland, and upon whom the disaster fell in the blink of an eye.

The reality was not quite what the people of our town had imagined: they had assumed that the Red Army would quickly cross the bridge and the three hundred meters that separated them from our town. But the Red Army, apparently secure in its occupation of the area, did not rush to enter our town. Meanwhile, the Polish government was crumbling and the town was left on its own for a number of days.

In that transitional time, the situation in our town was tense. There were rumors that the farmers in the area were preparing to attack the town, to riot, plunder, and rob. The Jewish youth recognized the need for an organized defense and a watch, especially at night. They were prepared to repel any attack by rioters, even though they did not have any weapons.

Then the Russians crossed the bridge over the Sluch River and entered our town, without firing a shot and without bloodshed. They appointed a sort of temporary authority then continued marching westward. All traces of the Polish government, which had dominated the town for twenty years, were erased at once; there were no more signs of Poles, of the police, of the border guards, or of curfews at night. The Russian language reverberated once again throughout the town, as it had in the days of Czarist Russia.

There were residents who were dissatisfied with the change in government, for example the merchants and the shopkeepers, who were concerned about their economic situation. The religiously observant, who had heard about the war on religion and about the oppression of religious people in the Soviet Union were, on the other hand, happy not to have fallen under the control of Hitler, even though very little was known of the horror that accompanied that reign of terror. Most of the residents were happy with the change: there was work for anyone who wished to work, and those with the talent could find office work that carried with it responsibility. Particularly in demand were office workers, managers, and bookkeepers.

Gradually, the shopkeepers liquidated their stores and a department store opened in the town. In the beginning, there were shortages of everyday items, so that when things finally appeared in the store, the residents bought up as much as they could afford. People began to hoard things such as soap, matches, kerosene and other items.

Fairly quickly things settled down, and the situation returned to normal.

[Page 48]

A few families, both Jewish and Christian, whom the government suspected of being criminals and sinners against the Soviet regime, were exiled deep into Russia. Those who were exiled felt that the decree was a great disaster. But at the end of the war it was possible to say, as Joseph did to his brothers in Egypt: "But as for you, you thought evil against me; but God meant it for good…" (Genesis 50:20). Thanks to their exile they were saved from destruction. After the years in exile, whoever wished could return to his home and his town.

Many of those survivors went to Israel; others to America and other countries. They know enough now to appreciate the great favor that was concealed in their being sentenced to exile. Regarding matters of religion, the youth shook off the burden of Jewish tradition, but their elders did not. They continued in the ways of Israel, praying day and night without disturbance. A suggestion was made to convert the synagogue to a club, but it was quickly rejected.

The school continued to exist, but sadly the language of instruction was Yiddish rather than Hebrew. The study of the Tanach (bible) was removed from the curriculum. Children continued their Jewish studies secretly, at home.

There was a significant rise in the influence of other cultures. Activities were renewed in the Polish club *Dom Ludowi*. Theatrical productions became more frequent, as did the screening of films. A big new library opened, and next to it was a reading room.

The overall value of the town went up, and it became a regional city and a center for government institutions such as the *Raikomparty*, the *Rayasfolkom*, a courthouse and other institutions. From all the surrounding area, from villages and settlements near and far, people came to the town to settle their affairs. The closest town, Mikashevichy, was included in the Lenin region and their residents made use of the government institutions there.

The government had many plans: to drain the Pulsia Marsh, to make the Sluch River suitable for transportation, and to establish a hydro-electric power station which would provide electricity to the entire region, but the government was not able to put any of these fine plans into effect. Less than two years after this new regime was established in our town, the Nazi army attacked the Red Army and put an end to everything.

Under the Nazi Occupation

The 22nd of June 1941 was a day of darkness and despair for most of humanity, and a disaster for our town.

Only in the afternoon did we learn of the attack of the Nazis, and we were all terrified. There were horrible rumors of the lightning-fast victories of Hitler's army: they had entered Brisk, they had occupied Baranavichy, and they had even reached the suburbs of Minsk…

Four weeks after the outbreak of the war, we still had not seen a single Nazi. In those days our town was filled to capacity with refugees from other cities and towns. They

[Page 49]

rushed to our town in the hope that they would be able to cross the river and flee to the Soviet Union, or to board one of the transport vehicles that evacuated the families of the Soviet clerks from our town.

But the Soviet border guards maintained their positions and continued to fulfill their duty along the banks of the river, refusing to allow anyone across. In spite of the excellent guard work, in the midst of the commotion many succeeded in escaping eastward together with those in retreat; even a few young people from our town were able to cross the river.

Many of those in retreat died on the way, some killed in bombings and some in other circumstances. In spite of those difficulties, there were many from our town, especially the young, who were willing to run eastward for their lives even though they didn't know and couldn't even begin to imagine what kind of treatment they could expect at the hands of the Nazi beasts.

As was mentioned, a few young people from our town were able to escape. A few days before their own retreat, the border guards spoke to us, urging us to remain until the rage had passed; they promised us that the Red Army's retreat from the place was just temporary, and soon they would return. The young people, therefore, should remain, carrying out acts of sabotage against the Germans: cutting telephone lines and putting other stumbling blocks in the path of the occupiers.

On July 17 in the evening hours, the last tanks of the Soviet Army retreated, together with the last remaining members of the Communist party in the *Rayasfolkom*.

Complete silence prevailed in our town. Anxiety about the coming unknown trembled in the air, and to the great despair of the residents the last retreating members of the Red Army blew up both bridges, one leading over the river and the other over the lake; dividing the town into two companies, one completely isolated from the other.

The next day, on Friday morning the 18th of July, the first Nazi bandits appeared in our town. They came from the town of Mikashevichy and the village of Hryczynowicze, entering the town by Podlipya Street. Immediately upon entering the town they established positions at the ends of the streets and pointed their machine guns towards the Sluch River.

That which we had feared had befallen us. Thus it all began. In the evening of that same Friday, with wild screams the Nazis summoned only the Jews, rushing them to the river and forcing them to work on the construction of a temporary bridge, over which would later cross cars, weapons, horses, and tanks. They also immediately demonstrated their cruelty to the residents: they hit, pushed and threw people into the river – why? Just for the sake of being cruel.

Suddenly a Soviet airplane appeared and bombed the bridge. No one was hurt, but the heroic Nazis were the first to run, frightened, and hide under the bridge.

The next day, on the Sabbath, for the second and last time a Soviet plane appeared in the skies above the town and dropped a bomb somewhere. Many of the Nazi soldiers and their officers, who happened to be out in the street at the time, panicked and ran to hide in the old synagogue.

[Page 50]

That marked the end of the Red Army's resistance to the occupation where we were. Two or three days later, we heard the echoes of cannon fire, but it grew fainter and fainter, and we knew that the Red Army had continued its retreat.

From that day on they forced us, men and women both, to work day after day, repairing roads on the other side of the river in the direction of the villages of Lyudenevichi and Zhitkovichi, places where we had not set foot in more than twenty years, since the establishment of the border along the Sluch River. Every morning we would set out, hundreds of men and women, equipped with rakes and picks, and we would work under the supervision of the Nazis – it was slave labor, done without recompense. If a day passed when we were not beaten, that was our wages.

We still didn't realize, even after we had seen the cruel way they treated us, that the Nazis were also likely to kill innocent people. The refugees who had come to our town from Warsaw and the surrounding area in 1939 had told us that the situation of the Jews there was very bad indeed: the Jews were forced to stand in separate lines, and in some places the order was given for Jews to wear the yellow patch on their clothes. But they had not said a word about the murder of innocent people.

The first victim in our town was Nachman Eleynik: he was shot by an S.S. man who had ordered him to bring wine and tobacco. Nachman was sick and lying in bed and was therefore unable to fulfill this demand quickly enough. The town was terrified. That murder taught us that to those animals, our lives were worthless.

On the evening of the same day, the same S.S. murderer ordered that eight young komsommols (members of a Soviet youth group) would appear before him and his friend. Among those eight young men were Shimon Schusterman, Shimon Beigelman, Kusha Gelanson, Minsk and others; they were shot to death that night in the yard of the Gmyna (city hall), all except for one: Ayzik Brodatski, who was able to evade them in the darkness and run away. They chased him all the way to the bridge over the lake (which had been repaired immediately after the Nazis entered the town). When he saw that escape was impossible, he jumped over the side of the bridge into the waters of the lake and drowned. He chose to die in the lake rather than fall into the hands of the murderers.

For many days the killers searched for him in every corner of town, even in the home of his bereaved parents. But the murderers were not satisfied with this; a few days later they slaughtered another fifteen people (among them, all the members of the Gorodetski family – five souls).

This is the story of the murder of that family: for no real reason a quarrel broke out between Chaya, the daughter of Gorodetski and Mrs. Hilkovic, the wife of the mayor at the time. Chaya spoke carelessly, telling her, "Do not imagine that your time has come to rule!" That same evening, the people of the town saw Chaya and her mother being led down the street by soldiers and policemen, heading in the direction of the hill behind the city on the way to the village of Steibelovichi. Before reaching the village, they killed the women and left their bodies lying in the road; so that people would see them and be afraid. The bodies remained there for twenty-four hours. Chaya's two small children

[Page 51]

(twins) and her brother were killed in their home the same day. The bodies of the two children were thrown out of the window. The next morning, when their bodies were found there were signs they had been gnawed on by pigs.

A few days later, Yudel Levin and a Christian resident were shot. Someone had reported to the authorities that they had predicted that Germany would be defeated in the war. Judah Golob and Yaacov Maslov, upon their return from their service in the Polish Army, were executed as soon as they returned to their homes and families. Young men from the town of Mikashevichy who had been released from the army were taken to the hill, shot and buried there.

After that the pace of the murders slowed down, and we wanted to believe that our lives would return to normal.

The Council (*Judenrat*)

By order of the Nazis, a Jewish council (*Judenrat*) was selected in our town, for the purpose of fulfilling the demands made by the Nazi government on the residents. The members of the Judenrat were: Aharon Millner, Yitzhak Kolpanitsky, Benyamin Starobinski, Moshe Reuven Zaretzki, and Yosef Rubenstein.

Bitter was the fate of those selected to those positions. The residents spewed insults and curses upon them. People had not yet given up on life; they cherished each and every one of their belongings. The Nazi robbers showered the council members with their demands for one thing after another. First they demanded all of the soap in the possession of the residents, after that the eau de cologne, then the watches, rings, gold, silver, sugar, cocoa, clothing, shoes, samovars, musical instruments – in short, every single thing that they saw and coveted.

And after all that came the worst demand of all – the residents were commanded to turn over to the government all of their cows and chickens. Thus was the supply of milk taken from the mouths of the babies!

The council was required to fill the position of an employment agency: they supplied the Nazis with the number of workers demanded by the beasts for cutting trees, pumping water, cleaning, repaving the streets and paths, and clearing the snow in the winter.

The Physical and Emotional Situation

There was great fear of killings, especially in the first months, and the situation - which already was awful – grew worse from day to day. But they couldn't take from people their will to live.

Although faces were gloomy and eyes filled with deep sorrow, hidden in the heart there remained a spark of hope that things would change; it was inconceivable that the current situation would continue forever.

There was nothing to eat: no meat, no milk (no one even dared to dream of eggs and butter), but in spite of that we continued to live somehow. People secretly traded with the Christian population. They traded in clothing, handkerchiefs, undergarments, and shoes taking in exchange loaves of bread, or a kilo of potatoes here, a cup of

[Page 52]

milk there. All of this, of course, was done in secret. Milk, eggs, meat and fats were expressly forbidden to Jews.

The allocated portion of bread, 100 grams per person, was doled out by the Jewish council. Every person was required to pay a head tax every month. A rumor was spread that the Nazis intended to lock us into a ghetto. Everyone understood what that meant, and people began to hoard food, especially bread (that is, flour and grains). Many among us did not have anything to trade with the farmers, and nothing with which to buy foodstuffs, and were clearly unable to put anything aside for the coming days.

The front line withdrew farther and farther from us each day, retreating deeper and deeper into Russia, beyond the eastern valley, which distressed us more and more.

There were days when we could see, to our sorrow, Nazi reinforcements passing through our town, various forces: infantry, mechanized forces, cannons, cavalry, tanks, and within them companies of S.S., all moving eastward, in apparently infinite numbers.

It is difficult to describe what we went through in those days, living in the grip of fear day and night. The young people would hide amongst the cornstalks in the garden or in the privy, peering out through the holes and cracks, following the approaching army with terrified eyes, frightened by their wild screams and the orders of their officers which could be heard from one end of the street to the other.

Hungering for even a scrap of bread, we were forced to watch satiated, healthy, red-cheeked soldiers gobbling with full mouths the geese and chickens they had stolen from us, and the pig meat stolen from our Christian neighbors, and finishing off their meal by guzzling wine. They would cut off the heads of the stolen chickens and force whichever young person they caught to pluck the carcass and prepare it for the cook pot. Occasionally the person doing the work was rewarded with the legs or the head. Immediately he would run home with his spoils and prepare a feast fit for a king. There were others, however, who in spite of their hunger, refused to eat anything that was not kosher.

Soldiers who passed through our town would pound on the doors and demand to be given wine, tobacco and other things which would pleasure their filthy souls. Those visits filled us with terrible fear.

Who can describe the sadistic abuse those predatory beasts used against our people? In the middle of their hard, exhausting slave labor, the old people were forced to get up and dance for them, and the young women were forced to strip and dance naked for them on the tables. They performed still other abominations which I can not bring myself to put to paper.

One day a company of S.S. soldiers passed through our town, tarrying for a couple of hours. The commander of the company called for the leading rabbi of the city, Rabbi Moshe Millstein, of blessed memory. He took the rabbi into the barber shop, sat him down,

[Page 53]

and ordered the barber to shave off half of the rabbi's beard, after which horrible act they forced him to sing for them. At the sound of the rabbi's beautiful voice, shaking with tears, singing the Kol Nidre prayer, the hearts of the Jews bled.

Like an arrow from a bow the rabbi ran home, his hands covering his cheeks. Even in those bitter, difficult days he did not cease his work; he would sit and study, day and night. He was a prophet who predicted that in the end the Germans would be defeated and overthrown. He was certain of it.

In the spring of 1942 whispers infiltrated our community that companies of partisans existed in the woods, daring occasionally to enter the villages in order to take hay for horses or obtain necessary items, then returning to the forests. It was told they entered the villages armed with rifles, machine guns and other weapons.

It was very difficult to believe. Could it be possible? There were Nazi soldiers and policemen at every turn, and they were well-equipped with ammunition and weapons. They watched every movement and governed with an iron fist. Could it be possible that in an area under their control, right under their noses, there could be operating a group of people who would dare to oppose them and rebel against them? Where did they come from? And how could they survive in the forests, especially in the winter? We heard rumors that a group of partisans had entered the nearby village of Khvorostov and taken control of the place for a few days, until they saw a need to withdraw. Another story was told in whispers, that our people who worked repairing the road to Mikashevichy had seen, not far from them, a company of partisans armed with weapons and dressed in the uniform of the Red Army. And once, we saw with our own eyes a company of Nazis establishing a position next to the Christian church, and lying in the trenches with their machine guns pointed towards the forest. They remained thus for two days. Why else would they take up a position of readiness – and against whom – when the Red Army was as far away as east is from west?

It was difficult to believe the rumors about the existence of a partisan company. But the rumors and whisperings did not cease, and in our hearts there glowed an ember of hope. If it was true, then the world had not yet come to an end. We began to doubt the boastful stories of the Nazis, who claimed that their army had already reached the gates of Moscow. They had made such claims when they first entered our city; now, ten months later, they were still at the gates of Moscow and not yet within the city?

Even a prisoner in jail was less removed from the world than we were. We had no radios, no newspapers, and no passersby. The only news we heard came from a deceptive source, the mouths of the Germans, and we did not believe their stories. We knew that in the towns closest to us, Mikashevichy, Lachwa, and Horodok, the Jewish communities still existed. But we had no communication with them, because none of us left our town, and none of them came to us.

[Page 54]

We had no knowledge of the activities in Jewish towns far from our location. We heard that in the cities of Pinsk and Luninietz, they had taken all the men away and they had never returned to the town or their homes. Nothing was known of their fates. It was said that they had been taken to a place of work. Our mental state was divided between two extremes; hope that we would be rescued on the one hand, and despair and hopelessness on the other. A few times there hovered over our town the danger of destruction and annihilation.

We remember fondly the German Max Fiershtenhauffer, a resident of our town for forty years, who knew each one of us and was a friend to every resident of the town, especially the children, and who was an honest and loyal man. More than once he saved our town from destruction – before it could happen he would run to the army officer and the S.S. and ask for mercy to be shown towards the Jews of the town who, as he said, were the best Jews in the world. And those evil men would grant his request and spare us, for his sake.

We also remember the wife of the town's minister, who took into her home the Kliger girl, daughter of a refugee from Warsaw who had come to our town. The girl remained alive thanks to her, for she claimed the girl as her own daughter.

The Ghetto

On the 10th of May 1942, the Nazis imprisoned us in a ghetto. They brought into our town the Jews from the neighboring villages and from villages farther away, such as: Khvorostov, Hryczynowicze, Garbov, Milevich, and many families from the Volka village. Altogether there were gathered about one hundred and fifty people.

The center of the ghetto was on the main road which came to an end at the bank of the river. The borders were: the lane next to the two-story house of Herzl Paperna and the corner of Podlipya Street opposite the lane. From there the border turned to the Street of the Gentiles and crossed that street until the end that reached the riverbank; that is, to the house of Mordechai Tziglig, cutting the house in two. That side of the main street was within the ghetto, and the other side ran along the Pulsia Marsh outside the ghetto. The area of the ghetto was the portion of the main street from the lake to the river, and half of the Street of the Gentiles parallel to it.

Within that narrow area were confined the Jewish residents of the town and the surrounding villages. Obviously it was terribly crowded, and conditions were difficult. Three or four families, along with all of their furniture and belongings were forced into a single apartment; men, women and children. Our mutual, bitter fate and the fear that hung over our heads brought us closer together. We didn't fight or bicker; in fact, the opposite. Everyone helped each other as best he could; since we couldn't help one another materially, we comforted one another.

Immediately after the order establishing the ghetto came the command to wear the yellow badge. We were required to put two badges

[Page 55]

on our clothes, both front and back: one over the heart and one on the right side of the back. It was forbidden to be seen outdoors without those badges. At the beginning, we were ordered to put a yellow Star of David on a white background on our sleeves. Afterwards, we were ordered to put a yellow Star of David on our fronts and backs, and finally we were forced to wear a circular badge with a diameter of ten centimeters (four inches). I look back now in wonder and amazement, how easily some of us accepted that order. There were even young men and women who rushed to be the first to leave the ghetto with their clothes decorated with the yellow badge, so others would see them.

The main street of the ghetto was always full of people. After the work day, young people would wander aimlessly in the street, visiting friends, unaware of the fate that awaited us all. As usual, the Jewish council continued to supply the Nazis with workers; they would leave in the morning and return in the evenings to sleep in their own homes. Of course, the economic situation, which had been bad enough before we were enclosed in the ghetto, only grew worse until things became unbearable.

Those confined in the ghetto were unable to continue their trade with the Christian residents. The ghetto was enclosed with barbed wire stretched between wooden posts which had been driven into the ground, and guards were stationed to ensure that no one left the ghetto. We were prevented from bringing any foodstuffs into the ghetto. Occasionally, a few of the workers were able to bring in a kilo or two of flour or potatoes hidden in their clothes as they returned to the ghetto from their work. They were able to do so at the post and on the watch of a kind-hearted policeman who was one of the young Christians of the town.

We came to know the policemen very well, and to distinguish between the good ones and the bad, and information about the guards on duty was passed from friend to friend: "Today a good man is on duty" or "A bad fellow, hostile to Jews, is on duty today – be careful!"

How did we live?

As was mentioned above, many people made sure to bring in foodstuffs on which they could live for a certain amount of time. Others were able to sneak things in on their return from work or other opportunities. For how long could we have lived like that, if we had been given the chance? It is difficult to answer that question. Every day our supply of valuable items used to trade for food grew smaller and smaller: clothes, undergarments, sheets, pillows and jewelry. Shoes also disappeared. We continued to live, somehow, if such an existence can be called living.

* *
*

Shortly before we were imprisoned in the ghetto, the Germans removed a group of young men from our town and sent them to work at the train station in Hantsavichy (near Baranovichi). The group consisted of about sixty professionals in the fields of construction, carpentry, and welding. They would send us greetings, and occasionally letters.

[Page 56]

On the 21st of May 1942 an order was given for all men between the ages of fourteen and sixty to gather in the field of the club on Lachwa Street. Of those gathered, one hundred and fifty men were selected and told to stand to one side. The remaining men were the feeble, the sick, and a few professionals who were needed to perform work in the town. We were told that they were going to send those of us who had been selected to join the first group of sixty men who were working in Hantsavichy, where the commander in charge of the work was located.

Many of us tried, by any means possible – pleas and begging – to be allowed to remain in the ghetto and not be sent to work. Those who were about to be sent away were envious of those allowed to remain in town. It was hard for them to be separated from their loved ones, to leave them and go who knows where, without knowing what awaited them there. And the family members – parents, sisters, brothers and children – cried bitterly over the fate of those who were leaving. Who knew when they would return, and when they would be seen again?

After all that, it never occurred to even one of us that we were parting forever, and that we would never again see our dear loved ones.

On the last night, the eve of our departure, no one closed an eye, and no one sought his bed. We were busy preparing for the journey. We were equipped with two or three loaves of bread and underwear. Those who were able brought valuables with them to trade with the Christian population of the place where we were being sent to work. These included head scarves for women, silk stockings, ribbons and similar items (based on the advice we received from the sixty who had set off to work before us).

Early the next morning, on Friday the 22nd of May we set off, a group of one hundred and fifty men surrounded by policemen walking towards Mikashevichy. Our packages followed behind in a wagon. All of these commands and troubles fell on our heads on a Friday; is there any possibility it was purely by chance?

The Nazis entered our town on the 18th of July – a Friday. All of the orders and decrees were given on Fridays. We were sent to Hantsavichy on the 22nd of May, a Friday. And finally, the bitter and hurried day - the day the people of our town were slaughtered – was the 14th of August, a Friday.

* *
*

When we arrived in Mikashevichy they put us in a fenced yard opposite the train station. The Jews of that town, which was a sister town to our own, were all of them familiar, good friends or relatives of the people of Lenin. They were not put in a ghetto but instead walked about freely. They rushed to bring us food, commiserated with us, and felt our pain.

[Page 57]

According to the Nazi's division of the area, Mikashevichy was not part of Lenin or White Russia; but rather was considered one of the areas of the Ukraine. The command there was different from that in our town, and there was no ghetto there. In the end they put us into two transport cars, seventy five men in each, and closed us in.

The darkness and crowded conditions in the car were intolerable. Most of us stood up, a few sat on top of their belongings. The next day we arrived in Luninietz and were taken to the ghetto to spend the night. The streets of Luninietz - which had formerly been full of life and gaiety, teeming with people, mostly Jews – were empty. As we made our way to the ghetto, here and there we passed by a solitary Christian or a policeman; they stopped and stared at the group of Jews burdened with all sorts of heavy packages, boxes and baskets.

As soon as we arrived in the ghetto we saw the evil that had befallen the Jews of Luninietz. There were no men to be seen or found in the ghetto, just women of all ages and children. Where were the men? No one knew. They were taken away and were gone…Among one of the few men left we found Brodinski, who served us tea.

The next day we reached Hantsavichy, where we found the sixty men from our town and a group of one hundred and twenty men from the town Pohost, near Pinsk. They put all of us into the small houses at the outskirts of town, houses that had once belonged to the poor people of the Jewish community.

After a few days they added another twenty men from our town, the last group of workers from our town. We were a work camp of three hundred and fifty people, and a new way of life began.

The Nazis crammed twenty-five or even thirty of us into a single room. We slept on long wooden benches on three levels, one above the other, with hay spread on them. In these crowded conditions we were ordered to maintain complete cleanliness, such that there should not be found – God forbid – any speck of dirt, and that there should be absolute orderliness. We were responsible for the cleanliness of the walls and the floor.

The Germans would perform frequent cleanliness inspections, and would suddenly perform surprise inspections of our persons, examining our skin and hair with a magnifying glass. And woe to the man on whom was found any bit of dirt or any kind of sore on his skin; he could expect to be shot to death. We were told that before we arrived two people had been put to death for this reason.

We did the best we could (though our ability was quite limited!) to keep clean. On Sunday, which was a day off from work, we devoted our time to cleaning, especially washing underwear.

[Page 58]

We had long ago run out of soap. We scrubbed our underclothes as best we could, and boiled them in water. They were not white, but they were clean.

We didn't lack for work. Everyone had to work every day; it was strictly forbidden to be sick. Professionals such as tailors, shoemakers and carpenters mostly worked in workshops to provide items for the Germans and the policemen. The rest of the workers were busy with various jobs: gardening, cutting trees, tanning leather, loading trains, and flattening and paving roads. For our labor our cruel captors allotted us 200 grams of bread and twenty grams of groats per day, nothing else.

Two hundred grams of bread is not enough to sustain a small child; it certainly wasn't enough for a grown man doing hard work. It is completely clear that such a miniscule portion of food could not sustain anyone, let alone a man doing hard physical labor.

Secretly, at great danger to our lives, we would bargain with the farmers in the area: coats, trousers, sandals, socks and handkerchiefs were given in exchange for potatoes, flour, oils, and sometimes eggs. We were in need of God's mercy, that He should protect us and rescue us, and ensure that the allowed basics would fall into our hands and not into those of our oppressors. We had hiding places under the floor and in the attics. When night fell we baked bread, secretly and at the risk of our lives, and divided it up amongst us. It tasted like paradise to us, and the more we ate of it, the more our appetite grew. It is well known that a few grams of bread do not satiate one.

It was then the season for picking blackberries, and we bought them from our neighbors in the yard. We made jam from the berries, sweetened with saccharine, to spread on our bread. On the way to our place of work we sometimes passed over fields of ripened grain. We took advantage of the opportunity, picking the grain and filling our pockets with the stalks. We ate them later, raw or roasted over a fire. This source of life and nutrition did not last for long, though. After only a few days a guard was stationed there; the owner of the field had issued a complaint to the area commissar, that the Jews had eaten a large amount of grain, and he demanded compensation for the damage we had caused.

The commissar of that place was Miller, and he had two deputies who were responsible for the execution of the work: the engineer Kolvic, and his friend Zigred. The first, Kolvic, wasn't bad. He had lived in Russia during the First World War and spoke Russian.

Among the officers, there were another two (ironically, members of the Nazi party) who were unusual amongst the gang of murderers. They were cultured men of conscience who, in their hearts, despised the actions of the Nazis and their cruel, murderous ways. We knew this from our face-to-face conversations with them, but what could so few do against the pack of vicious animals in men's form?

[Page 59]

They feared even their friends, who knew nothing of mercy even towards their own people, indeed even their friends. There was one officer named Koplavski (a Polish name?), a tall handsome man, who was by far the most cruel, evil and malicious. This officer was the scum of the earth, head and shoulders above the rest in his actions during the slaughter of the Jewish communities, and the leader in the torture and murder of martyrs.

* *
*

Among the many things the Nazis forbade the Jews were: to smoke, to eat fats, to walk on the sidewalks, and to enter the homes of Christians. All of these prohibitions were clearly posted on bulletin boards all over town. When we arrived in Hantsavichy we saw no Jews at all. We were shown a few mounds and told that the bones of the Jews were buried there. I cannot describe the despair we felt when we saw those mounds. But we knew from the farmers that in other towns, both near and far – Klatzk, Baranovichi and others – the Jewish communities still existed.

At times we were terrified for our lives because of the surprise inspections the Nazis would suddenly organize, usually in the middle of the night. They would take ten people from among us and stand them off to one side. They were hostages; the murders would kill them if they discovered that someone had run away from the camp.

There was no threat in these incidents; it's just the way things were. When these assemblies took place there were policemen posted all around us like a wall in the yards and lanes, and armed German soldiers stood at the ready. More than once we thought to ourselves, "This is our end." Once, not far from Hantsavichy, a German soldier was found dead in the road. They immediately gathered us together and told us what had happened, then threatened us that if there would be another killing of a German, ten Jews would be executed – ten Jews for one German.

Every day we saw people passing by, their hands tied behind their backs, on their way to be executed. Sometimes they were accompanied by Germans, but more often by policemen equipped with rifles and hoes. They killed many Polish youth, women with children, and White Russians. The news that reached us from the front by way of German broadcasts was all bad – like the lamentations of Job. Although we were convinced that the news of their successes was exaggerated, we didn't know for certain, because the Red Army continued to retreat.

Hitler's army occupied Sebastopol, and the Germans joyfully celebrated that victory with cheers and applause, while we turned our faces to the ground, depressed and full of despair.

One day, while we were in the forest, a young man from the city of Klatzk came running up to us, telling us that the Nazis had organized a massacre of the Jews in Klatzk. Only a few young people had successfully escaped the gunfire, when the Germans had set the city on fire on all sides. A few young hotheads from our group wanted to run away

[Page 60]

that same day after work, but the rest of us convinced them not to take such a rash step that could lead to disaster for all of us.

Every day our determination to run away grew stronger. It was clear to us that although the fact that we were in a work camp indicated that the Germans needed us, our fate was likely to be the same as all of the Jewish communities, and we understood that we should not deceive ourselves that we would transform the murderers into good men, and we could not just sit back with folded arms.

We knew that if we ran away it would bring about a disaster for our brothers, sisters and parents left at home. Our escape would speed the death sentence of the members of our community. For now, we knew they were still alive; policemen, the sons of the farmers of the area, would bring us letters from them. That knowledge and the awful thought that their precious blood would be on our hands – God forbid - virtually tied our hands and prevented us from running away from the den of wild animals. We were caught between a rock and a hard place or, more accurately, to use the allegory from our sages of blessed memory, we were the dove caught between the hawk and the snake.

We were tensed and ready for every blow. We made an agreement that if we were forced to run away, we would all go, with no one left behind; all three hundred and fifty men, an organized unit. It wasn't long before the hour for which we had prepared was upon us; the sudden push to run away immediately was the total destruction of our town, Lenin. <

The End of Our Town

Oy, how difficult and horrible is the chapter I am about to write. The wounds in my heart, which have healed just a little, are reopened and bleeding as I recall the horrific scenes that pass before my eyes.

Those final hours! The last moments! Who can imagine?! Who can describe to himself the thoughts that passed through the minds of our dear ones then?! Who among us has the strength to imagine himself in the midst of those old people, young people and children who stood and saw the atrocious death that awaited them, their grave open before them?! Who has the strength to imagine jumping into that grave together with them?!

* *
*

On Thursday evening, the 13th of August 1942, army reinforcements and policemen streamed into our town from the surrounding towns of Strubin, Hantsavichy and others. The residents of our town wondered, and didn't understand why those reinforcements had come. But the next day, Friday the 14th of August 1942, with the coming of the dawn, they realized what awaited them.

[Page 61]

The order was given to awaken all of the residents of the ghetto, from the youngest to the oldest, and gather them in the street not far from the house of the officer of the city (commandator), on the other side of the bridge over the lake. All of the streets and gardens of the ghetto were surrounded by soldiers and policemen with machine guns and automatic weapons of all kinds.

The soldiers and policemen searched every corner to ensure that no one escaped, grabbing by the neck those who dawdled or lagged behind. When the people had reached the gathering place, the Nazis arranged them in rows, four in each column. Mothers stood together with their children in an attempt not to be separated from them. Everyone tried to stay close to his family. Thus they arranged themselves in columns, each man with his family.

Everyone knew that they were being prepared for an inescapable death. They stood silently, frozen in place. Their hearts had turned to stone and they were unable to react in any way.

Young mothers, their babies still caught up in sweet sleep in their mothers' arms, whispered to them: "Sleep, my baby! Don't wake up. Sleep, my child, do not awake." The murderers approached them and separated out some individuals and several families from among the columns of those about to die. They separated those who would stay alive and put them to one side. They were professionals – tailors, shoemakers, and other artisans –whom the murderers felt they still needed for the time being.

Among those standing in the columns were a number of young women who, through some kind of instinct, snuck away from their positions and stealthily joined those set aside to live, as if they were the daughters of those families. Their shrewd instincts proved fortunate, and they were saved from death. Twenty-eight people remained alive: the artisans and their families, including the young women who joined them. As has been said, the murderers decided to keep them alive for as long as they found them useful, though as will be told later, a miracle happened and the twenty-eight managed to escape from the murderers and were saved from death.

Our people stood a long time in those columns with no hope of salvation as the killers loaded them group by group into trucks. They took them to the well-known bloody hill on the main road to the village of Steibelovichi, opposite the orchard of the Agarkov farm.

Deep ditches had already been dug there. At the edge of the ditches the cursed murderers undressed the people of our town and took their clothes and opened fire on them with their machine guns. Their shocked screams were heard by the Christian residents, who were eyewitnesses to the massacre. The bodies of our martyrs rolled and fell into the ditches. The killers arranged the bodies in layers, one on top of the other.

[Page 62]

And blood mixed with blood. The blood of babies mixed with that of their mothers, grandfathers and grandmothers. There is no doubt that some of them were buried alive. The trucks filled with living souls kept on coming, one after another, and the entire horrific massacre was completed within an hour.

* *
*

David Schusterman

As all of the Jews of our town stood in lines, a scant hour before they were executed, and while the Germans searched for and selected a few families of tailors, shoemakers and the like to keep alive for the time being and be put to work for them. Among those, they were prepared to keep the tailor David Schusterman and the barber Yaacov Afman alive. But the Nazis determined that the families of the two men were "too large" for their taste, they refused to allow the families of the men to remain alive. Schusterman and Afman gave up the opportunity to stay alive, saying that if their families were to be massacred they would join them.

* *
*

The Tanis family (who owned the pharmacy in Lenin). Nachum (or as he was called, Naum), from the city of Pinsk, who married Sonia the daughter of the pharmacist in Lenin, was considered to be a little bit sickly all of the time he lived in Lenin, and far from being a hero in either body or spirit. He would walk slowly in front of his house, taking small steps. His wife watched over him to be sure he wouldn't, God forbid, take sick. They were a very intelligent couple. They lived peacefully and watched over one another. They did not have any children. When they were loaded with the rest onto the trucks on what they understood would be one-way trip, they decided to die at their own hands rather than at the hands of the cursed Nazis. During the ride on the truck they swallowed some poisonous pills which they had prepared in advance, which put them to sleep forever.

[Page 63]

Yentel Starobinski, the wife of Betzalel, hid while the Jews were being awakened and rushed to the special gathering place from which they would go to be slaughtered. She hid under the porch of a house and lay there for awhile. After the killings, policemen who were searching and snooping around for money, gold and other valuables found her. They took her to the jail (a small building in the yard of the Gmyna). That night, she tore her nightgown into strips, wove it into a rope, and hanged herself.

* *
*

Nishka and Chaya Isers, daughters of Yisrael Aharon, and one other girl, a relative of Itka Winik, hid in the attic of Nina Obchinikov, and thus remained alive for several days. Nina, a Christian, had always been considered among the supporters of the Jews. Her only daughter had always been friends with Jewish girls.

In spite of that, one day she went with Sima Firshtenhauft (son of the German supporter of the Jews, Max F.) and reported the girls to the authorities, who came and took them away.

* *
*

Beshka, the daughter of Mordechai Tziglig, lived in the house at the end of the street. She also succeeded in hiding in the attic, after preparing enough food to last her for several days. She crawled into a hidden corner and waited. Some small Christian boys found her and reported her to her neighbor, Lender, who was used by the Germans as a policeman. He came with a few others to take her. She asked them to allow her to live, and promised to give them all of the gold she had. They asked for the gold first, but Beshka thought it over and told them that anyway they would kill her (she knew them well), and didn't give them anything.

As they brought her past the house of Efraim Goldberg, the building used to house the 28 people who the Germans had selected to live, they saw her walking by with her back straight and her head held high. She turned her head toward the window and bowed her head in a gesture of farewell as she passed by.

* *
*

Rachel Vacharbin, wife of Asher Golob, who had always been very energetic and opinionated, also managed to hide. First she sat in the bathroom of Aharon Migdalovich, later she moved to the garden of Yaacov Nemchania, who had lived opposite Efraim Goldberg. She lay down between the flowerbeds, and sometimes they would bring her a little food. She asked if they would hide her in the house of those who remained (something that was almost impossible because of the guards and the inspections). Once, when she stood up for just a moment, the Germans spotted her and took her away.

[Page 64]

* *
*

Eliyahu Tziglig and Layzer (Eliezer) Golob worked in the village of Moritz at the time of the slaughter in Lenin. After a few days they were brought back to Lenin. They were shadows of their former selves, their faces covered in stubble, filthy and broken down from the journey. All the way they had been cruelly abused and beaten; they had fallen down, gotten up, and fallen down again…

They took them all the way to the big bridge in order to kill them there; a pit had already been prepared. Olshevsky, the son-in-law of Max Firshtenhauft and someone who, ironically, was known to us to behave badly towards Jews, especially in the days of the Germans, went to the place to delay the execution. The Jews were put into the home of E. Goldberg, with those who remained; they all ran away to the forests together during an attack by the partisans. In a further touch of irony, the two were killed by the partisans during the infamous "oblawa" (chase). The partisans didn't want to accept them during the time of the oblawa since they were out in the forest then, and not in a partisan camp, and they were shot to death by Ivanov.

The youngest son of Eliyahu Tziglig, Noah, stayed alive thanks to Moshe Rabinovitch of blessed memory, who managed to grab him and hide him in his large cloak in a way that he went unnoticed; thus he remained alive. Rachele Kliger (daughter of the refugee, who was in Lenin), was also saved by a miracle thanks to the self-sacrifice and righteousness of the minister of Lenin's wife, who took her in as her own daughter. Noah and Rachele were sent later on by air to Moscow, where they live. Rachele was reunited with her father in Moscow.

The twenty-eight people whom the Nazis saw a need to keep alive for the time being were returned to the house of the Jewish council, in the former home of Avraham Yitzhak Chinitch. They sat and labored there under guard, expecting to meet the same fate as the other Jews of our town. About a month after the massacre, a partisan company attacked the town, occupied it and remained there for awhile. When they left the town, they took the remaining Jews of the town with them and burned the ghetto and its main street to the ground.

Most of the twenty-eight eventually made their way to Israel, where they made their homes. A few stayed in Russia, and a few immigrated to the United States.

The town of Lenin was completely emptied of its Jews, and no sign remains of their existence. A tradition hundreds of years old was wiped away. Gradually, house by house and street by street, the town of Lenin was built by a peaceful people who loved life, who worked and strove, and were satisfied with their lot. Then came the savage beasts and with one movement put an end to it all.

The Jews of Mikashevichy were massacred by the Nazis eight days before the Jews of our town were slaughtered. Two weeks after the massacre of the Jews of our town, the Nazis executed the Jews of Horodok and the Jews of Lachwa.

I cannot refrain from mentioning at least a few of the courageous acts of the Jews of Lachwa. Those acts deserve to be written down in detail from the memory of a witness and recorded in a book of the tales of the brave acts of rebellion in the ghettos. In the hope that it will be done, I provide here a few lines:

[Page 65]

the number of Jews in Lachwa was greater than that in our town. The men there, and also the young, were not taken to work camps. They were, therefore, prisoners in the ghetto. When the Nazis came to massacre them, the young people set the ghetto on fire, killed a few of the soldiers from the companies of Nazis that held the ghetto under siege, and ran away into the forests and swamps.

Only a few were saved and remained alive. Most were hunted down one by one by the Christian population around the city, who had always been known as Horchokim (named for David Horchok), and who were known for their heartlessness and cruelty. Those Horchokim caught the runaways and killed them with their own hands or delivered them to the Nazis. In spite of that, many of the runaways were saved and joined the partisans and were able to participate in the war of revenge against the enemies of humanity.

[Page 65]

B. Escape from the Forced Labor Camp in Hantsavichy

by Mordechai Zaichik

Translated by Amy Samin

The 14th of August 1942 was an ordinary work day, just another dark day of slaving for our enemies in the forced labor camp in Hantsavichy. No one knew how many more such days we could expect to survive, or for how much longer we would be sentenced to work strengthening the hellish death machine that was destroying our people. We tortured ourselves with the knowledge that every time we put our hoes to the ground, we were basically digging the grave of another Jew, and every time we hammered a nail into wood at the order of the Nazis, we were building the coffin of another son of our people.

But what could we do when our filthy captors were plotting to take from us the thing we held most precious, the souls of our women, our elderly, our children, back there in our town? We knew that even the slightest sign of rebellion on our part would result in their deaths. We were forced to continue.

That same Friday, three hundred and fifty people (two hundred and thirty from our town, and one hundred and twenty from the town of Pohost) set off to work, each at his task, divided into groups: one group for unloading and loading freight cars, another for repairing roads, and still more for other types of work.

I and my three assistants set out for the regional command post (which was housed in the former gymnasia). It was my task to install electrical wiring in the offices. My three helpers were Sandetz (a Jewish refugee from Warsaw), Gronet Segalovitch and Yitzhak Novick, the son of the cantor. I sent one of my helpers to the town to bring back replacement parts needed for my work. An hour later, he had not returned. I sent another of my helpers to look for him and bring back the parts – he also did not return. The same thing happened when I sent my third assistant to look for the other two.

I became quite concerned. Something must have happened, or was about to happen. We certainly weren't expecting any salvation or comfort. If something had indeed happened, it must be something terrible. Anything that could happen

[Page 65]

must be a calamity. At that moment, I recalled portions of conversations I had overheard between S.S. officers when they had been drunk and had lost control of their tongues. My worry only increased as I recalled a friendly conversation between myself and one of the thousands of S.S. officers, an older man who had not lost his human character, whose soul suffered and who despised the acts of his own people. In his words I caught a clear hint that our days were numbered and soon the end would come.

While I continued to work and my heart feared the worst, the regional deputy commissar, Inge Kolovitch, behaved in a convivial fashion towards me. He approached me frequently, expressing interest in the progress of the work and often engaging me in friendly, almost warmhearted, conversation. I was overcome with apprehension: this overly-friendly behavior made me fear that something awful was in store. Or perhaps I was anxious unnecessarily? Irregardless, that day he seemed completely different than usual with me.

As the day turned towards evening I returned from my work to the camp. Some inexplicable feeling urged me to hurry. On my way I did not encounter a single living soul; neither did I meet anyone in the streets.

I cannot describe the sight that met my eyes when I entered our living place. In the first moments I was completely astonished, and my senses were spinning. All of my roommates, twenty-five men, stood fully dressed with small satchels in their hands or strapped to their backs, their faces pale as death, frightened and agitated, some sobbing quietly. They all stood facing the door, the only exit from the room. Someone briefly explained to me that word had come of the horrible massacre that the Nazis had perpetrated in our town. All of the residents – women, old people, and children – had been taken out and slaughtered. We were all bereaved, orphaned. We had no parents, no brothers or sisters, no sons or daughters.

All of the ties that had bound us in our slavery had been cut. We no longer had any reason to submit to the yoke of the hellish creatures. We were ready, as one man, to break out and run away. We knew what we could expect; we had no illusions that most of us would be able to escape and remain alive. But what value did this life have - a contemptible life of slavery, bereavement and loneliness, whose limited days were in the hands of beasts?

We did not fear death, nor were we driven by a thirst for life when we determined to escape from the labor camp. Our motivation was our fierce will to rebel with all of our puny ability, against the rule of bloodshed and evil; to at least break free from the nest of vipers even if it put an end to our miserable lives. Yet, deep in our hearts burned a tiny spark of hope; "Maybe, just maybe, we would survive and be able to avenge the blood of our beloved families." That faint hope urged us to hurry, to run away and escape. But even in that horrible hour we kept our heads. We knew we must control ourselves and plan our actions wisely. We realized that an uncontrolled haste would ruin everything and only result in our disastrous destruction. In the light of day, even if we reached the forest and succeeded in making our way deep inside, our pursuers would find us and kill most of us; the rest they would take back to the camp and kill in various cruel ways. We knew that only under the cover of darkness could we conceal ourselves deep in the forest. We needed all of our emotional strength to control ourselves and not run away immediately, but to wait until the end of the day when darkness would cover the forest and provide us with concealment.

[Page 67]

I changed out of my work clothes into other clothes and equipped myself with the last piece of bread which I had been saving, and with a knife. We stood in a tense state of readiness. There were among us those who complained that the decision about the timing of the escape left only a very narrow window of opportunity, the instant of twilight when light turns to darkness. They feared that, because of unnecessary caution, we might miss our chance; that if we tarried until the police arrived to begin the first nightly guard shift, all would be lost.

There was not one man in the entire camp who, out of fear for his own life, tried to escape before the set time. And not a single one of the three hundred and fifty said, "I will worry only about myself, and the others can take care of themselves." The great tragedy that had befallen us brought us together, and the individual felt responsible for the whole. Everyone knew that to attempt to escape early would bring a sentence of death on the entire camp.

And so everything was until the moment arrived, when suddenly everyone began to behave as one who is trying to escape a sinking ship, with men pushing one another aside to try and reach the lifeboats, grabbing one another, getting entangled with each other, and in the end overturning their lifeboat. Each man was overcome with the urge to be the first to leave; or more properly, to not be the last to escape, thus being the one most likely to be captured by the cruel pursuers. The exit was blocked by the press of bodies. The pressure on the opening was eased after a moment, because some of us, seeing the situation, remained calm and simply jumped out of the window. In a short time we were all outside, and our escape began. We ran frantically, as if rather than using our legs to run we were carried by the wind. We jumped over the fences. We fell, got up, ran and fell again, and again got up and ran. Barriers were as nothing to us, and we overcame every obstacle.

Only about twenty men remained in place and stood without moving, pale and trembling. They stared at us, but did not dare to join us. One of them was a man from our town, Yaacov Kravetz (one of the people responsible for the work in the camp); he was tall, handsome and smart. He called after us in a loud voice: "Murderers! Thieves! What are you doing?! You are bringing down disaster upon us all!"

No one listened to him, no one heard him. We were running as if borne on invisible wings. Were not the pure souls of our loved ones urging and carrying us onward? Were not the eyes of mother, father, brother and sister winking at us, from deep within the forest, calling to us, "Hurry! Come to us quickly! Flee from the den of vicious beasts."

We ran one alongside the other, no man leaving his friend. Fathers ran close beside their sons, close enough to touch and to hear his breath – and if God forbid he should fall, that he should die before his eyes.

The heat was almost suffocating, and the running only made it worse. We passed the area of the gardens and reached the canals brimming with water. I was in the first row of runners; I jumped into one of the canals and dunked myself in the cooling water and felt relief from the heat. A few of the other front runners saw my actions and jumped in also.

Who was that breathing so quickly and shallowly? Yehuda Rubenstein. He was wearing

[Page 68]

a short winter coat, heavy and thick. In whispered gasps he complained that he had no more strength to run, that soon he would break down and fall. I called to him to take off his coat while still running and leave it behind. He heard me. I could hear the sound his coat made when it fell into the water of one of the canals. Others saw what he had done and did the same.

We were escaping, getting farther away from the city. From behind us came the echoes of the first shots. The air was split with the sound of the siren. The predators knew that their prey was escaping from under their destructive claws. It was no wonder they were summoning others, who hurried to respond. Three hundred broken-down, depressed, defeated, hungry and thirsty people of an inferior race had dared to rise up against their subjugators, people of the superior race!

When I heard the shots and the sound of the alarm, my heart rejoiced, celebrating the start of our victory over our enemies. "We dared, and we did it!" I smirked in the direction of the far-off killers.

Meanwhile, we had reached the forest. We threw ourselves on the cool ground, exhausted, to rest for a bit and catch our breath for just a moment. We recovered quickly, for we knew that the time to truly rest had not yet arrived. We stood up to take stock. We wanted to know who and what was with us. We discovered there were no more than twenty-three people from our group: twelve from Pohost and eleven from our town. Those were: Simcha Schneidman, Yitzhak Slutsky (from the village of Hryczynowicze), Yehuda Tziglig and his younger brother Yaacov, Nissel Rabinovitch, Eliezer-Aharon Kolpanitsky, and myself.

We continued to run away from the camp. While we ran we ripped the yellow tags from our clothing: we were free men, the camp was behind us. We slowed down; we were deep in the forest and darkness was falling. Three guides and leaders were chosen from amongst us: Rabinov, Feldman (both from Pohost), and the one who writes these lines.

Not one of us thought of saving our yellow tags for the coming days, as a memento. There was not one of us who even imagined he would stay alive for another day, and certainly not until the end of the war – for it seemed to us the war would never be over.

Our Wanderings and Hardships

Deep in our hearts we gave thanks to God for ending the day and bringing the night; and for having the light give way to darkness. I think none of us were ever as happy to see the coming of darkness as we were that night. The darkness would help us to evade our pursuers. We arranged ourselves in single file and progressed swiftly and silently by the light of the stars. We turned southwest, in the direction of the town of Pohost. We crossed the train tracks close by the station at Liusina. Throughout the night we made good progress, covering about twenty-four kilometers, thereby putting a good distance between us and Hantsavichy. We knew well that danger could come to us not only from Hantsavichy, for we were subject to a siege in every direction, and could easily encounter a company of the evil of the earth, who could descend upon us from any direction and destroy us. That thought never left us. In spite of that, we were happy in our achievement: we had distanced ourselves from our pursuers,

[Page 69]

who chased us with the wrath of snakes and the foaming mouths of ravening dogs, who proposed to devour us and take revenge on us for what we had done to them. We had spit in their faces in a way which would not be easy for them to wipe clean. The camp supervisors would be called to account for every person who remained uncaptured.

The coming of the morning light brought the Sabbath day. We looked into the faces of our friends and saw that in the space of a day, we had changed: we were gloomy, lifeless and withered, our eyes grown dim. The crushing news that had shocked us the day before, the stress of preparations for our escape, the wild flight, and the long march at night had all left their marks on us.

Broken and exhausted, we sat on the ground with our heads bowed. After we had recovered from the horrible message we had received the day before, which had overwhelmed our senses and made us lose our reason for awhile, and after the terrible fever of our emotions, which had given us the courage to rebel against our captors and the strength to run beyond the normal human ability, had dissipated, we were overcome by fear. After the storm in our souls, which had not allowed us even the briefest moment to consider what had happened, had calmed, we were able to stop and reflect on the events of the past twenty-four hours.

Now we knew what it was to be a bereaved widower and orphan, which had fallen upon us in one day. The thought squeezed my heart like an iron vise, for I was a lonely solitary man in this evil and hostile world, with no father, no mother, no brother or sister, no relative with whom to share life's burdens. The memory of those who, twenty-four hours before, had gone to their deaths filled my heart and tortured my soul. I wanted to know and to be able to imagine how they stood, aware and with eyes wide open, face to face with death. My imagination provided horrific scenes which were capable of destroying my sanity, breaking my heart, and paralyzing my brain. The pain in my heart tortured me: why hadn't I been with them, why didn't I go with them to that grave? What were our lives now, what hope had we for revenge? How could we, a small group of poor, exhausted, and broken down people, find the strength to avenge the innocent blood of our beloved ones?

Rage boiled in my blood. Oy, how I wanted to sink my teeth into the neck of...the whole world! To devour - and be devoured!

How jealous I was of the two young men from our town who suddenly began to cry. They sat on the ground with their heads bowed, tears streaming silently down their faces. They made no sound: no sobs, no sighs, no utterance at all. But their tears fell, silently watering the ground.

To my right sat a man about forty years old, from Pohost. I sensed his strange and restless movements. One moment he would raise his hands to the sides and up into the air, as if searching for something to hold on to. The next moment his hands fell to the ground, his fingers digging into the earth, again, as if searching for support. I looked at him from the side and saw his pale, trembling lips, his Adam's apple rising and falling, rising and falling. He tried with all his strength to hold back his tears and his sobs, fighting an internal struggle with his stormy soul. I feared that if he lost the battle with himself, and his howls were unleashed, our own would soon rise in response and the forest and surrounding area would be reverberate with the sound. The guide Ravinov foresaw the danger and called out, "Get ready to move out!" and added, "We don't know

[Page 70]

this place very well. We need to move deeper into the forest where it is more overgrown; there we will be able to rest and sleep a little. It will also increase our chances of finding a company of partisans – for my part, I have no strength to go on. For the last twenty-four hours, from yesterday morning until now, we did not eat a bite. Whoever has a slice of bread should take it out, and whoever has breadcrumbs; put them on the cloth I will spread out on the grass. We will divide them up equally amongst us. We are partners in our destiny; therefore we will be partners in all that we have. Now hurry, because the hour grows late."

We did as Ravinov told us. We chewed the stale, bitter bread, but it was difficult to swallow. There was a heavy lump in our throats, blocking them. After we had eaten what little we had, we got up and continued walking.

I cannot describe all of the hardships that befell us in our wanderings, all of the misfortune and troubles that found us, so I will be brief.

For a number of days, the first days of our wanderings, food barely touched our lips aside from a few blackberries and mushrooms that we found. We tried as best we could to walk only in the densest parts of the forest, and at night, so we wouldn't run into other people. More than once we lost our way, making mistakes and finding ourselves going around in circles.

Our planned escape – three hundred and twenty people – from the labor camp which was carried out under the tight security of the Nazi army, the S.S., and many policemen made an impression on the entire area and was a hard blow to the arrogance of the Germans who controlled everything. The German command could not forgive the officers responsible for the shame and disgrace brought to the entire military regime by their negligence. The command gave an order to use all available means to pursue us and to either return us alive or slaughter us. Large companies of soldiers and policemen went out to pick up our trail. The local populace was also enlisted for this task. They were promised various prizes - money, tobacco, salt, soap – for every escapee they caught and turned over to the Germans. Many of the farmers fulfilled this task gladly and with great devotion.

After a few days we learned to our sorrow that some of our people in other groups lost their lives through lack of caution. When they were overcome by hunger, they turned to a shepherd or farmer they had encountered and asked them for food. He pretended to be kind and merciful, promising to bring them food to sustain them and showing them a place where they should wait for his return. After about an hour he returned, leading a group of soldiers and policemen, who surrounded the place and opened fire on the escapees. They killed many of them and took the few who had survived prisoner and returned them to the camp, where a very cruel death which could only have been designed by the devil himself awaited them: they forced them to hang one another, brother to brother, father to son, friend to friend.

A few groups encountered companies of soldiers, policemen, or farmers a day or two after their escape. One big group that was captured included many people from our town, including our friends: Yehuda Rubenstein, Boaz Rubenstein, Yerachmiel Dvorin and Shmuel Zaretzki,

[Page 71]

the five Gelanson brothers, Yitzhok Kribitzky and his son Yankele, Mordechai Baruchin and his son Berele – all were captured and returned alive to the Hantsavichy camp.

The fate of our group was a better one, because in one night we were successful in putting a good distance between ourselves and the area where the Nazis were searching around Hantsavichy. Not only that, we were extremely cautious during our wanderings. We preferred to starve rather than ask farmers for food. We tried as much as possible to walk on untrodden paths, to make our way where no one else had set foot. We were extremely careful to walk silently, without speaking out loud. Thus we were able to make our way safely until we reached the partisan camps.

On the third day after our escape as evening fell, something happened to me that even now, as I remember it, makes the hairs raise up on the back of my neck. Even today I cannot forgive myself that, through my own stupidity, I brought such suffering upon myself. I suddenly found myself separated from the group. And for what? For nothing. This is what happened: that day near the village of Khutinitz we encountered a second group of our friends, led by Greenboim from Pohost, a wise man who, in the camp, was one of the people responsible for the work. We began traveling together, a group of about forty men. We were all hungry, and to our joy we discovered many bushes of ripe, juicy raspberries in the forest. We pounced on the fruit and, with shaking hands, took the edge off our hunger, and put some of the fruit into our satchels. The group finished picking the berries and began to move on. I had discovered a bush so laden with fruit that I couldn't bring myself to stop picking, and continued for a moment longer. Then I saw the back of the last person walking away. I immediately ran after him to try and catch up, but I could not find any of our people. I thought to myself: "Perhaps I didn't pay attention in which direction they turned." With my heart pounding, I turned to the left, in vain! They had disappeared! I didn't dare call out to them, for we were accustomed to keeping quiet. I continued to run in all directions and tried to follow the footprints of my friends – with no success.

A terrifying despair gripped me. "I'm lost!" I told myself. My fate was sealed in one moment, all for a few raspberries. On legs trembling from the exertion of running about, I searched for and found a small log and placed it under a dense bush, to provide myself with a hiding place. I sat on the log and stared at the ground. I don't need to elaborate on all that was going through my mind. I saw myself, alone in an unfamiliar forest without any idea where I should go, with no food, with no way to defend myself against the world, vulnerable to ambush from every side, alone against huge armies, policemen, and an infinite number of people who wanted to take my soul.

Man, like other creatures, apparently has a strong will to live, strong enough even to cheer the one who is facing the end. After resting for a few minutes, which felt like years, I got up to continue my wanderings. I roamed through the forest, still carrying a spark of hope in my heart that I would reach a safe place through my own, solitary strength.

For three straight days and nights I wandered alone in the forest. I will not recount here all of the

[Page 72]

miracles that happened to me in those days. A few times I encountered shepherds; as is well-known, they were allowed to kill me, but they didn't. Then there was the story of the farmer woman, who saw my boots (which were still in fairly good condition) and coveted them. She demanded I give them to her, and provided a pretty reasonable claim: "Of what use are they to you? In all likelihood, you'll be killed today or tomorrow. Better you should give them to me in exchange for a few eggs."

Who knows? If I'd had a weapon in my hands, perhaps in the bitterness that consumed my soul I would have killed her and her daughter, who supported her claim. An old shepherd surprised me when I came face to face with him. He showed me a path to take on which I would not encounter any Germans or their collaborators. I followed his directions and after some hardships in my wanderings I came to the Babruyka River. I crossed the river in the clothes I was wearing – and at midnight I fell into the hands of a guard made up of my friends, who were out making their nightly patrol.

I hope that everyone who reads these words will imagine and understand how great my happiness was to have found my friends, and how great their happiness that I had been found. They carried me upon their shoulders, for my wanderings had exhausted my strength, and they brought me to the stopping place of the group, which now numbered some eighty men as groups met up and joined together. Most of my friends were sound asleep, but I found a few by the campfire who were still awake. They gathered around me, and we hugged and kissed one another. They had already given up on me, believing me to be dead and eulogized.

When these memories come back to me, I find it hard to understand how, in the unbearable situation in which we found ourselves, there was a place for happiness! Could it have been that even in the midst of dark despair there were buried seeds of hope?

C. Among Partisans

Translated by Mira Eckhaus

In the large group I saw new faces: some of Lenin's people joined it, among them were: Nachman Migdalovich, Eliezer Kirschenzweig (Gronam Migdalovich's son-in-law) and others. However, the people who were with us from the time of our escape until I got lost and was cut off from them, were not among them. I was very sorry that I did not find among them Simcha Schneidman, Nissel Rabinovitch, Itzke and Hirshel Slutsky, and Eliezer Aharon Kolpanitsky. During my absence, the people of our town separated from their members in the group, and chose to follow the paths leading to our town.

At the time, our group camped in the forest near the village of Bogdanovka. Some of our men would go out every evening to patrol and roam the forests in the hope of finding partisan companies and join them. Indeed, we heard rumors about a partisan company in the vicinity, not far from us.

As a matter of fact, we were not sure until now of the existence of partisan companies; the stories about them seemed to us like beautiful fairy tales. It was not until we were camped in the Bogdanovka Forest that we heard from competent sources about the presence of such companies in the immediate vicinity.

Meanwhile, we spent the days sleeping too much, being idle and washing. The dirt and filth have already given their signals in us in a real way…

[Page 73]

The main problem was the economy of our camp, which counted at the time, as previously noted, about eighty people. For this purpose, we organized small companies, which can be called "commando companies". Night after night, one company would go out, each company in turn, to the nearby villages and farms and with various tricks, take from the hands of the frightened peasants everything that could be eaten: bread, flour, grits, salt, potatoes, butter, milk, and the like.

Only brave and talented guys were accepted into these companies. Nachman Migdalovich excelled in these actions. He knew how to talk to the peasants in their rural accent until it was not evident that he was a Jew, but he seemed to them to be one of them.

The tactics of this action were: the company went into action late at night while its men were loaded with sacks, jugs, buckets and other abject tools, as the Gibeonites did in the days of Yehoshua ben Nun. Each shouldered a thick stick tied with a leather strap, which in the darkness of the night seemed like a rifle; they would knock on the window of a peasant's house. When they would come over to see who the knocker was - and before they have had time to take a good look at their uninvited guests - they were given an order in a loud and energetic voice to bring out - for the partisan battalion - loaves of bread, butter, flour, and other foodstuffs. During the act, orders were heard in the courtyard, seemingly military orders given by officers to their soldiers. The owners of the farm also heard supposedly feet stepping on the spot as if preparing to walk. All these made an impression on the peasant and his wife as if hundreds of partisans were gathering at his yard. Scared and excited, he would try to argue that the quota imposed on him is beyond his strength, and beg to reduce it somewhat. After a short negotiation they would reach a compromise - and both sides were satisfied: the owners of the farm who managed to give less than what was imposed on them, and our people - for receiving what was given to them… Thus the company managed to visit several farms during the night.

Early in the morning, the company's men would return to the camp tired and exhausted, but loaded with food. Now it was the turn of the few women, who escaped the massacre in Pohost, to show their ability in the craft of cooking. However, the ingredients were monotonous and therefore we always ate a kind of soup, which we call "kalatusha" in the language of White Russia, (meaning: mixture), that is: a mixture of flour and water together with salt and fat, if there were any.

Ten days have passed since our escape - and we're still alive! We knew that many of the fighters were killed, but we did not know at the time how many were killed as well as their identity. The question of the "identity" of those who were killed did not bother us. We were all friends, and secretly wept for each one of us who was killed. However, the question "how many" did not give us rest. Indeed, that's why we ran away. That day we did not believe in the existence of partisan units. And without them we had no chance of surviving for many days; we fought because we chose death over being enslaved to the murderers. But now, after the existence of partisan companies was certain to us, our heart ached because not all our members were with us. Afterall, now a glimmer of hope has awakened in our hearts to live and reach the day when we can take revenge on our enemies and punish them.

And then, one day we were informed that our contacts had finally managed to meet with partisans,

[Page 74]

who expressed their willingness to meet with us and also set the date and place of the meeting - in the forests of "Bailoya Aziero" (the White Lake).

At midnight we all set off. We passed the long village "Bogadnovka", which seemed to us to have no end. We walked quietly. On the way we picked up more members, who would wander alone, among them were the brothers Moshe and Gronam Lezbanik, Moshe Shapira (Liva Golob's husband) and others. Our group grew to over a hundred people.

Our mood was uplifted despite being tired from the toil of the road and lack of sleep, because we didn't sleep at all that night. We knew that something new and encouraging awaited us, and that for this thing we were going through these tribulations: we went to see those wonder men, the partisans!

Early in the morning we arrived in the deep of the forest, and suddenly we all stopped walking, as if by command. A Russian partisan, a young man, broad-shouldered, firm and flexible, suddenly appeared in front of us, as if he had emerged from under the ground. He was wearing a short coat, boots and a winter hat with the "star"| on it - the symbol of the Red Army, and in his hand, he held a submachine gun. We stood surprised and excited.

And then a young partisan girl came and stood next to him. She was dressed in a similar outfit to the partisan, and she too held a submachine gun in her hands.

Both welcomed us with a warm greeting. After that, they served the little children who were with us (the children of the parents from Pohost), cups full of cream. We stood wondering: where did they get cream in the forest and in such a large amount?

The welcome was cordial and encouraging, but what followed brought us bitter disappointment and discouragement.

They informed us immediately, frankly and without delays, that they cannot annex us to them, since we are large in number, about a hundred men, including women and children, we have no weapons and they themselves were sent here by their base which is somewhere far away, in order to carry out a certain operation. "Stay here", they said, "and wait for the instructions that will come to you from the headquarters at our base".

For three consecutive days we stayed in the same forest and waited for instructions from the headquarters somewhere, all those three days we didn't eat anything, except for one slice of bread that we managed to get.

We sent delegation after delegation asking them to take us in or give us some help. We did not receive a response, and the members of the delegation did not return to us either - they were accepted into the regiment. After many efforts on our part, some more of us got to be absorbed into the partisan regiment. Most of these lucky ones were craftsmen in professions such as carpentry, shoemaking and the like. Some also received weapons and joined a fighting unit. Among those who were accepted into the regiment were also some people of our town: Moshe rTzrukovich, Yaakov Schusterman (Beigelman) and others, and the rest were people of Pohost. Lipa Yoselevsky, who now lives in Israel, told me that he and Kirschenzweig had previously been accepted into the ranks of the partisans, but that a short time later, for some reason, they had to leave that regiment, which was under Tsikonkov's command, and look for another place that would accept them.

[Page 75]

After all, about twenty-five of our people were accepted into the ranks of the partisans, and the rest were given an order and an advice by the headquarters of the regiment: an order - to leave the place, the areas of operations of the regiment: and advice - to advance to the east, because there, according to them, there are many partisan regiments, which would be able to receive small groups of ours, and in addition, according to them, it was a safer place.

When we said goodbye to the partisans, they gave us as a parting gift one rifle and twenty bullets. The rifle was of an old type: a kind of a short rifle, which was called "Urez", and the bullets were wet and unfit for use.

Exhausted, after three days of fasting, we left the forest where we hoped to find a rescue and were disappointed. We headed east, in the direction of the Baranovichi-Luninch railway. Our tendency was to cross the railway and enter the areas we were familiar with, around our town of Lenin... Maybe there, close to home, we will find advice and resourcefulness. As if a destroyed house could be a source of support for its owners...

A group of seventeen people set out to follow this path, most of them were from Lenin: Yaakov Epstein, Yaakov Ginsberg, the brothers Moshe'l and Gronam Lezbanik, Shmuel Migdalovich, Binya Gurevich, Hoshea Nathan Macon, Gedaliah Pixman, the two Taktash brothers and myself.

(Yakob Ginsberg held the rifle, carried it, and did not give it to anyone else during all our wandering time.)

Armed with this "firearm", we started our journey. We usually walked at night, - sometimes during the day - through forests and swamps. Sometimes we were lucky and we found a good place to sleep in piles of hay, we prepared for us a soft and warm substrate made of fragrant hay. But most of the time we weren't fastidious and we would sleep in the swamps, without any substrate. Sometimes the moisture would seep through our clothes and onto our skin. And we had a miracle: none of us caught a cold or got sick. In our situation then, some kind of illness could have brought a great disaster upon us.

What did we survive in those days? This is a question for which I have only one answer and it is: Oh, woe to such a survival! Once, on our way we passed a field full of potatoes - and it seemed to us that we were the happiest people in the whole world. With trembling hands and a gluttonous appetite, we pulled the potatoes out of the ground to prepare a feast fit for kings. We baked them far from the place of our camp and in the thick of the forest, so that the smoke of the fire would not reveal our whereabouts. We divided the baked potatoes among us equally and we ate them with great appetite and joy.

The two Taktash brothers were in charge of baking the potatoes. They were experts in this, and none of us resembled them.

We pumped water from deep within the earth. Around Polisia, in the swamps, one does not have to dig a deep well. Even a small hole can yield water for drinking and even washing. I was in charge of the water supply. My penknife served as a digging tool for me.

[Page 76]

For several days we progressed without mishaps and without incident, except for one incident worth telling about.

One of the Lezbanik brothers was almost killed, not by the enemy's hands or by his destroyer, but by our rifle, the famous "Urez", and by us, and more precisely, by me. This is how it happened:

Many times, being, of course, in the thick of the forest, we tried to shoot with this rifle, in order to see whether it works properly and we can trust it in case of a need. None of us managed to get out of it either a shot or the sound of a shot. Some of us blamed it on the bullets, which were wet, according to them. Most of our people rejected the use of the tool itself and gave up on our "weapon", and yet we didn't throw it away, and comrade Yaakov Ginsberg continued to carry it.

And I couldn't sit calm and accept that fact. I had to investigate and discover the reason why it refuses to fulfill the role for which it was created. I disassembled it, tested every part of it, assembled it and tried to shoot it; again, I disassembled, tested, assembled and tried to shoot it - but in vain: it did not shoot. In short: our "weapon" has lost its value and all the comrades looked at it with contempt and disdain.

One day we all sat in a circle, the people sat and fell asleep, all of them, except for me - I was messing with our rifle. Its stubbornness did not give me rest, and here, after I almost gave up on it, I pressed the trigger once more. A tremendous thunder of gunfire pierced the air, and the bullet missed the head of one of the Lezbanik brothers by few millimeters.

The thunder of the shot was very loud, its echo in the forest was enormous, and this happened suddenly, therefore, it is no wonder the people woke up from their sleep in fear and panic and started running in all directions. They were sure that a Nazi company attacked us and opened fire on us.

After a panic calmed down and our people learned that it was our "weapon" that caused this tremendous noise and that it was the one that made the forest trees move and woke the sleepers from their slumber, its value increased immeasurably in our eyes and Yaakov Ginsberg clung to it with more strength and affection.

The weapon fired only once. But now it was clear to us that it was because all the bullets were wet, except for one, the same one that almost murdered one of the Lezbanik brothers.

We were very happy about Lezbanik being saved from death, but the next day Gronam Lezbanik caused us great sorrow. He was on guard that day, when we were about to leave the place and move on, we couldn't find him. We looked for him around as much as we could in our condition at the time - and we did not find him. He disappeared. It was difficult for us to move from the place without our member, but we had to. Staying too long in one place meant risking being caught, and the mysterious disappearance of one of our comrades also put fear on us. Maybe he was captured by the Nazis?

After two days of walking, we arrived at the railroad. In the evening, we succeeded

[Page 77]

to move to the eastern side of the railroad. It was a daring operation. A short distance from the "Luyshtashe" station, while seeing Germans, policemen and officials, we crawled one after the other, we climbed and got on the dirt mound of the railroad and on top of it we rolled down towards the other side, some into bushes and some into pits surrounded by various wild plants.

As early as the morning of that day, we unknowingly stuck our heads in the predatory animal's mouth, and only by a miracle we were saved. We didn't know exactly where we were and the name of the station near which we were. This information was very necessary for us, so that we would know where to go. Three of us went out to explore the area: Yaakov Epstein, Yaakov Ginsberg and me. All the rest of our men camped in the woods not far from the railroad. The three of us made our way to the big building we saw in the distance.

Early in the morning we entered the courtyard of the building. And here a Christian boy about twelve years old appeared and came towards us. He was horrified when he saw us. We asked him: What is this building? And he answered us with his teeth clenched together in anxiety, that this is the "Luyshtashe" railway station, and that there are many German soldiers inside the building.

We needed a lot of self-control to pretend to be calm and quiet and to hide the terror that attacked us upon hearing these things. We quietly left the yard and entered the forest. There we started a panicked run. We ran and the rest of our comrades, those who rested in the forest, ran with us. They ran without knowing the reason for it, and only after we had run a decent distance from the place of danger did we stop and tell them what had happened to us.

And again, we wandered: we moved eastward, to our surroundings; we were in the area of villages that were more or less familiar to us.

We arrived at the village of Balut. And how great was our joy, when we suddenly found the lost one, Gronam Lezbanik, walking in the middle of the street.

We passed the village of Krasnaya Volya, followed by the village of Dobraya Volya, and entered the famous Richin Swamps, which is the "jungle" of the Polisia Swamps, which stretches for many kilometers in length and breadth, and has always been used as a place of refuge for criminals, thugs and all those persecuted by the authority and the law.

We were familiar with the rivers and paths in this environment. We were born in the area of the swamps, we grew up there, and also worked there in the forest business. Among us there were those who had already passed through this "jungle" throughout its length and breadth and knew its exits and entrances. Here we met peasants who came to our town and knew some of us. There were also good people among them, who welcomed us and provided us with food. Well, our economic hardship was alleviated a little. But we didn't trust them with our safety. We knew that many of them were only pretending to share our sorrow and that their hearts were not with us. And in addition, we clearly saw that even the righteous among them were afraid that, after they welcomed us, we will stay at their houses permanently; we did not condemn them for it.

[Page 78]

We had no moral right to expect them to endanger themselves because of us, since the death penalty was expected for anyone who provided shelter to Jews.

And so, we had to continue our wanderings, and this time we were no longer hungry and thirsty, but satiated and full. There were some young people among us who eagerly filled their bellies to excess, as if they wanted to make up for the deficit in the days of famine. These did not eat but devoured, and had a serious upset stomach. We were still in the heart of the Richin Swamps, when serious stomachaches attacked Gdalike Fixman. He fell to the ground near a pile of hay, writhing in his agony and pain, and unable to move from his place. We stood around him helpless and without the means to render him any help and ease his suffering and pain. But we did not want to leave him alone. He moaned and begged: "Leave me alone! Here I will perish and die. And you, do not risk your lives because of me, go!" (days later I met this Fixman. He was a partisan in Zorka's regiment, in the village of Rafin, and I was then still moving from regiment to regiment, from commander to commander, and I could find no refuge).

We reached the village of Heritsinowitz, about twelve kilometers from our town, and found a small group of our people there: the three sons of Yaakov Tziglig and the Segalovitch brothers. They joined our group.

Some from our people entered to tour the village, they returned and brought a lot of news from a very reliable source, from Fyodorowitz, a communist and friend of the Jews of our town. He told details about the massacre in the town. He also listed the peasants who had engaged in robbery and looting and informed us who did the Nazis leave alive to serve them. He advised us to advance further to the east, because there our chances of being absorbed into the partisan regiments would increase. We listened to his advice, set off and headed east. And despite the fact we walked in the area of our villages, a great deal of caution and luck was still required. Mortal danger lurked for us every step of the way. Even in the remote villages we might encounter wandering soldiers and policemen. Only at nightfall could we be more certain that we would not meet them in the villages, because they would usually spend the night in the towns and the concentration points.

One day we heard the bitter news about one small group of Henzwitz refugees who perished in a place where they considered themselves almost safe, that no evil would befall them. There were four of them: Yitzhak Warshal, Herschel Goldman (who was the husband of Yocha Rossumka), the pharmacist's son, and the fourth - Sander Shuster's son-in-law. They were captured alive by the Germans in the village of Khvorstov near the town during the partisan attack on that village and brutally murdered by the Nazis.

The bottom line: our lives were in danger. Death lurked for us everywhere. We didn't know who to beware of and who to trust: here is a farmer who welcomes you, as if he shares in your trouble, also brings you bread to satisfy your hunger, but who can guarantee you that he is not full of hate and plans to take your life. And here is another story about two of our comrades, Lipa, the son of Hiska Mishelov and the son of Eliezer Golob, who were captured by the peasants of the village of Khvorstov and imprisoned in the basement in order to hand them over to the Nazis; in this village there were many farmers

[Page 79]

who collaborated with the Nazis. Partisans who happened to be passing through that village took these two out of their hands and showed them the way to the village of Domanovitz. When they came to that village, the two entered the village school to spend the night there. But when they entered, they were greeted by the Nazi murderers, who were at that time in the same building - and murdered them.

Israelik Gorodetski was seriously injured in the leg by policemen who fired after him, and despite his injury he managed to escape from his pursuers and crawl to the village of Khvorstov. One peasant took pity on him, fed him, watered him and offered him a straw bed to lie on and rest. After the wounded man fell asleep, the compassionate peasant set fire to the hay bed, set his guest on fire, and immediately ran to the Nazis to brag about his actions, hoping to receive a reward from them for his dedication and loyalty to them.

But the Germans, instead of presenting him with a reward, turned to him with a moral reprimand: "How could you kill a wounded man, who came to ask you for help in a difficult situation! Your sentence is death because you are a villain". And so, they did - they killed him.

The Germans had their own logic: they saw in the peasant's act something like trespassing, a kind of violation of their rights, given only to "distinguish" people to commit heinous and depraved acts and a Russian peasant, ignorant and rude, should not imitate their actions!

* * *

We reached the river Lan. In the distance we saw a group of people bathing in the river with their clothes and weapons lying on its bank. Who are the bathers, we wondered, what is expected of them, we had to be very careful. We went around them, we spied, and to our joy we found out that were partisans who went into action. We also found two of our people among them, and they were Ze'ev (Walwel) and Yehuda Tziglig.

We envied our two members who were able to find shelter for them, and we continued to wander. We passed the villages of Rehovitz, Moritz and Garbov and reached the Slouch River. That is the same Slouch River - the former border river between Russia and Poland. We crossed it. The water was already cool, the autumn days were near.

And so, we arrived at the village of Anantzitz, a place where we were warmly received. We entered the peasants' houses, and they fed us. This village was located in the partisan area, which covered a large and extensive area and included over a hundred villages. The partisans were the masters of this area, not the Germans. We passed the villages of Domanovitz and Kirov and came to the village that bears the name "Kaadika", where we found a real partisan regiment, which was organized in all aspects: weapons, equipment and kitchen.

Among these partisans we also found a familiar face, our neighbor in the town, Grigor, the son of Kirilo, known as "Bablach". Grigor escaped from the town several days after the Germans entered our town, and no one knew where he disappeared to. We also found Daniel Konick's son there. Two of us were accepted into this regiment.

A company of partisans, led by commander Chinitch from the town of Strobin, took us through an area that was considered a dangerous place, between the villages of Sosna and Kuzmitz. There camped

[Page 80]

strong German units, who guarded the railroad tracks. We walked all that night, and in the morning, we crossed the Aresa River and arrived at the village of Bibotka (Klinovka).

In the nearby village of Pelicin, we were ordered to stay there and wait for instructions from the brigade headquarters, instructions that would seal our fate.

For ten days we waited for the instructions and they did not come. The members were desperate, and no longer expected a comprehensive arrangement. So, they scattered to different places, each went to try his luck alone.

Of our entire group, only a small core of four members survived, and they were: Nahum Parpliuchik from Mikshevici, the two Lezbanik brothers and myself. We decided to continue our search together, leave the village and continue wandering together until we find an arrangement. We postponed leaving the village until the next day.

And while we were discussing what to do, suddenly three partisans appeared on horseback and one of them, their leader, ordered us to march ahead of them in the direction of the nearby grove. When we came to the grove, the commander dismounted from his horse, the loaded machine gun in his hand, and ordered us to stand side by side. He informed us that an order had been issued from the main headquarters, that anyone who is found wandering and does not belong to any partisan unit – in sentenced to death by shooting.

He didn't give us time to explain to him what we were doing in the village and for which purpose we were wandering, instead he aimed the machine gun in front of us and repeated his order, that we stand side by side, just as he ordered.

Gronam Lezbanik did not want to obey. He kept his composure incredibly and claimed that he would not line up, because it is the same fate for us: to die lined up in a line, or everyone wherever he stands.

I remember that I didn't say anything. I thought about how this world is run and, more importantly, about its leader…. about the irrationality of everything that is done under heaven. We lost everything we had. We gathered courage and bravery and burst out against the world's masters. And in our hearts, there was one and only hope to avenge the blood of the pure and holy. We went through thick and thin and survived. And now, when we were already on the verge of fulfilling our ardent desire, death came to us in such a foolish and stupid way, not from the hands of our enemies, but from the hands of those for whom we wish, as redeemers and saviors!

Nahum did not speak either: he sobbed quietly. But Moshe Lezbanik served as our speaker. He started talking continuously, like we had never heard him talk before. He argued, explained and pleaded. In addition, he took out of his pocket pictures of his murdered wife and children. He continued arguing that life was precious to him only so that he can avenge the blood of his family members, and while he was speaking, he was bold and approached the commander in front of the machine gun, and showed him the pictures.

At this moment the miracle happened. The commander's finger on the trigger of the machine gun seemed to move a little: the shot hesitated to come. His gaze rested for a moment on the pictures. He looked at us, some kind of a human emotion awoke in him. He slowly lowered the barrel of the machine gun, and ordered us in a rage to leave the village of Pelicin immediately and beware of appearing in his sight again.

It goes without saying that we quickly got out of his sight. As I walked, my lips involuntarily murmured the words of prayer, which were habitual in my mouth: "What are we? What are our lives? What is our grace? What is our righteousness?

[Page 81]

What is our salvation? What is our strength? What is our heroism?… And the spiritual superiority of man over animals does not exist because everything is nonsense!

I remembered that, like us today, a young white rooster was once saved from death in our house. On the eve of Yom Kippur, my mother told me to get me a chicken from the coop for atonement. I caught hold of the young white rooster and already started spinning him over my head. At that moment a miracle happened to this rooster. Mother looked at it and exclaimed: No, not that. It is still very young. Let it grow up. Find another one instead of this one". I immediately let go of him, and he hurried away from me with a screech of irritation and joy, maybe he then recited the prayer of humility in the language of the birds: "What are we? What are our lives?…"

Well, we escaped for our lives and continued our wanderings. We passed through many villages until we arrived on the eve of Yom Kippur in the village of Andriyevka.

Gronam Lezbanik managed all the calculations. We could trust him. In all the days of our wanderings, he didn't eat any non-kosher food, and he was careful with a light mitzvah as if it was a severe one. In our situation, this required exceptional bravery and supreme devotion.

In the village of Bobnovka we found Moshe Shullman standing guard at the entrance to the village properly with a rifle in his hand. Oh, how much we envied him. When will we also reach such greatness?! All our requests and pleas to be admitted to any unit led to naught. Every commander we would turn to would dismiss us with good advice and with the same phrase that was well-known to us: "he has no weapons for us", or: "he has already put a number of Jews in his unit, we should turn to that commander, who is stationed with his unit in the nearby village. He will surely welcome us with open arms". And so, we were thrown like a game ball from commander to commander.

We almost gave up on achieving our goal, and bitter thoughts began to gnaw at our hearts: Well, why are we suffering for? What is the purpose of all this passing between life and death? What is the point of this march through dangerous places if we cannot penetrate the ranks of those who are fighting against the oppressors of our people? And we were certain that if we only got to see these wonderful creatures called by this magical name – "partisans" - we would be happy. How bitter and hard was our disappointment!

One Saturday evening we came to the village of "Rafin" where we found Hirschel Rubenstein and his two sons - Isaac and Moshe; Matos Rubenstein and his son Eliezer. They all worked in a flour mill. The only mill that supplied flour to the entire partisan area.

The partisans demanded that we help them saw trees, we all approach the work except for Gronam, who declared that he will not work. He does not work on Shabbats. Everyone looked at him with bewilderment and curiosity: from what world did this same strange creature come from?! They argued with him and insulted him, but he insisted: on Shabbat he does not work - and indeed he did not work.

We were surprised that he didn't pay with his life for his refusal to do so.

In the same village we also found Lipa and Shekhna, the two sons of Mordechai Mishelov, as well as Gedaliah Pixman, who begged us in the past, that we would leave him alone and let him die near the hay bale in the Richin Swamps.

[Page 82]

We also left that village upset. We did not receive an attentive ear to our pleas in it either.

We arrived at the village of Albin, the location where the main headquarter parked. We were not saved there either. We passed through many villages in our wanderings. In the village of Hamin Rog, we found in Plushevsky's regiment - Shmuel Migdalovich, Leibel Schwartzman and Herschel Shuster. After lengthy negotiations, Plushevsky agreed to accept two of our members, the two Lezbanik brothers, into his unit.

And so, we remained only two: Nahum and I. We stood motionless, one facing the other. Without saying anything, we understood what was going on in each other's wounded and bleeding heart. Will our wandering days end one day? Maybe we were destined to wander in this world of chaos without end and without purpose?!

And as if it wasn't enough for us that commander Plushevsky was fed up with us, the wrath of the regiment commander Nikolai Nikolayevich, who was known to everyone for his hatred of the Jews. He forbade us to spend the night in that place and expelled us out of the village in a fit of rage and with murderous intent.

In the village of Zagalia, in Patrin's regiment, we found Zabar (the husband of Bracha Zaretzki). Gronam Migdalovich (Risha's grandson), Hoshe'ale Riklin and Sommer Hoy – the lucky and happy ones!

In this village we found something that was new to us: Baruch Slutsky and his son and another family from the town of "Oratsia", who were not taken in by the partisan units, lived in the school building and existed outside of any military framework.

* * *

Desperate and heartbroken, we arrived at the village of Slavkowitz, which served as the center for the partisan units stationed in three nearby villages. Here at last came the end of our wanderings and our troubles. Commander Gulayev accepted us to his regiment. It was thanks to a woman's right and her request of him: the landlady with whom Commander Gulayev lived was our savior angel. She listened and heard from me the stories of all our troubles, wanderings and sufferings. After that she did not let go of him and asked to annex us to one of his units. To her aid came the Jewish partisan, Gulayev's right-hand man, a guy from Sevastopol, Yapim Havkin. (This young man later died a hero's death).

And here, when I was already on the verge of suicide, literally, came my salvation. One word from Commander Gulayev's mouth changed my situation in an instant. All the hardships and troubles were over, as if they never existed. Full of hope and energy, I was ready to go on the threshold of the new life.

I am a partisan

I can't boast of the first reception I was given in the forest to which I was brought the next day after I was accepted into the partisan unit. It was neither cordial nor encouraging; on the contrary: there were moments when I was almost ready to flee to where my feet would take me and even to the gates of death.

When we got to the thick of the forest where the partisan units were camped, the moment I got off the wagon, a young partisan approached me, barefoot, with a large Mauser gun in his belt - some sort of commander, probably -

[Page 83]

and greeted me with harsh words and insults: "are you the one Gulayev received to the unit? An engineer! Someone who studied in France! What need do we have of you? Who needs intelligent people? Intelligent! Educated people! To hell with it! We need fighting people! Not intelligent rags! damn it!"

At the sound of his insults and curses, many partisans gathered around us. Everyone came forward to mock and curse the new guest. One uttered a word of contempt at my expense to the point of making the audience laughing at me, and another one emitted a sharp and barbed joke, and all I wanted at that moment was to disappear. Then, the stream of insults was changed to a broader and more general channel: Jews! Cowards! So-called warriors! Now they come when evil has touched them, and where have they been until now?!

I looked to the sides to see where my help will come from. Will there be someone who will put an end to this murky flow of words, or save me from standing near it. I saw some of our members who joined the unit a few days before me. These were: Yaakov Epstein and the three sons of Yaakov Tziglig. They were standing some distance from us. The heard all the insults and curses, but they too, apparently, did not want to say anything and enter into polemics with the group of the scumbags.

I was rescued from this situation by a respectable partisan, with the rank of lieutenant, the Ukrainian Rizenko, who after some time was appointed the commander of the regiment, as well as the Jew Vishnyavsky from the town of Lusk, Bobruisk district. Those who attacked me received a decent amount from these two until their claims were silenced. The Jew Vishnyavsky had a strong position in the unit and was among the respectable ones, as he fled to the forest in the first days of the Nazi occupation, and was one of the first organizers of this regiment, the Gulayev's regiment.

The Jewish partisans in the campaign

Much has been written about the actions of the partisans and their life in the forests. I will therefore only write here shortly about our actions, the survivors of Lenin, the refugees of the Hantsvitz labor camp, in the ranks of the partisans, a short article about the acts of heroism, the courage of the few who remained alive, and of the many who died a heroic death in their war against the enemies of our people, the scum of the human race and its atrocity.

Our small town had about a thousand Jews. We are, therefore, can be proud of the fact that two hundred and ten of them dared to perform such a heroic act: to break out against harsh masters, who have order and a disciplinary regime. Admittedly, there were conditions that helped us - the concentration of men and only men, in one place, and most of them were middle-aged people, yet such an operation required courage, organization and above all - social discipline. There was not one among us who cared for his soul and life, and not one who would think of betraying his friends in order to save his life. And after all, there were about twenty people among us who did not join us and did not escape with all the escapees, and their opinion was that our escape would danger our lives as well as their lives! They argued with us, tried to convince us, but could not come up with something that would dissuade us from doing what seemed to them to be an act of madness

[Page 84]

and craziness. They stayed in the camp and knew very well that in the future they would be held accountable for not informing the Nazis of anything…

Thanks to all of the above, the Nazis did not notice us during the first hour of our escape. They realized what happened only after we managed to move a considerable distance from the camp and reach the forest at nightfall.

Many of the fugitives were caught and murdered before they could avenge the blood of the martyrs. Many died in the first days of our escape, in the vicinity of the villages Kotinitz and Malkovitz. Unfortunately, among them were many of the young, sturdy, strong-willed and brave guys who could have done great things if they had reached the ranks of the partisans. They died before they had a chance to act: Starobinski, Eliezer Pesetsky, Bunia Tziglig, Shmuel Zaretzki, Benny Leivik Kravetz, the five Glenson brothers, and other guys like them.

And those who remained alive and were absorbed into the ranks of the partisans contributed a lot. Many of our members excelled in all kinds of operations of sabotaging the enemy's systems and in battles. They showed courage and self-sacrifice while fulfilling all the difficult roles and all the tasks assigned to them without paying attention to the dangers involved in their execution.

And furthermore, the elderly people, some of them sixty years old and older, also did not sit idle. They brought, directly or indirectly, great benefit to the partisan regiments. They were busy with the regiment's economy: they were working in the camp and in the field, in supplying food, processing leather, tailoring, shoemaking and the like.

Many of us were absorbed into the partisan units in the vicinity of Slutsk, Bobruisk, Starobin Zitkowitz; a few of us found a place in the regiments that camped in the vicinity of Barnowitz, Luninz, Pinsk.

As already mentioned in our book, the attitude of the rural population in White Russia to the Jews was not bad. Fair relations prevailed between the Gentiles and the Jews. In some places, such as around our town, there were good neighborly relations. Thanks to this we were able to move and wander from village to village, to find shelter and food in the peasants' houses until we found shelter in the partisan units.

Of course, in some places the situation was not so good. It has already been mentioned above that in the village of Hvorostov, which was near our town, there were Christians who handed some of the Jewish partisans over to the Nazis. Also, the Christians around Turov and Davidhorodok were also known for their hatred of the Jews (they were called "Horotsoks" after the town of Davidhorodok). The White Russians around us also despised the "Horotsuks", they would condemn them for their wickedness and cruelty and would avoid coming into contact with them.

Regarding the attitude of the Christian partisans and their commanders to their Jewish friends, it can be said that, in general, it was not bad except from several exceptions.

In the Komarov (Kurzh) division, in the vicinity of Pinsk, there were several regiments whose commanders did not affectionate the Jewish partisans, and the situation of our members, who were absorbed into these regiments, was sometimes

[Page 85]

very bad. Some of our members were murdered by their unit members while carrying out operations; some of them were murdered due to false accusations that were stitched up to them. The members of our town Israel Goldman (the son-in-law of Yaalov Kravetz) and Lipa ben Elikum Slutsky were also murdered in this way. They were shot after they were accused of being involved in robbery.

The attitude towards the Jews was better in those units whose main nucleus was Soviet military personnel, those who were separated from their brigades after the first blow the Nazis struck them, and remained stuck in the forests.

In general, the requirements that were presented to the Jewish candidates as conditions for their acceptance into the unit were much more severe than those presented to the non-Jews candidates.

First of all, they demanded we will have our own weapons. They would greet us with a barrage of questions: Where is your weapon? Why is it that you sat in the ghettos without lifting a finger for your release? and sometimes demanded from a Jew, as a condition for his entry into the ranks of the partisans, to kill a German or a policeman and take his weapon. The Christian candidate would be received with open arms, and they would not ask him about his weapon.

Some of them justified their excessive demands from us by the fact that we, the Jews, have a special reckoning with the murderers who were destroying our people. "You", they said, "should and must do everything in your power, and beyond your power, in order to destroy those who destroy you; you must dedicate and sacrifice your lives in this war. It is your war".

We did not argue with them about this, and we did not contradict their words. Because at the heart of the matter, we shared the same point of view; after all, we were always ready to sacrifice our lives for the sake of war against the impure enemy; This is why we didn't get tired of our lives, this was the purpose that kept us alive. Our lives, a life of wandering in a world of chaos, had no value to us except the hope of somehow taking revenge on the abominable Nazis.

We had only one request from the commanders of the units, that they put us, first of all, in the ranks of the partisans and give us weapons like theirs, so that we can carry out the holy task of avenging the blood of our people.

And this thing was not always given to us. Some of us were indeed admitted to the partisan units, but they were not given weapons simply due to the lack of weapons in the partisan units.

Therefore, for many days, we were forced to work in the economy of the units; we knew that this work was necessary for the general cause, and that without an economy an army could not exist, but it was not our desire. Our desire was to be part of the combat unit. And every one of us who worked in the economy, considered himself as disadvantaged and inferior. I was also occupied for several weeks as a woodcutter and water pumper for the partisans. After that I was assigned a higher role, the role of a shepherd. My assistant was a Jewish guy from the town of Lusk, and sometimes I was given a second assistant, Gedaliah Tziglig from our town.

After many pleas I was allowed to be included in a combat unit. How happy I was when I became

[Page 86]

a partisan with equal rights to all the partisans in our regiment, the Gulayev regiment, which first camped in the village of Slavkovits and then moved to the vicinity of Starobin.

The members of this regiment were our townsmen - Yaakov Epstein, the three Tziglig brothers, Nahum Parpliuchik as well as several families from the city of Halusk, Bobruisk district.

Not far from our regiment, Tsikunkov's regiment was stationed, where Haim Slutsky, the four Segalovitch brothers and Yehuda Shuster's son were taken in. Not far from us, many more members of our town were found in partisan units, such as Hoshea Natan Macon and Chaim Aharon ben Chishka Mishelov, who camped in the village of Zaielni in Zelezniak's regiment (Tsiklov Brigade). After the defeat of the Nazis, Chaim Aharon was taken to Russia to work on the railroad, and stayed there. Among them was also David Latocha, Baruch's son, who was killed in the battles over Berlin in the last days of the war.

In Pakush's regiment in the village of Liaskowitz were found our townsmen Eliyahu Sadovski and his two sons - Hirshel and Shlomo, as well as the two Topchik brothers - Yaakov and Bunia. I would see these from time to time because I would often go to the village of Reffin to the mill to charge the accumulators for our radio. Every time I came there, we would gather over a cup of schnapps, as was the custom of partisans, and we would reminisce about our town and homes that no longer existed. We would talk continuously until we couldn't bear it any longer because clouds of grief weighed on us - and we burst into tears. That's how we sat, we told storied and wept in memory of our town Lenin and everything that happened to us, until the time of parting came.

In Zorka's regiment, which was stationed in the village of Reffin, I found Gdalke Fixman, the brothers Lipa and Shekhna Mishelov as well as Herschel Rubenstein and his sons and Matos Rubenstein and his sons, (as mentioned above) and others.

Moshe'l Lezbanik and his sister Feigel (who was among the twenty-eight people, whom the Nazis left alive after the massacre, to serve them, and who were saved from the death that expected them thanks to a partisan attack on the German garrison, who fled and left the town in the hands of the partisan occupiers). Both worked at the main headquarters; Moshe'l also worked as a photographer.

In the vicinity of Kworostov Rachowitz, in the brigade named after Budioni, in the Komarov brigade, many people from Lenin found there a shelter, here are the names of some of them: Yaakov Yulevich, Yaakov Ginsberg, Yitzhak ben Osnat Macon (died in a battle), Dvorah Yulevich, her husband Gilek, and their son, the cantor Novick Moshe and his sons, Alter Warshal, Yitzhak Reingold and his sons.

Our missions and operations were: attacking Nazi companies from ambush, blowing up essential bridges, destroying the railroads, taking control over wagons that were transporting soldiers to the front or cargo wagons loaded with military equipment, in short: sabotaging the enemy's systems.

We were also privileged to participate in real battles against the enemy, and quite a few of us died on the battlefields; quite a few were also died heroes' deaths in the various sabotage operations.

Even among those who were busy providing food there were many who were killed or injured, because also these occupations

[Page 87]

required courage and bravery. The method of supplying meat, for example, was: robbing herds under the noses of the Nazis. In one of these actions, David ben Ya'akov Tziglig was injured.

I came out safe and sound from all the military operations and battles, including the big and well-known battle that took place in the village of Panitz, where we had many losses. Even in the middle of the battles I had the feeling as if I was immune to the impact of the bullets, and sometimes I didn't try to be careful enough about them either.

In the last days of the war, we visited a lot on the Miksevichi-Zytkowitz railway line and we often came to blow up that track. David Tziglig and I received, among other outstanding people, certificate of excellence for successful bombing operations.

On our way to the aforementioned railway line, we would pass through the villages in our vicinity, villages that were well-known to us, and it was impossible to recognize them anymore because they were almost wiped off the face of the earth. All that remained were piles of ruins, the remains of charred trees, water wells - and wild grass, thorns and brambles covering everything.

Few lonely peasants lived in wooden huts covered with dry branches and straw stalks. These huts often stood on the banks of the river. But how our hearts ached as we approached our town. We were standing on the other side of the river and we looked towards the houses that were once our homes. There was a terrible silence! A silence that appalls and shakes the soul. As if it was a cemetery! And sometimes it seemed to me that I was not looking into an empty space, but there were also eyes that were directed at me, mute and silent eyes, the eyes of mother and father, brother and sister - and I hurried to get away from the place. I couldn't resist that wondering look. It was unbearably difficult. I hurried to blow up, destroy, sabotage and ruin…

On our way we met with our friends, the people of our town, soldiers of other regiments. The goal of their journey - which was also the desire of every bereaved Jew - revenge, sabotage, destruction and ruin. We are happy to see them alive and to hear about those who were still alive, bitterly mourning the missing, honoring the memory of those who sacrificed their lives.

Wherever we went, in all our actions and operations, when we went to sleep and woke up in the morning, we were accompanied by the figures of our loved ones, the martyrs. We have always heard them shouting at us and demanding from us to revenge their death!

We did not spare our lives; We wanted to take revenge on our enemies; we knew well that we were not able to do to our enemies even a fraction of the things that they have done to us.

We found great satisfaction in every successful sabotage we managed to perform in the satanic enemy's systems. We found some comfort in every German who fell into our hands and plead for his life. Each of them would claim that out of necessity he joined the army and out of necessity he fought, and that actually he sympathizes the communist regime, and that he knows very well that Hitler will be defeated at the end of the war…

At the end of 1942, huge Nazi forces made a major attack on the partisan area with all types of weapons at their disposal, rifles and heavy tanks. We had many

[Page 88]

losses. We fought them for many weeks. Many of us sank into the swamps. The Nazis in their war against us also practiced the "scorched earth" method. They set fire to many of the villages that served as shelters for our people. The villages were burned: Domanovitz, Moritz, Milewitz, Zeliotsits and the other villages around Lenin, our town.

In 1944, the Nazis returned once again besieged the partisan area, surrounded the area from all sides and attacked it severely. Among the heroes of the partisans who died in this difficult battle were many people from our town. Some of the names that I know are: Hirshel ben Eliyahu Sadovski, Hanan Epstein, Baruch Slutsky and his son, Yitzhak Salutsak and his son, and others whose names I do not know. All of these were killed in the vicinity of the city of Lusk and in the forests of Liaskowitz.

During this period, Gedaliah Kaplan and Matos Rubenstein also died in the forest, from diseases.

On June 22, 1944 - exactly three years after the outbreak of the war - while we were camped in the forest near the village of Rubetsky Lies, we heard the heavy artillery of the Red Army. They bombed the city of Bobruisk. We listened to the melody of this fire dance - and our hearts beat fast. We knew it was the end of the evil enemy, and that our salvation was approaching us with bold steps. On June 29, 1944, on the fifth day of the week, after a hard battle, we entered the town of Starobin, where we remained until the arrival of the Red Army, which disbanded our regiment in the last days of July.

Many of us were immediately sent to the front near Warsaw. Ugly and difficult battles took place there. Our men were thrown into the hard war machine and most of them died there, after many hardships, upheavals and wanderings and after they were saved countless times from the hand of death that lay in wait for them at every step.

And the number of those of us who survived was small. Some of us remained in Russia, but most of our people crossed the border and reached Germany and Austria. From there, few immigrated to the United States, while most of our people came to Israel and live here with us.

In summing things up, we, the people of Lenin, are allowed to say that we did everything we could do. We did not shame the memory of our martyrs. We sacrificed our lives, so that we would avenge their pure blood. Many of us fell and died the death of heroes, they knew for what and for whom they were sacrificing their lives. And when they closed their eyes forever, they saw in their mind their fathers, their brothers, their sisters and their sons, who were murdered and buried alive, looking at them satisfied with their actions, saying: Well done!…

* * *

I will tell only a little about the acts of heroism committed by the people of our town, because none of us recorded or cared to count all our acts. And the little I know only by chance came to me from the mouths of reliable eyewitnesses.

Moshe Shullman, Hirschel Rubenstein's son-in-law, served in Shweykov's regiment: he entered the regiment as a private partisan, and despite being Jewish, reached the rank of company commander (rota).

[Page 89]

And it was not for nothing that he earned this rise - he was responsible for the blow up in huge explosions of a considerable number of trains, wagons and bridges. He was an exemplary saboteur, and received several high certificates of excellence. He was one of those, who in their courage and their acts of heroism, raised the appreciation of the Jewish partisan in the eyes of all.

Yaakov ben Hanan Epstein first entered Gulayev's regiment and was later transferred together with Baruch ben Yaakov Tziglig to the Barnowitz area, where a new brigade was organized under the command of Sukhorukov.

He also excelled as an experienced and daring saboteur, and he brought down more than one train on the Brisk Barnowitz line. He carried out a very successful attack on a train carrying German pilots near the Lyushtza train station. For this act, he was awarded the medal for "courage" (now lives in Israel).

Caliger was a refugee from Warsaw, who came to our town and settled there. A blond, God-fearing young man. It was said about him that a day did not pass without putting on a tefillin, even in his wanderings in the forests. An outstanding saboteur in Pakush's regiment, in brigade 225. In the fall of 1943, the Germans made a major attack on the village of Holofenitz. The losses of the partisans were heavy, because they were overpowered by a huge force of Germans. Caliger was among the fallen in that battle; he died a hero's death.

Eliezer Kirschenzweig (who became famous during the Peshitik trial), the son-in-law of Grunam Migdalovich, a resident of our town, was together with his friend Lipa Yoselevsky (now lives in Israel), one of the first initiators and organizers of the escape from the labor camp in Hantsevitz. They first spent a few days in Tsygankov's regiment, and were then transferred to the well-known Batya brigade… Eliezer Kirschenzweig was a firm and strong young man who has done many commendable deeds. Courageous, fearlessness and always ready to embark on any high-risk operation. In the last time he went on a tour with two Christian partisans, he did not return. The two Christians, his members on the tour, said that he was shot by the Germans, but news reached us that he was murdered by these two members.

Zeev (Walwell) Zavin and Yehuda Tziglig, may he live long life, in the regiment named after Kaganovitz, the Komarov Brigade, initiated and organized the attack on the Nazis in our town, about a month after they murdered the congregation of our town.

They, the two guys, initiated and planned the attack, were the guides to the attack company and the pioneers who went at the head of the attackers and launched the attack on the German garrison and the policemen who were camped in our town at the time. In this surprise attack, several Germans and policemen were killed, and those who survived escaped from the town in panic. The partisan company entered the town and controlled it for a while, and the two guys, Zavin and Yehuda Tziglig, did even more: they gathered the twenty-eight people, the professionals that the Nazis had left alive for their use, they brought them to the forests, where they were absorbed into the ranks of the partisans, and almost all of them came to Israel, where they are now, together with their survivor, Yehuda Tziglig.

[Page 90]

A brave act of heroism was done that night by the partisan from our town, Beryl Ginsberg: he entered the bedroom of the Hooftman Grossman, who had a loaded pistol under his pillow, put his hands on the neck of the evil one and strangled him.

* * *

Grunam Segalovitch, one of the four Segalovitch brothers, who was in Tsikonkov's regiment, showed uncommon courage in all his actions and operations. He excelled in battles as a machine gunner and an excellent sniper. His older brother, Eliyahu, fell in a battle. And also, Hirschel Meir Isers (remained in Russia - in Minsk) was considered one of the most outstanding machine gunners. He is credited with a fairly large number of killed Germans.

Shmuleik Mishelov was killed a few days before the eve of our release; a mine was hidden near Sagozalek's house in our town, and he was afraid that someone would unknowingly step on that mine, and proceeded to disassemble it and remove it, to prevent a disaster (he considered himself an expert in dismantling mines). Suddenly there was a huge explosion noise and Shmuel was killed on the spot. At first, he was buried near the place of the explosion, but his fellow battalion member, Haim Simcha Rovnitz, later moved him in a cart and buried him in the mass grave in Christi, on the Gritsinowitz-Dobrodereba road, (reported by Haim Simcha Rovnitz, who was with him and they were together in Mishka Lubnov's regiment, the brigade by Budioni; he is now in Israel).

* * *

I have tried to tell some of the stories of heroism committed by the partisans of our town, the acts that I have seen or heard from reliable eyewitnesses. Of course I don't know everything. I am sure of one thing: even these partisans from our town who did not receive high certificates of excellence, did as much as they could in sabotaging the systems of our evil enemy. None of us was negligent in this holy work. None of us waited for the order to be given. Everyone wanted to be the first to do it, everyone saw the task assigned to him as a great privilege.

And the two elders from our town, Yitzhak Reingold and Israel Slutsky, who are now in old people's home on Avoda Street in Tel Aviv, or: Eliyahu Sadovski and Moshe Novick (the cantor), won't they also be counted among brave-hearted heroes? On the day of our escape from the labor camp, they were already about sixty years old, and they dared to act together with the young people, to wander through the forests and swamps, to deal day and night with the dangers that lie in wait for us at every step, to join the partisan regiments and to be active and effective there as well; otherwise - they would not have come this far.

Because the partisans acted according to the rule that says: everything that does not add - detracts, and it had no right to exist in the audience of partisans. And all the means were kosher to get rid of idlers. And they were not at all liked by the audience of partisans.

* * *

[Page 91]

My thanks are hereby given to all those who provided me with reliable and clear information, and to all those who helped me raise the sacred memory of each of the members of our community and compile lists of those who were massacred in our town and murdered in other places; the memory of our partisan heroes who were killed in battles with our enemy and perished in the forests while wandering from place to place.

Also, my gratitude goes to those who helped me compile the list of partisans who remained alive, the few who remained abroad, as well as the many who are with us in Israel.

These lists will be a testimony and a memory to all the members of our town who remained alive and a memorial to all our loved ones who were slaughtered by the Nazi beast[a].

And in this perhaps we also fulfilled our duty to a small extent regarding the residents of our town who are no longer alive.

Partisans

First row (top: standing (from the right): Yaakov Ginsberg, Shmuel Zaichik, Shlomo Sadovski, Mordechai ben Zaichik, Yaakov Yulevich
Middle row (from the right): Israel Slutsky, Lipa Topchik. Yaakov Epstein, Mordechai Zaichik, Shlomo Glenson, Yaakov Beigelman, Yaakov Topchik
Sitting in the bottom row (from the right): Eliyahu Sadovski, Haim Simcha Rovnitz, Yitzhak Reingold, Masha Shuster and Yehuda Shuster]

Original footnote:

a.   The lists are given in "Hapinkas", at the end of the Hebrew section of this book (the editorial).

[Page 92]

D. Standing at the mass grave

by Mordechai Zaichik

Translated by Sara Mages

After a lot of wanderings a strong desire stirred in our hearts to see what remained of our town, and visit the graves of our martyrs. We entered the town through the road leading to the village of Ioviche and walked by a mound of a burnt building. At first this building was used as a hospital and later, during the days of the Nazis, as Lenin's military headquarters. We cast a glance at the old cemetery on the left side of the road. It stood naked, its trees were cut down, the gravestones were scattered, many were missing and the fence was destroyed. The narrow minded murderers also disturbed the dead sleeping in the earth. The Nazis cut down the trees and used them to fortify their military headquarters, for shelter and protection against the partisans' attacks.

We arrived to the outskirts of the town. Our eyes explored and searched for the tower, the first buildings and the trees on both sides of the street – but there was no a sign of them.

The silence of death prevails wherever you turn. You can only hear the sound of frogs croaking in the "Polotza" swamp, like the old days … you feel discomfort in your heart and endless grief attacks you. Our eyes can see now what we couldn't describe in our imagination.

I close my eyes for a moment, and it seems to me that I see the streets, the houses, and the faces of my townspeople, the faces of my friends and acquaintances, and the faces my family members - just for a moment – and everything disappears - where are you?

Weeds and shrubs cover both sides of the street. Some rise to a height of a meter and a half, and inside those weeds you see, piles of bricks, scrap iron, rusty cans, scraps of clothing and scorched shoes – everything is covered with moss.

And the streets aren't streets at all. They became very narrow, just like a path in the weeds.

We arrive to the lake. Something survived from the bridge. We cross it to the other side and see the foundations of Bresler's big house. Here and there a charred tree is rising. And again, here are the foundations of the pharmacy and the pharmacist's apartment, wild plants and weeds, endless weeds.

In Lachwa Street only the foundations of Gelanson's store and the brick houses survived, and also the foundations of the building on the way to Agarkov's farm.

And you want to run away, to hurry and run. You can no longer stand and see the devastation and destruction. As if the ground is burning and scalding the soles of your feet

And I'm running away ... where to? To my father, my mother, my brothers and sisters, my relatives and friends, they are all there in the martyrs' mound. It is the mound on the way to the village of Herizinivich, the mound in front of the fruit garden. There, old and young, women and children, brothers and sisters, relatives, friends and beloved parents, found their rest in two pits…a mass grave for one thousand souls, our beloved souls.

And here we stand still next to the grave, we only see the two long pits that have sunk to the ground – and we can't believe there is room for a large number of people in such a narrow strip of land…

We are very sorry to leave this place. But we leave the town after we saw

[Page 93]

with our own eyes that this terrible thing really happened and it wasn't just a nightmare. No. This terrible tragedy really happened to us! - - -

In 1946, a number of young partisans from Lenin, led by our friend Shlomo Gelanson came and erected a temporary fence around the graves. The mass grave is still waiting for a proper fence and a memorial monument.

Recently, the surviving farmers built a few small wooden huts in each street, and returned to work their land.

Near the mass grave

E. The Lonely mound

by Menashe Ben-Yisrael (Yulevich)

Translated by Sara Mages

Inside the forests,
between fields, meadows,
a dirt mound is rising
on our beloved brothers.

Long is the mound,
hiding a thousand martyrs;
fathers and sons,
grandfathers and great-grandsons.

Isolated and desolated,
in a blood-soaked earth,
lonely and orphaned,
away from the community.

There is no one to pray on their grave
take pity on their dust,
saturate it with tears
and lament their memory.

They will be mourned from a distance
their names will be dedicated
with broken hearts and tears
by their surviving sons.

Rest in peace,
you will be remembered forever,
a mighty God, who resides for eternity,
will avenge your blood.

[Page 94]

F. The partisans' attack on Lenin

by Yehuda Tziglig

Translated by Sara Mages

A.

On 15 March 1941, I was drafted to the Red Army and served to the day when the German army attacked the Red Army. I was worried about the welfare my family members and their fate and fled to my house without receiving permission from my superiors. A few days later, our town was taken by Hitler's soldiers. I was among those who were sent by the Nazis to work in the town of Hantsavichy.

And here came the bitter news about the slaughter of our community, about the loss of our loved ones, for whom we worked in hard labor that shattered our bodies and souls. Our vicious employers deceived us. They told us that as long as we submit to them in the labor camp, nothing bad would happen to our loved ones that we left in town. We saw ourselves as hostages in the hands of the murderers, pawns for the lives of the helpless souls in our town. All the time, during the many hours of work and the few hours of rest, we envisioned our children, our women and elderly, spreading their arms towards us begging: "continue to work, any kind of work, don't rise against them so you won't bring our demise!" – and we continued to suffer the torments of body and mind.

Suddenly everything was lost! We were lonely and we had nothing in this evil world. None of us shattered his head against the wall and no one lost his mind. The lust for revenge attacked all of us, and turned into a burning fire in our bones. It united us. We were three hundred and fifty men, and we decided to unload the burden of our vicious employers, to escape to the forests and wander on the roads leading to the partisans' detachments.

We didn't argue a lot because we were pressed for time. Only a few remained in the camp because they didn't find the courage in their hearts to take the dangerous step. We decided to organize in groups, which would run in different directions to make it harder for our enemy to chase us. There wasn't an informer among us. According to the agreed signal we broke into the forest, each group in its assigned direction.

Many of us were caught by the soldiers who were summoned to chase us. They were executed together with those who remained in the camp. Many were caught after wandering days and nights in the woods. They were caught hungry and thirsty by Russian and Polish farmers, and handed over to the Germans. Around sixty men were able to escape and joined various partisans' detachments.

My friend Zev Zavin and I were lost in the forests for several days. We crossed the lakes of Polesie's swamps until we arrived to the village of Herizinivich. One night, we arrived to a camping location of a partisan detachment, and met a number of young farmers that we knew from our village. The company's commander, Pavel Tekovitch, who was a farmer from the village of Zlozin and knew my late father well, said that he was willing to accept us to his company provided that we will carry out the following task: to derail a train. If we accept the task – we would be equal members in his company, if not – "He would send us on the road that our Jewish brothers took…" This farmer didn't know and didn't sense that we waited and wished for such a mission.

We answered him: - we will do it because we can.

[Page 95]

The commander taught us in a nutshell all the theory of using explosives, complimenting us at the same time: "The Jewish brain is a smart brain, and you're quick learners"! ---

We left for the location of the mission with several soldiers from his company. The soldiers were ordered to show us the way and make sure that we will carry out the mission that was imposed on us.

This commander knew how to spare the lives of his subordinates, and was pleased with the opportunity that fell into his hands - two Jews, tortured and feeble, hungry and thirsty, after they tramped days and nights in the toxic swamps. It was better to sacrifice their lives than the lives of his loyal troops.

He walked with us for some distance and never stopped talking and explaining the great value of the sabotage mission that was assigned to us.

We tramped in the Polesie's swamps, crossed lakes, and got closer to the railroad tracks. I won't describe the details of the operation, but the point is that we were able to derail a large freight train, and as we were told, there were forty-three cars in it. From there, we ran back to the location were the company was based. The commander expressed his gratitude and informed us that from now on we were members of his group.

We were very pleased that we were given to opportunity to hurt our enemy, but so far we haven't satisfied our revenge.

B.

I told the commander: Look, our people are naked and barefoot. I know that after the massacre in our town the Nazis didn't leave a large number of soldiers, and that they moved their headquarters to the train station in Mikashevichi. We will attack the town, conquer it, and find the best in it.

It wasn't easy to entice him: being cautious he didn't hurry to risk his company. But I didn't leave him alone. I talked, and continued to talk, until I convinced him. He contacted other detachments, and a military force of one hundred and twenty men was established.

Our weapons' inventory was low: we were short of guns and had a few bullets. Days passed until we filled in the shortage. And I – I couldn't wait. Impatiently I looked forward to the day when I will be able to avenge those who robbed our bereaved town of her sons and daughters.

One evening, I was summoned to the partisans' commander. This time I was introduced to a man that I haven't seen before. Later learned that he was given the command of the united brigade. He turned to me and said: "I found out from your commander Pavel, that you initiated the military action that we are preparing for now. Therefore, you will also start it. I order you and your friend to go, explore the town, and bring us detailed information on everything that is happening there. No one besides you knows how to do it.

Zavin and I left for the road where death stalked us at every step. At midnight we reached a small hut that was standing a distant of about a kilometer and a half from Lenin. We knocked on the door. A Christian woman, about 40 years old, opened the door. We entered quickly before the woman changed her mind and closed the door in our faces. We found another person in the hut, an old man lying on his bed, sick or feigning sickness. The woman was shocked at the sight of her two guests who were armed from head to toe. Apparently she knew

[Page 96]

that we were Jewish, and this knowledge increased her amazement and confusion. The old man crossed himself in his bed and his lips whispered a prayer – or maybe - a curse ... The woman stood frozen in her place and her speech was taken from her.

We had to take an advantage of her confusion before she was able to recover, and turned to her with the question:

- Where is your husband? Serving the Germans?

The woman took a deep breath and began to talk in a weeping voice:

- No, no! We don't serve the Germans.
- Where is your husband?
- I don't have a husband. I had a husband, but he died many years ago.
- And the Germans visit you?
- Why should they visit? Why visit? After they took everything from us, the pigs and the chickens.
- But we know that you visit the Germans in the city, that you serve them.
- No, No, shouted the woman. I don't like them…I hate them.
- Let's see if you are telling us the truth. Tell us how many of them are in town and in which houses do they camp.

She told us and it was clear that her words were words of truth, and as she continued to speak also her fear started to fade. When she realized that we were listening to her and trusting her words, she started to talk animatedly. From her words we found out that the number of Nazi murderers isn't very small, and we needed to prepare ourselves for quite a serious fight.

They were housed in the section of the street between the houses of Baruchin and Yakov Kravetz. Their headquarters and storeroom were in Rodnitzki's house next to Yisrael Gelanson's house.

I returned to the brigade commander gave him everything that we learned. He warned me for the second time, and said: you know that you are responsible for the news that you brought me, and also to the results of the military operation. If you lead us into a trap I would behead you the way I behead a dog and you would die like a dog. I answered him: I'm in your hands and I will do all that I could. I know the outskirts of the town and I believe in our success. He shook my hand, put ten soldiers under my command, and we were assigned to be the company's advance team. We moved in the darkness and arrived to the center of our town. I posted the soldiers in their positions as I was ordered by the commander. He ordered us to begin the attack at four in the morning when we see the red flare signal. At three o'clock in the morning everyone stood at his post and at his aim. All of that was done in absolute silence, and the murderers didn't feel and didn't notice all the preparations. We waited impatiently for the zero hour.

Finally the red flare was shot and we started to shell the town from all sides. The shelling continued unabated until eight o'clock in the morning, but the murderers barricaded themselves in the house and it was difficult to break into it. And here we found a barrel of gasoline. Crawling, we rolled it under the house of Yosef Zaretzki of blessed memory, and ignited it. A moment later the house was engulfed in flames and the murderers started to flee. I was given another mission, to break into the storeroom in Rodnizki's house. I threw two grenades through the windows. We entered the house after the sound of the explosion ended, and saw that all of the town's property was piled there,

[Page 97]

including gold and silver. Our brothers and sister brought all this to the murderers who assured them that by doing so they will redeem their lives and lives of their family members.

The Nazis fled for their lives from the burning town leaving more than ten dead.

C.

I turned to the commander:

- I've done everything that was assigned to me – give me a few hours off!
- Time off?! – The commander wondered - why do you need time off?
- I want to wander in the town's streets a little. Maybe I'll find some Jewish survivors.
- And why do you think that there are survivors after the robbers' death actions?
- I heard that a number of people are still alive, the woman who gave us all the information told me – and her information was true and accurate.

The commander saw the excitement in my words, understood me and answered:

- Well, go and may God help you, but be careful, the town is burning and here and there you can encounter a Nazi murderer or even several of them.

I took off and ran to the ghetto between burning embers and suffocating smoke plumes. Next to Kosha Gelanson's house I met a young man wearing a policeman's uniform. He lived the village of Plostevich and was a Nazi employee. When he saw me, he remained in his place like he was nailed to the ground. Without thinking much, I shot the Nazi employee with the modern weapon that I obtained from his employer. Wonderful weapon! The evil employee fell before he could speak. I continued to run. I crossed the bridge over the lake and came to our house at the edge of town. And here I stand in front of our house and I don't hear anything. A deathly silence prevails in the house which was emptied from its inhabitants. I remembered that this was the house where I spent my childhood, where I grew up, where a loving mother hugged me and a father's hand stroked me. I stood in front of the house – and my heart moaned inside me. I made an effort to walk away. And here came the priest's wife, whose house was next to our house and told me that there are over twenty Jewish survivors in Avraham-Yitzchak Chinitch's house. I quickly rushed over there, and a few minutes later I saw myself surrounded by people from our community. Yehudah Shuster and his family, Nuska's daughter with her twin babies in her arms, and her husband.

I was surrounded by all the survivors of our community. Their eyes were upon me as if I was their savior. Nuska's daughter kissed me crying: "What should I do? Where should I go and how could I save my babies?"

My heart was bleeding, I comforted them and encouraged them saying: "He who saved you will also rescue you in the days to come".

What else could I do for them when I only had one loaf bread and a packet of butter? I gave them to babies' mother.

While I was talking to them Moshe Rabinovitch and his family arrived. He threw himself on my neck crying and kissing. He also asked me where they should go and what they could do.

I gave them instructions on how to get to our company's assembly point, but immediately changed

[Page 98]

my mind and accompanied them all the way to the assembly point because I was afraid that our soldiers will hurt them.

At the assembly point I was ordered to burn the town.

The first house that I set on fire was Hillel Epstein's house, where half of the town's property was piled up. Walking away, Herman, Henka's brother, came towards me. The killer's sons had a hand in the massacre of our community. I killed him and avenged the blood of our pure and holy – the member of our community.

After that, Zev and I went to the graves of our martyrs, the member of our community. The graves rose just above the area around them and the blood streams were not erased. Next to one of the graves we found a pile of women's hair. Both of us stood there crying.

Meanwhile, the Nazi murderers recovered a little after their hurried flight and started to attack us.

We were forced to depart from our loved ones for eternity, and returned to wander in the forests and in the swamps.

Zev and I promised each other, that if one of us survived he would tell his friends about his friend. Therefore, I'm asking that his name will be written in our town's book.

I only wrote about a few of things that I saw and experienced. I can't write any more because it shocks me to the depths of my soul. I remembered them, and my heart is crushed in unbearable grief and depression.

Editor's Note: All references to Polesie and Polotza swamps probably refer to the Pripyat River and Marshes. Polesie was the name of the Polish Province that existed between WW1 and WW2 and encompassed what is now SW Belarus including Pinsk and Lenin. Partisans conducted much of their activity from the relative safety of the swamps.

[Page 98]

G. Wandering (The escape from Mikaševičy)

by Zvi Tzukrovitz

Translated by Sara Mages

In memory of my mother, sister and brother,
who were killed by the murderers.

One day, after the German invasion, I sat next to my house in the hours before noon. Suddenly I heard aircraft noise from the east. They flew at high altitude, but I noticed the swastikas on their wings. I thought to myself: "They are flying to destroy Russian's cities", but they changed direction and started to drop bombs along the railway. Out of panic I slid off the bench, ran passed the dining room and the kitchen, and fled to the adjacent forest through the back door.

After I ran a few hundred meters, I remembered my wife and my child. I retraced my steps, helped my wife to dress our child, and we fled to the forest. I waited until the all-clear signal was given, and we returned home.

This was the first - and the only - bombing on Mikaševičy since the war broke out on 22 June, 1941. Immediately after, people started to leave their homes around the railway and the factory, and came to seek refuge with Getzel Kravetz and his sister Alta Weisblat because their 12 room house stood at the edge of town near the forest.

[Page 99]

Among the arrivals were – Yosef Ben-Chaim and Yehudit Slutsky with his family and his father; Berel Shuets from the village of Sinkavich with his wife and his son Sender ,who came from the Polish army which was defeated and dispersed by the Germans. A number of families came after them, and the house was filled with noise and weeping. Getzel and his wife ran between the refugees and tried to fulfill their needs as much as possible.

The elderly Dr. Gitler, who was respected and loved by all who knew him, also arrived with his wife, but there wasn't an empty room for them. Alta Weisblat invited him to her house. Dr. Gitler's roommate was Lipa Rubenstein whose wife and daughter found a place with Gina, the wife of Sender Weisblat who was at that time in the Red Army.

I found Lipa lying on a bench, turning, out of nervousness, an old newspaper with his hands. By the look in his eyes and the movements of his hands I immediately noticed that this person, who was quiet by nature, was struggling with the question: Should he leave everything and wander, or stay put…It seemed, that he decided to stay.

The days were days of inaction because of the state of the war, and this argument took place: Should we travel east with nothing or stay and wait for the mercy of the Germans. Lisa Rubenstein said: "We won't go anywhere, especially to Russia, to starve there for a slice of bread, and what will I be able to give my daughter to eat there? ". Feiwel Shuster, the tailor, said something like that: I sewed clothes for the Tsar, later I dressed Pi³sudski, some time ago Stalin, now it would be necessary to sew for Hitler". Feiwel Ben-

Nachum from Lenin said: "The demon isn't so bad; the Jews may even do good business with the Germans". Dr. Gitler expressed his opinion: "I'm old. Why should I be afraid? I'm just a doctor. I was never interested in politics. What would the Germans do to me?". The fatal mistake was… that they compared the new Germans to those from the days of the First World War…

It happened on a Saturday morning. The factory manager ordered to load the train with everything that could be loaded. Getzel Kravetz entered his home a bit panicked, walked from to room and began to arouse those who were asleep. All that night, a sleepless night, he oversaw the dismantling of the machines in the factory. At dawn, the manager told him that all the clerks, who weren't residents of the town, were leaving the place. Any worker, who wants to join them, can take his belongings with him. He also made up his mind to leave.

Getzel's wife, Hannah, didn't like to hear about it. She expressed her unwillingness with a number of claims: She will not travel during the war - they will bomb us on the road; in addition to that - no one is traveling; and the most important thing - today is Saturday – how will she get to the station!? Getzel had one answer to all these claims:"I will not stay. When the Germans enter, they will hang me first because I was the foreman who dismantled the machines in the factory". His wife gave up and began to pack what she could. In the meantime, Getzel brought a horse and cart and started to load it.

On the way he grabbed a liter mug, which was used for hand washing, and muttered

[Page 100]

while walking: "We'll have something to draw water for drinking on the way". Slammed the door and left without saying goodbye to those who stayed.

At first, I decided not to travel since it was necessary to prepare fresh food for our nine months old son, something that we couldn't do in a train car. I went to say goodbye to those who left, and saw that a lot of families were leaving in addition to the Kravetz family. Apparently, they decided to follow him. I was worried that the station will be bombed with so many people in it, but everything went smoothly and the train moved off.

Meanwhile, the factory workers started to rob the food warehouses and the abandoned food shops that were left unattended. There was also fear of pogroms against the Jews. Everyone locked himself at home, closed the blinds, and waited for things to come.

Late in the afternoon we heard a number of great blasts from the direction of the factory. As we learned later, Russian soldiers blew up the large steam boilers. This caused fear, and everyone began to worry about his fate and the fate of his relatives. I already regretted that I stayed. I should have traveled together with my in-laws, or go to Lenin to be with my brother and my relatives. I decided to leave on the next day, at the first opportunity. In the morning I went to the station. A locomotive with two small freight cars stood on the rails. I asked the stoker where he was going, when, and if I could join him. He replied that he was heading to Zaskevichi in an hour, and to contact the officer in charge of the train for travel authorization. The officer, a young Russian, told me that he needed to take care of some matters, and take with him the entire garrison. If there is space left he would take me with him. I went home and told my wife. She started to pack a few things. I told those who stayed that we were leaving. A few tried to persuade me and prevent me from leaving, but I made up my mind. It seemed to me that earth was burning under my feet, and that every moment that I stay might seal my fate. In the yard, Dr. Gitler turned in Russian: "I'm too old. I won't be able to travel in a freight car. If one of my sons was with me I wouldn't have stayed here. My heart predicts trouble - - - and indeed, he knew what he had predicted.

We parted from the people and left.

When I arrived to the station I saw the locomotive and the freight cars. Soldiers were lying around holding bayoneted rifles in their hands. A soldier lit a pile of straw and set fire to the petroleum that spilled from the tanks. Beams of fire broke out and smoke billowed up. Suddenly, there was a terrifying explosion - it turns out that the great boiler was detonated in the power station. There was noise in town and cries were heard from every side. The soldiers added to the commotion and started to shoot in the air. In all of this, I saw Mendel Ben Hillel Zaichik whipping his horse` which was harnessed to cart loaded with belongings. Heleina Topchik (the nephew of Shlomo Topchik from Lenin) was holding two children and a baby on his arms. His wife ran after him with their three other children. When he reached the car, he pushed

[Page 101]

the children inside and then raised his wife and the children that were with her. Also Arke Temkin and his son Herzl crawled inside. A few more people and children managed to enter the car. Schatz, the baker, threw his three sons and hurried to get his wife and daughter, but he was too late. When the officer saw the confusion that aroused in the town, and the havoc around the cars, he ordered the driver to move fast.

It is difficult to describe what happened later in the car. Arke Temkin hugged his son and both of them cried and shouted:"We no longer have a mother!" It turned out that he sent his wife to a sanatorium in the vicinity of Baranavichy. When the war broke out he tried to reach her a number of times, but each time he was forced to return. Heleina Topchik also hugged his children and cried: "How they left naked and with nothing!" Schatz's sons also cried "Father, mother" and wanted to jump from the car, but we didn't let them. And so we arrived to the bridge over the Sluch River. Here, the officer ordered us to get off. He returned two hours later and the two cars were filled with officers and soldiers, wars refugees from the Brisk battlefront. We piled up and pushed between them. Later, the bridge was blown behind us, and we continued to travel.

When we arrived to Zaskevichi I boarded another train. About half way between Homyel [Gomel] and Kijów [Kiev] I entered a third train where I met Getzel Kravetz and his family.

[Page 101]

H. Seventy years of sufferings and hardship

by Yitzchak Reingold

Translated by Sara Mages

I was born in Lenin in 1883 to my father Yehudah and my mother Henya. In 1903, when I turned twenty, I was called to serve in the Russian Army. A group of twenty-one young men traveled to Turov to report before the medical review board. Nineteen were released, and only Elyakim Migdalovich from the village of Herizinovich and I – were accepted to the army. From there I was sent to Baranovichi.

The five months of basic training were difficult and bitter, as it is known to all who endured this period of hell in the Russian Army during the days of the "Tsar". We rested a little after we were sworn in and promoted to the rank of "Veteran Soldier, but not for many days. In February 1904, the Russo-Japanese War broke out. A battalion from our regiment was sent to the battlefield in the Far East, and I, a soldier in that battalion walked to Minsk. From there we were transferred in crowded rail cars that were designed for horses. The trip from Minsk to the Far East lasted forty six days. We arrived to Magadan during the days of Passover. There were seven Jews in my company, and all of us received Matzot from the city's small Jewish community. From there we left by foot for the battlefield. We walked for nine days, more than forty kilometers a day, loaded with weapons and food. We were fed up with our lives. Ten days after leaving Magadan we came into contact with the enemy - the Japanese. The boasting,"We have only to throw our hats at them", was proven to be wrong very quickly. The "reception" was so warm that we fled with the skin of our teeth. We relaxed when we were a distance away from the enemy. I suffered for six months. After I was wounded in my right leg and in my arm, the heavens took pity on me and rewarded me with a release. Meanwhile, my parents and the members of my family were rewarded with a greeting from the "next world". This is the story: My friend, a Christian who knew my parents' address, informed them in a letter

[Page 102]

that I was lost. My parents turned to the town's rabbi, and he ruled that they should sit on the ground for seven days, according to the custom of mourners, and read "*Kaddish*" in memory of my soul. My parents have done as they were ordered. They mourned me for more than two months and they would have continued, but I wrote my parents many letters and I never forgot to write the date. And this is how they found out that I was still alive.

After I recovered from my wounds I was sent to one of the convalescence companies in Harbin [China]. From there, I was sent to serve in a sanitary train that traveled for many months. This time I was lucky, I had food and money. When I learned about the great fire that broke out in Lenin in 1904, I sent my parents six hundred Rubles, and the builder, Reb Eliyahu Dolgin, built them a wooden house.

Additional events and accidents happened to me until I returned home. In one train collision I was thrown from the carriage and landed a distant of twelve meters. I was saved thanks to the sandy soil on which I was thrown. Many cars were crushed, and many people were killed and injured. Four months before I was released, I was seriously burnt in a sauna from the steam that rose from the hot stones after a bucket of water was poured on them. The doctors told me that my end was near, but continued to take care of me with dedication, and with God's help I recovered. In 1906 I finally returned to my parents' home. From Vladivostok I traveled for thirty two days in a **fast** passenger train!

When I came home my situation was good. Surely, I didn't have a lot of money with me, but on the other hand I was given a permit to settle outside the Pale area. The value of this permit was greater than the value of money. A short time later, I got married and had three daughters. My father passed away in 1914.

When the First World War broke out, I was among the first recruits and was sent immediately to the battlefront. I spent sixteen months in this hell. I was buried in dilapidated foxholes under a barrage of German fire, until I was wounded in my left arm. Four years after I was recruited I returned home alive and well - to my elderly mother and my wife and children. I also found eight additional children in my house. These abandoned children were my sister's children. Her husband was in the United States and she died young in our home during the war, and left us her eight children.

Difficult days arrived to our townspeople, and twice as difficult to our home. I had to support my children and the orphans, and I was powerless. We only had bread to eat. Hunger controlled us until the heavens took pity on us, and a good angel appeared in the form of a messenger from America. He took the orphans from us and brought them to their father across the ocean. With love and blessings we took them out of our house. We accompanied them to Warsaw, they arrived safely to their father and forgot us.

From 1920 to 1946 we didn't receive a letter or a greeting from them. Only twenty six years later, after I lost everything that was precious to me, and after I arrived lonely and lonesome to Italy, I received a letter of condolence from my niece, Dvora Kolton. "My beloved uncle" she wrote me, "I'm glad that you survived, don't despair and don't loose your mind. You're not the only one in trouble. You're one of the survivors of the six million Jews that the enemies put an end to their lives. Don't worry. We'll take care of you and provide you with all your needs" .I was very happy with this letter and I wrote her something like this: My dear sister's children, your letter brought me comfort and encouragement and I was happy in my grief. The heavens will bless you. I don't need any material help. I just ask you for one thing - encourage me in my loneliness, support me and delighted me with your letters.

[Page 103]

Write me often about your life and about everything that is happening with you". They answered my letter immediately, and it was their last letter. I continued to write them week after week – but never received an answer. To my last letter, in which I poured my bitterness and anger that they weren't answering my letters, I received a short answer: "We don't want to know anything about you". With this they parted from me, and I – I asked about their well being and got information from sources unknown to them. I know they are alive and well and wealthy. In short – they have a good life.

Now I live in a nursing home in Tel-Aviv. It wasn't easy to find a place in this home.

After much trouble I found peace in this house.

Woe is me, that in my old age I don't have a grandson or a granddaughter to sit on my lap and warm my heart with feelings of love, because I'm lonely and lonesome like the heath in the desert.

*

In 1941, when the German murderers arrived we saw ourselves on death row. On the first night they murdered seven young people in our town and raided the town to rob, loot and rape. They took me and my oldest son out of the house and ordered us to load a wagon with hay. Feivel Strigatch and Eizel Behon worked with us. The pile of hay was close to the wagon, and we didn't do a sloppy job. Two Nazis, armed with heavy wooden clubs, stood next to us and hit our legs with heavy blows when we passed them. I don't have the strength to describe what happened to us.

I lived in our town's ghetto together with my family and children until Passover eve 1942. On Passover I parted from my loved ones. I wouldn't forget this parting to my last day. On that day, they sent me together with my two sons and my son-in-law to the labor camp in Hantsavichy. Two hundred and thirty people from our town were in that labor camp. Our daily food ration was 200 grams of bread and half a liter of soup. We worked for a whole camp. Death stalked us at every turn. We worked in hard labor out of hunger. The anguish and fear of death lasted from Passover to the first of Elul – until the bitter fatal day - when we learned that our beloved family members – children, women, and elderly - were killed in a brutal way. We learned about the brutal massacre in our town early Friday morning and immediately broke through the camp's fences and fled to the forests.

For four months I wandered lost in the forests together with my two sons and my son-in-law. During the day we hid in the forests lying sprawled out with our faces pressed to the ground. At night we wandered lost holding hands. We followed the stars and ate mushrooms and berries. We wandered until we came across a partisan detachment. We joined it and stayed with it for two and a half years, until the arrival of the Red Army. My two sons joined the Russian Army to avenge the killers of our nation. My young son fell in the Battle of Warsaw, and I don't know the fate of my oldest son. I was left childless- - - It's hard for me to bring to light what I went through during my seventy years of life, I only wrote very little....

Translated by: B. Forman 5714 [1953]

[Page 104]

Partisans Who Survived

Arranged by Mordechai Zaichik

Translated by Jerrold Landau

Yitzchak Reingold	(in Israel)
Yisrael the son of Nachum Slutsky	"
Eliahu Sadovski	"
Shlomo Sadovski (his son)	"
Chaim-Simcha (Rovnitz)	"
Yehuda the son of Chaim Shuster	"
Masha (his wife)	"
Golda (their daughter)	"
Zelig (their son)	"
China (there daughter)	"
Mordechai the son of Aharon Leib Zaichik	"
Shlomo the son of Yisrael Gelanson	"
Yaakov the son of Shlomo Topchik	"
Yaakov the son of Moshe-Aharon Schusterman	"
Yaakov the son of Chanan Epstein	"
Yaakov the son of Nachum-Natan Yulevich	"
Yaakov the son of Eliahu Ginsberg	"
Yitzchak the son of Eliahu Ginsberg	"
Mordechai the son of Leibl Zaichik	"
Moshe Novick (the cantor)	"
Yeshayahu (his son)	"
Yehuda the son of Leib Tziglig	"
Netayahu Natan the son of Mordechai Maykin	"
David Shalom the son of Berl Tzukrovitz	"
Rachel the daughter of Meir Derl Shuster	"
Shlomo Bauman (son-in-law of Aharon Shkliar)	"
Chaya-Risha the daughter of Alter Gurevich	"
Shlomo the son of Izak Behon	"
Lipa Yoselevsky	"

Mordechai the son of Naftali Kravetz	(Russia)
Getzel (his son)	"
Masha the wife of Elyakim Slutsky	"
Shimon Slutsky (Bena)	"
Ovadia the son of Yeshayahu Slutsky	"
Chaya the wife of Leizer Rabinovitch	"
Lyuba Rabinovitch (her daughter)	"
Yosef (Yossel) Rabinovitch (her son)	"
Berl Venderov	"
Michael (his son)	"
Alter the son of Yitzchak Varshel	"
Yitzchak the son of Moshe Novick	"
David the son of Yaakov Tziglig	"
Baruch the son of Yaakov Tziglig	(Holland)
Nachman the son of Avraham Migdalovich	(Russia)
Chaim-Dov the son of Mosheke Migdalovich	"
Avrahamke the son of Mosheke Migdalovich	"
Hershke the son of Mosheke Migdalovich	"
Moshe the son of Nachman Eleynik	"
Yitzchak Schusterman	"
Avraham Schusterman (his son)	"
Yeshayahu Schusterman (his son)	"
David (Dochke) the son of Zelig Tziglig	"
Shlomo Tziglig (his son)	"
Chaim the son of Gershon Slutsky	"
Shmuel the son of Chaim Berl Migdalovich	"
Hirsch Meir the son of Yisrael Aharon Isers	"
Ben-Zion (Bunia) the son of Chanan Epstein	"
Mordechai the son of Avraham Migdalovich	"
Buma (Avraham) Rappaport (the son-in-law of Zalman Bresler)	"
Noach the son of Eliahu Tziglig	"
Leiba Riklin	"
Yeshayahu Riklin (his son)	"
Aharon the son of Shaul Rovnitz	"
Benia the son of Yitzchak Reingold	"
Reichman (the son-in-law of Y. Reingold)	"

[Page 105]

Hershel the son of Yaakov Slutsky	(Russia)
Shlomo the son of Tamara Kravetz	"
Hershel the son of Tamara Kravetz	"
Shoel Slutsky	"
Shmuel Holtzman (the son-in-law of Nachum)	"
Chaim Aharon the son of Moshe Mishelov	"
Yisrael Chinitch (from Breznik)	"
Lipa Chinitch (his son)	"
Chaim Chinitch (his son)	"
Michel the son of Yaakov Kerzner	"
Chaim Berl the son of Hershel Lipchik	"
Berl the son of Yosef Ginsberg	"
Zhama the son of Yisrael Gorodetski	"
Ben-Zion (Bunia) the son of Shlomo Topchik	"
Chaim Shebrin	(New Zealand)
Freidel Shebrin (his son)	"
Chanan the son of Yehuda Shuster	(Canada)
Sara the daughter of Baruch Slutsky	"
Dvora the daughter of Nachum-Natan Yulevich	(Argentina)
Yosef Hillel (her husband)	"
Chaim (their son)	"
Hershel the son of Meir Berl Shuster	(United States)
Grunem the son of Moshe Segalovitch	"
Betzalel the son of Moshe Segalovitch	"
Avraham the son of Moshe Segalovitch	"
Moshe Shullman	(Canada)
Feigel the daughter of Yaakov Lezbanik	"
Grunem the son of Yaakov Lezbanik	(United States)
Lipa the son of Mordechai Mishelov	"
Chaim the son of Alter Yulevich	?
Hershel Rubenstein	(United States)
Meir the son of Mendel Migdalovich	(Russia)

[Page 109]

The Sacred Community

(Kehilat HaKodesh)

Synagogues

by Mordechai Zaichik

Translated by Sara Mages

The Old Synagogue

The old synagogue was built in 1870 in place of another house of worship, a smaller one, where they continued to pray until the construction of the synagogue above it was completed (only then, they dismantled the walls of the smaller synagogue).

The old synagogue was built from the finest wood that they received at a discounted price from Count Wittgenstein, the forests' owner. The town's governor of those days, R' Mordechai son of R' Mendel Tziglig, paid for most of the expenses. There were many seats around the three walls, in the middle, and also around the *Bimah*[1]. *Aron HaKodesh*[2] was decorated with beautiful wood carvings. The women's gallery was on the second floor. Inside the synagogue was a small room that was used by the *Minyanim* [3], and by the worshipers who arrived late. The town's senior residents prayed there. Most of them were poor craftsmen and simple folks. The Rabbi and the Cantor had a permanent place in the southeastern corner.

The building was spacious and was built on an area of 400 square meters. During the last years, it was necessary to support the ceiling with strong wooden pillars.

The synagogue, besides being used for prayers, was also the location where all sorts of disagreements and personal conflicts, which sometimes ended in a "fist fight", were decided. Official parties in honor of the country's national holidays, first of Russia and then Poland, also took place there. The "preachers", who happened to be in our town, also carried their talks there.

A Jew, who wanted to pour his heart before his Creator, chose to do it in the old synagogue without interruption or hesitation. There, it was always possible to meet someone sitting wrapped in a *Tallit* and *Tefillin*, studying the *Gemara* or another book

The New Synagogue

The new synagogue was built in the years 1900-1904, at the beginning of Podlipia Street, on the left side. It was much smaller than the old synagogue, but more beautiful. Its walls were painted with beautiful colors, and *Aron HaKodesh* was decorated with beautiful artistic carvings of various lifelike fruits and vines. The wealthy residents, the intelligentsia and the proprietors' sons-in-law, who recently came to town, prayed there. Only a few of the town's veterans prayed there.

The atmosphere in the new synagogue was freer. The small room next to the synagogue was used for talks and political debates on current affairs.

In the winter, during the long Sabbath nights, when it was cold outside and pleasantly warm inside, it was customary to come after the Sabbath meal to hear the weekly Torah portion from the Rabbi.

[Page 110]

Simple Jews and Torah scholars crowded around the tables, the study was interesting and included interpretations, legends and sayings of the generation's sages, and brought great pleasure to the listeners.

The new generation also found its place in the synagogue. Boys ages 14-15, sat tight on the benches and listened to the fascinating stories of their older friends. About robbers, jokers and thieves, the heroes of ancient Russian fairy tales like Ilya Murametz, Alyosha Popovich and others.

They also came to the synagogue to beg God for help in time of trouble. In the case of someone's mortal illness or disaster, the women came to beg for mercy and for the patient's recovery and salvation.

Translator's Footnotes:

1. Bimah - A platform in the synagogue on which stands the desk from which the Torah is read.
2. Aron HaKodesh – The Torah Ark.
3. Minyan (pl. Minyanim) – Quorum of ten men required for certain religious obligations.

[Page 110]

Cantors and Ritual Slaughterers

by Avner Golob (Yonai) and Avraham-Yitzhak Slutsky

Translated by Janine Sherr

A

The first "shochet"- ritual slaughterer- in the town, as recalled by R' Avner Golob, was Reb Herschel Hashkowitz. Reb Mordechai Tziglig and the famous wood merchant, Zeldovich, brought the "chazzan-shochet"- cantor and ritual slaughterer, Reb Yisrael Chaim HaCohen, to our town. Immediately, a dispute broke out.

Those who supported Hashkowitz refused to eat from the meat of Reb Yisrael Chaim; even the local rabbi would not eat from his meat.

After several days the matter was resolved; the first shochet was allocated a monthly salary and, in the meantime, R' Yisrael Chaim, the cantor-ritual slaughterer, who was a clever, cheerful, energetic, and sociable man, managed to win over the people of the town.

He had a strong musical background and was skilled at conducting a choir. He also composed his own melodies that were soon adopted by the community. In fact, many of his tunes were sung in the factories by the tailors, seamstresses, and other workers. On the High Holidays, he would lead the prayers, accompanied by a large choir, which he had trained over the summer months. Yitzhak Slutsky writes that the melodies composed by Cantor Yisrael Chaim continued to be popular even in the United States, where they were often sung by former residents of our town during community celebrations.

R' Yisrael Chaim's joyful spirit animated all the religious celebrations in our town, including weddings, circumcisions, and ceremonies for the Redeeming of the Firstborn Son. R' Yisrael Chaim spread happiness wherever he went.

He made a decent living as a shochet; his home was lovely and spacious. He was blessed with three sons and five daughters.

Even in old age, he maintained his sense of humour. It is reported that on his deathbed, he told the doctor who had come to visit him: "Esteemed doctor, I am fully aware of my condition. I think I am about to die because I ate too much of the afikoman!"

B

Mordechai Zaichik:

As mentioned previously, R' Avner Golob (Yonai), our community elder, claimed that he could not remember any cantor-ritual slaughterer in our town before R' Herschel Hashkowitz. But Mordechai Zeicik remarked: I heard from my father that the first "chazzan shochet" was actually a man named Leibke Zeichik, who came from Minsk. R' Herschel Hashkowitz only arrived later in the town.

After the passing of R' Yisrael Chaim, the town remained without a chazzan for many years, since their shochet (ritual slaughterer), Eliyahu Aaron, was not a trained cantor.

However, the town was not left empty-handed. They still had several outstanding prayer leaders (who had pleasant voices, even though they were not trained cantors): there was R' Chaim-Berel Migdalovich of the Old Synagogue, and Avraham-Yitzhak Chinitch and Mordcha-le Steinbok of the New Synagogue.

For a brief period of time, R' Yaakov Shmuel, the son-in-law of R' Yisrael Chaim, served as the community "chazzan-shochet". He was a handsome man, courteous, and of fine character, and was beloved by the entire community. His excellent reputation was known far and wide, and he was soon offered a position in a city seven times the size of our town. Our community was very distressed when this dear man departed from our small town. Unfortunately, we could not compete with the big city, which was able to offer him a higher salary and better living conditions.

[Page 111]

Cantors, Sextons

by Mordechai Zaichik

Translated by Sara Mages

Since the population of our town was small, the cantor also had to be the ritual slaughterer and the *Mohel*, but the emphasis was placed on cantillation. If the cantor didn't excel with a pleasant voice, he should, at least, know how to play a musical instrument. It was important that he knew how to pray accompanied by a choir, and that his prayers would please the worshipers.

The choir had to accompany him in the High Holidays prayers, and also with the reciting of "*Selichot*"[1]. On the first day of Rosh Hashanah he prayed in the old synagogue, and on the next day – in the new synagogue. On Yom Kippur he prayed "*Kol Nidre*" and "*Ma'ariv*"[2] in the new synagogue, and on the next day – all day in the old synagogue.

Every year something was changed in the prayers' melody, for fear that the previous melodies won't arouse the heart …

Therefore, it is understood, why the town's residents couldn't imagine how cantors in other towns prayed unaccompanied by a choir!

The cantor received a special payment for praying with a choir during the holidays and the High Holidays, and he also organized it every year. In addition, the choir supported and helped the cantor:

[Page 112]

He was able rest while they sang, and on Yom Kippur, during the "*Avodah*"[3], the two senior singers raised him from "*Keriah*" [kneeling down].

Most of the worshipers, who liked the cantor and his music, belonged to the old synagogue. It was customary that the worshipers of the old synagogue came to the new synagogue on Yom Kippur, to hear the same songs that they heard the day before.

Lenin's first cantor and ritual slaughter was R' Lcibke. He was followed by R' Herschel Hashkowitz, who also served as a *Melamed* [teacher], because he couldn't make a living as a cantor and a slaughterer alone.

Later came R' Yisrael-Chaim. For a certain period of time there wasn't a special cantor, so, there were local readers like R' Chaim Berel Migdalovich. The cantor Yakov Shmuel, who was considered to be a Lenin man, prayed a number of times and his prayers were very pleasant. His music to the prayer "*Ki Hem Chayenu*" (from the prayer "*Ahavat Olam*" [eternal love] that is recited during *Ma'ariv*) was sung for many years even by other cantors.

The cantor Leibel Gershon made a huge impression with his method. He came to our town accompanied by a large choir, among them, a baritone, alto, and a soloist who always wraps a muffler around his neck. The cantor and the choir sang according to notes (just like in the city). The townspeople liked him and he was accepted as a cantor and a ritual slaughterer. Out of the choir he only kept the alto.

This cantor, who had a beautiful tenor voice, was a healthy chubby Jew with a yellowish beard (his strength excelled in particularly when he laid a bull for slaughtering in one pull). He came to our town from Minsk at the beginning of the First World War, and stayed with us for 5-6 years. His rendition to the prayers, "*Kawokores Rohe Edro*" [like a Shepherd] and "*Va-y'hi b'yom hashlishi*" [on the third day], is worth noting.

When he left Lenin, R' Feibel Chinitch, who originated from Starobin-Slutsk, was accepted by the town.

He was a handsome Jew with a thick black beard, a Torah scholar who was familiar with musical notes. Although his voice was not developed, his prayers warmed the hearts. He also prayed accompanied by a choir. His cheerful melody to "*Yitgaddal veyitqaddash shmeh rabba*" [May His great name be exalted and sanctified] after the *Ne'ila* [locking] prayer was the town's favorite. It felt like he refreshed the people after a day of fasting and serious prayers. The whole community sang with him.

R' Moshe Novick served as a cantor after him. He arrived to us from the small town of Snov near Baranavichy-Klyetsk. He served as a cantor and ritual slaughterer until the German invasion. He was imprisoned, together with others, in the labor camp in Hantsavichy. He escaped from there, joined the partisans, and now lives in Israel.

The Sextons and their helpers

The salary of a *Shamash* [sexton] in Lenin's synagogues was very small. In order to support a family – wife and children – he had to work in side jobs like teaching the *Gemara* to older children, and also a little in… butchery. In addition, he had seasonal jobs like: lashes on Yom-Kippur eve, and so on. But of course, all of them were not enough to make him rich….

All sorts of sextons passed through our town, and we will tell here about the most interesting:

[Page 113]

In the old synagogue there was a sexton assistant by the name of Talya Kanik, who always swept the synagogue's floor, brought water or chopped wood for heating. He was short, and came to us as at young age. His speech wasn't clear and fragmented, and we barely understood him. But over time, when we became used to him – we understood him. According to him, this defect came to him when he served as a soldier in the army and was wounded in the war.

During the winter, when it was extremely cold, he sawed thick pine trunks with many nodes that were difficult to split. The children watched with curiosity as he carried the wood to the cellar where the furnace, that heated the whole synagogue, was located. Generally, he was quiet by nature, but when the children annoyed him too much – his strike was bad.

His "helpmate" was a very short fat woman, shorter than him by a head, and her face was black and shiny…

It was interesting to watch this unique couple, when they sat at the threshold of their house near the synagogue and talked.

The woman, among her other virtues, was completely deaf, but it was possible to hear her two streets away…

Their most serious conversations took place on Fridays, and their contents were on current affairs: The holy Sabbath is approaching and we still don't have fish and meat ...

Once, in the winter, the *Shamashit* [female sexton] Alte, went to the well near the synagogue. She slipped on the ice on top of the well - and rolled into the well which was about ten meters deep. By miracle she wasn't seriously hurt. She got stuck in the well, sitting in the icy water, because the well was exactly the size of her body ... somehow they pull her out of there.

In his last years Talya complained of earaches and headaches, and he passed away a few years later.

[Page 114]

Jewish National Fund troop in Lenin

Translator's Footnotes:

1. Selichot - special prayers for forgiveness. They are usually said on fast days and also during the period preceding Yom Kippur.
2. Ma'ariv – a prayer service held in the evening.
3. Avodah – service - liturgy for the *Musaph* [additional] prayer on Yom Kippur.

[Page 117]

Daily Life

The "Office" and the Farm

by Mordechai Zaichik

Translated by Sara Mages

The estate, which was located one kilometer southwest of the city, covered a large area. It belonged to Agarkov, who spent most of his days abroad or in Southern Russia and rarely came to visit it. It was built according to a well designed plan: At the center stood a beautiful perfect house, the "White House" ("Bia³y Dom"), whose windows were decorated with various carved ornaments. Agarkov and his entourage stayed there during their few visits. Next to it stood the "Red House" that was built entirely from red bricks. The offices and the service-buildings concentrated a distance away from them. Around the center, but a considerable distance away, stood the houses of the officials and the employees. Two beautiful manicured boulevards – a boulevard of pine trees and a boulevard of birch trees- extended from the center to the entrance gates.

A large fruit garden stretched along the estate. Every summer the administration office leased the garden to a Jewish resident. The tenants sold the fruits in town, and in a blessed year the fruit was also sold to other cities.

The town's residents visited the estate frequently and walked in its boulevards. The entry to the estate and the access to bears' cage were free. Many came to see the bears and give them pieces of sugar or other delicacies.

[Page 117]

Characters and Customs

by Mordechai Zaichik

Translated by Sara Mages

It is permitted to point out with a certain pride, that there were tradesmen in our town Lenin who were learned not "ignorant".

Many tradesmen and cart owners used to interweave sayings and verses in their speech and debate chapters from the Book of Yeshayahu, and there were also those who were proficient in Talmud

1. **Yisrael Gelanson**, or as he was called Yisrael the blacksmith, worked all of his life in his smithy. He dedicated his free hours for the studies of the *Gemara*, which he knew and understood well.
2. **Binush the shoemaker**, a tall quiet Jew who walked with his hands clasped behind his back. He used to spend most of his time studying a "*Tractate*" [a section of the Talmud dealing with specific subject], and he also knew a chapter in the *Gemara.*
3. **Chaim-Cheikel**, a simple God-fearing Jew who worked very hard all the days of the week. It was possible to see him stepping heavily in the mud in his bulky boots, carrying a skin that he just stripped from a young calf. But on the Sabbath, he cleaned up the filth, threw the worries of the week behind his back, and dedicated the whole day to the synagogue. From his place next to the

pillar he recited psalms, and the congregation repeated after him. Surely he knew *Tehillim* well, and his recitation of the psalms became his "strength".

The cart owners also excelled in their Jewish knowledge. The passengers, who had the opportunity to travel

[Page 118]

with them on the long muddy road leading to the train station in Mikashevichi, weren't bored thanks to the sayings, verses, legends and tales, that the carters amused their passengers with.

They even talked to their horses in a special holy-language, in the style of "Tevye the dairyman"...

I should also mention a special character, and he is Bezalel Zaichik or Bezalel the "Greek" as he was called.

This nickname was attached to him because he was one of the "Kidnapped" (Cantonists) from the days of Czar Nicholas I, when Jewish children were abducted, placed in the army and served for 25 full years! He was kidnapped at the age of 11 and served for 25 years in all kinds of army barracks. Despite living for so long among the Christians – so he said – he almost never ate non-Kosher food and never desecrated the Sabbath.

In the army he reached the rank of "Feldfebel" [Sergeant], which was considered to be a high level military rank, especially for a Jew.

His appearance was the appearance of a real military man, erect with a well-developed body. From his time in the army he kept his abusive language that he used when he was angry.

In 1928, when the Polish general Skladowski visited Lenin, Bezalel Zaichik approached him together with the rest of the delegation. He introduced himself and asked for a pension for the many years that he served in the Russian Army. At the same time, he showed the medals that he won during his military service, and told the general that he participated in the suppressing of the Polish rebellion of 1863. The matter angered the general and he shouted: What?! You fought against us and you demand a pension as a prize?! It is obvious that Bezalel Zaichik never received a pension...

He reached an old age and he was healthy and fully conscious to his last day. He died in 1933 at the age of 94.

[Page 118]

The Village Jews

by Mordechai Migdalovich

Translated by Sara Mages

Dedicated to the memory of the martyrs - My father Eliyakim son of R' Ovadia; my mother Miriam daughter of R' Yitzchak Rubenstein; my sister Sarke; my sister Sheindil and her child; and the rest of the Jews, who lived in the villages, whose life, life of honest workers, were cut by the defiled Nazi beasts. And in memory of my brother Yitzchak, a Red Army soldier, who fell in the battlefield among those who fought the murderers of our nation.

There were many villages around our town Lenin, where a number of Jewish families lived among the White Russian farmers. Those Jews earned their living from the labor of their hands. Most of them were tradesmen: blacksmiths, tailors, shoemakers and carpenters. One or two earned their living from a tiny store that supplied the farmers' needs. Some traded with anything that came to their hands. They wandered around the villages - in a horse-drawn cart or on foot – to the farmers homes and granaries, and bought everything they could lay their hands on. They brought their merchandise to the town and sold it there.

[Page 119]

I was born in the village of Herizinovich, a distance of fourteen kilometers from Lenin.

The road from the town to the village passed through lakes and swamps. The transportation into town wasn't easy or convenient. The road flooded when the snow melted in the spring and during the rainy autumn days, and the water covered the wagon's wheels. We knew how to walk across the slippery wooden beams that were placed in the swamp. We used to walk on them equipped with a long stick. When necessary, the walker leaned on it, sinking its lower end near a tree trunk, and woe to the one who stuck his stick into the bogy swamp – then, that person fell head first into the swamp. Although I was careful and accustomed to this walk, I often slipped on the slippery beam and fell into the deep swamp. I fell seven times and held on to the beam seven times, I climbed, empted the water from my boots, and kept on walking on the beams until I arrived to the village. There were fifty to sixty farmers' huts with straw roofs in the village. They were arranged in two rows on both sides of the street. There were two or three wells in the middle of the street for drawing water.

The home of the "richest" Jew in the village, Chaim-Yakov Ginsberg, stood out among the huts. He was a simple Jew, but an experienced trader and a supplier of cattle cars to Warsaw (towards his old age he immigrated to the United States, to his sons and daughters who lived there. He left two daughters in the village, both of them widows who perished along with the members of our town. They are: Liba and her children and Yentel and her children).

My grandfather, Ovadia Migdalovich, and his two sons – my father Eliyakim and my uncle Avraham – earned a living from their work in small trade and excelled in their hospitality. They received every passing guest with kindness and happiness. My mother Miriam served the meal to the guest with a warm welcome, and when she found out that a Jew was staying in a Christian home, she went to look for him and bring him to our home.

These village Jews, despite their hard work and worries about their income, did everything they could, and over their ability, to educate their children. Two, three or four Jewish families, that God graced them with small school age children, had to bring a teacher, pay his wages and support him.

The first teacher that was brought to our village was Avrahamle, who was known by his nickname "The organized". He was the son of Eliyahu Slutsky, a resident of the village of Puzitz. He was tall and had long legs. I remember that one morning I saw a person sleeping on the couch between the table and the wall, and his legs were hanging down to the floor. My mother realized that I was wondering who and what he was, and told me that he was the "rabbi" who came to teach us reading. He taught us for half a year. Two years later, during the days of the First World War, he was called to the Russian Army. He was sent to the battlefield and didn't return to his home. It is unknown if he fell in the war or died in German's captivity behind "barbed wire".i. Later, he graduated, with honors, from the teachers' seminar in Vilna. A few years later, he became famous as one of the finest teachers and outstanding educator in *"Tarbut"* schools in Poland. He died a martyr's death in the city of Kremenets among the other martyrs of our nation.

Our second teacher was Moshe, son of Reb Aharon-Leib Zaichik. Later, he graduated, with honors, from the teachers' seminar in Vilna. A few years later, he became famous as one of the finest teachers and outstanding educator in *"Tarbut"* schools in Poland. He died a martyr's death in the city of Kremenets among the other martyrs of our nation.

Also our third teacher, Eliezer son of Yosef (Yosel) Zaretzki, had a high school education,

[Page 120]

rewarded with superior teachers. Also our teacher, Eliezer Zaretzki, fell under the cruel hand of the reaper...

After he spent half a year in our village, he traveled abroad where he studied medicine and became a good doctor. He provided free medical help to the poor in our town and in other cities.

How our village, which was cut off from other settlements and stuck in the swamps, was rewarded that two inspirational gifted young men would come to teach a number of children?

Time caused it. These were the days of the First World War, which brought in its wake satiety to the village and hunger and shortage to the city. These young teachers weren't paid in money but by foodstuff: flour, potatoes and other vegetables, that they gave their parents in the town. The families of these young men had food to eat, and we were rewarded with superior teachers. Also out teacher, Eliezer Zaretzki, fell under the cruel hand of the reaper...

After the First World War, the situation of Jews in the village worsened. The few members of our village couldn't bear the heavy burden - paying the teacher's wages and supporting him.

The few Jewish families in our village had another burden besides their children's education: they couldn't provide their religious needs without help from the outside.

For the High-Holidays it was necessary to bring a cantor from the town, who could also read the Torah to blow the Shofar. It wasn't easy to find a person who was perfect in all of them. There were years when three men were brought for that purpose –a cantor, a reader and a blower. This matter cost the village people a lot of running around and a lot of money, because it was necessary to pay each person for his travel and for his sacred work

During the last years we found a man who knew everything. The veteran teacher R' Aharon-Leib Zaichik, who prayed the *"Musaf"* [additional] prayer, read the Torah and was a regular Shofar blower in Lenin's old synagogue. In addition to those, he also knew to say words of admonishment and awakening before *"Kol Nidre"* to the small congregation of rural Jews, who stood and listened attentively to his great words.

I also remember a year; when the members of our village couldn't compromise on the distribution of the payments for the religious needs. They traveled to town for the High-Holidays to pray there with the community and left the daughter in the village to protect the house and everything in it.

It was a rare case. The Jews of our village always reached an understanding and organized their public affairs together. They were innocent people. They lived from their hard work until the predators arrived and put an end to their lives, their work, their happiness and grief together.

Natives of our village were rewarded to come to Israel to see the revival of our nation and our people.

[Page 121]

The Sluch River

by Mordechai Zaichik

Translated by Jerrold Landau

There were various bathing places in the town. The Sluch River flowed close to the town. Its waters were clear and light, and it flowed calmly in many places. The Jewish children loved it and flocked to it. They threw themselves into its bosom, and played in its lapping waters until they got tired. Then the river ejected them to the shore, where they would spread themselves out on the sand or the soft grass, rest, and then return to the river.

Thus did the Jewish children spend hour after hour – from the water to the shore and from the shore to the water, until they heard the voice of Mother standing on the porch of their house, calling: "Moshe, Yaakov, where are you? Come home!" The children would be silent and not answer, so as not to reveal to Mother where they had spent the day. They would return home in a roundabout manner, with faces of complete innocence. It was not only the cheder students who loved the river, but all the residents of the town.

Old and young awaited the bathing season in the summer. The set bathing area was next to the bridge over the river. To the right of it, about 200 meters away, the women bathed. The river was not deep there. A person of average height was able to cross it on foot. The men bathed to the left of the bridge, right next to it. There, the river was deeper, and only those who knew how to swim would dare to venture forth from the edge of the river to the middle, or to swim to the other side.

There were many people in the town who excelled at swimming. Some of the young swimmers would sometimes go under the bridge, overcome the strong currents and dangerous eddies between the wooden pillars, and venture as far as the bathing place of the women. They would go to it, but not enter it. Nobody would dare enter the women's bathing place. In those days, there were not bathing suits in the town, and a youth who crossed the border would bring disgrace upon himself.

The bathing places were crowded with people on Fridays. The bathers were different than those of the other days of the week. For the most part, they were adults and the elderly. The youth who knew how to swim, headed by Zelig the son of Mordechai Yulevich, crossed the bridge to the other side of the river, and distanced themselves about 1.5 kilometers to the "Bein Haalonim" (Among the Oaks) . There was a beautiful beach there, with a steep slope. The river was wide and deep, even at its bank, and the bather would immediately fall into deep water when he descended from the beach and dipped his foot in the water. In short, this was a bathing place for those who knew how to swim.

Suddenly, to everyone's surprise, Reb Moshe Tomashov, a man who studied Torah day and night, appeared. Even he permitted himself to leave his book for an hour, and to enjoy himself by bathing in the river in honor of the Sabbath. In honor of the Sabbath Queen, he, the serious Jew, permitted himself childhood enjoyments. He demonstrated his ability to swim well. When did he learn this? During his youth? Was he also once a boy? Did he at one time also spend hours on the banks of the river?

However, it is proper not to be suspicious of proper people. We are sure that when he finished his bathing, he would go to the bathhouse to immerse in the mikva (ritual bath) in accordance with his holy custom. He would then return to his simple house, sing enthusiastically

[Page 122]

the "Song of Songs" and sanctify himself to greet the Sabbath day. Then he would once again close himself in the four ells of study and prayer.

One would think about the bathers and ponder: what was the great enchantment of the river and its cool waters. The Jewish community, burdened with worries all of their days, toiling to earn their livelihood – took off all of their clothes and simultaneously removed all of the heavy burdens under which they were buckling. They jumped into the bosom of the river, and they enjoyed themselves and disported themselves as children – they returned to their childhood…

The river was a friend and brother to our town. From it, we drew the pleasant spirit of life that restored the souls. Then peace returned between Russia and Poland. The peace treaty that was signed in the city of Riga stole the blessing of the river from the town. According to the treaty, the Sluch River became the international border. Half of it was in the bounds of Poland, and the other side was in the bounds of Russia. The bridge over the river was also divided into two halves and two booths were erected on both sides: one for the Polish border guards and the second for the Russian border guards.

At first, the Polish government established a bathing place near the bridge. It was small, and there was a fence in the middle of the river that divided between the two regions so that nobody would sneak over the boundary. Only very few came to bathe with such bathing conditions. After some time the Polish authorities saw that soldiers of the Red Army would come to bathe on the Russian side of the river, and they would engage in conversation with the bathers of the town. After they saw this, bathing in the river became completely forbidden.

With time, any wise person was wary of approaching the river, for they knew that a suspicious eye was watching out for those who approached. Informers from one side and Red agents from the other side wandered about town, and at times it was difficult to distinguish between them.

Thus did our river betray us. It turned an angry face to us, restricted our steps, distanced relatives from each other, and separated those who were together.

It was sevenfold bad and bitter for us on that terrible day when the dark, impure troops of the Nazis came to us. That day, the river closed off the escape route of many refugees and did not let them cross the border – the border that divided between annihilation and salvation.

[Page 122]

The Lag Baomer Celebration

by Yocheved Amit (nee Forman)

Translated by Jerrold Landau

At any time of trial and tribulation, the comforting adage would be in the mouths of every Jewish man: "We will yet have days when we will joyously tell about all of the tribulations that we endured". This adage, full of faith that the bad days would pass and good would come, strengthened the aching hearts and breathed faith and comfort to the downtrodden.

Alas, something different was decreed against those of my age. Our hearts are pained as we remember the days of youth. The agony and pressure is almost unbearable. Nevertheless, the desire to write memoirs overcomes this.

[Page 123]

My years of study in the school of our town were spent in a large, spacious home in the center of town, surrounded by a spacious yard (which in our day was the home of the shopkeeper Tetel Oko). It had been built years ago by one of the wealthy people of the town. Approximately 120 children boys and girls of our town studied there. I am certain that I can serve as a mouthpiece for all those of my age, my friends from the school bench, if I state that we loved this school with all our hearts, with its fine protocols and exemplary cleanliness, and with the studies that we studied calmly and with desire.

Our school had a tradition of Zionist Hebrew study for many years. The teaching staff who taught during my years of study included: Reb Aharon Leib Zaichik of blessed memory (he was murdered by the accursed Nazis on the day that they slaughtered the people of our town); and may they live, Mr. Meir Boktzin, and my father Ben-Zion Forman (both living today in Israel). In 1918, the well known pedagogue Yitzchak Katznelson (not the poet) was added to the staff. He arrived in our town from the far off city of Berdiansk. He was sent to us by the center for culture in Kiev, and he led our school for more than a year with great ability and wisdom. We studied the following subjects there: Hebrew, Bible, arithmetic, geography, physical education, singing, as well as the Russian language. The cantor conducted the singing lessons.

During the time that Katznelson was the principal, our school held a Lag Baomer celebration that left an unforgettable impression. There was a fine parade in the schoolyard and afterwards a procession through the streets of our town. 120 students participated, marching in rows of four. This parade was a sign of the days of freedom that had come upon us at the end of the world war and the fall of the Czarist police which had restricted all of our steps and deeds. Here were Jewish children going out without asking permission from the police, marching upright before everyone. They passed through the streets, each class with its blue and white flag. They were signing songs of Zion, and all the townsfolk, young and old, men and woman, Jews and gentiles, were watching the parade and accompanying them with hand clapping and shouts of joy and mirth!

Thus did we parade through the main street, cross the bridge over the pond, and go all the way to the council building (Volost). From there we retraced our steps over the river. We crossed the bridge and traversed the forest until we arrived at the Green Mountain (a small valley that was approximately 15 meters higher than the area around it and was called the "Green Mountain" by the youths who loved a joke.)

The school continued to exist even during the difficult times that came upon us after that. It displayed its power of endurance through all changes of governments – Poles, Bolsheviks, Ukrainians, and around again – that passed through our town. The principal Yitzchak Katznelson left our town, for he was invited to direct a large school in one of the cities of Volhynia. Our school continued to educate the children of our town, to impart in them the values of Hebrew culture and to instill in their hearts the idea of the renaissance of our nation in its land.

We owe thanks to this school for the young generation that arose in our town and merited for the most part to actualize Zionism in body and spirit. They arose and made aliya to Israel – with the language of our people, the Hebrew language, living on their lips.

[Page 124]

The students of the Tarbut School on a Lag Baomer excursion, 1930

[Page 125]

A Winter Eve Wedding

by Michael Rechavi

Translated by Jerrold Landau

Memories from my childhood

A winter evening descended upon the town. The snow covered the streets with a thick, white, soft covering. Even the pond was covered with a thick sheet of ice and snow. The haystacks and wood storage attics were covered with a thick, white blanket, whose edges were decorated with icicles. The bright stars were beckoning…

The sounds of the violin, flute, drum, and cymbals were echoing from one of the houses on the street. The street was lit up with great light that night. This was before electricity had reached our town, but the women hastened to place burning candles in the windows of their houses to light up the way of the bride and groom to their chupa (marriage canopy) and to thereby express their good wishes and blessing that the path of that young couple through life should be full of light, joy and gladness. After they did this, they went out to the lit up street to fulfill the commandment of entertaining the bride.

Tulia the assistant shamash (sexton) hurried to the storage place of the synagogue to take out the chupa canopy. The children hurried after him and offered their assistance, so that they would be able to help hold up the poles during the marriage ceremony.

The groom was already standing under the chupa. His friends, the joyous youths, were standing opposite him, winking their eyes at him and making funny faces at him to see if he would be able to control his nerves. Indeed, the groom stood strong, calm, without responding to the funny gestures of his friends. There was not even a trace of a smile on his lips. They were already bringing the bride. The entire town accompanied her to the chupa, everyone with a lit candle in his hand.

– Who were the in-laws?

– Do not ask, for all the people of the town were in-laws. Everyone was rejoicing, and making the bride and groom happy.

– Was this the wedding of wealthy people?

– Not necessarily. This was not the well-known band from the city of Turow who was leading the procession, and not even that of Kozhan Horodock , but rather the local "Capelia" at the head of the procession. He was the barber-musician Efraim, who put down his razor and scissors at night and took hold of the violin and bow. To his right was the drummer whose name was also Efraim. To his left was the youth playing his flute. They played to the best of their ability, and the town was joyous and mirthful.

All the people of the town had gathered around the chupa next to the old synagogue: men, women, youths, elderly people and children. The cantor was singing and leading everyone. The men sung after him, while the women were wiping their eyes with the edges of their winter kerchiefs out of joy.

Mazel Tov! Mazel Tov!

The wedding moved from the synagogue to the home of the bride. The bride, groom, and marriage party marched at the front. The musicians were playing loudly. An elderly woman was dancing in front of the couple. Children were running around and attempting to peek at the faces of the bride and groom. The entire town was marching behind the couple… The violin was being played with feeling, the flute was trilling with a still, small whisper.

[Page 126]

In the Counsel of the Poor People

by Sarah Fogelman (Kolpanitsky)

Translated by Jerrold Landau

On one of the streets of our town, in which the majority of the residents were Christians and where there were only a few Jews, there lived a family with young children. The father, who was weak and sickly, was not able to provide his family with proper sustenance. Hunger and want often frequently visited the family.

The father would go around to the villages of the region on Sundays in order to provide food for his family. He would make the rounds in the villages for six days, and the mother would be burdened with caring for the children. She was a small, thin woman. She toiled from early in the morning until late at night in order to assuage the hunger of the nine children and the elderly father who was also supported at this impoverished table, and he lived together with the entire family in this single room house.

Indeed, as in any small town, every woman of our town knew what was taking place and what was found in the oven of all her friends and neighbors. The neighbors of the mother of this family would support her: one with a measure of flour on Thursday to bake challas for the Sabbath, another with a glass of milk for the sick child or to restore the soul of the old man so he would be able to get down from his bed, and the third with a jug of sour milk to spread over the fried potatoes. With all this, the small, thin woman had to gird all of her strength, exert her mind with great energy, and keep her hands busy without stop in order to sustain their hungry souls.

Everyone who knew her was amazed at the great diligence and energy of this mother, for despite the many concerns, this small, poor house excelled in its cleanliness. The path to the entranceway was always sprinkled with clean yellow sand. The woman was always busy: washing sheets, patching the clothes of the children, cleaning and polishing anything that needed to be cleaned or polished, or preparing lunch for the family – for the most part a soup made out of grits and potatoes.

I knew this home and its residents well. The children were my age, and I would go to play with them. I was often present as the children were eating around the table, as they were waiting anxiously for a morsel of bread. At times, one of the children was not satisfied with his portion (it seemed to him that the portion of his older brother was thicker than his piece…) The mother would chastise the complainer with a chastisement accompanied by sighing and weeping – and she would return silently to her toil.

I remember that at the sight of the hunger and desires of the members of this household, and at the sight of how they ate with an appetite and were concerned with every crumb of bread – a strange appetite would also be aroused within myself, the satiated one, and if the woman would give me a morsel of bread, I would devour it while it was still in my hands…

The children would wait anxiously for their father to arrive on Friday. They would go out to greet him and to help him carry the sack on his shoulders that contained the food provisions that he had toiled to obtain.

The woman made peace with her lot, and waited for the time when the children would get older and the heavy burden that she bore would be lessened. It was not in vain that she comforted herself with this hope: her two eldest sons studied and became professionals.

The living room served as the workshop for all of them, and this too did not affect the cleanliness and order in this home of the impoverished toilers. The two beds were made, with white clean sheets spread over them. The pillows were spread with bright covers that were embroidered by the mother in days of yore, when she was still a girl or when she was engaged.

[Page 127]

Two beds and the wide elevated platform of the oven served as the sleeping place for all the residents of the household. The mistress of the household never forgot to change the embroidered, ironed pillowcases with regular pillowcases every night. Similarly, she removed the nighttime pillowcases from all the pillows at night and replaced them with the pretty covers.

Thus was the life of this family (and the lives of other similar families): a life of poverty, toil and suffering, a life of trust and hope for good days. They were silent in the face of their suffering and toil. They did not curse nor complain, and they also kept their trust and hope hidden in the depths of their hearts. In suffering, toil and difficulty they raised their children and educated them to Torah and livelihood. They guided them on a proper, modest path, and merited to see them living off the toil of their hands in an honorable fashion.

This went on until the profane enemies put an end to both their despair and joy. Their joy and worries, suffering and toil, happiness and mirth all ended. Whatever these working hands built up, raised and nurtured, day after day and year after year, with patience, suffering, agony, creative joy , hope and life – the murderers came with their profane hands and destroyed everything – man, beast and tree all together. Everything went down into a communal grave – in your midst, my town of Lenin…

[Page 127]

Father Johanns– A Righteous Gentile
(Lines to the image of the town's priest)

by Eliyahu Shalev

Translated by Sara Mages

Every year in the autumn, during the recruitment season, the new recruits from the villages used to gather in town to behave wildly and have a drink in the tavern. While they were trying to unwind, they teased the Jews and tormented them. In one of these seasons, when the new recruits gathered in town, the town's anti-Semites tried to incite them to perform acts of violence against the Jews. The matter became known in time, and the Jews turned to the priest with a plea to influence the recruits not to carry out the inciters' scheme. The priest promised to help. He assembled the young men in front of the church, spoke to them, calmed them down, and in this fashion he prevented a riot in town.

A similar thing happened at the outbreak of the First World War when all the reservists, up to the age of forty, were recruited. Among them were many dangerous types, who wanted to attack the Jews and rob their property. Also then, Father Johann assembled them in front of the church, took out the icons, and headed the procession holding a thurible in his hand. He walked and pulled them out of town where he blessed them. He parted from them with words of appeasement and sent them to the county seat. And so the town was saved from trouble.

*

The body of a murdered Christian was found on the road from the town to one of the villages. The authorities picked on a Jew, a resident of the village, and accused him of the murder. The investigation began. From time to time, the Jew was forced to come to the county seat for an additional investigation, and his life was in danger. They turned to Father Johann and asked him to do something for the Jew, because he knew him and knew his integrity. Surely, he fulfilled his promise: he went and testified that one of his parishioners confessed to him that his hand was in the murder. Since then, they ceased to harass the Jew.

[Page 128]

During the winter, the boys went out at dusk to the big lake in the middle of the town to skate on the ice. The teacher, R' Yehudah Rubenstein, walked on the ice to cross the lake. One of the Christian boys tripped him with his leg, and the teacher fell on the ice. At that moment a voice was heard from the bridge "come here"- Father Johann shouted to the Christian boy. The boy came to him and in a crying voice apologized that it happened inadvertently. "You bastard", the priest said in anger, "I saw with my own eyes that you did it on purpose. Go ask for forgiveness, next time, you'll receive the appropriate punishment for such an act".

*

It happened after the Russian Revolution when chaos reigned in Polesie. The "Whites" wandered around the area. It was dangerous to leave the town because different gangs dominated the roads and the forests. They robbed passers-by and killed them. From time to time they also came to town, and sometimes they became unruly. The principal of the Russian school where we studied wasn't a resident of our town. He left during those troubled days because he was afraid of the gangs, and Father Johann was appointed as a temporary school principal.

One morning, when we came to school, we found a message written in big letters on the main door: "Beat the Jews and save the homeland". We, the Jewish students, started to investigate and search for the writer. After a long search a Christian student gave us the writer's name.

We decided to teach the owner of the message a lesson. We lured him into one of the classrooms, locked the door behind him, and started to beat him with strong blows. His shouts reached the teachers' lounge and the ears of the principle Father Johann, who came early to school on that day. He hurried to the location of the act and knocked on the locked door. When we heard his voice, we let the student go and fled through the windows.

The priest turned to the weeping student and asked him to tell him what happened. He told him that the Jewish students attacked him and wanted to kill him, and gave him the names of his attackers.

Immediately, we were summoned to teachers' lounge to report before the school principal. There, he asked us for the meaning of our act, and explained to us that we could be brought to justice for such a bad act. We listened carefully to his words and his admonition, and then we told him about the message that was written on the door. We asked him to come out with us and see it with his own eyes.

He went out and saw it. He let us go and called the student, the young thug, to come and see him in the teachers' lounge. We didn't hear what the principle told him, but after a while, the student came out from the room with tears in his eyes and a wet cloth in his hand and erased the wiring from the door with his own hands.

Our victory was complete.

The next day we saw the boy's brother, who was an engineer in Agarkov's farm, a typical anti-Semite and a member of the "Black Hundreds"*, knocking on the principle's door. Also this time we didn't hear what he said to the principle and what the principal said to him, but we saw him leaving the teachers' lounge accompanied by the priest- principle who said to him in an angry voice:

"As long as I'm here, I will not allow and will not permit such acts"!

*

[Page 129]

The home of the Rabbi, R' Yehudah Trotzaki of blessed memory, was about fifty paces behind the old synagogue. This was the range of his daily walk, to synagogue and back

When he and the priest met on the way, the Jews stood and watched the meeting with curiosity. The priest took off his hat, approached him, greeted him and asked with interest what was happening in his community. The Rabbi, who didn't know the country's language, answered with a hand gesture and said: "Thank God, thank you". The priest blessed him, cleared the way for the rabbi, and the Jews enjoyed the respect that the priest gave the rabbi. The rabbi walked saying to himself "a true lover of Israel".

When the priest found out that the rabbi broke his leg and fell ill, he came to visit him and asked with interest about his illness and his recovery.

*

When the Russian Revolution broke out, the Bolsheviks took over and started to harass the clergies, including Father Johann. They confiscated all of his property, including his cows, and he was left naked, hungry, and in great poverty. My uncle Avraham Yitzchak Chinitch of blessed memory, who was already in America, sent him thirty five Dollars right after his first request, to buy a cow and have money to live on. There wasn't an end to the priest's delight. He wrote a letter of thanks to my uncle in America and asked him to send him his picture so he could put it between the icons of all the saints. My uncle, who was a religious man, didn't fulfill his request.

*

When the Poles occupied the town, it remained in Poland after the signing of the peace treaty. The priest returned to his role as the spiritual leader of the Provoslavic Church. When the priest celebrated forty years of service, a group of clergies headed by an archbishop gathered in town. The priest received a Jewish delegation and praised them in the presence of all the important clergies. The Jews gave him a gilded bound Bible with an inscription that he kept as a precious memento.

* *"Black Hundreds" - Russian reactionary, antirevolutionary and anti-Semitic groups formed in Russia during and after the Russian Revolution of 1905.*

[Page 129]

Chaim Grune Yente's

by Avrom – Yitzchak Slutsky (United States)

Translated by Sara Mages

He was a handsome Yeshiva student, tall, strong, flexible and straight. His pale bright face was adorned with a light narrow beard.

All the townspeople knew that he was a great scholar. He sat in the old synagogue and studied together with R' Yitzchak, the son of the old rabbi. He was named after his wife: Grune-Yente. They had a daughter, Michal, who is living in the United States.

As I remember, his mental illness was expressed by his solitary walks in the roads and paths out of town. At that time he was already separated from his wife and daughter. He was liked by the town's children, who gathered around him and drank his words with thirst. He told them various short stories, legends and proverbs. The little children weren't the only ones who liked him, also the adults and the young students. The forests' merchants and their clerks liked to chat with him and greatly enjoyed his sharp sayings. When he appeared in the street, they surrounded him with affection and talked to him. Obviously, he wasn't short

[Page 130]

of small change and meals. He never degraded himself by begging for money or by asking for a gift. On the contrary, it was a great honor for a man that R' Chaim agreed to take a coin from or eat at his home. On the Sabbath and on the holidays he was a regular guest of R' Zechariah Slutsky (R' Zechariah had an established claim to that).

Many clerks of the forest trade lived at the home of Baruch-Yakov Baruchin. Pesil, Baruch-Yakov's wife, turned to Chaim in the present of her guests, and asked him to tell them something. He didn't think long and answered her:

- I wonder about your father. I knew him as a Jew who observed the commandments and the Torah. How he allowed himself to violate one of the most serious 'don't' in the Torah?!

- What is the 'don't', that according to yours words my father allowed himself to violate? Pesil wondered.

- It is written in the "Ten Commandments" – "You shall not make for yourself a *Pesel* [idol]!", and your father created himself a Pesil, answered Reb Chaim.

Chaim's name was also famous among the Christian population. They also knew that it was possible to hear a sharp answer from his mouth. A number of farmers, who came from one of the nearby villages, told that they met Chaim on Sunday when they walked from the village to the church. They turned to him and said:"Chaimke, we have to kill you".

- What for and why? - ask Chaim in amazement.

- Because Lenin's Jews – the farmers answered – killed our God.

- God forbid - Chaim replied as if he was serious - Lenin's Jews didn't spill his pure blood, but Starobin's Jews committed this murder.

Pinchas Kaplan, a forest merchant, was gifted with a sense of humor. He used to tell various jokes and also liked to hear a beautiful saying. One day, he sat on Ben-Zion Tziglig's porch together with other people. Suddenly, Chaim walked by, and as always, he was lost in his thoughts and in his hallucinations. Pinchas turned to him and said:

- Chaim, please tell us something nice and I'll give you a Ruble.

Chaim answered:

- Well, I'll ask you a question, and the person who will answer it properly will win all of my assets. He took out a twenty Kopek coin and said: "this is all of my property, it is all before you".

- Ask Chaim ask, and we will listen, answered Pinchas Kaplan.

- Please hear me, Chaim opened his speech, I've just arrived from a trip along the riverbank. I climbed on the bridge and looked into the water. I looked at them pretty well and was surprised to see a second Chaim, who looked like the Chaim who is standing before you right now. His shirt collar was open as the collar of my shirt, and the leather strap that held his pants to his waist was exactly like the leather strap around my waist. He was exactly like me, but he stood with his feet up and his head down. So, tell me why the other Chaim needed a leather strap? When he stood in that manner his pants couldn't fall without it.

[Page 131]

The people, who were sitting on the porch, started to answer this way and that way, but Chaim wasn't satisfied with any of their answers. They turned to him and said:

- Let's hear what you have to say

And Chaim answered:

- It is very simple. If the other Chaim didn't have a leather strap around his waist, the pants of the Chaim who is standing before you would have fallen off.

Chaim had a special attraction to the river and its water. It was possible to see him standing by the river bank looking at the small fish swimming back and forth. At times, he used to sigh from the bottom of his heart and cry:

- It would have been better if I was a small fish among these small fish, then I could have escaped from my terrible headaches.

He knew how to swim very well and saved a number of children from drowning during the swimming season.

Mr. Aharon Singalovzki, who knew Chaim very well and had a lot of conversations with him, said: a living encyclopedia walked in Lenin's streets, which is Chaim the "crazy". He was knowledgeable in the six orders of the *Mishnah* and *Poskim*, in "questions and answers", and the entire sea of rabbinical literature. He knew very well the history of our nation. He didn't draw his knowledge from the history books but from the sources. With all of that, this wonderful man knew that we liked him and appreciated him very much, because he was sick. At times he complained about it. As far as we remember him, he was quiet and polite, but an elder from Lenin, Mr. Avner Golob, said that he used to go wild during the first days of his illness. Once, Moshe-Yakov Temkin saw him running wild in the street. He tried to calm him down, but Chaim slapped Moshe-Yakov in the face. A few hours later, Chaim calmed down, came to Moshe-Yakov and asked for forgiveness.

When he felt better he divorced his wife, who immigrated later on to the United States together with her daughter. Chaim remained lonely, and since then slept at the home of Yehiel Temkin.

[Page 131]

Bere'le the Bookseller

by Yitzchak Slutsky

Translated by Sara Mages

No one knew from where this man came to the town of Lenin and for what reason, and when he was asked about it, he avoided giving a clear answer.

Some said that was forced to leave his hometown, somewhere around Vilna, for family reasons. There were those who said, that his town's rabbi ordered him to be a wanderer in a foreign land because he committed a sin. Some whispered that this man was involved in a political movement, and escaped his town from the agents of the Tsarist regime. It was impossible to believe that this uneducated man had a position in a political movement.

He was short but sturdy, and his beard and mustache were slightly trimmed. His boots, with the folded gaiters, were polished to a shine, an act of a soldier.

[Page 132]

If someone from our town wore such shoes, and put a hat with a shiny visor on his head –our townspeople would scorn him, and see in it a sign of imitation to the way the young gentiles dressed in the city. But no one wondered about him because he was weird in his manners, and everyone attributed his habits to his unknown place of origin.

When he arrived to our town he settled in the small room in the new synagogue, and became a helper to Mordechai Steinbeck, the head sexton. All the cleaning work was done by Bere'le the bookseller, and everything was sparkling clean. Everything that came to his hands was fixed. This man loved to work and made sure that everything was clean.

On Sabbath eve, after his hands gave the synagogue the look of a parlor, the head sexton would appear dressed in sparkling clean Sabbath clothes, wearing a hat and sometimes a top hat. His beard was combed and his mustache was made. He lit the lamps and the candles with a gesture of greatness, like he was saying: "Surely, I'm an educated man but I'm not ashamed to be a sexton, and I don't see any degradation in it. On the contrary, I bring the duty of a sexton to a higher level".

As can be learned from the nickname bookseller, Bere'le had another occupation: he sold books – Siddurim, *Tkhinot* [supplications], Tehillim, Mezuzot, Tallitot and Tzitziot. He also sold reading books in Yiddish, the stories of "Hershale of Ostropolerand others. He kept his books in locked boxes that he stored in the synagogue's "eastern" benches. When the *"Cheder Metukan"* [reformed school] was opened, he became a textbook supplier and saw himself as the only bookseller in town. Woe to the one who failed, and brought back a Hebrew book for his son or daughter, when he returned from a business trip to Minsk.

Bere'le also had another business: he was a water drawer, especially river water for the town's privileged, and who boasted that hard well water won't reach their samovars, only soft river water. When they invited a person for a cup of tea, they promised and assured him, that he'll only drink river water. Bere'le was an inventor. In the summer he installed two wheels to a barrel, harnessed himself to the barrel, and pulled it to the town. In the winter he attached a small sled the same barrel.

Bere'le the bookseller had another occupation: he was a night watchman. He also fulfilled this duty with joy and elation. There was no one like him when he wandered in the town's streets at midnight, announcing with the Purim gragger that he held in his hand, that "He who keeps Israel will neitherslumber nor sleep". The sound of the gragger was rhythmical and measured. This duty gave him a lot of pleasure. He saw himself as the patron of the town, as if the town's security was placed in his hands, because Bere'le had a great imagination.

Bere'le was also a collector of weird items: empty match boxes and materials that he stored in the synagogue's attic.

As no one knew from where and why he came to our town, no one knew why he suddenly left and disappeared. Some said they saw him around Vilna, old and tired, begging from door to door---

[Page 135]

Educational and Cultural Institutions

Educational, Medical and Sanitary Conditions in Lenin

By Avraham Yitzhak Slutsky

Translated by Esther Mann Snyder

Education That Was Cut in the Bud

The name of our town, Lenin, is not found on geographical maps. The town was located on the banks of the Slutz River, a tributary of the large river, Prifet. It was one of hundreds of small towns that were in the Pale of settlement in Russia, during the reign of the Czars. There was no industry or crafts in this area and many other sources of livelihood were closed to the Jews; also living in the villages and acquiring land was forbidden to the Jews. Therefore, it is not surprising that poverty was rampant in all the towns in the Pale of settlement.

Some people in our town worked in transport and haulage; in the winter they would haul wooden planks from the forest to the banks of the rivers which were covered with ice, in order to float them downstream when the waters flowed in the spring after the ice had melted. These men would buy horses at the beginning of the winter for this seasonal work that started after the swamps and the rivers froze and were covered with snow, and ended with the melting of the snow and ice in the spring. Then they would sell their horses and were left without employment and income during the whole summer. The condition of the craftsmen - tailors, shoemakers, hatters and the like - wasn't much better than the haulers. This was also the status of the grocers and "merchants", as it were. The life of the residents, except for a few, was very difficult.

The depressed material state influenced, of course, negatively the general progress of our town in those times. In my childhood days there was no advanced study for a child or a lad. Both the resources and the awareness of such a need were lacking. However, years later our town was known for its progress and served as an example to other towns in the area for its proper "heder" which, after a short while, became a proper elementary school. However, during my childhood the children of our town studied only in the traditional "heder", where most of them barely learned to read the "siddur" - prayer book, or as it was called in those days: they learned "ivri" - reading Hebrew and a bit of writing. Thus an ignorant generation of boors grew up. One cannot blame this on the children and not even on the teachers; on the contrary, there were several teachers who had broad knowledge. The poverty of the parents was the reason for the poor education of the children, and many families were forced to remove their children from the "heder" at the age of eleven or twelve and sent them to learn a trade, or took them into the forests and swamps to help their fathers in packing and unpacking the heavy wooden planks. The youth had to help with the burden of making a livelihood for the family. Who knows how many talented children could have been successful in different fields if their spiritual and educational growth hadn't been stopped. I, myself, for instance, continued to study in the "heder" much longer than my friends. My father and mother struggled with their poverty and made a great effort to pay for my tuition, especially with the best teachers. However, at the age of fourteen my parents - who could no longer afford to pay for my education - sent me to the carpenter Avner Golob, who now is in Israel - to learn carpentry. Such was the case with most of the children in our town.

[Page 136]

It was only natural that the poverty and crowding that existed in our town, especially among the Jews, had a negative effect on the health of the populace. Thus, all kinds of diseases such as infections and epidemics afflicted the people. The whole town was crowded into a small area surrounded by water and swamps. Many homes had no bathrooms. Consequently, the sanitary conditions were very poor, which led to the rapid spread of various contagious diseases, especially among children. Without adequate medical aid, this situation took many sacrifices among the children. As I remember, almost every home suffered some loss - one infant, two or even three. Frequently, fires broke out. This curse was due mainly to the extreme closeness of the wooden homes. I witnessed a great fire that occurred in our town in 1904, in which most of the buildings burned down. One characteristic fact should be mentioned: after the conflagration the authorities demanded that the buildings be rebuilt with larger spaces between the houses and with proper sanitary facilities; according to this plan the number of homes would have to be reduced. The residents viewed this decree as a severe hardship and they decided to send a delegation to the governor of the province in Minsk. Elyakim Slutsky was one of the members of this delegation that succeeded in presenting the pleadings of the residents to the governor who was willing to repeal the evil decree. Thus the town was rebuilt as in previous years and the houses were even more crowded together.

Medical Assistance

I remember two people who tried to care for the health of the residents of our town. They were R' Hershke and R' Yisrael. They were both medics but the residents honored them by calling them Doctor. They were both dignified and pleasant, although their knowledge of medicine was meager because they had never learned in an official medical school. They diagnosed diseases according to the stories and complaints of the sick, and the medications - powders, tonics and pills - they made themselves. The masses believed in them and trusted in their abilities. Many were cured apparently due to the psychological influence of their belief and trust. However, such miracles occurred only to those with minor illnesses, while with the serious illnesses results were poor.

An old woman, Shaine-Rahel, is well remembered as she aided the health of the people with methods known only to her. Most of those who sought her help and medical treatment were from the carriers, porters and others who dealt in hard work. She knew how to knead with her fists those whose stomachs and intestines hurt from the hard work of lifting and carrying heavy loads. She would cure anthrax by placing a honey mixture on the affected area while on a regular tumor she would place a grilled onion. In such conditions people continued to live, as it were, and exist and also - to die ...

[Page 137]

Cultural Life

By Mordechai Zaichik

Translated by Esther Mann Snyder

A

Schools

Since the years after World War I, the Tarbut school, which was connected to the Tarbut center in Warsaw, existed in our town. Each year about 150 pupils studied there in 4 - 5 grades and one preparatory class. There was no kindergarten in Lenin; the children started to attend school at age five.

Most of the teachers were from other towns and were sent to us by the Tarbut center in Warsaw; these teachers remained with us between one to four seasons. The exception was the old teacher, A.L. Zaichik who lived in the town and continued teaching for almost 50 years.

For the 18 years of its existence, male and female teachers of all types stayed in our town. Actually, even before this there was a school that was founded around the year 1900. It was located in a separate building, on Lachva Street (among Christian houses), and next to it was a large playground. This school was divided into grades and had four teachers who taught according to a prescribed plan. Between lessons there were recesses announced by a bell. In addition to Bible, the children learned secular studies: grammar, arithmetic, geography, history (Jewish history), language (Hebrew), etc.

Of course, the Tarbut school was more suited to the new times. Other subjects were added to the curriculum: gymnastics, singing and more. It must be said that the discipline was less strict than before, but despite this the pupils were polite and advanced in their studies.

After completing the Tarbut school, the youth from families of means continued their studies in the Hebrew gymnasia in Pinsk, the Teacher's seminar in Vilna, or the professional school ORT in Brisk.

There was also a Polish elementary school with seven grades; Jews also studied in this school, especially in the higher grades.

B

The Tarbut Library

The meeting place of the youth was in the club of Tarbut, a place where one could read every night many different types of newspapers and magazines in various languages. Also, meetings were held there, debates and lectures given by emissaries from Eretz Yisrael.

Next to the club was a fairly well stocked library and in addition to books, it held magazines and periodicals. Many readers visited the library.

The club had another advantage, and that was that it was a place where youth from poor homes as well as youth from well-off and educated homes met and talked together.\

There were three Zionist political parties in the town: Betar, the General Zionists, and Hashomer Hatzair. Of course, there were arguments and disputes between them, but matters never reached serious clashes.

[Page 138]

The First School in Lenin, 1913

In the center of the bottom row, the teachers: Aharon-Leib Zaichik (killed by
the Nazis), Haim Shalev (Nakritz) (in Israel), Yoshke Boktzin (in America).
In the top row: second from the right: Asher Tcherin (son of Avraham Yitzhak),
the tenth - Mishal Schmelkin son of Zashama (died in Israel), the fourteenth -
Yaakov Yulevich (son of Nahum Natan), the fifteenth - Dov Migdalovich (son of
Moshe Nisan), the nineteenth - Menashe Yulevich (son of Yisrael), the third from
the left - Elka Kolpanitsky (daughter of Bezalel).
Second row, first on the right: Haim Slutsky (son of Yisrael), fourth - Eliyahu
Nakritz, fifth - Nahum Nakritz (sons of Isser), sixth - Dov Zaichik, seventh -
Mordechai Zaichik (sons of Aharon Leib), eighth - David Golob-Yonai (son of
Hunia), thirteenth - Masha(daughter of Yitzhak).
Bottom row: first on the right: Menashe Latocha (son of Moshe), thirteenth -
Pinhas Zaretzki (son of Moshe Reuven), sixteenth - Tzvi (Hirshl) Grib (son of
Arye), second from left - Sonia Rubenstein (daughter of Shayma). All are in
Israel.

[Page 139]

The Tarbut School, 1928

In the top row: Shimon Schusterman, from Moritz in Argentina, Yitzhak Yulevich son of Alter. Moshe Boktzin(in Israel), Yitzhak son of Assana, Avraham Lilenberg (in Israel).
Second row from top: Leah Margolin daughter of Libbe, Babel Chinitch daughter of the Cantor (in Israel), Hannah Chinitch daughter of Shmuel, Hannah Zaretzki daughter of Reba, Batya Zaichik daughter of Aharon-Leib, Sarah Zaichik daughter of Shaindel.
The third row, the teachers: Yehuda Rubenstein, Pepperberg Morsha. Meir a(in Israel), Aharon-Lev Zaichik.
Bottom row: Shmuel Mishelov, Tcharna Vacharbin (in Israel), Zema Schneidman.

[Page 140]

C

Theatre, music

They started producing plays in our town in the period of what was called "m'chabei aish" - the fire station. That was a building that was 20 meters long and 8 meters wide, and in which was stored equipment needed for putting out fires, such as: barrels, a 2-handled pump, ladders and also metal helmets.

When it was time to present the play, all the equipment was removed. Then chairs were collected from the people, the stage was decorated with greenery and thus the hall was prepared for the play. All the town excitedly awaited the performance.

The first plays that were presented were historical: "The Selling of Joseph" and "David and Goliath". At a later time other plays were performed - even The Miser by Moliere.

The Performance of the Miser by Moliere August 19, 1923

From right to left: Esther Rubenstein (Israel), Yosef Shub (died in Warsaw), Meir Boktzin (Israel), Batya Rosomacha (killed), Tsila Baruchin (Israel), Moshe Zaichik (killed), Moshe Schmelkin (died in Israel), Yaakov Graeib (U.S.A.).

[Page 141]

After the fire station was demolished, the plays were held in the halls of the Russian government school, which were large and spacious.

At a later period, when the Polish government built a hall for public use (dom-ludovi), the plays were held there. This building had a special hall with a stage that was intended for this purpose. During the years many different plays were performed, including: "G-d, Man and Satan", "Hasia the Orphan", "Motke the Thief", "The Dybbuk" and others.

The actors were from the town and some of them were quite talented. Meir Boktzin successfully filled the task of director and make-up artist; he was a teacher and also knew how to draw.

A movie film was first seen in our town in 1923 and the audience was amazed. In later years, one film was shown each week although there was no special hall for these performances.

In contrast there was a regular orchestra that played at performances and dances held after the plays, that lasted until morning.

Before a performance - when a special license was given for staying in the street which was a chance to remain outside, something that was not allowed on regular nights. The people of the town and especially the youth suffered from this prohibition.

The Orchestra
Conducted by M. Zaichik, 1926

[Page 142]

A police car passed through the streets every evening and hunted those who were violating this prohibition. A first time offender had to pay a small, nominal fine, or he ended up spending the night in the police station. Anyone caught several times was charged in the District police in Lubiniatz and his punishment was much more severe.

It was difficult for the youth, of course, to remain without social activities in the evenings, especially in winter when it became dark early. Groups would gather in one house for reading or some other entertainment. But returning home was a serious problem. They had to be very careful and use various tricks to avoid being caught by the police. Sometimes they would find the police near the door of their home. If the "offender" managed to enter his home quickly and close the door, then he was saved because the police were not allowed to enter the house.

In the winter, when every step was heard on the frozen snow, there was the advantage that one could the police approaching. Of course, it could be the opposite: the policeman stands and quietly waits for his approaching "victim". Then. one heard the command: "Stand! Who goes?" Either way, it was interesting and even thrilling for the youth.

D

Sports

The interest in sports started in our town in 1923. At first only a few were active in sports and they were youths who studied out of town and returned home for summer vacation; they were joined by some of the local youth.

"Trumpeldor" Soccer Team (Urgana, 1924)

Standing (from the right): Yitzhak Chinitch (Argentina), Meir Temkin (USA), Shlomo Graeib (Israel), Ben-Zion Tziglig (died in Holocaust), Zvi Graeib (Israel), Mordecai Zaichik (Israel), Haim Pederaski (died in Holocaust), Hanan Yitzhaki (Vacharbin) (Israel), Asher Golob (USA), Dov Zaichik (Israel), Moshe Zaichik (died in Holocaust).
Sitting (from the right): Feivel Tzukrovitz (died in Holocaust), Yitzhak Slutsky (Israel), Menashe Yulevich (Latocha) (Israel), Dov Migdalovich (Israel), David Bresler (died in Holocaust).

[Page 143]

The most attention was given to soccer. In the early years we didn't have experienced players, therefore the players didn't have special uniforms. Only after several years a soccer team was formed in our town, that was given uniforms, and knew the rules of the game. For the first time, there was a separate Jewish team, after that a mixed team of Jews and Russians was formed that played against the Polish teams from the border army. The Polish team always beat the mixed team, although the latter learned from them how to play well.

The mixed team reached its top form during the years 1930 - 1933 and achieved good results in its games with the stronger teams from Mikashbitchi and Lakhva, beating Lakhva 2:0.

In addition to soccer other sports activities included swimming and ice-skating.

E

Places for Hiking and Entertainment

Places for walking and hiking were not lacking in our town. Before World War I and before the setting of the border, it was common to walk, especially on Shabbat and holidays, to the other side of the bridge, to "The Green Hill", to "The Factory" (zavod) or to the Observation Tower (mayak).

The Green Hill was closest. It was 8 - 10 meters high and its circumference was 30 meters. However, for our town, whose environs were flat and filled with lakes and swamps, it seemed quite high. On the way to the Green Hill, the boys would often catch snakes, carry them with their heads down, until reaching the hill where there were many ant-hills. They would throw down the snakes down among the "millions" of ants who would attack the snake who tried, in vain, to escape. In just a few minutes all that was left of snake was only the skin.

On the road to the Observation Tower, we passed the factory, which wasn't really a factory but the remnant of a tar furnace. The tower was built at the beginning of World War I, on a hill and not far from the river, 3 kilometers from town and reaching a height of 100 meters. Only the courageous youth dared to climb to the top. They could climb it or use ladders from one floor to the next. A few did this with a wooden stick in their hand and when they reached the top they would throw it down to the ground and it sank completely into the ground. Those who climbed up so high looked strange to those who remained on the ground and vice versa.

Around the tower there was a large pine grove that gave off a clean, pleasant scent. After the war, when it was forbidden to visit the area, grass and weeds grew on the road. Then, the people would walk towards the hospital (bolenitza) which was on the road to Yavitz. There, also, was a pine grove with dry clean air.

Mostly, people walked on the road leading to Makvitz, which was 3 kilometers away from town. This was a "romantic" path especially in the autumn, when the leaves of the oak trees would fall and padded the road as a soft rug.

[Page 144]

A pleasant place to stroll was also the garden next to the estate. The owner of the estate - Agarkov - lived with his family most of the year out of the country and only clerks and workers remained on the estate to supervise it. Many different types of fruit grew in the garden that won a reputation for their quality in the area and were also sent for sale to other countries.

There were two splendid houses on the estate - one was white and had windows decorated with beautiful wooden carvings, and the second one was built entirely of red bricks. The rest of the estate had houses for the clerks - one made of birch and the other of conifer and also well-tended paths. Between the thick trees could be seen wild goats; there were also bears in cages.

The entrance to the garden was through Lakhva Street and also from the road leading to the village Stabeliyevitz and Haritzinovitz.

The garden was leased each year by the Jews of Lenin who put up guards to protect it. When the fruits ripened they were sold and some were put away for use during the winter.

An Unsuccessful Purim Party

By Avraham-Yitzhak Slutsky

Translated by Esther Mann Snyder

During my childhood years the cultural conditions in our town were very undeveloped, although there was no lack of cultured people; on the contrary, there were not a few who knew Torah studies or were highly educated. However, there were no cultural institutions such as a public library, etc. Those who learned Torah had their own books and libraries that they loaned to each other. But there was no place for some of the youth, those who came from poor families, who wanted to read. Sometimes, one of the owners of a private library would be charitable enough to loan one or two books to one of us, if he felt that person would take care of the book and return it in good condition.

If a travelling bookseller came to our town, the townspeople would hurry to him - boys and girls - and buy a novel by Shem"er, a book by Elyakim Tzunzer or a book of adventures and jokes by Hershele Maustropoli. These books usually were read on Sabbath eves among the family or at parties of friends. Newspapers also were available, in Russian, Hebrew and Yiddish. But even these were bought mainly by the middle class. Due to the slow transportation and postal service, the papers reached us two or three days late. Often, three families were subscribed together to one newspaper that was passed from one to the other. The poorer families would hear the news of the world in the synagogue between Minha and Maariv [afternoon and evening prayers] from one of the intelligentsia; they would gather around him and hungrily listen to his report.

The Sages said, "When scholars vie wisdom increases." We, the youth of the lower class were jealous of these privileged persons, and three of us - the late Shlomo Dolgin, his friend Mordechai son of Hoshea Tziglig

[Page 145]

and myself subscribed jointly to the Yiddish-Bundist newspaper, the "Falkszeitung." We read it diligently ourselves and also shared it with relatives and acquaintances.

Some attempts were made to hold cultural activities but nothing came of them. Perhaps I should tell about one such activity that sheds light on the people of our town, their dealings and the sparks of spiritual light within the everyday life of routine and poverty.

The "gabbai" (sexton) of the old synagogue (I don't remember if it was Mordechai Mandelbaum or Eliezer Vladovski) brought a bookbinder from Pinsk to bind the worn books in the synagogue. He was a learned man, happy and energetic. He didn't want to spend his rest time doing nothing but rather devoted this time to cultural activity. He quickly organized some of the youth including the two daughters of the cantor-shohet, Yisrael-Haim, whose names were Tzivia and Devora, and suggested that we perform a theatrical play.

The young people happily accepted the suggestion and enthusiastically started working on the project. They began learning and memorizing the lines of the play, The Witch by Goldfadden. I, who was in the cantor's choir, joined the cast of players along with some others from the choir, Abba son of Moshe Eliyahu and Avraham, the cantor's son. The young bookbinder from Pinsk decided who would play each role and the rehearsals were held in the home of the cantor, Yisrael-Haim. We met at night three times a week for rehearsals and the Pinsker directed us with talent and devotion.

I remember that Manya Migdalovich studied for the role of "Mirele." We were busy all through the winter with preparations for the performance and things were going well. Each one of us knew his or her lines well and we were hoping to succeed. Indeed, the first performance before a small audience went well. Therefore, we were ready to perform the play that would be held in the fire station building before a large audience. However, our hopes were not fulfilled because the young Pinsker finished his job of book binding and returned to his home a week before Pesach. Without our experienced director we dared not go onto the stage. Our group of actors separated, each one going back to his work but with a heavy heart over the pleasant dream that had faded away.

However, the wonderful efforts of that young Pinsker were not in vain. After a year, we started cultural activities, this time without external assistance, but by our own efforts. We organized ourselves to perform the Purim play, "The Wisdom of Solomon." We rehearsed on Sabbath days during the whole winter, in the home of Zelig Yulevich, the son of Itche Noah. Zelig's son, Zalman, also had a role in the play. They lived in the courtyard of Ben-Zion Tziglig.

Shlomo Topchik played the role of King Solomon. I think that Shlomo Dolgin took part in the play. Other participants were Isser Yulevich (son of Matos), Avremel Migdalovich, the son of Beryl the carpenter, and many others whose names I don't remember.

I was given two roles: one was "Bat Sheva" and the other was "David." Of course, with one small stone I could fell "Goliath the Philistine." The rehearsals went very well and we all knew our lines perfectly.

Purim arrived and we went out into the street with make-up and dressed as royalty with crowns and swords made of paper, accompanied by Ephraim with his clezmer (clarinet) and Ephraim the drummer. All the people

[Page 146]

of the town - children and adults - among them also non-Jews, joined the parade. They hesitated to let us enter a Jewish home in case the crowd might break the windows out of curiosity to look inside.

The first show was performed in the home of Beryl the sexton. So many people entered the house that there was barely room to move. When we finally managed to leave the house, each one's costume was wrinkled and tattered and everyone was missing some part of his costume.

In short, we saw that all our efforts had failed and that the income we had hoped to gain, which was to be given to the Talmud Torah (the elementary school), was never received... We barely managed to perform the Purim play in a few homes. In the home of Noah Rubenstein we received 5 rubles and we were honorably invited to perform the play the next year.

In short, we had a double failure - spiritual and material. But we were consoled by the fact that it wasn't our fault, but due to the local conditions of the time and even more we blamed our audience who were not used to such activities and didn't know how to behave. We said, all beginnings are difficult, but without a beginning there is no activity. We will continue and achieve, and in time we will see success.

Who would have imagined that this Purim play would cause a political problem? And this is what happened:

A few days after Purim, the Prista (head of the town) ordered Ben-Zion Tziglig to come before him in the "Volosat" building (village council). When he appeared before the council, the Pristov said to him: You are one of the honorables of your community and who is like you in this town, therefore I want to hear from you about this game. Why did youth dressed in royal clothes and gold crowns appear in the street? Is there not a connection between this appearance and the revolutionary movement? You surely have heard about the doings of the revolutionists in the big cities, about the punishments imposed on those who do such deeds and about the prisons that have been prepared for them. Hasn't the time arrived for me to take such action against this group of youth?

Ben-Zion Tziglig explained to the Pristav that it was only a traditional Purim play, customarily played by Jews from the time of Ahashverus until today and there isn't even a hint of revolutionary activity nor such a movement in our town.

The Pristov was satisfied with this explanation, but warned him that such acts should not be repeated. He doesn't object to Purim and he doesn't mind if once a year also the Jews can enjoy a bottle of liquor and get drunk - why not! But no such games. Surely, he doesn't doubt the honesty of the words of an honorable Jew like Tziglig, that there was no bad intention of the actions of the youth, but even so, the game shows desecration of royal clothes and ridicule of gold crowns. The Pristov ended his warning by saying, "Such actions shall not be done in my jurisdiction!"

[Page 147]

Educational Institutions

by Zelig Yulevich

Translated by Esther Mann Snyder

In Memory of my sister Haya-Kraina and family and my sister Mina and family who were murdered by evil persons.

Our town could be proud of its achievements in the field of education, both general and Jewish; if the Hebrew/Jewish school had not been destroyed by evil people, it would have celebrated – four years ago – the jubilee of its establishment.

In 1903, the "Improved Heder" was opened in our town, and it developed and improved until it became a real Hebrew school, that taught the children Torah and knowledge, the values of Jewish education and culture in the spirit of Zionism and pioneering fulfillment (*hagshama*). Indeed, many of the town's youth fulfilled the ideal of Zionism with their body and possessions – they left the town and went to Eretz Yisrael, became acclimatized and integrated. There is almost no family, among the 270 families in Lenin, that doesn't have descendants in Israel. Almost all of them arrived with knowledge of Hebrew and knew how to speak it and thus didn't need evening classes.

The founders of the "Improved Heder" were the teachers – Nissan Bergman, Yehuda Rubenstein, Aharon-Leb Zaichik. Yehuda Rubenstein was about 63 years old when the school was established but even at this age his spirit inspired the school in its first steps and he was the one who raised it to its high educational and cultural level. This man was superior to many among us in his broad knowledge; he knew Hebrew and its writings, ancient and modern literature; he was a grammarian and philologist, a cultured person who had polite manners. He was fond of the young members of the community and those seeking knowledge were welcome in his home. The youth would visit often and listen to his thoughts and ideas.

In Yehuda Rubenstein's home and that of his son, Noah Rubenstein, who dealt in lumber, the youth met the writer A.A. Kabek who had come to say farewell to his sister, Libbe, Noah's wife, and their family prior to his leaving to go to Eretz Yisrael.

***

The "Improved Heder" didn't take the place of the smaller heders. Although most of the children studied in this school (about 120 – 150 pupils), some parents, but not many, preferred to send their children to the traditional heder.

A. R' Avraham Aryeh's

The teacher Avraham Aryeh's had a special heder. You can surely say about him that he was of the students of Aharon the Cohen: "Love peace and seek peace…love people and bring them close to the Torah." (Avot 1:12). He had a great love for "Humash' (the five books of the Bible) and Rashi.

Rashi! He would call out with wonder and pleasure. Rashi is everything because what would we do without him. Without him we would be like those lost in the desert. We would not truly understand a chapter of the Bible

[Page 148]

nor a page of the Talmud; we would grope in the darkness even over the simplest verse in the Bible or an easy section of the Gemara (Talmud) without him. Rashi came and illuminated all these matters. But, he used to add, one had to understand even Rashi himself, because his commentary had hidden and concealed ideas that not everyone was able to find and decipher. Sometimes, for example, he would meet someone in the synagogue or in the street, grab his collar so he couldn't run away and tell him about a very interesting Rashi interpretation.

The Bible for him was not just the Bible but "our little Bible-le" that has everything, all the seventy-seven wisdoms all together. Rashi's commentary was holy to him, but for R' Avraham Aryeh's, there was some room for his own interpretations, as the Bible has so many different aspects. During the reading of the Torah in the synagogue, between the *aliyot*, he would go from one person to another telling his interpretation of one verse or another. When he looked for someone to tell of his interpretations, he didn't discriminate among people, whether a scholar or an unlearned person. The listener would listen, the main point being that R' Avraham was able to tell his new interpretation.

It's obvious that he had a great love of everything in the Bible, the biblical "fathers" and the land of the fathers. He was very familiar with the land of Israel as if he had traveled it himself. He learned about the land and knew it well through his studying of the Bible and also the Mishna. Every morning after prayers he read a chapter of Mishna to the people gathered. He would say, "When I read the Mishna, I imagine myself as if I lived in Eretz Yisrael, walking among the vineyards, sitting in the shade of the vines and tasting all of the things that Eretz Yisrael is blessed with."

Despite his meager livelihood, he knew how to live with dignity. Rumor said that R' Avraham could manage a whole week with a loaf of bread and pickled herring, and that he was an expert in splitting a match stick into four pieces. I knew that there was a lot of truth to these stories and respected him even more. He was not miserly; he knew how to be thrifty, to balance his expenses according to his deficient livelihood. Thanks to these qualities, it was pleasant to meet with this Torah scholar in the street or the Synagogue. He didn't wear silk or fine clothing, however his clothes were always clean and never had any dirt or stains.

B. R' Yehuda Rubenstein

And there was another "heder; the "heder" of the distinguished teacher, R' Yehuda Rubenstein. As we mentioned above, R' Yehuda who was over the age of sixty, helped two younger teachers, Nissan Bergman and Aharon-Leib Zaichik in establishing the school. After only two years R' Yehuda left the school and opened a heder for those who had already graduated from the school, and it became sort of a continuation class. R' Yehuda was a man of wide learning and knowledge and was a pioneer in Jewish/Hebrew and secular higher learning in our town. In addition to his students, a group of youth used to come to his home and listen to his words, or read Hebrew newspapers or read a book that was not to be found elsewhere. He also had a small library for children. Sometimes, we were lucky enough to read a letter that was sent from Eretz Yisrael, written to him by the very hand of the writer A.A. Kabek

[Page 149]

who was related to him by marriage as his son was married to Kabek's sister.

On Sabbath days R' Yehuda read from the Torah in the new Synagogue. And sometimes he would agree to the request of the sexton (gabbai) to lead the Musaf prayer service. His reading was very good and his prayer a pleasure. Those who knew Hebrew paid close attention to his careful, accurate reading.

R' Yehuda Rubenstein

In addition, his external appearance attracted respect. He stood tall and straight, his beard was shaped like that of M. Nordau, his clothes were clean, his boots polished and he walked easily and with grace.

He had two daughters and one son. His daughter Feigl (Zipporah) was married to a clerk in the forestry business. They lived in Mikashvitzi, near the train station. Feigl was outstanding in her good-heartedness. She and her daughter, Liova, were murdered by filthy murderers. Her son Shlomo, his wife and children remained in Russia. Her son, Dov, lives in Israel.

R' Yehuda's second daughter, Tima, was also married to a clerk in the forestry business. He name was Sender Chinitch and he was born in the town of Strobin. For some years he was a gabbai in the new Synagogue. They died in the holy grave of the Jews of Lenin.

R' Yehuda's son, Noah Rubenstein, had a wide and deep knowledge of Hebrew, was proficient in the Bible, had much knowledge in Talmud and knew foreign languages. He dealt in forestry, succeeded and became a well-know lumber merchant. He married the sister of the writer, A.A. Kabek. His home was a meeting place for scholars and writers. Due to him our town was privileged to see famous writers strolling the streets and sitting in the shade of the forests.

Also the wedding of Kabek took place in our town and it drew many writers and journalists. The residents were proud of this and thought: "Don't view us as residents of a small town who are stuck in the mud – high-level people from their exalted positions came to our town."

In 1912, Noah Rubenstein gave his home to Zalman Bresler, and he and his family moved to Pinsk where he bought a beautiful, spacious home. During World War I, the newspaper "Hatzfira" had a financial crisis and thanks to the financial aid of Noah the newspaper continued to appear and did not close down.

Noah Rubenstein's two daughters, Rahel and Hadassa, and his son Naftali were among the founders of

[Page 150]

Mishmar HaEmek. In 1936, Noah and his wife Libbe moved to Eretz Yisrael. He liquidated his assets in Poland and brought his possessions and business to Israel. However, not much was left due to the limitations placed by the Polish laws and the directives of Grabeski.

He was buried in Mishmar HaEmek. His widow, Libbe, settled there and didn't leave even in times of attack.

In Lenin, after the death of Yehuda Rubenstein, a group of parents took upon itself to find teachers for the higher grades. Most of these teachers came from other towns.

[Page 150]

The "Heder" of Teacher X

by Haim Yonai

Translated by Esther Mann Snyder

In 1908 teacher X was invited to come to teach in the "heder" which had two high classes and the total number of students wasn't more than fifteen. One of them was Shlomo, the son of Noah Rubenstein. Noah used to visit the "heder" at least two or three times each month. He observed the arrangements and sanitary conditions, listened to the lessons, checked the students' notebooks, looked over their written papers, tested some of them and was proud of their knowledge and scholastic achievements. He even looked into one child's ear, scolded another for the manner he held his pen or for unkempt hair. He would rebuke a student until he turned red from embarrassment in front of the teacher. After all this, he would praise the teacher in front of the students, encourage us students with kind words and praise. He would distribute sweets and candies, and leave with the blessing of "shalom" and wishes for success in our studies and deeds. He asked the teacher to accompany him for a few steps. When they left, we watched them from the window and according to their facial expressions and hand movements, we would know whether Noah Rubenstein was satisfied with what he saw and heard or perhaps he had some comment that would lessen the praise he had given to the teacher before the pupils.

After a while, the teacher returned and his expression … well, sometimes it reminded us of the story of Yaakov in the Bible, who fought with the angel and was victorious, but hurt his thigh and walked with a limp…

Thus, our classes were supervised by Noah Rubenstein. I didn't know then and even today I am not sure whether Noah appointed himself or he was asked by the parents.

We, the pupils, were very interested by the visits of Noah Rubenstein, which were a special experience for us. Our school routine was broken for about two hours when he visited. We watched with curiosity as the young teacher tensely answered the questions posed. Sometimes the supervisor had a different opinion as to the interpretation of a difficult passage from the Bible, or understanding a section of the Talmud, or in a rule of grammar. More than once we witnessed

[Page 151]

an argument between the two. I remember that we pupils prayed in our hearts that the teacher would be victorious -_ his victory was also ours. Once, during such an argument, I asked Shlomke, Noah's son, "What do you think, who is winning?" Shlomke answered with confidence, "Our teacher will be right."

Finally, the two took leave with affection and friendship. We knew that Noah felt affection for the young teacher, and the teacher respected the supervisor.

Noah Rubenstein left the town a few years later and moved to Pinsk, and from there he moved to Warsaw. From there we heard the sad news that my friend Shlomo had died, at a young age, only eighteen years old. We, his friends from the "heder", mourned him bitterly. He had been a faithful friend with a good heart and soul. May his memory be blessed.

[Page 151]

The Lenin Branch of "Tarbut"

by Dov Zaichik

Translated by Esther Mann Snyder

Our town cannot be described without mentioning, among other public institutions, the branch of "Tarbut." It had a library of about 600 books, mainly in Hebrew and Yiddish. Most of the books, which covered many fields of interest, were serious works, such as the classics and the books of contemporary authors; every important work that was translated was immediately acquired, among them all the volumes of the literary magazine "HaTekufa." In the reading room were to be found issues of these newspapers, "Heint" (Today), "Mament," "Farvarts" (from America), and the weeklies "Welt-Shpiegl," "Literarishe Bletter", "Kvila" (a Zionist paper written in Polish and published in Lvov), and others.

The library fulfilled an important role in the life of the youth in our town, as it was the only meeting place for all ages. The club council had representatives from all the political parties. Books could be borrowed three times a week; suggestions for choosing books were often given by my older brother, Moshe z"l when he was home on vacations.

The establishment of the library preceded that of the reading room; its basic collection was donated by the members and for a short while was placed in a small bookcase in the home of Leah Rubenstein. Later the books were transferred to the entrance hall of our home, until the branch of Tarbut was organized. Then a room was rented in the home of Gelanson where the books were kept and which also served as a reading room.

The assistance of the member, Hershel Migdalovich in organizing the branch should be noted. He served as the first chairman of the committee which also included Leah Rubenstein, Moshel Temkin, Haim Pederaski, Shlomo Graeib and this writer. The income from theatrical performances and dances were donated to the branch and were the basis of the book budget, maintaining the reading room and subscribing to newspapers. Part of the expenses were covered by membership dues from the readers.

[Page 152]

We remember with gratitude all those who helped in organizing plays and projects and who voluntarily worked very hard. They include: the member Meir Buktzin, who was a talented director and make-up man; the amateur actors, our orchestra with the participation of my two sisters (deceased), and others, who should live, Yaakov Tzukrovitz, Lipa Mishelov, my brother Mordechai, the writer of these lines and others, and lastly those who lent their chairs and benches and those who moved them for the performances. On the evening before each performance we would go from house to house collecting chairs and putting them on a cart attached to a poor horse. We held the performances in the hall of the fire department near Shmalkin House – and later in the town Meeting House (Dom Ludovi).

Late at night, after the performance when we stayed up most of the night, our first task was to return the chairs and benches to their owners, while the audience went home very late to "grab" some sleep. A small group usually helped with this task: Tzvi and Shlomo Graeib, Moshel Temkin, Shlomo Gelanson, myself and a few others.

On Simhat Torah, a "minyan" was held in the reading room of the clubhouse and all the donations were given to the branch and the Jewish National Fund (Keren Kayemet L'Yisrael). From the synagogue we paraded in the street to the branch with the Torah scroll and after the prayers we marched back. Everyone who took part in this celebration will never forget it. It should be mentioned that the attitude and appreciation of the Rabbi and the elders of the community to us was very favorable, certainly because we were respectful towards our parents and to our elders.

In later years the branch moved to the apartment of Lilenberg, in the house of Herzl Papareno; slowly, slowly we added young members who lovingly set about continuing the work of this educational institution. Those who endeavored were Avrahamche Lilenberg, Moshel Bavkin, Tcherna Vacharbin, Nasha Schusterman and they were assisted by Yisraelik Tziglig and others.

Worthy of mention are the active members who devoted themselves to the work of the branch and actually supported it, including Avner Avineri (Schusterman), who was active until he left for Eretz Yisrael, despite the fact that he lived far from the town. Before his aliya, he donated to the branch a wooden engraving that he had done. Others who deserve mention are Pinhas Zaretzki, Nahum Golob, Menashe Latocha, Sender Weisblat, Moshe Tzukrovitz, Leah Mishelov and others.

Many participated in our assemblies and in the "Questions and Answers" parties that were popular.

My heart fills with pain and trembling when I remember our young, who were and are no longer. They were youth who were known and admired in the whole district and in the north due to their good knowledge of Hebrew, their belief in Zionism, the parties held for national causes, their interest in all the current problems of the lives of the Jews in Poland and the world at large.

I think that while reading these words each one will stop for a moment and remember the young men and women, dear and modest, who were devoted to lofty ideas but were not privileged to fulfill them in the land of our fathers.

May their memory be blessed.

[Page 153]

Active Members of Tarbut

[Page 154]

My Town, Lenin

by Tsila Zaretzki, nee Baruchin

Translated by Esther Mann Snyder

I loved my town, Lenin, although I didn't remain there. I lived there only during my childhood because while I was still young, my older sister, Feigel, took me to Moscow to continue my studies.

Whenever I returned to visit our home in Lenin, it was a pleasant experience. Although I preferred the big city with its advantages and lively cultural scene, I still had a strong connection to my town.

Memories of the years I studied in the "heder" starting from age 6, awake in me warm feelings. At first, we studied for a time with Feivel, the son-in-law of Haim-Beryl the sexton, and we managed to reach the 10th letter of the alphabet, "yod." After Feivel went to America, Heneh Sokolovski from Mokriva took his place. The "heder" was held at that time in the home of Mordechai-Leib Tziglig. I remember that often during rainy days whenthe mud was deep and we weren't able to cross the street, Sokolovski would carry each child in his arms to the heder, while his boots were covered in mud.

Also this teacher did not stay long and we transferred to the "improved heder" of the teachers Yehuda Rubenstein, Nisan Bergman and Aharon-Leib Zaichik. We progressed well in our classes, especially in Bible (Tana"ch), math and Russian language.

The school set time for examinations, usually in the summer. The examiners were parents of the pupils or guests who spent their vacation in Lenin during the summer months, like my brother-in-law Moshe Medursky and Mr. Aharon Singalovski. We, the students, studied hard for the exams and waited impatiently for the grades received.

An evening of readings and recitations done once by the students of the higher classes left an indelible impression on me. It was organized by Mr. Singalovski and held in the home of Herzl Papareno.

This event was the beginning of our appearences on the stage and it gave us courage later to put on plays, as was common in the big cities. According to knowledgeable people these performances were a success.

*

Unique things in our town of Lenin: who among those of my age doesn't remember how much we enjoyed being released from classes and spending time in the beautiful nature surroundings. We loved walking on the long bridge above the Slutz River (which we called humorously, "Navski-Prospect"). From there we continued to the hill called, "the Green Hill," climbed to the top and looked out at the thick pine forest surrounding it. And how much we enjoyed the pleasure of swimming in the river near the oak trees, at the spot named "dovnik" or "the white beach." How lovely it was to go out on Lag B'Omer, accompanied by the teachers, for a hike in the forest that surrounded our town on all sides. I remember the special experience of the winter days

[Page 155]

when we went out in the evening with lights made of oiled paper, made by each child. We loved to skate and slide on the ice and walk through the falling snow flakes, melting on our faces, or to make snowballs and throw them at each other.

However, the youth didn't want to remain within the confines of our town and anyone who had the means left to go to a bigger city, near or far, to learn more and find a profession. Even when we were in the big cities, we were proud of our town and could always prove that it had a great advantage in terms of interpersonal relations and its love of Zion.

Whenever I visited Lenin, after being away for a long or short while, it seemed to me that the houses had become smaller or more fallen in, and despite this it was still charming in my eyes. The opposite was true, my yearning for her grew stronger. The custom of labeling people with funny names which existed in the big cities hardly occurred in Lenin. If someone did use a funny term about another, it wasn't due to a bad attitude but just a silly joke.

I can see in my imagination each of the people of our town, and I know now to appreciate the qualities and good character that all of them possessed.

*

It is very difficult to reconcile to the bitter knowledge that all that was dear to me was totally destroyed. I heard many stories from eye witnessed how the people were tragically killed by the evil enemy – may their name and memory be erased – the dear members of my family and all the people of the town and how the town was destroyed and burned down.

Great is the pain that burns in me and the heart refuses to accept condolences, because the grief is great and the pain and sorrow are difficult to bear. We don't even have graves of our dear ones to visit.

The memory of our town and its residents will remain forever in our hearts.

[Page 156]

Orphans "Soup Kitchen" established by the Tsentos
Society

Movie Benefit held for Orphans Society "Tsentos"
(1925)
Standing, right to left: Bashke Tziglig, Mordechai Zaichik,
Esther Mandelbaum, Shmuel Graeib, Shaindel Rubenstein.
Sitting, right to left: Meir Boktzin, Hanan Vacharbin

[Page 159]

Parties and Youth Organizations

The Beginning of the Zionist Movement in Our Town

By Avraham-Itshak Slutsky

Translated by Oren Yulevich

The first signs of the Zionist movement were seen in town immediately after the first Zionist congress in Basel. Educated youngsters, Yeshiva students and secular students were the first to be caught by the Zionist idea; they held to it and did their best to spread it in our town. It can be said that as the days passed, many people accepted it. Some memorable movement activists: Yehoshua-Mordechai Tziglig, Jacob Greenberg, Zalman Bresler and Avraham Meir Paperna, of blessed memory. The movement members and other supporters met in the attic belonging to Moshe-David Greenberg, of blessed memory; or at Ben-Zion Tziglig's house. They were very active in educating the children and youth in the Zionist spirit and ideas and organized Young Hebrew Readers after school class. During class, Slutsky was sometimes assigned the Reader role and he would read out stories and news from the "Little World" child magazine. Movement activists began spreading Anglo-Palestinian bank shares, vigorously and enthusiastically. Only a few people could afford the 10 rubles; therefore two-three people purchased a single share jointly. Draws were arranged in order to enable the less fortunate to own a share: twenty people each paid one half of a ruble each and the draw winner received the share.

A young Christian, Albert, the son of a clerk in Agarkov court, who was always hanging around with the young Jews, heard of the draws and wanted to take part in them. He paid the one half of a ruble and won. He was offered 10 rubles for the stock, but he refused to accept them and kept the shares. He held on to them like a precious gift that brings good fortune to its owner.

Reb Zelig Singalovski and his wife Frida

The Zionist movement grew stronger with the Singalovski family's arrival in town. Zelig, the head of the family, was an important clerk in Agarkov estate management. His only daughter and five sons went to high schools and colleges in various cities in Russia. On school vacations they would come to their house on the estate grounds.

On a Nahamu Saturday afternoon, an announcement was made: one of the boys, Aharon Singalovski, will give a speech at the new synagogue. He was already known as a gifted speaker. On the appointed day, the synagogue was full and crowded. The speaker spoke passionately and touched many listeners' hearts. When he finished many approached him, and hugged and kissed him. Yakov Latoucha, who will ever be remembered, did even more: he lifted Aharon and wept tears of emotion.

Then the great man, the great scholar Reb Isar Nakritz, of blessed memory, took the stage and started preaching passionately and with much excitement for Zionist awareness, actions and deeds for the Settlement of the Land (Israel o.y.). His father-in-law, Reb David Gerayev, was shocked to hear his son-in-law. He raised his voice, anxiously: "Is it possible?! That this son-in-law of his, the family pride and jewel, had been trapped?! Had he given his hand to those youngsters who do not wait for the messiah anymore and joined those who pray for the end?!". Other community elders zealots raised their voices too and the turmoil increased. Reb Isar had to cease speaking and left the stage, embarrassed. The meeting was dispersed.

However, the seed Reb Isar had sown, bore fruit: his son Haim Zelig Shalev immigrated to Israel in 1919, founded a mosaic and marble tiles factory –Mertsafia. Haim Zelig brought his parents, Reb Isar and his wife, to Israel; and all his brothers and sisters.

Aharon Singalovski now heads the "Ort" organization of which he was a founder. His brother, Yehoshua Singalovski, served as a teacher in a Jerusalem seminary for many years and was known to all the college students as Mr. Y. Avizohar. Sara Singalovski, Yehoshua and Aharon's sister, lives in Israel now.

[Page 161]

The "HeHalutz" Movement

by Herzl Tzukrovitz

Translated by Sara Mages

The founder of "*HeHalutz*" [the pioneer] Movement in Lenin was Hershke Migdalovich.

A short young man with a dark complexion, his hair was curly and a smile graced his face. He was pleasant and humble. I've never seen him scolding someone, because he always explained his words with grace and pleasantness. He graduated a vocational school for carpentry. Since he was an intellectual young man he acquired knowledge in management and organization. The topics of the conversations with him were different and diverse - all streams of Zionism and all forms of pioneering, congresses, art, etc. Not everyone participated in the discussion because not everyone was familiar with the subject in question, but everyone listened to him with great interest.

He took upon himself to organize this movement under quite difficult conditions. First - because the movement couldn't hold meetings of political nature without the authorities' permission, second - because of the contempt of the local Jewish population, third - the indifferent attitude of the youth.

Most of the youth were craftsmen and worked in physical labor, therefore, *"HeHalutz"* was the natural place for every boy and girl from a working family.

Hershke overcame all the obstacles. On weekdays small groups met secretly in private homes, and on Saturday they left in groups of two or three in the direction of the *"Bolnica"* (hospital) or on the road to Makovitz - and met at the designated spot. The risk was great. Any suspicion, even the smallest, could have resulted in a severe punishment. The town's proximity to the border has worsened the situation, and everything with a political scent could've been interpreted as a relationship with the Soviet regime across the border.

The meetings, which were illegal in the eyes of the authorities, continued until the organizers were able to obtain an official confirmation. A hall was rented and there was no need to hold the meetings in secret.

The results weren't late to arrive. The members started to show interest in *hakhshara* [pioneer training]. Ziril Shosterman was the first to leave for a *hakhshara* Kibbutz near Kobrin. Six months later she was approved for immigration and immigrated to Israel. Many members followed suit and immigrated to Israel. Among them: Yakov Tzukrovitz, Moshe Gurevich, Zelig Behon and others who joined a kibbutz. Others settled in various cities in Israel.

[Page 162]

"*HeHalutz*" chapter in Lenin
21 Tishrei, 5692 [2 October, 1931]

[Page 163]

"*HeHalutz*" Movement in Lenin

[Page 164]

Betar

by Ben Shamai

Translated by Sara Mages

Two young men in our town, both seventeen years old, and they are Y.B. and D.R, were captured by the ideology of the Betar Movement. The names - Jabotinsky, recruitment, legion and headquarters - appealed to them and spoke to their hearts. They turned to the main headquarters in Warsaw and asked for propaganda material. The headquarters filled their request and sent them the material. The two young men sat and studied the material, read it carefully, and decided to open a chapter of Betar in Lenin.

They turned to the Polish district governor and asked for a license. The license was granted in April 1930, and immediately, about two dozen young men and women met in the woods near the Jewish cemetery, and declared the founding of the nest.

This organization wasn't "created out of nothing" since most of the townspeople were Zionist. The youth worked faithfully and with great devotion for the "funds," and was aware of every Zionist activity. A strong organizational framework for Zionist activities was created with the establishment of the nest.

A short time later, a crisis started in our organization. Several young people left and established the "*Halutz*" movement. In this manner, two organizations, which fought a stubborn and bitter struggle to acquire the local youth to their ranks, were established.

However, Betar overcame the crisis and started to work energetically. Active members came to the aid of the founders, and they are: Moshe Bavkin, Yisrael Tziglig (both were killed in the war), and Avraham Lilenberg (who lives with us in Israel). The organization, which contained nearly thirty members, didn't aspire to expand. As mentioned, our first activities took place in the forests around the town. When autumn arrived, the top floor at the Lilenberg's house was rented, and Betar was rewarded with its own club. It was a meeting place for games, reading and study. Lessons in the Hebrew language and the history of Zionism were also given there.

A short time later, Y.B. returned to his studies at the seminary for teachers in Grodno and D.R left, with the main headquarters' permission, for pioneering training. The management of the branch was given to Moshe Bavkin, Yisrael Tziglig, Avraham Lilenberg and Yitzchak Kolpanitsky who returned to the town after he completed his studies at the vocational school in Brisk.

D.R immigrated to Israel. His way wasn't easy, but he saw the fulfillment of some of his aspirations.

These few words will be a monument on the graves of these young people, who dreamed the dream of resurrection, but didn't live to see its solution because they were devoured by defiled killers.

[Page 167]

People and Personalities

Rabbis

HaRav R' Yehudah Turetski Zts"L

By Mordechai Zaichik

Translated by Sara Mages

We don't know who the first rabbi of our town was. It's only known that in the years, 1830-1860, a rabbi already sat on the Rabbinate chair in Lenin, but no one remembered him in our time. Prior to 1830, the Jewish community in Lenin was small and poor and wasn't able to support a rabbi.

Anyway, HaRav R' Yehudah Turetski, who ascended the Rabbinate chair in 1860 and sat on it for sixty six full years, endeared himself to all the residents of our town. He studied the Torah day and night to fulfill the saying "You shall meditate therein day and night." He only stopped his studies when he taught the laws of *Kashrut*, mediated between litigants who voiced their claims before him, officiated at a wedding, sold leavened food, etc.

[Page 168]

He lived in poverty and distress all his life. His financial situation slightly improved in the last days of his life.

The rabbi wasn't only respected by the Jewish community, the Gentiles, in the town and its environs, also respected him. The priest Johan, who visited him often, also expressed great affection towards him. During the rabbi's illness, the priest spent many hours next to his bed and talked to him on various subjects with the help of a translator. Of course, the Gentiles saw the rabbi as a holy man and when they met him in the street they greeted him with great respect.

We already said that he sat day and night and studied. When he encountered a difficult issue, he got up from his chair and paced slowly, back and forth, until the matter became clear to him. Then, his face lit up and he returned to the open page before him.

However, when the members of his community came to ask his advice, recount their troubles or ask him to mediate between rivals – he put his handkerchief on the open Gemara, welcomed them warmly, listened to them and found a word of comfort and encouragement to strengthened feeble hands and inspire hope in the heart on a difficult day. He made peace between rivals in the most wonderful and amazing way! He preferred a compromise on judgment.

As long as the rabbi saw that his help, advice and arbitration assisted those who turned to him, he wasn't sorry he had to cancel the study of the Torah. However, when someone bothered him with nonsense and idle talk, he held out his hand and said: "Well, well, Good night! Good night to you! Shalom! Shalom!"

Rabbi Yehudah Turetski had four sons and three daughters. All were talented and educated. R' Itche (Yitzchak), R' Aba, R' Shmuel–Michel, R' Moshe and his three daughters: Sheindil, Ethel and Basha.

R' Itche died at the prime of his life from a venomous snakebite. R' Moshe was a rabbi in one of London's neighborhoods. R' Shmuel–Michel, who was known by the name "The Karliner *Dayan*," was appointed to served as a judge in Pinsk. He was kindhearted, well–versed and sharp. He dedicated his book of sermons, in which he gathered his father's sermons, commentaries, proverbs and sayings, to his father.

His daughter Ethel resided in the town of Petrikov on the Pripyat River. Basha and her husband, R' Yakov the slaughterer, l resided first in our town and later left for the city of Minsk. Sheindil and her husband, R' Hillel, resided in Kazan–Haradok.

R' Yehudah passed away at the age of 96. One winter day, when he left his house to go to the synagogue, he slid on the frozen snow, fell and broke his leg. The townspeople summoned the surgeon, Yavsienka, from Minsk. The doctor came with his assistants and nurses and treated him with great devotion. Despite the rabbi's old age, he managed to mend his broken leg and heal it – and there was great joy in town.

However, a few days later, the rabbi stumbled for the second time, fell and broke the same leg. The surgeon was summoned again, but this time he had to amputate the leg. Our beloved rabbi didn't have the strength to withstand this surgery and passed away.

A heavy mourning fell on the town which was orphaned from its good and amiable father. There were many days of mourning and eulogy because the man was loved because of his righteousness and great love to the members of his community.

Many rabbis and important community leaders came from towns, near and far, to pay their last respect to our rabbi and accompany him to his resting place. He was eulogized by Rabbi Itzale, the rabbi of the town of Lachva; by Rabbi Walkin, the rabbi of the city of Pinsk, and others.

[Page 169]

HaRav R' Yehudah Turetski Zts"L

by Yitzchak Slutsky

Translated by Sara Mages

Our town was awarded that for over sixty-six years a beloved and humble Jew, who loved people and was loved by them, served in its rabbinate. Although he wasn't considered to be an active man and didn't distinguished himself as a speaker and preacher – the secret of his good influence on the townspeople was his pleasant manners, his humility and great love to the entire town.

He lived in a house that belonged to the community and stood behind the synagogue. His apartment was quite spacious, but poverty and shortage prevailed in it. He came to serve in the rabbinate in the days when poverty was the lot of most of the townspeople. Prosperity came to town when the office of the landowner, Agarkov, expanded its activities in the timber trade and employed many of the town's residents. By that time, the rabbi was already used to his poverty and didn't complain until the situation was unbearable…

Once, during the winter, at a wedding feast at the house of one of the town's notables, the old rabbi sat at the head of the invited guests – the town's rich and important homeowners. Also the slaughterer-cantor, R' Yisrael Chaim, and his choir, came to delight the bride and groom with their singing. When the guests were in a cheerful mood, the rabbi turned to the dignitaries and told them that he's freezing in his apartment because he doesn't have the means to buy wood to heat the oven… The rabbi's simple words deeply touched those who heard and caused uproar in town. Is that possible?! The rabbi is in such distress, suffering in silence – and no one noticed that!

The residents of the town were immediately called for a meeting, to consult on how to improve the economic situation of the rabbi, and the correct advice was found:

Till then, the rabbi's income came from the yeas that every housewife purchased on Thursday for the baking of the Sabbath *challot*. Until the meeting, the price of a portion of approximately ten grams of yeast was two kopeks. At the meeting, it was decided to raise the price of the packet to three kopeks and to also give the rabbi the right to sell the Sabbath candles which, till then, were sold in each grocery store. The shop owners didn't want to give up their right willingly, but after heated arguments were forced to surrender to the will of the crowd – and the sale of the Sabbath candles was transferred to the rabbi's house.

And the Sabbath candles of our townspeople illuminated and also warmed the rabbi's house.

[Page 170]

Rabbi Moshe Tomashov

by Chaim Shalev

Translated by Sara Mages

R' Moshe son of R' Zundel Tomashov Zts"L

When we come to place a memorial monument for our beloved town, and when we raise the memory of the men of virtue who lived and were active there, the image of my teacher and rabbi, R' Moshe Tomashov Zts"L, rises immediately.

I don't remember when I was introduced to him for the first time, but from that day I learned to know him and felt his entity. He was a little fat, had a long beard, his hat was slumped over his eyes and his coat hung over his shoulders. When he walked from the old synagogue to his home, his mouth murmured a prayer, and when he met a Jew he shook his head and said *"Gut Shabbos! Gut Shabbos!"* (twice), and continued on his way and his prayer without waiting for an answer.

I was his student for four consecutive years, and when I was in his presence I got to know him well and understand his nature, habits and way of life. Every day, summer and winter, he woke up from his sleep at four in the morning, sat and studied until *Shacharit* prayer. When prayer time came, he walked a long distant to the old synagogue even though the new synagogue was closer to his house. He came to the new synagogue for *"Kabbalat* Shabbat" and for *Maariv* prayer at the conclusion of the Shabbat services. He greatly extended his prayer and emphasized each word as if he was counting gems. He started with "*Ma*

Tovu," ended with "*Ma'Amadot*," and continued to read a chapter of *Mishnaiot* before the audience. Although it was much to the chagrin of a few, they didn't dare to speak up and ask him to shorten his reading. On weekdays, after the *Shacharit* prayer, he returned home to eat his fill, which, most of the time, consisted of dry cake with a glass of goat milk. I remember that he made sure to collect all the crumbs and eat them, maybe out of poverty and savings, or maybe out of piety. He began teaching after this meager meal. We opened with a lesson in the Gemara. Naturally, there were those among the students who were talented and those who had a blocked brain. He worked harder with the latter and literally "chopped wood." Most of the time the students didn't understand the lesson, but the rabbi was stubborn and repeated his lesson one hundred and one times until something entered their brain.

[Page 171]

Towards evening, at twilight, we studied the *Tanach* – or, as we used to say then – "the twenty four" [books of the Holy Scriptures]. This was the order of studies all the days of the week, and only on Friday the studies lasted until eleven o'clock in the morning. On this day, we engaged in easy studies: we read the weekly Torah portion, the *Haftarah* in "*Taamei Hamikrah*" and "*Shir Hashirim*." On Sabbath eve, the rabbi allowed himself to engage in easy matters and told legends and jokes. On the Sabbath, R' Moshe didn't engage in everyday conversation and if it was necessary to say something, he said it in a few words in Hebrew. On the other hand, the rabbi allowed himself to speak in Yiddish in matters that were related to study, prayer and the explanation of an issue in the Gemara. Because of his humility he didn't eat any delicious food that he could keep for the Sabbath. If someone gave him a cake, or any other pastry on Thursday or Friday, he turned to his wife and said: "Keep it, Base, we'll bless it on the Holly Sabbath." Yet, on weekdays, he managed to complete the number of blessings that he blessed every day, up to one hundred and one.

I'm unable to count and describe all his noble qualities. All the good qualities that our Sages counted in a noble man were folded in him in their entirety and connected together. He was humble, frugal, loved peace, fled honor, was far from envy and hatred, and loathed profit (he never demanded tuition from his students). He accepted everything with love and defended every person. The highlight of his virtues was his great love for all the Jewish people, but his love for the society did not detract from his love for the individual. If someone told him about a person who has sinned or committed an offense, he did not believe the story and said: "your eyes must have deceived you and you didn't see it clearly."

He didn't hurt the dignity of a person and forgave an insult. His love of the Torah exceeded all bounds. Once, a student burst out and slapped him (the rabbi) on the cheek (today, forty-seven years after the act, my whole body trembles when I remember it). The same student, who was frightened and scared after his act, decided to correct the distortion and started to work diligently on his studies. However, it only lasted for a few weeks. The student gradually forgot the incident, returned to his evil ways and neglected his studies. Rabbi Moshe told him: "Slap me on the cheek again so you can pursue your studies."

Even though the rabbi was constantly situated within the world of Torah, prayer and piety, he was a sociable person and was interested to hear the news from the world. He liked jokes and wise sayings and was gifted with a sense of humor. I remember, once, on Passover eve, when all the Jewish women were busy with the preparations for the holiday - with the polishing of the tableware and the cleaning of the house, R' Moshe turned to the home of my uncle, the son of R' Avraham Yitzchak Chinitch's sister, on his way home from the synagogue. There, he was given a cup of coffee and a pastry, and after he finished eating the refreshments he hurried to leave. They asked him – "why are you in such a hurry?" He answered them with a smile – "You understand, today is Passover eve and Base, my wife,

[Page 172]

is angry and needs someone to pour out her wrath on. If I stay here, she wouldn't have anyone to scold and raise her voice on."

R' Moshe was childless, his wife was sickly and suffered from all sorts of pains and aches – and the order of the house was neglected. The floor was washed twice a year – on Rosh Hashanah eve and Passover eve. However, the rabbi excelled in a great deal of patience and never complained. In all the years that I came to his house I've never heard him complain, he received all the sufferings that came to him with love. Only once, on a winter night, when we, the students, got him angry and drove him crazy, he erupted with anger (I only saw him doing it once). He took off his silver watch and said: "Base, take the watch and sell it, I will expel these demons – and God will have mercy." When we heard his words, the fear of death fell on us and we repented, if not for long.

We used to do all acts of mischief. In the hot summer days, when the rabbi lay down for his afternoon nap, we used to slip away to the river shore which was behind the rabbi's house. We collected all the fishing boats of the Christian fishermen (they were made of a thick wooden beam which was hollowed in the middle), tied them together into a raft, sailed to the middle of the river and played and enjoyed the water.

When the rabbi awoke from his sleep and saw that none of us was in the classroom, he went to the river shore and called: "*Shkotzim*, enough! Hurry up, enough!" We struck a deal with him: "Rabbi, we will come back if you promise not to beat us." He promised, we returned, and he kept his promise.

His knowledge in the Talmud was amazing. When he was asked a question, he walked to the bookcase, took out the Gemara, opened it and pointed: here it is. It was said, that he finished the Six Orders of the Mishnah and Talmud thirty six times.

After I returned from the army I came to him every day to study a page from the Gemara and then, so to speak, already as a friend. There was no limit to his happiness. He used to give me a cigarette - it seems to me, that it was his only pleasure out of all the pleasures of the world which were strange to him and he did not enjoy them.

In the summer, he used to go on Sabbath eve to bathe in the river in honor of the Sabbath, and then he showed the wonders of swimming: swimming on the back, swimming under water, trimming of the toenails while swimming, and more. When he became ill and was confined to bed I was his helper during the day and also at night. One day he said to me: "My son, would I be able to walk again before God in the lands of the living?" I told him: "Rabbi, what are you saying?! It's clear to me that you will get better with God's help. After all, we are standing in the middle of *Masechet Eruvin* and we need to finish it and start another tractate." He answered me: "my brother, Mordechi–Yoshe, died at the age of 72 and today I'm also 72. I doubt that I will live longer than him." And as he said, so it was: he passed away on the same week.

Many accompanied him to his resting place. They said that Lenin had never seen such a well–attended funeral.

[Page 173]

The Rabbis – R' Nachman Wasserman and R' Moshe Millstein

by Mordechai Zaichik

Translated by Sara Mages

HaRav, R' Nachman Wasserman, came to serve in the rabbinate in our town after the death of R' Yehudah Turetski. He was a Jew with an imposing figure, clever and well–liked. His house was always full of townspeople who came to consult with him, ask "questions" or litigate before him in monetary matters.

R' Nachman was a talented speaker and when he delivered his sermon on the Sabbath the old synagogue was full to capacity.

However, he didn't stay in our town for long. Shortly thereafter he moved to the city of Stavisk near Łomża.

As was customary in Jewish communities, the chapter of electing a rabbi started immediately after the departure of R' Nachman and lasted six months. The townspeople, who split into two camps, couldn't reach an agreement between them. When a rabbi was found, one side was satisfied with him – but the second side disliked him, what was good in the eyes of the second side – was rejected by the first side – and so forth. Meanwhile, our town was awarded to hear various sermons. Each rabbi, who came to present his candidacy for the rabbinate, gave his sermon, and since many candidates – young and old – came, an abundance of sermons and speeches rained down on our town. The old synagogue was filled to capacity on Sabbath eve, on the Sabbath and also on weekday evenings. Men, women, boys and girls came to listen and see the candidate. Obviously, each candidate came and gave his best sermon, and the members of our community weren't tired of hearing and listening. A few of us, who were quick to listen and comprehend, were probably able to go to one of the towns in which the rabbinate chair stood empty and orphaned, give a high quality sermon and present their candidacy to the rabbinate, if… if they wanted to…

However, the abundance of sermons didn't make the members of our community any wiser. On the contrary, the more they've heard, the more they got confused and didn't know who to choose and who to despise. Finally, the members of our community overcame their confusion and HaRav, R' Moshe Millstein, who was nicknamed "R' Moshe'le from Warsaw," was elected rabbi of our community. He was a handsome young rabbi, was a great scholar and knew several languages. He had a fine voice and many loved to hear him when he taught and when he led the prayers at the synagogue. He was involved with people and knowledgeable in world's affairs. His five children were beautiful. He sat on the rabbinate chair for thirteen years and was the last rabbi of our town. He was murdered by the defiled murderers together with the members of his community, his flock.

The Holocaust chapters already told about the troubles and torture that he endured in the hands of the defiled Nazis, and the abuse he had suffered when he was still alive.

To his dying day he predicted, with great confidence, that the evil regime would fall and proved it with conclusive and logical evidence that were taken from the world of politics in which he had an extensive knowledge.

[Page 174]

R' Avrom –Yitskhok Chinitch

by Avrom –Yitskhok Slutsky

Translated by Sara Mages

R' Avrom -Yitskhok Chinitch

He was handsome and tall and all, who saw him for the first time, stood in amazement and said: "Did Dr. Herzl rose from his grave?!" because it was the image, the height, the facial expression with the beautiful black beard, and also the beautiful shapely lips.

He was one of the six son–in–laws of David Graeib and had a good and secure income. His spacious house, which stood in the center of the town, served as a hostel for passerby. He devoted himself to public affairs and was the one who initiated the building of the new synagogue. Thanks to him an elaborate building was constructed and for many years he was the *Gabbai* [beadle] of this synagogue.

He was also gifted with a pleasant voice and many enjoyed hearing his prayer when he led the prayers at the synagogue, especially on the High–Holidays.

His sons immigrated to the United States and settled there. In 5681 [1921], he also left the town to join his sons in United States. There, he was appointed rabbi of one of the synagogues in Brooklyn.

After the First World War, when the economic situation in our town worsened and many of its residents suffered from shortage, R' Avrom–Yitskhok Chinitch organized the support of our townspeople in the United States to the needy residents of our town. Nothing stopped him from action. Despite his old age he participated in all the meetings of the former residents of Lenin, even winds and heavy rain did not stop him.

All the great activity for the benefit of the needy of our town was concentrated at his house, and all the concern for the town leaned on his shoulder and the shoulder of his daughter Itka. Both worked over their ability. The former residents of our town, who saw the good deeds of the father and daughters, treated them with great respect, affection and gratitude.

After his death, a large funeral was held for him in Brooklyn and renowned rabbis eulogized him. The members of his community, the former residents of Lenin in the United States who were orphaned, mourn him…

[Page 175]

Loyal friends

by Eliyahu Shalev

Translated by Sara Mages

In memory of my father my teacher, R' Yisrael–Isar HaLevi Nakritz z"l, and R' Zalman (Zama) Schmelkin z"l

"But he gives grace to the humble" (Proverbs 3:34). Both were born in Slutsk and both were excellent Yeshiva students in Yeshivot Valozhyn and Słobódka. Both were proficient in *Shas* and *Poskim* and had great knowledge of Hebrew and secular literature. Each owned a permanent seat by the eastern wall among the "faces" of the community and its dignitaries, and both chose to turn down the Sabbath with the "common folks" at the table between the back of the *Bima* and the door. Both treated the child the way they treated an adult, the poor as the rich, knew to consider the views of each and point out an error in a pleasant way and convincing evidence.

A loyal friendship prevailed between them. Both sat on a bench and talked and an audience, mostly young, stood around them and listened to their conversation. The topics of their conversations were: ancient and modern literature, explanation of difficult verses in the Bible, the commentaries of Ibn Ezra and his riddles, witty and serious issues in the Talmud and matters of utmost importance in the political world.

Despite their friendship, their path split in the education that they've given to their sons. My father z"l gave his sons a traditional Hebrew education, national and Zionist, because he himself was one of the first members of "*Hovevei Zion*" in our town. R' Zalman gave his sons a general secular education which contained a lot of sympathy for the revolutionary movement in Russia.

Yet, my father z"l and R' Zama z"l knew to respect each other's opinions.

The two were divided in their opinions after the outbreak of the First World War: R' Zama z"l said that he was sure that Germany will win the war and its victory would bring salvation and blessing to the entire world. This victory is especially important for the Russian Jews, because it would release them from the regime of Czar Nicholas and his discriminatory laws against the Jewish residents. R' Zama z"l based his opinion on all sorts of imaginary evidence and proofs. My father z"l argued against him that Germany will fall and Russia, France and England would win the war, and proved his opinion with logical reasoning.

It goes without saying that R' Zama z"l had the upper hand for many days. All the mighty victories of the German Army in the battles were his victories. He used to come to the synagogue in a celebratory mood and call: "Didn't I tell you that Germany would win, now you can see with your eyes that all my words were verified."

My father's situation wasn't good. He was on the defensive and claimed that the victories in battle are not the victory in the war, and only at the end of war it would be possible to know who won and who was defeated.

Every morning my father z"l read a page in the Gemara before an audience of students, and Talmudic legends from the book "*Ein Yaakov*" between *Mincha* and *Maariv*. Every Sabbath, before sunrise, he read the weekly Torah portion before an audience of workers. His listeners, his fans, devoured his words, which were in the spirit of the love of Zion and love of Israel, because he explained them well. At the same time, R' Zama z"l sat at the table, which was situated at the opposite wall, and preached to a crowd of young people about Moshe Rabbeinu, the first socialist.

[Page 176]

In those days, the revolution broke out in Russia, the Tsarist regime was eliminated, and R' Zama z"l saw the revolution as the essence of everything. My father z"l was skeptical and didn't believe that the revolution would bring salvation and redemption. Then, the relationships between the two friends worsened and the friendship came to an end.

When R' Zama z"l was asked to voice his opinion about R' Yisrael–Isar, he answered: "Yes, he's a great scholar, but he can't break free from his early opinions that their time has already passed." When my father was asked to express his opinion on R' Zama z"l, he answered: "Great scholar, but he deviated from the path."

With the Balfour Declaration my father began to believe that the days of the Messiah arrived. He was happy when his son, Chaim Shalev (Nakritz), immigrated to Israel. I immigrated after him.

In 1923, many young people started to leave Israel because of the severe economic crisis of that time. Among those who left were also a few from our town.

My father z"l was worried that we would also get caught in the panic of departure, especially after he found out that we already received a "demand" from our family in the United States. He immediately started to send us a letter after letter and warned us not to be hasty. "The country is only acquired with agony and sufferings" he wrote.

After we wrote him that it never crossed our mind to leave the country, he wrote us a letter in which he expressed his joy, hope and confidence that the bad days will pass quickly and we will live to see better days in the country.

My father z"l immigrated to Israel together with my mother. Their children, who preceded them and were based economically, were able to accommodate their parents and allow them a life of dignity and well–being. Since my father z"l didn't have the burden of livelihood, he continued to study and teach a page of Gemara before an audience. At first he taught at the synagogue of "*Merkaz Baalei Melacha*" and later at "*Beit El*" synagogue. My father taught in our town for thirty–five years and twelve in Israel.

[Page 177]

R' Yisrael Isar HaLevi Nakritz

by Chaim Shalev

Translated by Sara Mages

Born in Slutsk 28 Kislev 5626 (1866)
Passed away in Tel-Aviv, 20 Tevet 5697 (1937)

My father of blessed memory

My father, R' Yisrael Isar, was born in the city of Slutsk on 28 Kislev 5626 (1866) to his father, R' Azriel Zelig HaLevi Nakritz, and his mother Chaya. He was orphaned from his father at the age of seven.

His mother was a simple woman, but she cherished scholars and respected them. She sacrificed herself for the education of her sons and economized in order to teach them the Torah. His name came to fame at an early age. He was a diligent student with a perfect memory who never forgot anything and when he entered the Yeshiva he became famous as a prodigy. He fulfilled the way of the Torah literally: "Bread with salt you shall eat, water in small measure you shall drink, and upon the ground you shall sleep; live a life of deprivation and toil in Torah…" and took upon himself the burden of the commandments with love. He was known as a simple and honest man since his early youth, placed himself under greater restrictions, was righteous in all his deeds and fulfilled the will of his Father in Heaven.

When he married my mother z"l, Mrs. Chana, daughter of R' David Graeib from Lenin, he moved to live in this town and established his home there. His father–in–law, who was a prosperous merchant, guided him in the laws of life and the ways of the world, and opened a store for him. Soon, my father z"l emerged as a wise, honest and intelligent merchant, and a man who says what he thinks.

He never lived a life of wealth but lived a life of honor – respected people and was respected and loved by all. Was humble by nature, escaped from power and honor and was satisfied with little. He was lenient and generous all his days, his soul couldn't get enough Torah and wisdom, and his straightforwardness bordered on zealousness. He didn't allow himself to deviate, not even a tad, from the path of truth in his trading and negotiation with people. Not only that he didn't believe that "it's permitted to deceive a Gentile," he also claimed that there's no greater mistake than that, and there's no specific law on this issue in our sources. Therefore, not only the Jews, but also the Gentiles, respected him and said: "You can trust Isar with your eyes closed!"

He was God–fearing, careful with a minor *mitzvah* as with a major one, and with that, an ardent Zionist and a significant intellectual. When he was a Yeshiva *bocher* he earned his education in an hour which is neither of the day or the night. Because of his poverty he didn't have the means to purchase his own books, so he sat and copied a full Yiddish–Hebrew dictionary by hand. He was one of the subscribers of "*HaTsefirah*"[1] and "*HaZman*,"[2] and also read a Russian newspaper and the best Russian literature. His Zionism was a bone of contention between him and his father–in–law.

[Page 178]

In the days when the Colonial Bank was founded, he preached Zionism from the synagogue's *Bimah* and excited the hearts to purchase shares. His father–in–law, R' David, who opposed Zionism and believed that the redemption of Eretz–Yisrael would be in the hands of God and the secular Zionists cannot bring the Messiah by human force – interrupted his son–in–law's speech and removed him from the stage. This open clash led to a difficult conflict and the friendship ceased for a year, until they reconciled.

His love of the Torah was an unconditional love and he never used it for a personal gain. He was a popular man who loved people. All his life, at first in the Diaspora and towards his old age in Israel, he tried to teach and plant the love of the Torah in the hearts of the masses in his usual manner – calmly, in moderation and in a voice full of sweetness and pleasantness. In his town, in Lenin, and later on in Tel–Aviv, he gathered around him a large crowd of students who drank his sweet words with thirst, enjoyed his explanatory power and his clear and instructive remarks which were seasoned with proverbs and poetic phrases according to the place, time and period.

His visionary soul, which longs for words of Torah and words of the living God, is folded in his commentaries on the Torah and *Mishnah*, sermons and *Hadranim*[3]. We, his sons and grandsons, pray that we would be able to publish his writings in a book. In this bundle of pages he expresses his devotion to the

Torah and his desire to distribute his knowledge. His writings are sealed with a seal of a Jewish man, who believed, in his heart and soul, that: "The Torah will only endure in the person who gives his life for it."

"A woman of valor is the crown of her husband" – so was Chana, my mother z"l, to my father. Even though their livelihood was meager and scarce, my father z"l didn't know shortage all his life thanks to her devotion, practicality and cleverness. My mother z"l helped him in matters of livelihood and even assumed the burden of managing the store. She ran her home with wisdom and love – baked her own bread, cooked, washed, sewed, and looked after the children. And not only that, she didn't complained and wasn't angry at her husband who immersed himself in business and the world as it exists, and set a regular time for the study of the Torah. But, "She does him good, and not harm, All the days of her life" [Proverbs 31:12]. She was proud that his candle didn't go out at night, and that: "Her husband is respected in the gates, When he sits among the elders of the land" [Proverbs 31:23].

After his sons immigrated to Israel, he didn't rest until both he and my mother z"l were brought to country. He was "lovesick" for the Land of Israel since his early youth, but this love didn't sever the faith and the feeling, which pulsed in his heart, that: "There is no Torah like the Torah of the Land of Israel, and there is no wisdom like the wisdom of the Land of Israel."

He was sixty when he came to Israel weak and exhausted. His sons supported him with honor. Even here he quickly took his rightful place. Those, who came to the synagogue ("Beit El",) smelt the scent of the Torah and gathered to hear his lessons. Even here he used his special measure of humility and fulfilled the practice "Humility is a fence around wisdom." He showed understanding to the soul of the young generation and honored the builders of the country and its pioneers. He didn't treat them out of zealotry, but out of understanding, forgiveness and faith in the righteousness of their actions.

My father passed away in Tel–Aviv on 2 Tevet 5697, at the threshold of his 72 year of his life, as his wife, four sons, his daughter, daughter–in–law and grandchildren stood around his bed.

"An honest and humble man studied the Torah all his life" – so is written on his tombstone.

Translator's Footnotes:

1. *HaTsefirah* – The Morning or The Dawn – was the first Hebrew newspaper in Poland.
2. *HaZman* – The Time – a Hebrew newspaper published in Russia.
3. *Hadran* (Aramaic "we will return") – a term indicating both the celebration held on the completion of the study of a tractate of the Talmud (*siyyum*) and the type of discourse delivered on that occasion

Reb Zalman Schmelkin

by Yitskhok Slutsky

Translated by Sara Mages

R' Zalman Schmelkin, or, as he was called by the people in town and the surrounding area, Jews and Christians – "Z'ama" – was a son of an extensive and attributed family in the city of Slutsk.

He studied in a "*Heder*" in his childhood and in a Yeshiva in his youth. He was given the title "*Illui*" [prodigy] in "Valozhyn Yeshiva" where he was a classmate of H. N. Bialik and the illustrious rabbi, Rabbi Chaim Ozer Grodzinski. He acquired a broad and comprehensive education in the Bible, the Talmud and its commentators, and in all the treasures of Jewish science.

Later, when he saw a different way than his, he turned secretly to secular studies and within a short time acquired a broad knowledge in Russian literature. This self–educated man became a treasure trove of Torah and knowledge, which merged in him in a wonderful way, because he was gifted with a quick perception, a sharp mind, wit, an exemplary memory, iron logic and wisdom of life

Above it all, R' Zalman was liked by us because of his noble qualities: his simplicity, nobility, modesty, social relation to others and cleverness.

His sharp sayings, his manners and his negotiation with people were full of wit, healthy intelligence and deep knowledge of life and people.

His knowledge in the Talmud was amazing. Talmudic law led him to read and explore the theory of Roman law. In this manner he acquired, through self–study, a thorough knowledge and expertise in civil and criminal law which was in effect in Russia. Expert judges and well known lawyers listened to his explanations and remarks.

His way was to always to stand by the side of the weak. He was always ready to give advice and assistance to those who have lost their assets, and managed to save the oppressed from his abuser. After a thorough review and a detailed study of the problem, he was able to find the "weak point" on which he based his claim against the abuser.

[Page 180]

Dr. Yisrael (son of Zalman) Schmelkin

He owned a permanent seat at the "new" synagogue next to the eastern wall among all the town's dignitaries. However, the humble preferred to remain in the shade and we never saw him go up to his place among the notables.

We always found him behind the *Bimah* at the table of the "common folks," or on the balcony in the summer. He felt himself free there, as if he was at his own home. There, he conducted friendly conversations on current affairs, and his audience, mostly the members of the young generation, drank his words with thirst. His unwavering loyalty to the principles of justice, equality and democracy, and also his deep understanding in the suffering of the simple Jew, earned him the respect of all the townspeople.

By the way, there, behind the *Bimah*, he had a permanent interlocutor, his equal – R' Isar HaLevi Nakritz.

How did R' Zalman Schmelkin arrive to our town? R' Chaim Paperny travel to "Valozhyn Yeshiva" and asked the head of the Yeshiva to chose an outstanding young man for his granddaughter, Sara–Leah, daughter of his son Herzl.

After his marriage to Sara–Leah, Schmelkin began to engage in the lumber trade – the most important industry in our town which was surrounded by virgin forests. He educated his sons and daughters in high–schools and universities, a matter that wasn't easily done during the "*Numerus clausus*" period of the Tsarist regime. His son, Dr. Yisrael Schmelkin, who passed away several years ago in the United States, was one of the few Jewish students who were able to graduate two faculties, science and medicine, at the University of Moscow. His daughter, Dr. Tehila Schmelkin, may she live long, who lives in the United States, studied dentistry. His daughter Chaya and son Eliezer continued their studies in Moscow after they were cut off from their family when the Polish border was placed. His young son, Moshe, a medical student at the University of Bratislava (Czechoslovakia), arrived to Israel after the Nazis took over the Republic of Czechoslovakia. He worked for many years at the laboratory of "Hadassah Hospital" and received a certificate of excellence from the Municipality of Tel–Aviv for his important discovery in blood types. To our sorrow, he died at a young age from a severe heart disease. May his memory be blessed. The only family member, who wasn't able to receive a higher education due to her poor health, was his daughter Feigel who suffered from asthma since childhood. After the death of her parents, she joined her family in Moscow and died there at a young age. May her memory be blessed.

R' Zalman wasn't always successful in his businesses. There were also periods of decline and crisis. However, he didn't despair. He continued his way of life and

[Page 181]

the education of his sons in high–schools and universities continued even after he got into trouble because of his debts.

Five to six years before the outbreak of the First World War, the winter was late in coming and the rivers and swamps didn't freeze. The traders' time table was disrupted, they weren't able to sell their merchandise and comply with the terms of their contracts. This crisis also affected R' Zalman Schmelkin.

According to the terms of his contract, he had to bring several thousand Rubles to the management of Agarkov's estate by a certain date, but he didn't see the possibility of raising such a large sum of money by the fixed date.

One clear day, an inspector, who was accompanied by several forest guards, appeared in the patch of forest where he began to cut down trees. He ordered the workers to stop their work on the basis of an order given by the management of the estate for the non–payment of the amount determined by the contract.

R' Zalman Schmelkin was very surprised by this act. According to his calculation he had two weeks to submit the payment. However, he accepted the decree, returned home, took out his contract with the management of the estate, and with great joy determined that the cessation of the work in the forest was a mistake. He didn't think for long, sat by his desk and drafted a lawsuit against the landowner. He demanded a compensation of six thousand Rubles for the financial and moral damage cause to him due of the hasty act of the landowner.

It was a first time that a landowner appeared as a defendant in the District Court by a legal demand of a Jewish merchant. For reasons of prestige it wasn't fitting for a noble landowner to litigate with a Jew. The management of the estate recruited the best lawyers and ordered them to do everything in order not lose this trial. However, all their efforts have failed, and all their claims and long debates didn't help. With his healthy logic, R' Zalman Schmelkin managed to overcome them in the District Court and also at the Appeals Court. This trial made waves in the entire area and R' Zalman Schmelkin's fame grew day by day.

The management of the estate filed an appeal to the Supreme Court because they wanted "drag" the issue and buy time so they will not have to pay the large amount awarded to the stubborn Jew. They wanted to bother him even more, especially after his financial situation deteriorated because of this trial.

One summer day, a carriage, which was harnessed to three mighty horses, stopped in front of the rabbi's house, R' Yehudah Turetski Zts"L. Milinritz, the estate manager, descended from it and entered the rabbi's house. The whole town was abuzz: What had brought the chief executive for a sudden visit with the elderly rabbi who isolated himself in a world of *Halacha* and study? All sorts of speculations sprung up, and there were many arguments on this issue among the local residents. Eventually, it became clear that the estate manager came to ask the rabbi to intervene in his trial with Schmelkin. He hinted to the rabbi that if he could persuade his opponent to compromise with him – it would greatly benefit all the Jews of the town which lies on his land.

R' Zalman Schmelkin, who was in a tight situation, didn't want to hear about a compromise and demanded an unconditional surrender according to the terms of the State Court judgment. And now, there was a new conflict that no one wished for.

At that time, R' Zalman Schmelkin built his new house on the lake shore, on the other side of the bridge, on land that its ownership was disputed between the management of the estate and the farmers community in the town.

[Page 182]

The management of the estate, who wanted to get even with R' Zalman Schmelkin because of the shame he had caused them when they were charged in court, filed a legal claim against him. It demanded him to demolish his house, which was built, according to their claims, on the estate's land and without its consent.

However, R' Zalman Schmelkin not only knew how to prosecute, he was also an expert defender. He mobilized the treasure of his knowledge in law and trial and proved that he built his house under an agreement with the farmers' community who was the rightful owner of the disputed land. The plot, on which his house was built, was part of the land known by the name "*Vigum*," meaning, grazing area, which was granted to the farmers when they were freed from slavery in 1861 and belonged to the community from which he received permission to build his house. In its judgment, the District Court recognized the farmers' ownership of all the disputed area which covered thousands of "*desiatinas*"[1]. This ruling saved R' Zalman Schmelkin's house from demolition, but he aroused a lot of anger among the town's Jews because many have lost the right to graze their cattle in this area. The farmers took advantage of this ruling, fenced off the whole area and didn't allow the Jews and their livestock to enter.

After the October Revolution, his eldest son, Dr. Yisrael Schmelkin z"l who a doctor in the Russian Army during the war, was appointed physician of a match factory in the city of Rechitsa and the whole family moved there. R' Zalman Schmelkin was appointed Justice of the Peace, but he didn't serve in this capacity for long. A civil war broke out and he returned to his town, Lenin, which was seized by the Polish Army. In 1921 Lenin was annex to the Polish Republic.

To get used to the new situation, R' Zalman Schmelkin tackled the study of the Polish language with a youthful vigor. He studied the laws of the news country day and night, memorized the rules of the Polish grammar, and in a short time was able to resume his activity in the Polish courts.

His health deteriorated towards his old age. His vision, which was impaired over the years, weakened and he lost his eyesight. He undergone several surgeries but all the efforts of the famous doctor, Dr. Pins from Warsaw, to restore his eyesight have failed. Dr. Pins, who was also a Yeshiva *bocher* in his youth, became very attached to his patient and spent a lot of time talking to him about religious topics. Despite his serious condition, R' Zalman Schmelkin was in a good mood and full of sense of humor. Once he asked Dr. Pins: "What is between you and Aharon HaCohen?" He asked, and he replied: "Aharon HaCohen made an *Eygel* [calf] out of gold and someone is making gold out of *Oygel* [eyes in Yiddish]. The answer hit the mark because Dr. Pins became very rich from his practice.

After he became blind, R' Zalman Schmelkin kept to himself in his home. Every day I spent a lot of time talking with him and read before him from the newspaper. He never lost interest in the events that took place in the big world and in our little world. At times, when he remembered a certain issue from the Talmud, he asked me to take out a tractate from the bookcase and open it on a specific page. Then, he showed me with his finger the place where I have to look for the necessary issue, and I read it before him. I was quite surprised by his clear memory which didn't disappoint him to his last day.

He died suddenly after a short illness with heart disease.

[Page 183]

Translator's Footnote:

1. Desiatina (*plural* desiatinas) – An old Russian unit of area, approximately 10,925 square meters (the Treasury/official desiatina) or 14,567 square meters (proprietor's desiatina).

R'Dov-Ber Baruchin

by Tzila Zaretzki

Translated by Yocheved Klausner

R'Dov-Ber Baruchin
(Died 5 Tishrei 5680 – 29 September 1919)

   The Jews of our town who survived the Holocaust and now live in Israel or elsewhere, remember well my father **Dov Ber Baruchin** z"l, as a very distinguished person, whom all residents of our town regarded with love, respect and appreciation. Indeed his renown was undisputed.

   He had a blessed influence on his children. He implanted in their hearts, since their early childhood, love of Zion, as well as aspiration and longing for Eretz Israel.

   I remember that a Hebrew newspaper was always present in our home: *Hamelitz* or *Hatzefira* and later *Hatzofe*. My father and my uncle Baruch-Yakov z"l were subscribed to the *Tushiya* Books. Under the guidance of our father z"l we absorbed a spiritual sense of life; he was happy that God blessed him with children who aimed to acquire knowledge and education.

   I can still see before my eyes the image of our father absorbed in reading the *Tanach* [Bible] – whenever he had some free time from his businesses. This book never left his desk, and he demanded us to read it as well, day by day.

I remember the Sabbath evenings, when we, the children, were waiting impatiently for the Sabbath meal to end, so we could slip out of the house and run to town (we lived across the lake) and join our friends. However, our father z"l always began reading for us a chapter of the Bible or a legend from the Talmud before the festive meal was over; his reading, beautiful and full of feeling, touched our hearts and distracted us, preventing us from going out. As we listened to his reading and his stories, we enjoyed them so much that at the end we did not miss the parties and our friends.

As far as I remember, our father z"l never punished us; all of us regarded him with awe – not fear but love and respect. We felt that his eyes were watching every one of us – he knew our character and qualities, so that he always found the right way to guide us best.

We loved to listen to the stories about the days of his childhood, his study at the Yeshiva, how he and his friend Lifshitz managed to hide, under the open Talmud volume, books in German and Russian, which they read secretly. This friend finally left the shtetl and went to Germany, where he completed his studies at the University. To express his appreciation he dedicated to my father z"l

[Page 184]

his doctorate dissertation. My father kept the Diploma among his letters and documents and I liked sometimes, when my father was not home, to look through his papers in his drawer. Once I was pleasantly surprised when I found my letters, which I wrote to him from Moscow, in Hebrew. I was glad that Father was interested to keep my letters at that time.

I remember walking many times with my father from the town to our factory. The walk took about an hour; I was never bored during those walks and did not notice the distance. These times were very interesting and instructive for me: my father taught me the names of every tree and enriched the lessons with stories from the Bible and the *Midrash* about animals and plants.

My father was alert to any new event in our Jewish and Zionist world. With his encouragement, my sister Beila z"l and her children made Aliya to Eretz Israel in 1913, to secure for the children an education at the Herzliya High School in Tel Aviv. He hoped that this would open the way for Aliya for the entire family. Among his papers I found an exchange of letters with Nachman Sirkin z"l, concerning our Aliya: he intended to buy a plot of land and wanted to know how many people will be needed to cultivate it and whether the sum of money he had would suffice. However, WWII forced my sister and her children to leave Eretz Israel since they were Russian citizens. My father's wish was not fulfilled.

Great is my sorrow, knowing that my father did not live to see the new Aliya to Eretz Israel, and even greater that he did not see my own Aliya in 1925. I can still hear his words of farewell to Efraim when we parted. He was excited and had tears in his eyes: "Do not cry – you should be happy and joyful; go with success and pave the way for all of us."

He was full of life and energy, not knowing that death was waiting for him: two months after Efraim left, my father died on 5 Tishrei 5680.

My mother Elka (died 3 Tevet 5687), daughter of Yehuda Tziglig z"l, was a modest woman. She knew to read and write Yiddish, to say the prayers and read *Tzenah Ur'enah*. But the blessed influence of our father z"l could be observed: she was always busy with work around the house, and hated idleness and gossip. She was never too curious about her neighbors and acquaintances, was blessed with good qualities and gave charity in secret.

I often saw her pack a basket with food. When I asked for whom she was preparing it, she always replied "none of your business." During her last years, before my Aliya when my father was no longer alive, she increased her charity work, without any of us at home knowing. Chana-Feigel was one of her most frequent visitors – and every time she brought another "order".

I heard her asking my mother to prepare fresh, unsalted butter, fish cooked in butter, baked food etc. When I asked Chana-Feigel, just out of curiosity, for whom she needed those things, my mother answered curtly, as was her custom: "none of your business." After she died, when I visited the town in 1937, I heard from the neighbors about her many deeds of charity.

May both their memories be blessed.

[Page 186]

In Memory of our
Dear Grandfather and Grandmother

by Chaim Shalev

Translated by Yocheved Klausner

R'David son of R'Chaim Graeib z"l - died in Lenin, 8
Marcheshvan 5680 (aged 88). Mrs. Shprintze daughter of
R'Efraim Berkerman z"l - died in Lenin, 10 Av 5681 (aged
86). My Grandparents

Our grandfather R'David was not a great scholar, nor was he very knowledgeable in the Talmud and its commentators. He was content with studying *Ein Yaakov*, the Mishna and the weekly Portion of the Torah [*parashat hashavua*]. He was a God-fearing and honest man, and kept strictly all commandments. He cherished *Talmidei Chachamim* [Jewish great scholars] and fulfilled the word of Our Sages, in the

Tractate *Pesachim*, 49: "One should sell everything he has, and marry his daughters to scholars of the Torah" – his six daughters were married to persons who were Torah scholars as well as generally educated, people of good deeds and diligent merchants. He loved in particular the *Mitzva* of candle-lighting at the beginning of the Sabbath day: When Sabbath approached, he would walk through the streets of the shtetl, even when he was already old and his legs were weak and aching, and announce in a loud voice "Sabbath is coming, the Day of Rest is here" and urge the Jewish women to light the Sabbath candles.

He had about fifty grandchildren and great-grandchildren, and the people in town used to joke: when one of his grandchildren came to his house, he would pinch his cheek and ask

[Page 186]

playfully and lovingly: "child, what do you want?" Indeed, his house was always full of boys and girls, sons-in-law and grandchildren and great-grandchildren, family relatives and guests. On holidays, when the prayers in the synagogue were over, the entire family, old and young, would gather in his house for *Kiddush*. The refreshments were fit for a king – cakes and cookies and other goodies from the blessed hands of our grandmother. The joy was especially great on Purim, when all members of the family gathered for the festive Purim-meal, to eat and drink and sing the songs, until after midnight. The Purim meal at my grandfather's house was a great sight to see: the sounds of joy and happiness filled the house, rose through the walls and were heard in town from end to end.

Our grandmother, a kind and modest woman, possessed rare and special qualities. She was an admirer of Torah scholars and was always busy with her charity work. In addition to her seven children, six girls and one boy, she raised many orphans, members of the family, and kept in her house her daughter Beile, a widow, and her three children: Eliyahu (died in Lenin of tuberculosis), Mendel (perished with his family during the Holocaust, in Lodz) and Yehuda (perished with his family during the Holocaust, in Pinsk). Her daughter Sarah lived in her house until she married (died somewhere in Russia).

Our grandmother was a pious woman; she helped relatives, neighbors and others and cared for the sick, with compassion and devotion. She donated large sums of money and her home was always wide open to assist the tired, the poor, the depressed and the hungry. Day and night was her heart attentive and ready to support and help, as much as she could and even more.

During the *Days of Awe* [Rosh Hashana and Yom Kippur holidays] as the Jews from the neighboring villages came to our town to pray, entire families would stay in her house, which consisted of only one big room and a spacious kitchen, and nobody complained. The house was always filled with light and joy, and our grandmother welcomed everyone with a pleasant disposition and a cheerful face. For years and years she collected money from the residents of the town, and finally used the money to buy a Torah Scroll for the new synagogue. There was no end to her joy and happiness when the scroll was brought to the synagogue – she organized a festive gathering and was happy as on her wedding day.

Our grandmother loved her grandchildren very much and, unlike our grandfather, she knew all of them – their characters, their weaknesses and their needs, and tried to fulfill their wishes. She gave them *Chanuka-gelt* ["Chanuka money"] kindly and generously.

With her own hands she would spin kosher threads for Tzitzit and give them to the people in town; she would also prepare candle wicks for those who studied Torah at night, or early in the morning. We should remember that electricity was non-existent in town at that time, and people would study by the light of candles or a kerosene lamp hanging from the ceiling. This way she felt she shared the Torah study with the learners.

Our grandparents lived a life of contentment, faith and peace of mind. When I remember their pure personalities and their way of life, filled with love of the Creator and love of Man, modesty

[Page 187]

and confidence, I understand the words of our Sages (Tractate Berachot, 60:1): "Old Hillel was walking on the road to town, when he heard loud cries from the direction of the town. He said: I am sure it does not come from my house." At first, this saying sounds strange: Hillel, the most modest man – how can he be so sure? The reason is this: he taught his family to accept everything with love and without complaint. He was convinced that the members of his family would not raise their voices, but accept their troubles without complaint…

R'Israel Glenson

by Shlomo Glenson

Translated by Yocheved Klausner

My father R'Israel Glenson was a handsome man, with wide shoulders and a beautiful white beard.

"R'Israel the blacksmith" was a Jew who combined Torah and work – and the local rabbi once said that in his soul he carried a spark of the soul of Rabbi Yitzhak Nafcha, one of our great Sages.

Encouraged by the rabbi, he "read" [taught] a Mishna lesson every morning after the first *Minyan*. On Saturdays, the study group was divided: half of the people learned with the Rabbi, half with my father z"l.

On weekdays at *Mincha* [the afternoon prayer], he would leave his work and hurry to the synagogue, to read for his listeners from the *Ein Yaakov* book. By the end of the evening prayer *Maariv* he would hurry home and retire, so that he could rise at dawn and study the daily page of the Talmud. This was his custom day by day.

On Sabbath eve, before candle-lighting, my mother Lea, may she rest in peace, lit the big kerosene lamp, which spread the light over the room until midnight, when my father studied a chapter of the Talmud, with his friend R'Chaim-Yosef the *shamash* [synagogue attendant]. At one time there was a discussion between my parents whether to donate a Torah Scroll to the shul or buy a set of the Talmud, and our rabbi decided for the Talmud.

When my father was about 30 years old, he climbed on a chair in the synagogue to reach a book, was hit by lightning and he went into shock; of course he was given first aid right away, by the means available at the time, until he was conscious again; in six hours his hair turned white.

During many years he served as *Gabbai* [treasurer, supervisor] in the synagogue, and until his last day he was *Gabbai* of the *Hevrat Mishnayot* [Mishna Society]. He died in 1938 at the age of 74. He left three sons and grandchildren. Two of his sons and their families were murdered by the Nazis. One son and one grandson live in Eretz Israel.

[Page 188]

Reb Aryeh Graeib

By Chaim Shalev

Translated by Sara Mages

Born in Lenin 1859 – died in Tel–Aviv 1945.

R' Arye, son of R' David Graeib, was born in Lenin in 1859 where he was raised and educated and lived for seventy five years. His two sons, Tzvi and Shlomo, brought him to Ertz–Yisrael in 19.8.36. They fulfilled the *mitzvah* of honoring one's father generously and supported him to the day of his death in Tel–Aviv in 1945.

R' Arye was tall, had a sturdy body, and was a good looking person. Was a vibrant man, loved life, was very active, and honest in negotiations with people – allies and non–allies. He gave to the poor and has done many charity acts in secret. Not only that he fulfilled the commandment of *Hazal* "Don't withdraw from the public," he engaged, all the days of his life, in public needs in trust, love and happiness, as a man whose opinion was involved with people. After the First World War he was the person in charge of the aid and relief funds from the donations of former townspeople who immigrated to America and was crowned in a crown of a good name. R' Arye was a member of Chevrah Kadisha, has done true charity to hundreds of people, restrained the passion of those who tried to extort money from the relatives of the dead and in this way prevented the disgrace of the dead. He used to say: the name "Chevrah Kadisha" should be adequate to its doers – pure and holy in their deeds, lifestyle and nature.

Was a wealthy man all his life, had great assets and many businesses. Towards old age, when he became impoverished, he didn't mention the days of his wealth, didn't boast about his ancestry, but behaved with modesty and humility. When his sons placed him in a nursing home, he didn't complain and always served as an example and symbol in his good and convenient temper. He was lovable and acceptable by all his friends to the institution and took part in the fate and the condition of each of them. He stayed away from controversy and useless arguments.

He was known for his great affection to *arba'at ha–minim* [the four species] especially to the – *etrog* [citron]. When he was able to get a fine *etrog*, full of splendor, there was no one happier than him. In Lenin, the proprietors used to buy *etrogim* from the town's rabbi who received them from the nearby city of Pinks. In the days when they expected the arrival of the shipment of *etrogim*, usually at midnight, R' Arye wasn't tired or weary to stand on guard, and when the shipmen arrived, he carefully selected the most beautiful and best quality *etrog* for himself. If he was busy and was unable to welcome the arrival of the shipment, he woke up early in the morning,

[Page 189]

impatiently ran to the rabbi's house and knock on his door so no one would be ahead of him. How great was his joy and pride when he received an *etrog* from his nephews in Eretz–Yisrael – at that time his face shone with joy and delight. When he was granted to immigrate to Eretz–Yisrael and to fulfill this mitzvah here, on the ancestral land, he didn't spare money to obtain the fines *etrog*. He reached the height of enthusiasm on Simchat Torah after he drank a number of glasses of happiness and was in a state of "alcohol intoxication." He hopped and skipped like a kid with a Torah scroll close to his chest, stamped his feet until sweat dripped from his shining face. He sounded quick beats with his toe and forearm and sang in a loud and joyful voice "We shall rejoice and be merry on Simchat Torah, for it is for us strength and light!"… Indeed, the Torah was his tree of life and in its shade he sheltered all of his life.

Reb Aryeh Graeib, who reached a ripe old age, symbolized, in a nice way, the character of a Jew of past generation who feared God, kept his commandments and all his actions were for the name of God. Even though there is no "intention in commandments," he didn't perform light *mitzvah* or a weighty one without a good intention. All the days of his life he worked his Creator with love, faith and joy.

Reb Yitskhok Dannenberg

by Mordechai Rubenstein (Migdalovich)

Translated by Sara Mages

A.

Our town, Lenin, has won that R' Yitskhok Dannenberg and his gentle wife, Mrs. Ester from the family, moved there in order to set up a factory in our area that was rich in forests. He produced medical turpentine and other products from the pine trees that were in them.

On his mother's side, R' Yitskhok Dannenberg was the grandson of the genius, R' Itzele of Volozhin zt"l, and from her he inherited the great love to the Torah and its learners.

His grandfather, R' Aharon–Leizer Dannenberg, immigrated to Israel and has done for the building of Jerusalem. He built an almshouse for Torah students, and even today there's a Beit Midrash in our capital named after him. His father, R' Chaim–Arye Dannenberg, built in Stavisk, near Bialystok, a row of shops, rented them to learned shopkeepers and dedicated all the rent for the support of Torah students. This generous project existed until all the town's institutions were destroyed in the terrible Holocaust of the Second World War.

Chaim–Arye endowed the Torah education, love to the Jewish nation, and love to Eretz–Yisrael to his son R' Yitskhok.

[Page 190]

A native of Sṭavisk̦, a Yeshivot student, a scholar in Judaic studies and general education, a loyal Zionist and a dedicated activist – found a fertile ground in Lenin. In a relatively short period he surrounded himself with a circle of friends, acquaintances and students. He worked with them in the public area, especially on behalf of the funds: "*Keren Kyemeth leisrae*"l and "*Keren Hayesod.*" Who had the power to refuse to give promissory notes in favor of "*Keren Hayesod*" when Yitskhok asked for it? – with his bright and tender eyes, which peered from under the lenses of his glasses, with the delightful smile of this Jewish nobleman – he opened their hearts and their pockets. He also new to combine a pleasant homerooms word "at the right time" and success was guaranteed.

He sent his only daughter, Chava, who lives in Israel, to study at the university in Jerusalem after she received her high school diploma from the Hebrew Gymnasium in Pinsk. He carried his longings to his beloved daughter in secret and in modesty, to say: this is how a Zionist Jew must behave.

Before the outbreak of the Second World War he made plans for the future – the liquidation of his business and permanent residence in his desired country, but he wasn't awarded do so.

May his soul be bound for eternity in our renewed life in our homeland, and in the hearts of friends and those who honor his name.

B.

My parents' home was full of interest. As descendants of ancestors who were mighty Torah scholars and God–fearing, they always found content and spiritual elevation in their life.

Our house stood on the main road between Mikashevichy and Lenin. It served as a hostel for every passerby, was a meeting place to the wise, for those who sought knowledge and wanted to learn the theory of Zionism. All hungry for wisdom, all thirsty for knowledge found what they had desired in it, but also the hungry left our home satisfied. All, who were tired from the road or from hardships, found serenity in it, the sufferer found solace and the depressed straightened his back in the present of my parents z"l, and those consumed with despair left our home comforted and with hope. It was a convalescent home for the sick and elation to the oppressed.

My parent received everything, big as small, with love, happiness and understanding. In their devotion and tender character they instilled the faith in God and in humans. They saw in every Jew a treasure full of *mitzvoth*, like a pomegranate. Only people with noble qualities, that their hearts are brimming with light and human warmth, like my parents z"l who were gifted in them, were able instill such faith in the heart of the humans in our world. It is possible to establish a home like ours, which was a glorious Jewish home, only when the mistress of the home is a woman of valor like my mother z"l. She worked hard with a lot of energy and was always willing to welcome guests, rich and important, and also poor and needy.

My mother z"l excelled in her special dedication to others. When she was in her parents' home she was always willing to dedicate herself to them. She supported her husband, and without the help of my mother z"l, my father z"l wasn't able to realize his principles and aspirations. Only with her help he was able to sacrifice himself to such an extent, for the benefit of others, and acquired great honor and good name in the entire province.

In this manner they achieved their world which is crowned with great honor and glory.

Their daughter, Chava.

[Page 191]

Reb Aron-Leib Zaichik

by Mordechai Rubenstein (Migdalovich)

Translated by Sara Mages

Among the lofty figures rises before my eyes the glorious figure of my rabbi and teacher, R' Aron-Leiby Zaichik, whose name is associated with the history of the education of the generation in our town. He instilled in us the love for the Hebrew language and the values of Judaism, and taught fathers, sons and grandsons for fifty consecutive years. In instilling reading and writing to the little ones, *Chumash*; and Rashi, *Nevi'im* with commentators, Talmud to the adults, he drew the holy spark from every word and verse and gave it to us, the children.

As the owner of a superlative memory, he remembered events and facts that his students experienced and not one he recognized in a grandson the qualities of his grandfather or his father - who learned the Torah from him a generation or two ago.

We, his students, admired him and loved him even though that, not once, we were burnt by his ember when he lost his temper. And what is surprising about that? After all, he taught, almost every day, about 50-60 boys in one room and at daybreak, before the prayer, he taught the older boys in preparation for their *Aliyah La'Torah* and the reading of the *Haftarh*.

He did not accept wholeheartedly the establishment of the modern school by *"Tarbut"* in our town and the young teachers, graduates of the Teachers Seminar who were sent to the school by the center in Warsaw. He saw in them kind of a "foreign element" that wasn't consistent with his way of teaching, especially with the beginners. At the end, he reconciled with the official school principals who, by the way, treated him with courtesy.

A student of Minsk Yeshiva and the famous Mir Yeshiva, a great Torah scholar and was on the verge of receiving a rabbinical ordination. He didn't accept, to the depth of his soul, the "new pedagogy and didactics," and not once he poured his bitterness before his former student, and I tried to understand his spirit.

He lived frugally even though he had many students. Many were late paying tuition and others didn't pay him at all, some paid a pittance and with cash equivalents... Yet, it never occurred to him to deny the Torah education to a boy. He lived a life of hardship and sorrow but his ambition was to give his sons a higher education - even abroad - which was difficult and daring at that time.

He was an exemplary prayer reader and served in this duty in the Old Synagogue for many years. He was a constant companion to the rabbi, R' Yehudah Turetski zt"l, until the day of his death.

In the years before the Holocaust he was invited by my father and the rest of the Jews of the village of Grichinovichi to serve as a prayer reader and a shofar blower during the High Holidays. Because of his difficult situation he was forced to separate, with great sorrow, from his family and the community of worshipers at the synagogue and move to the village for the days of the holiday. However, these days probably fulfilled his soul when

[Page 192]

he gave a sermon before the *"Kol Nidrei"* prayer, and his words, which came from the heart, entered the hearts of the village Jews.

May these lines be a memorial for the soul of R' Aron-Leib, the soul of my parents, my sisters and the members of our village, Grichinovichi, who were not granted, like many others, to see the rebirth of the nation and the redemption of their homeland.

May his soul be bound in the bond of our life for eternity.

Dr. Aron Singalovski

by Y. Klinov

Translated by Sara Mages

My first meeting with Aron Singalovski took place in 1921 with my arrival to Berlin after I left' like many others, the Soviet Union. Since then, I was in contact with the deceased and was in his company for thirteen years.

People from various Jewish-Russian circles gathered at that time in Berlin. Some thought that it was just a way station, until the storm passes, and with the change of circumstances and political regime in the Soviet Union most of them will return home. However, in the meantime, Hebrew and Yiddish authors, activists and political leaders, found temporary shelter there. It was the representation of *"Yeḳopo,"*[1] *"Emigdirekt"* [Emigration Direktorium], and a bland of *"Vaad Hakehillot"* [a council of communities] that was born in Moscow, together with the representative of the "National Secretariat" of the Ukrainian Jewry, the "OZA" company and others.

Aron Singalovski settled in Germany already before that, and at this stage he was entirely devoted to "ORT" which eventually became his life's work. He left the general political system, the internal Jewish political front, and subjected himself to the question of the restoration of the nation, to constructive work and the distributing of the work among the Jewish masses in all countries. In 1919, a chapter of "ORT" was established in Berlin with Singalovski's help and with the help of German Jews.

Over time Aron Singalovski became one of the most prominent personalities in the Zionist-Socialists party, or S.S by its Russian initials. It is the Jewish Territorial Party that was established in light of the political stalemate in the Zionist Movement after Herzl's death. It wanted to solve the Jewish question by looking for a place for a Jewish autonomy somewhere in the Diaspora, and not in Eretz-Yisrael. Singalovski acquired

[Page 193]

himself a special popularity in the S.S as one of the best speakers. At that period he was known by the name, "Aron Czenstochower," and participated in all the organizations of the party. He was active as a speaker and writer. In 1913, when I arrived to Switzerland and started to visit the university in Geneva as a student, I still found echoes to the enterprise that was established by the initiative of Singalovski-Czenstochower in Zurich.

In 1910, Singalovski published in Berlin - with the participation Z. Shneur, Dr. Seligman, Dr. Harash and Shemaria Gorlick - the Jewish weekly "*Freitag.*" He also published booklets about current problems. There was a special charm to his lectures. He was especially accepted by the academic circles. In a later period - when the Russian Revolution, the February Revolution, broke out - he took an active part in the unity of Jewish forces in Russia. It wasn't easy to stand out in the Zionist Socialist party. There were powers in the party like Moishe Litvakov, who later moved to Yavasakim and published the Jewish Communist newspaper - "*Der Emes*" [The Truth] and also Yosef Kamorany (Lestschinsky) from the "*Bund.*" However, Aron Singalovski stood the test. His extensive education (the owner of a university diploma in the legal profession and philosophy), the power of his dialect, his organization skills - earned him a prominent place in the party's hierarchy.

But, as mentioned, in the years that I knew him in Berlin, he was no longer active in the political arena. He was only immersed in two things: matters of culture and the development of "ORT."

In the 1920s, he was also placed at the head of "ORT," as a president.

* *

For Singalovski, the activity of "ORT" wasn't just to provide aid, but the most important social movement in modern Judaism. An extraordinary zeal was manifested here and a particular **ideology** emerged. He lectured on various subjects, especially at the "Shalom Aleichem" club, and was able to talk about any subject. However, the conclusion that it's necessary to move Jewish workers, with the help of "ORT," to productive occupations was always emphasized. He was also a collector and among others he collected material about the efforts of Jewish communities in the Middle Ages to teach craft to the Jews. It did not matter to him that the motives of the communities hundreds of years ago were totally different, for him, there was an instinctive expression of feelings that nested in the heart of the Jewish Diaspora from time immortal, and the 75-years of existence of "ORT" served as evidence in our times.

When the Jewish settlement was established in Soviet Russia, Dr. Singalovski, who was very close to Dr. Rozen, the representative of the JDC in Europe which developed the Jewish settlement in Russia, left for a visit to the Soviet Union to see, with his own eyes, what was happening in the wide camp of Jews behind the curtain. When he returned, he lectured about his journey at the "Shalom Aleichem" club. It was before Birobidzhan's plan was born. Singalovski visited the Jewish settlers in Crimea. He praised the experience of the Soviet Union government and I remember an episode from his lecture "My most depressing impression" - said Singalovski - was the sight of a Jew plowing with an ox. Imagine: this Jews, who yesterday was probably a merchant, who lived in a city and was accustomed to a completely different pace of life - this man, who wants it all, became a colonist in order to get rid, once and for all, from the curse of the status of Lishntzi who was among those who denied the rights in the Soviet Union - he

[Page 194]

had to adapt to the tempo of the bull's work, proceed very slowly because at that time there was a shortage of horses. To me, it was a tangible tragedy of a Jew and bull…

With the arrival of Hitler's Holocaust - when the full work of independent and public Jewish organizations in Germany came to an end, including "ORT," Dr. Singalovski moved the center of his activities to Paris and Geneva. Also here - and maybe especially from here - he succeeded in improving the activity of "ORT." This personality, who was equipped with the knowledge of languages, who understood how to tie maintain contacts with all the factors in the world, was able to purchase, shortly after the war, a very respectable statues for "ORT." When it was no longer possible to develop activities in the countries of the Soviet Union, the campaign moved to undeveloped centers, to North Africa, to Persia, and thousands of young Jews acquired their craft and became productive elements. One idea didn't give Dr. Singalovski rest: the Jews not only need just craftsmen, they need "high quality" craftsmen, the finest quality among the working population. The school that was established by "ORT" in Geneva was one of the institutions that were designed to illustrate this lofty goal. Singalovski, the wise man, was quite flexible: when he realized that the country of Israel was established. Singalovski - despite his former political objection to Zionism (elements, who were in favor of staying in the Diaspora, usually concentrated in "ORT") - established a line of institutions in Israel and our country became one of the bases of his work. He kept in touch with central figures in the county and inserted a line of people to the action. And indeed, he didn't change his political views and didn't deny his past, but he knew how to get used to the new situation which came into being within the Jewish nation with the establishment of our country and we saw him here quite often. He succeeded in his mission also in Israel, and he was only worried what would happen next. Volodymyr Groysman, one of the activists of "ORT," said in his eulogy on the deceased:

- When we walked, some time ago, in the quite streets of Geneva, he suddenly said: But what would happen to our work after us? Who will continue the action that was created? - - -

And Singalovski added: - "I can't sleep at night when I think about it"…

Dr. Singalovski's heart predicted and knew what it had predicted, as if it felt that his end was approaching.

* *

A small detail:

In 1930, Zalman Reizin published in Vilna the "Lexicon of Yiddish literature, press and philology." All the writers in Berlin were asked to answer in a questioner about their biography and their works. In the same lexicon, in the term "Singalovski Aron," it's written among others: "In his youth, when he was a high-school student, Singalovski published the Zionist Cartography leaflet."

So he began…

[Page 195]

Moshe Ben Aron-Leib Zaichik

by Mordechai Zaichik

Translated by Sara Mages

In his youth he already had en experience in the field of education, a profession that his father engaged in. In the days of the first war, at the age of about 13-14, a skinny boy with a load of knowledge in Hebrew, mathematics, grammar etc. he traveled to the villages near Hryczynowicze and Horostov to serve there as a teacher. He received his wages in foodstuffs which greatly helped the economy of the family.

In 1922-3, he traveled to Vilna and was accepted to "Tarbut" Hebrew Teachers Seminary which was recently established and was kind of a continuation of the former Teachers' Institute (Utshitalsky Institute). He paved the way for others to follow him and attend a continuing education program in Vilna, Grodno and Pinsk.

When he was accepted to the seminar he already had a rich past, both in studies and experience as a teacher. He studied with great teachers and intellectuals such as: Professor Regensburg, Dr. Tzerna, Gutman, Orinovski etc. During his studies he also earned his living by giving private lessons.

In 1925, upon completion of his studies at the seminar, he immediately received the position of principal of "Tarbut" school in Dubrovitsa near Sarny, a place where he stayed for several years. He moved to

Volodymyr and also there raised the school to a high level. After seven years of work he was invited to Kremenets and there he lived to his last day, meaning, until the extermination of the city's Jews.

He was among the outstanding school principals in Poland. He was dedicated to his work and established a generation of young school graduates with high level and a beautiful spiritual development. A generation of Zionist pioneers who were devoted to the idea of the founding of the State of Israel. He was also one of the activists in the Zionist institutions and enterprises.

He was also offered the position of superintendent of schools, but he didn't accept this offer which involved many tedious journeys.

When he visited our town, his birthplace, during his vacation he brought with him the spirit of the Hebrew culture. The older students took advantage of his stay in Lenin to study literature, *Tanakh*, natural sciences, etc. with him for a few weeks.

At times, he also lectured at the synagogue about matters of Judaism, Zionism and culture.

His friends and students, wherever they may be, will always remember him with admiration and emotional mourning that he was cut down at his prime, at the age of less than forty, by the Nazi murderers in the city of Kremenets. May God avenge his blood.

His brother, Mordechai

[Page 196]

Reb Aron Migdalovich

by Moshe Migdalovich

Translated by Sara Mages

My father, R' Aron Migdalovich, was called, R' Aron Dabes, by our townspeople after the name of his mother who was called by all: "Di Babe Dabe" [midwife Dabe].

In the two nicknames, of father and grandmother, there was, God forbid, no insult or contempt. Insulting nicknames weren't common in our town. Most of the residents of our town were called by their given names and surnames. Grandmother was called by that name because she worked in maternity care most of her years. Indeed, she was not a certified midwife and her treatment methods were very old, as was customary in those days, but her dedication and kindness stood for her and all the members of our town, men, women, and children, treated her with respect and affection.

My father was called by her name because he was orphaned from his father when he was a baby of six weeks. His mother raised and educated him, and planted in his heart the feeling of love towards people and all the virtues in which this wonderful woman excelled at.

My father was modest and humble, God-fearing and friendly. Everyone respected him for his honesty and righteousness. He was known that his yes is yes, and his no is no. That he was faithful to his word and wouldn't change it.

He loved the Torah and studied and taught it in his free time from his work. He was a member of " *Hevrat Mishnayot*"[*Mishnah* study circle] all his life. Our house was open to anyone who wanted to hear from my father a chapter of "*Kitzur Shulchan Aruch*" or a *Parasha* from the weekly Torah portion. Our community appointed him to manage the community register, he fulfilled this role with great precision and made sure to record every episode and every event - easy, serious and important.

He was an active man and helped to organize public institutions such as : "*Linat Tzedek*," "*Bikur Cholim*" and "*Gemilut Chasadim*." He built the almshouse in our town, was a member of "*Chevrah Kadisha*" and had the right of possession to hold the annual members party in our home, at our expense.

Once, an article about my father's activities for the benefit of the public in our town appeared in the newspaper "*HaMelitz*." During the holidays he passed before the Ark and read from the Torah. He always read the *Selichot* on Rosh Hashanah eve. Every year he passed before the Ark and no one objected to it.

My father's kindness stood out in his negotiations with people. A quarrel never broke out between him and another member of our community. He ran away from controversy and didn't discriminate between people. Everyone was equal in his eyes: rich and poor, small and big. His attitude toward the working class was cordial. People came early to his door to pour their hearts before him, to ask for his advice and for any help he could give them.

Every Saturday evening the wagon owners - Yakov son of Baruch Zaichik, Eliyahu son of Asher (Asher's), Yisrael-Aron, Isar Broch's, Mordechai-Leib and Yehusua Zaichik, got together. All of them work in a cooperative. Father was their bookkeeper not for personal gain.

My father made a living from a department store. The store wasn't big and there wasn't great abundance in it. During the First World War, and in the years of changes and revolutions that followed it, the situation of all traders and shop owners in our town worsened.

[Page 197]

They suffered from lack of cash. All the shop owners ran around the town's streets looking to borrow money for a few days, promising the "benefactors" to return the loan on the set date. They couldn't always keep their word. My father excelled and it and always kept his word. He borrowed from that, paid off to that, and always on the day and the time that he took upon himself to return.

In the difficult days our mother helped our father to support the family. Even though she had to take care of the children and the housework she began to bake bread for sell. She was a good seamstress and had a lot of customers.

My parents suffered a lot of grief: their son. Yosef, a clever and talented young man, was an avid swimmer. He drowned on Friday, 21 Tamuz 1909.

In 1918, their son, Yitzchak, returned from German captivity. He spent about ten weeks in our home and then left by foot for the train station in Mikaszewicze in order to travel to Minsk to receive his documents and also clothes and financial support that were given by the government to those who return from captivity. The farmers from our town, who return from captivity, left before him. He walked behind them so he could catch up and travel with them to the city of Minsk. A distance of about five kilometer from our town he met our nephew, Arka Raska's. He stopped and told him where he was going. A Christian stood next to them and listened to their conversation. Arka said goodbye and walked away. The gentile stated to walk with our brother and advised him to walk through a shortcut in the forest. They entered the forest and there the Christian killed my brother with a hand grenade.

Days and weeks have passed, all the Christians returned from the city of Minsk but our brother was missing. The Christians said that they didn't see him on the train or in the city of Minsk. Our heart said that a disaster had happened to him.

In the intermediate days of Passover, after the snow melted, Christian shepherds came and told that they found human bones about eight kilometers from the town.

Many members of our town left to the same place. We frond the remains of a human body and identified, without a doubt, that these were the remains of our brother, Yitzchak z"l, who fell at no fault of his own.

Our brother, Chaim David, a talented clerk in the Russian government during the days of the Czar, helped many members of our town. During the Second World War he volunteered to the army. He fell in battle.

Our sister, Bil'ke, her husband, Yakov Golob, and their children were murdered by the Nazis in the city of Starobin, the Sluck District.

Our sister, Ester, aspired to immigrate to Israel. She received a certificate but didn't manage to leave on time and was murdered by the Nazis.

Our brother, Feibel, the diligent type, sat day and night and studied *Posekim* and *Shisha Sedarim*, was a ritual slaughterer and a successful preacher. He fell in the hands of the Nazis in the city of Yanova.

Our father z"l passed away on 26 Heshvan, 5700.

Our grandmother, Babe Dabe, passed away on the Sabbath. All the townspeople accompanied her on Saturday evening with thousands of candles.

May their memory be blessed.

My parents have been awarded that they have a name and a remnant in Israel. Two married sons, two married daughters' and grandchildren.

[Page 198]

Reb Eliyakim son of Ovadiahu Migdalovich
Miriam daughter of Yitzhak and their family members

by Mordechai Rubenstein (Migdalovich)

Translated by Sara Mages

I commemorate my honored father, Reb Eliyakim son of Ovadiahu Migdalovich, a beloved and modest man, with a warm and sensitive heart, who extended his help to the needy in secret.

All his days he made a living with integrity and raised his five children to the Torah and good deeds. He pleased with his prayer when he passed before the Ark and brought the worshipers to spiritual uplifting. Was devoted to the idea of the redemption of the Land of Israel even in the days when he was in Japanese captivity in 1903. He always dreamt about immigration to the Land of Israel together with his friend Joseph Trumpeldor. Since his childhood its landscape was etched in his heart and close to his soul, from the *Chumash* and *Nevi'im*, more than the area where he lived all his life.

I also commemorate my honored mother, Miriam daughter of Yitzhak, whose only desire was to do acts of charity and good deeds. With candles she searched for hawkers and passersby in order to feed them and provide them with a place to sleep so they wouldn't return home empty-handed on the Sabbath, and all this with a special grace and hospitality. I remember my sister, Sara, and my sister, Sheindil with her husband and her young child, who were murdered and buried in a mass grave together with the rest of the town - its men, women and children.

I wouldn't forget the noble image of my brother, Yitzchak, who survived the Nazi inferno, joined the Red Army and was missing from among its ranks.

My town, I still see you in my imagination, you're spread like a carpet and adorned with greenery. I see all your residents - among them relatives and friends. All of you are so dear to me with your weaknesses and quarrels, celebrations and tragedies - you were like a big family, and as one family you have been lost on a bitter and impetuous day.

Aron Millner

by Mordechai Rubenstein (Migdalovich)

Translated by Sara Mages

A.

Aron Millner z"l was born in the month of Menachem Av 5654 (1904) in the town of Drahichyn-Polesie near Pinks. His father, the great rabbi, R' Zev, served as a rabbi in Pinsk. In 5673 he left for the town of Sarnik, a place where his father was appointed *Av Beit Din* [Chief of the Court].

At the end of the First World War, Aron left for Bialystok to study at Beit Midrash "Tachkemoni," that was established by "Mizrachi," and completed his studies with the genius, R' Shlomo Polachek (the "Meitscheter *Illui*"), who, a that time, was the heat of "Tachkemoni."

His diligence and passion for the Torah and knowledge were extensive, especially in the *Tanach*, *Midrash* and words of legend. He studied day and night until he memorized the *Tanach*, in its entirety, with the commentaries.

He worked as a teacher at schools, and most recently at "Tarbut" Hebrew Gymnasium in Pinsk, a place where he endeared himself on the public as an excellent speaker and a dedicated activist to anything sacred about Eretz-Yisrael and the Jewish community.

[Page 199]

Aron Millner appeared in Lenin like shimmering dew at dawn. He married Chana, daughter of R' Yosef Zaretzki z"l, a respected and dignified man who earned his living from a department store and was a "reader" in the new synagogue. It is easy to imagine how Aron, the fine young man, the Yeshiva student with soft and dreamy eyes, felt when the burden of livelihood was imposed on him. The sudden transition from the world of nobility of Beit HaMidrash to the world of work and negotiations was a crucial step for him. It wasn't easy for him to adapt to the new status, but he bore his pain in silence and patience.

When he came to us he immediately befriended the town's young people and won them over. With his modesty and noble virtues he conquered the hearts: young and old, people loved him and admired him because he was an honest, uncorrupted friendly man who never hurt his friends or disrespect their dignity.

As the moving spirit in all the cultural-public activities in town he excited himself and others, He worked hard for the expansion and the strengthening of the elementary school "Tarbut" that didn't enjoy any state aid and only existed on tuition that was paid by the parents. His heart was open to the depressed and the weary, helped near and far with all of his soul and his heart. His being exuded grace, love of humanity and love of Israel.

A very special event is engraved in my memory: indeed, today it is just an ordinary act without any special meaning, but it wasn't so 17-18 years ago in a remote town in the Diaspora, the story was as follows: with a special permit from the town's rabbi, R' Moshe Millstein zt"l, Aron was allowed to read the Torah and the *Haftara* in a Sephardic accent on Simchat Torah - the first time in the town's history. The rumor has spread and many worshipers started to flock to the synagogue from all corners of the town and listened attentively. The elderly listened open-mouthed and there was no limit to the enthusiasm of the young. The singing of *Haazinu*,[listen] was supreme: the melody, with all its cantillation notes, penetrated the hearts and awaken the most hidden cords, and it echoes in my ears to this day.

The last years of his life and the bitter end of Aron, the good and the benefactor, is a horrific affair. His fate was very cruel to him and sentenced him to exhaust the cup of sorrow and grief to the end. After the occupation he was "appointed" by the rule of evil and malice to the role of "head of the Judenrat" - and was forced to carry the bodies of two murdered Jews to the cemetery which stood a distance of two kilometers from the town. He was among those who were "responsible" to fulfill all the murderers' demands in silver, gold and clothes and in the period of the ghetto he was also forced to rule on capital cases - selecting people to hard labor in Hancewicze. Without a way out, Aron fulfilled his role and his heart bled until he was awarded to be "redeemed": in a large mass grave of the town's martyrs that he

[Page 200]

dearly loved. He found his rest together with the members of his family and his two small children.

May his memory be blessed and may his good and pure soul be bound in the bond of life.

B.

When he came to us from Sarnik he was a Yeshiva student with the full meaning of this term - young in years and old in wisdom - saturated in the Torah and rich in external knowledge. After the wedding in 1931, he sat at his mother-in-law's house and helped her to run the business.

He liked to read from his early youth, he read a lot and even had a decent library in the concepts of those days in our town. He was a Zionist at heart and soul and active in all the projects and funds that were connected to the Eretz-Yisrael. He was cautious and moderate by nature. he walked sedately and spoke with calm and humility. He endeared himself to people in the first meeting with his good smile that was always upon his face. No one ever saw him angry and he dealt in public needs with faith, devotion and integrity.

During the Holocaust he was "appointed" by the Nazis as "head of the Judenrat" - this appointment caused him endless anguish. When the town's Jews were sent to hard labor at the camp in Hancewicze, he begged before the murderers to add him to the list of deportees, but they rejected his plea, they did not want to lose him and forced him to continue to fulfill his harsh and cruel job - to satisfy their demands that grew by the day. His end was as bitter as the end of his brothers to fate - he found his rest in a big mass grave together with the members of the community that he loved and served with love, holiness and trust. Respect to his memory!

Mordechai Zaichik

Editorial Footnote:

1.   *Yeķopo - Yidishn Gegnṭ-Ķomiṭ-eṭ- -* the Jewish committee for the aid of victims of war.

[Page 200]

Eliezer Kolpanitsky

by Leah and Sarah Kolpanitsky

Translated by Jerrold Landau

Much has been written and much more will still be written about the martyrs of our town who were murdered by the Nazi evildoers during the time of the Holocaust. However, who will memorialize those who fell to the hands of other murderers even before the Nazi beast trod the face of the earth? They remain anonymous, and what will the future generations know about them? Let us erect here a monument to some of them, even if this will only be with a few words.

In those days, we lived in a village near Lenin. How great was my joy when one day we moved to Lenin itself, and my feet crossed the threshold of the cheder for the first time.

Our parents were not especially happy to leave the village. They conducted their quiet lives there for many years, among the neighboring farmers with whom a mutual relationship of respect and esteem pervaded. I often heard it said: how good and quiet are the farmers of the village and the entire area.

However, very soon we were bitterly disappointed. Suddenly, rumors spread about killing and murder that had quickly reached the town of Lenin.

The first victim in the town was Yitzchak the son of Aharon Migdalovich. He was found murdered on the route to Lachwa. The following people fell after him: Yaakov Eliahu the son of Alter Kolpanitsky along with Eliahu Chinitch, Yaakov Rubenstein ("Yakeh"), Uriah (Ura) from the village of Tymoszewicze, Aharon Slutsky from Pozheche, Yisrael Aharon the son of Hershel Meir, Shlomo Dolgin, and the two Eisenstat brothers.

[Page 201]

Eliezer as a child

That year, Eliezer the son of Betzalel Kolpanitsky was also murdered. His death was mourned grievously not only by his family and relatives, but also by all the residents of the town. Fear and terror took hold of everybody. Nobody left the door of their houses, and people avoided traveling on the roads.

Eliezer Kolpanitsky was a young youth, handsome, refined, with a warm Jewish heart. He was connected to the town and its residents. He mastered both Torah and wisdom. He was blessed with artistic talents. His hands took hold of the painter's brush and he would sing with his sweet voice. When he was a student in the faculty of medicine in Kiev, he would return home during the vacations. He would often serve as the prayer leaders in the synagogue on the holidays and enthuse the congregation with his enthusiastic prayers. His heart was always open to give advice and counsel, and his eyes were open to any place that required his assistance. He once assisted a family with many children who lived in poverty. The eldest daughter, aged 14, went without education and any purpose in life. Eliezer started to diligently help this poor family. Along with his friend, he turned to the wealthy residents of the town, and even to the Christian notables, asking them to donate what they could for this purpose. His mother Dina was even asked to exert influence over the parents of the girl to agree to permit her to travel to Kiev with him in order to learn a trade, so that she could support herself. The girl's parents were happy at this advice, and after a few days she set off for Kiev along with Eliezer. He placed her in a business where she also learned the sewing trade. She would study knowledge at night. The girl began to earn her livelihood, and even sent support to her parents. Her parents did not forget what Eliezer did for them, and always recalled that their daughter was saved from degeneration thanks to his dedication.

Eliezer played a large role in the cultural life of the town. He assisted in the organizing of the library, the founding of a choir, arranging plays and all other communal activities. He taught Bible and literature to the youth, and planted the love of Zion in our young hearts. Everyone who knew him knew that he was destined for greatness and prophesied a bright future for him. Indeed, he was a source of pride and glory for his parents Dina and Betzalel, and all the residents of the town.

However, bitter fate decreed otherwise. Eliezer was cut off while still young in years and full of energy, ideas and plans for the future. He was about to conclude his course of studies, and he returned to Kiev at the end of his vacation. Along the way he found out that the Balachovche gang of murderers was approaching Lenin, with their hands sullied with blood and full of booty. Eliezer stopped his journey and remained in the city of Turow, for his conscience did not permit him to continue on his journey when there was the danger of ambush for his family and the residents of his town. He, along with 17 other youths from the region, decided to go to Lenin to protect it. The rabbi of the city warned the youths to refrain from doing so, for there was a great evil in front of them, but they stood by their decision. Along the way they were arrested, accused of espionage, and taken out to be killed in cold blood.

Eliezer was one of the many who fell in sanctification of G-d and the nation, and he is one additional link in the chain of Jewish martyrdom.

May their memories be a blessing!

[Page 202]

Yitzchak Kolpanitsky

by Mordechai Rubenstein (Migdalovich)

Translated by Jerrold Landau

{Photo page 202: Uncaptioned. Yitzchak Kolpanitsky.} Yitzchak the son of Betzalel Kolpanitsky was a man of action. He was a diligent forestry merchant, upright and pleasant in mannerism. He spoke calmly and in good taste. His family moved to Lenin from the village of Pozheche. About 40-50 years ago, Reb Betzalel sent his sons to schools in the cities of Russia with the intent of imparting in them Torah and erudition. The son Yitzchak mastered general and Jewish knowledge. He studied accountancy at a high level. He was active in the communal arena, and one of those who bore the burden of the maintenance of the Tarbut School in our town, that existed until the time of Soviet rule.

Even though the Tarbut School consumed large sums, remained without any government support, and that in those days a public Polish school existed that did not require tuition payments – 90% of the students of the town found their place in the Hebrew school, which was the glory of our town.

Thanks to the dedication of a number of activists who concerned themselves with the maintenance of the institution, free Hebrew education was made possible for those students who could not afford any tuition at all.

The following activists should be remembered positively along with Yitzchak: Mordechai Borochin, Yerachmiel Dvorin, Tzvi Yekutiel Gelanson, Binyamin Starobinski, Moshe Reuven Zaretzki, Yaakov Lezbanik, and others, who did not hesitate to give private pledges in order to ensure that the budget would be covered.

Yitzchak and his co-activists bore the yoke of education with all of its difficulties. They maintained and sustained the school as the apple of their eye. There, children were educated in Zionism, in understanding the values of the nation, and in the Hebrew language. It is appropriate to note that Yitzchak continued to bear the yoke of the maintenance of the school even after his children concluded their studies and transferred to the Tarbut Gymnasium in Pinsk.

Yitzchak of blessed memory served as the director of accounting at a government institution during the period of Soviet rule. He had

[Page 203]

the possibility of leaving along with the army which was retreating from the Germans, and perhaps he might have thereby saved his life. However, he did not agree to leave his elderly parents, his wife and his children behind. He went up in the inferno along with all of his beloved family, and the entire holy community of Lenin.

May his memory be a blessing.

R' Yosef–Noah Rabinovitch
Mrs. Itka daughter of R' David Graeib

by Meir Boktzin

Translated by Sara Mages

R' Yosef–Noah, son of R' Yakov, son–in–law of R' David Graeib, was tall, skinny, slightly bent, had a strict expression and bushy eyebrows that underneath them were intelligent piercing eyes which looked with love and mercy. He was articulate and encouraged his listeners with his great charm.

He wasn't a splendid speaker and didn't belong to those who wrapped their intentions with poetic phrases. He expressed his deep ideas with a few logical and sincere words that forced the listener to treat them with dignity and respect and be convinced by him. For that reason he was always invited to be the arbitrator in various financial and family matters – a duty that he fulfilled not for a personal gain.

[Page 204]

These words – "So said R' Yosef–Noah" – were enough to calm the rival sides, to straighten the painful problem between them and bring them to a friendly agreement. Everyone knew that he was an honest man, fair and impartial, loved peace and pursued peace.

Not only the Jews respected him, the non–Jews also greatly honored him: the farmers, with whom he conducted his business, saw him as "*Nash* Yosel" – our Yosef, because he always treated them with honesty and beyond the letter of the law. Once, one of the farmers lost a promissory note that R' Yosef–Noah gave him against a loan. The farmer came and poured out his heart believing that had just lost his money. R' Yosef–Noah invited him to come with him to the Council House and there he asked him to confirm before the clerk that he indeed lost his promissory note. On the spot he took the full amount of the debt and put it before the farmer so he could take it. Seeing this, the farmer was shocked and amazed and began to cross himself and beg: "Yoskale, take your money and return it to me on the date written on the note." He no longer wanted another note, he believed his word.

He made sure to fulfill the commandments and prohibitions as written in "*Shulchan Aruch*." His flour mill, which supports him and his family, was closed on the Shabbat and on holidays, and even more so, during the week of Passover. The farmers were already used to it, and even though there were many flour mills that belonged to Christians in the area, they didn't want to hand over their grain to others. During Kerensky's days, when food councils were established, R' Yosef–Noah was chosen by the local farmers as director of the local committee because they treated him in complete confidence.

There were also several yearly employees at the mill such as: a miller, mechanic, stoker, etc. R' Yosef–Noah paid their salaries handsomely and they were loyal to him with their heart and soul. When there was work in the mill that didn't require experts, he didn't want to take advantage of his employees and did the work on his own without listening to their requests to go home and rest and they would do the work themselves. He used to say to them "You don't get paid for this work and I don't want you to work for me for free." Besides the salary, he also gave them a bonus pay at every opportunity. R' Yehusua Tziglig z"l, who worked in the mill as a stoker was, in fact, a member of his family.

All the needy in town knew his kindness. He mostly gave charity in secret so no one would know and not to embarrass the needy. He gave generously to all the needy in town and didn't differentiate between Jews and Christians.

He was always careful to show respect to others without, God forbid, offending anyone. Once, there was an incident, on the Sabbath, after a prayer, when the sons–in–laws of R' David Graeib and their wives, turned, as they usually did, to the house of the aforementioned David to bless on a glass of wine and eat a cake. While they were chatting about this and that – on matters of the place and the problems of the world – Chaim Zelig, grandson of R" David (today Mr. Chaim Shalev) intervened and made a comment during a conversation. His uncles, the scholars, the great intellectuals, and his aunts got angry at him: "how dared he to interrupt such an important conversation about matters of supreme importance!? R' Yosef–Noah interfered in his defense when he said: "Wisdom isn't in the elderly – young people can also think and make sense and we shouldn't defer and embarrass the youth because, after all, they're the foundation of the world."

Even though he was busy in his busses he always found time for the Torah. In the summer and in the winter, he woke up early and after he washed his hands and said the Dawn Blessing he sat and studied until it was prayer time.

[Page 205]

He had the right to pass before the Ark during the *Mincha* prayer on Yom Kippur and he didn't give it up when he already felt the terrible disease from which he left the world.

For many years he suffered from stomach pain. This pain, he used to say, came to him from *"Achilat Yamim"* with different housewives as was the case during his youth, when he was a Yeshiva student. He healed for many years but it became worse during the Russian Revolution and the death of his beloved elderly father–in–law, Ben–Zion Volichkin, who left behind a young widow, his daughter Basha, with five children (the last two – twins – were born after the death of their father). The impact of these events was so intense that he became ill with stomach cancer and died while he was still young – only 54 years old – on 12 Iyar, 5679. May his soul be bound in the bond of everlasting life.

* * *

Mrs. Itka, daughter of R' David Graeib z"l, wife of R' Yosef–Noah z"l, was a kindhearted woman. She, the housewife, was a real help to her husband. She was beautiful, good, clever, and excelled in all the virtues. She ran her household with courage, cooked and baked, washed, decorated and cleaned, guided her children in the ways of the blessed God, and especially excelled with a heart of gold. She distributed alms to the poor generously and walked from house to house, with one of her friends, in all types of weather, to collect donations for the needy. Who was the needy – she never revealed. She used to say – "You want to donate – donate, more than that you do not need to know so as not to shame." With the arrival of autumn she pickled cucumbers and chopped cabbage in big barrels – especially for the poor. During the days of Hanukkah she mostly fried goose fat. In the summer she made jam from different vegetables so she would have something to revive the soul of a poor woman who just gave birth or a needy patient and distributed to everyone generously. The desperately poor sat at her table and she always, summer or winter, fed them to satiety.

She was a loyal and compassionate mother to her children and took care of them since birth. When they grew up she was tormented with their torture and happy in their celebrations. She worked very hard to support the family of her daughter, S., who remained with her husband and her children in Poland and she herself traveled to America after the death of her husband in 1920. Not a month has passed without giving her money and clothes. She always demanded her children in America, who send their generous help, to increase the aid to the children and grandchildren who were "suffering in Poland." She made a lot of efforts to bring her daughter's family, but she was unable to do so. Finally, she convinced her children in America to help to bring their sister, brother–in–law and the children to Israel. She thought to settle in Israel at her old age so she could live among them. But fate decided otherwise. When she learned that they already arrived in Israel, she held a banquet in honor of the occasion and from a lot of joy her heart strings burst. The loving maternal heart stopped beating; it couldn't stand he joy that she had felt when her children finally reached safety.

The memory of our beloved father and mother would never be erased from our hearts! We will always mention them with reverence because they have done the impossible for us, and with their death they ordered life to their children.

May their souls be bound in the bond of everlasting life.

[Page 206]

Yehudah son of R' Shlomo Rubenstein

by Mordechai Rubenstein (Migdalovich)

Translated by Sara Mages

Yehudah, or as we used to call him –Yeedel Chana's – was orphaned from his father, R' Shlomo, when he was still a teenager and a student at the Russian School in Lenin. Honest, shy, was left at a crossroad after his death of his father. Without the means to continue his education he tried, together with his mother, to open a fabric store in their specious big house that later turned into a hotel. However, the special nature of the young man, his excessive honesty on the one hand and the lack of commercial daring on the other, caused a rapid liquidation of the business. Since then, he devoted himself to private studies, almost without teachers, and at the same time engaged in teaching children whose parents couldn't send them to a high–school out of town.

Soon the word had spread that Yehudah is a gifted teacher and educator and invests his heart and soul in his students, especially in literature and reading, and also in all areas of science. In a short period of time he was accepted as a teacher at the local Hebrew School. At the same time he studied in special classes in Warsaw and other locations, especially during the months of summer vacation, until he reached his desired goal – becoming a certified teacher. Since then, new horizons opened before him. The Hebrew Teachers Centre in Warsaw recognized him as a teacher and educator with extensive knowledge who was fit to serve in well known schools, such as the Hebrew School in Kletsk and other locations, until he was appointed director of the school in Ludvipol (Wolyn). At the same time he decided to build a family and tied his life with his friend to the profession, the teacher Rivka Koch from Wlodzimirerz (Wolyn).

In 1939/40, during the Soviet occupation, he was appointed principal of the Yiddish School in Kletsk that contained about eight hundred students. From his letter to me which begins in the words: "I now work as a principal of a Jewish school…" I read between the lines his share of mental torture – a dedicated and loyal Zionist, who educated children to the love of the Hebrew language, the values of the nation and its holiness – fate imposed on him to be a teacher in a Russian school, teach Stalin's doctrine and deny in public everything sacred and precious…

He was taken to hard labor in Hancewicze by the defiled Nazis, but managed to escape from there together with dozens of townspeople. However, the murderers' bullets got him in one of the forests during the first days of the escape, and no one knows the location of his burial to this day.

May the noble memory of the scholar, a good example to justice and honesty, a beautiful spirit and a good heart, will shine to us, and may his pure soul be a torch to all his students, acquaintances and admirers. His wife and his daughter also perished together with all of Lenin's martyrs.

[Page 207]

Moshe Schmelkin

(died 1 Iyar, 5711)

by Yakov Berger

Translated by Sara Mages

Six years have passed since we accompanied the beloved and unforgettable Moshe'l on his last journey. From the days, steeped in sorrow and intolerable pain at the beginning of the summer of 1951 when we, members and friends, stood around his bed and witnessed his struggle for his life…

The life, that he loved so much, has been cruel to him. He loved the beautiful, the righteous and the pure – and believe in man.

Since then, the shining image of Moshe'l lives in the hearts of our many close friends with its special and endearing charm.

The stations of his life were memorial stones to his unforgettable image:

Bratislava, 1932: In a student meeting, students of the Faculty of Medicine from Poland, he took the stage to speak and in a moment the packed hall burst into a storm of complaints and a bitter debate of reckoning...

His strength wasn't in words, but – in a shout. In the storm of overflowing emotions those who came from nearby, me included, wanted to know: who is the man? And the answer was given, either seriously or sarcastically: this is a wonderful man who cares for each member, fights for every just cause, a man of the "*Lamed Vav*" (by the way: it was always possible to get a loan from him, but it wasn't necessity to return it).

And indeed, he knew how to struggle for a just cause with great dedication, to find the human core, the personal and the intimate in every political question and differences of opinion. I remember his war in favor of the students–members who were caught in the communist propaganda. The university authorities demanded to disclose their names as a condition for further studies and the stay of many. In his war against the communist worldview, his struggle for every denial on the state of national revival, he was prepared for any personal sacrifice to ensure the right of those caught in deviation – to continue their studies even if it risked the right to study for approximately four hundred students. "All Jews are responsible for one another." The secret of national partnership and the lifelong covenant of a persecuted nation, above all differences of opinion and thoughts that divide the nation...

The end of 1933 – the days of the founding of the Academic Association of Socialist Zionist, "*Arlosoroffya*," and the power struggle in the student unions "*Achdut*"["Unity"] and "*Samopomice*" ["Self Reliance"] in Bratislava. Moshe'l didn't know tiredness. He was involved in every meeting, discussion, debate and a gathering. His personal identity with the work for the idea, and for the movement, knew no bounds. He gave himself in his entirety...

[Page 208]

From here – to the labor movement, the united party "*Poalei Zion*," "*HaHalutz*," "*HaOved*," and the "League for Working Eretz Israel." It was natural that he found his way to the Zionist labor movement, to the camp of workers and the fighters for a new society. He, who was close with every fiber of his being to the oppressed, identified with their struggle for a better life. He saw himself as a living limb of the Labor Zionist Movement who fought and built the foundations for a society based on equality and honesty. How great was his suffering when he saw a sign of weakness and deviation from the ideal that he kept in his heart.

However, at that time the disease already showed its signs. He didn't want to acknowledge it, didn't pay attention to its first signs and didn't take care of himself.

In Bratislava, 1935, he had frequent asthma attacks and became very weak. In those days I moved to live with him in one room and saw his suffering and agony closely. However, he knew how to hide its signs, and more than that, his reflections on its future development. Only a little here and there he emitted a comment from which it was possible to see his mental suffering. Sometimes, sadness took over him for short periods, but very quickly he knew how to show restraint and move to his special way of life...

The melody never left his mouth. He sounded jubilant in the morning after a night of breathlessness and recurrent attacks.

Everyone knew him and respected him: the newspaper seller, the waiter, the neighbors, the workers at the institution, one or the other. The lecturers and their assistants, the members – always surrounded him, sought his company, and he knew how to help everyone with understanding, by explaining their situation, with a sound advice and a good word. Many sought his company and told him about their difficulties, disappointments and special problems...

Indeed, a wonderful man who cares for all, understands, explains and advises, but he didn't know how to take care of himself and find advice...

March 1938, the terrible days of the rise of the Nazi oppressor, the occupation of Vienna, the threat to Czechoslovakia, the suffocation and the sense of impending disaster. The days of the rise of the Socialist Zionist Movement, and the masses flow into it. Moshe'l takes part in every consultation, in every discussion and any crucial decision and his opinion is heard – because the members knew that the man is beyond all personal considerations and only the common good and the good of the movement are before his eyes

Munich's days, the threat of war and the changes in Bratislava, the tide of racial hatred and fascism is rising and threatens to flood everything on its way. There are no illusions in the movement's leadership and everyone is ready for the worst, to the disaster that may occur at any moment. Moshe'l doesn't shrink from participating, even though he was a foreign national, in the activities that are now carried underground and indirectly – in the students' summer colony, in the *"Halutz"* camp, in the *"Oved"* colony and in the party's conference in Nitra. He participates in all the discussions, vibrant, and infuses from his spirit and enthusiasm on everyone who comes in contact with him.

I remember that one day I brought before him the need to worry about his safety and his life. After all, he has a brother and sister in the United States and he could ask them for papers, for a visa and the possibility of travel for a transitional period to America until the rage of the war will pass, until he will be able to immigrate to Israel. His response was brisk: he wouldn't "immigrate" to America. He wouldn't look for a rescue and shelter with relatives that he loved so much, but he will immigrate to Israel together with the members and only in his own right – as a proud Socialist Zionist fighter!

I welcome him at the port of Haifa. How great was his excitement, how his face beamed when his feet stepped on the soil

[Page 209]

on the homeland... but here he had to struggle for his place at work, in the society, and the struggle was difficult and saturated with great bitterness...

In "Hadassah," in Tel;–Aviv, in his work as bacteriologist, Moshe'l refuted any doubts in his ability. He was able to contribute a significant contribution to the research of hidden factors in the blood – an important scientific discovery, even if it was made, almost at the same time, in the United States. His friends' joy to his discovery was tinged with a sense of the injustice done to Moshe'l and his grief. One of the head doctors claimed to be the first to discover it. The struggle has just begun and Moshe'l learns the difficulties of life, not from stories and not from friends who come to receive his guidance and advice, but from his flesh... His war is, first of all, to the justice that is trampled before his eyes and then to his personal right...

The municipality of Tel–Aviv gave his a prize for his discovery, and *"Harefuah"* [a medical–scientific periodic] published the results of the research in his name and the name of his opponent. But Moshe'l didn't hold a grudge at his rival – and out of patience and understanding he also knew how to find the bridge to the man's heart because it was his exalted feature.

The disease started to show its signs, but all the urging of friends were in vain. He didn't know how to take care of himself, to care for his own health. He who cared so much about others his friends and patients in "Hadassah," treated himself and his health with great cruelty. Any request from a friend, that he should change his way of life, was dismissed by a hand movement, by a melody, a joke or a saying – sarcastically or bitterly – that he has nothing to lose…

We invited him to a Purim party, his last holiday. He promised to come on Passover, for the "Seder," as he used to do a number of times, but he was unable to fulfill his promise: the disease prevailed and confined him to his hospital bed…

Did he know his condition? In one of the visits I told him that if he cannot come for Passover, he would have to spend the holiday of Shavuot with us. But his only response was an abolition movement of the hand: "Who know where I would be on Shavuot"…

He pure soul left on 1 Iyar.

May his soul be bound in the eternal life of the nation!

R' Yisroel son of R' Menashe Latocha

by Menashe Ben–Yisrael

Translated by Sara Mages

Thirty years ago I said goodbye to my father. Then, I hadn't imagined to myself that we were separating forever. His image is hovering in my imagination the way I saw him on that gray winter morning when I separated from him before my immigration to Israel. He stood still and pale, and the speech was taken from him from excitement. I understood his feelings. It was difficult for him to separate from his only son. His lips moved slowly: "Go in peace and take care of yourself."

He was an honest Jew with a gentle soul, a specialist in his profession, treated every person, big and small, with friendship and warmth. His talks were accompanied by humor. He read a book every free moment from his work and had a special liking to the Bible, especially – to Isaiah. He always found the current meaning of what was told in the Bible.

In his last letters he expressed his desire to the Torah.

[Page 210]

R' Yisroel son of R' Menashe Latocha

And indeed, what he wasn't able to obtain as a young man because of the harsh conditions and the need to take care of his family, he got later on his own. He was God–fearing but not fanatical. Once, when my mother threatened that she wouldn't give me breakfast because of a delay in the morning prayer – he stood beside me and said with a smile: "You cannot explain to the child the obligation of prayer with threats, he should know that there's no existence without the Creator the world and we have to thank him in good faith"… His spoken words, which were said calmly, entered my heart.

He was a national Jew and was devoted to Zionism. He always asked: "Would I be able to see the sun of Eretz–Yisrael and its radiance?

However, fate didn't want him to see the country that he dreamed of. On 9 Av 5692, he passed away in Warsaw after an illness.

R' Yisroel son of R' Menashe Latocha

by Mordechai Rubenstein (Migdalovich)

He was known in our town by the name, "R' Yisroel Hanyes," after the name of his wife, Hanye may she lives, who lives among us in Israel. R' Yisroel took very little interest in the business of his hostel and the hostess was his wife. He walked as if he was daydreaming, as if he was shaking off the hustle and bustle inside his house. He was surrounded by a storm of noise, masses of farmers from the vicinity, the yard was full of wagons and horses. He lived his life in this atmosphere and not a speck of dust stuck to him. He walked in world of the Almighty with great sensitivity and influenced others with his pure spirit and the look in his eyes that caressed the surroundings.

When the Sabbath and the holidays arrive, when tranquility descended on his house, he walked slowly to the synagogue, curling his blond mustache and greeting every passerby.

I sat next to him in the synagogue. He used to explain to me – according to his interpretation – chapters of poetry with good taste and awe to the beauty of the prayers, and the words were pleasant and convincing.

R' Yisroel was also versed in the ways of the world and knew how to shed light on what was happening in the various socialist movements.

He sent his only son, Menashe, to Eretz–Yisrael when he was still a young boy with the hope to join him shortly. However, he wasn't able to fulfill his desire and was abruptly plucked from the land of life at his prime.

His blessed memory is kept in the hearts of his many admirers and friends.

[Page 211]

The humble of the earth

by Meir Boktzin

Translated by Sara Mages

Among our townspeople, who fell before Hitler's evildoers, were Jews, men and women, who lived their entire life as if they were hidden by a shadow and they deserve that we will bring their memory in the memorial book. They weren't great scholars, weren't known for their piety, weren't among the masters of the town and their place wasn't among the "proprietors." They were far from national or socialist activity and didn't intervene in public affairs.

They were simple Jews, "ordinary" Jews: shoemakers, tailors, carpenters, etc. who sat all days of the weeks in their homes – next to their working table, or traveled in the neighboring villages and dressed and put shoes on the farmers. They abandoned their work only on Friday afternoon and returned to their homes to bless the Sabbath. By the way, it should be noted that some were engaged in acts of kindness, supported their fellow men and encouraged their health and their livelihood.

Leivick Horowitz David Tziglig

Leivick Horowitz the shoemaker and David Tziglig the tailor – or Leivick Zeliches and Dutschke – as the two were known by their nicknames. Both were small craftsmen who suffered a lot of during the First World War. For four long years they were poor unfortunate Jewish soldiers in the Russian Army which degraded the Jews. Every day they faced the dangers of war and humiliation that were their lot. They spent four years in the battlefields under a barrage of shells and exploding mines. In many occasions the Angel of Death stood before them and not once they were wounded and bled. The two – Leivick and Dutschke – vowed that if God would help them and they will return home safely, they will devote their time to help and encourage the poor and the sick with money and food, and provide them with medicines as directed by the doctor. They fulfilled this vow truly and faithfully as stated: "With all your heart and with all your soul."

Every Sabbath eve and holiday eve, in the summer and in the winter, in the scorching heat, heavy rain or in the frost, you were able to see the two of them, the lanky tall tailor Dutschke and the small shoemaker Leivick, walking from house to house to collect the weekly contributions for the sick and the poor. Our damp town didn't have a shortage of poor patients who needed medical help, nutritious food and even clothing. Indeed, the address for help was with these two. From time to time their friend, Yodel Schuster, participated in this *mitzvah* work of "*Bikur Cholim*" and "*Linat Tzedek*" (the last miraculously survived together with the members of his family and lives in Tel–Aviv).

In every wedding, in every *Brit Milah* or just a celebration, the three were seen walking among the guests and collecting their donation for "*Bikur Cholim*." On Purim, these good Jews had the "right of possession" to hold a "Purim play" with the participation of the children that they trained two months earlier for the presentation of the traditional images of "David and Goliath" or "the sale of Yosef." They took them to the homes of the rich Jews and collected substantial funds for their goals. Every homeowner and every housewife saw it as their honor to welcome the "Purim players" with a nice coin and Purim sweets.

[Page 212]

Sometimes there were also exceptional cases, when there was a need for large sums than usual and "*Bikur Cholim*" wasn't able to bear the expenses. Then, these two went after the town's intelligentsia and urged them to stage a play for the benefit of the fund. These responded generously – under the condition that the craftsmen will help with the arrangement of the stage and collect the required clothing from the townspeople. Leivick, Dutschke[1] and Yodel, abandoned their jobs for a few days and did everything they could. Indeed, the revenue from the presentation of the play saved the life of the dying. Many patients, who recovered and live today with their families in various countries, now mention, with tears of thanks in their eyes and a heartfelt sigh, these beloved activists.

Miriam Gellman

Another gentle and compassionate soul, who was hardly known in town because her good deeds were done in secret and obscurity, was – Miriam Gellman – the "elderly pharmacist" as she was called by the townspeople. Mrs. Gellman, being an intelligent woman, a city–dweller with a high Russian education, segregated herself, for unknown reasons, from the Jewish population in Lenin. She didn't take part in matters related to the local Jewish population and didn't even make friends with the town's richest women. She had a secret warehouse of clothes and shoes for men, women and children, and distributed them in the strictest confidence by her special messengers among the needy. Every Thursday she baked, quietly and secretly, challot for the Sabbath, cookies, pots full of fish and roast beef, and other delicacies, and sent them on Friday with her secret messengers to the needy in town. Indeed, she was considered to be the greatest righteous in town. She gave free medicines to "*Bikur Cholim*" under one condition – that her secret wouldn't be revealed. In this manner the rich woman – Maria Gellman, the "elderly pharmacist," continued to live. Thus, she was – one of the "*Lamed Vav*."

Chana–Feigel Mednik

In this brilliant group of gentle souls, which were hidden by a shadow in our town, we can also include the elderly woman, Chana–Feigel Mednik – or "Kushiche" after the name of her husband Kushe (or Yekutiel the builder). She was a mother to six sons and two daughters. Most of them were married and parents to children but, unfortunately, she didn't derive pleasure from them. Most of them left the world while she was still alive, some were lost from the world as soldiers in the First World War, some died as victims of malignant diseases, and she herself remained childless at her old age. However, she didn't let fate break her with its heavy calamities and didn't throw herself on the arms of despair. With all the warmth of her heart she devoted herself to acts of kindness and charity, helping the sick and the needy, and encouraging the widows and orphans with her warm and smiles. She was busy, days on end, from morning to late hour of the evening, collecting alms, food and clothing for the poor and the sick. She never asked anyone to help

[Page 213]

her in her good deeds because she has done everything by herself, with her own strength. She ran everywhere and collected alms for the poor: in the cold, snow and heavy rain. She waded in the swamps to visit the sick, encourage them with her warm smile and good words, or helped a woman who just gave birth with good food, washing, the replacing of bedding, took care of the young children, dressed them and sent them to school. She never said a bad word and with her smile and pleasant manners was a mother to poor children and the unfortunates.

Footnote:

1. We received information that Dutschke also survived and lives in Russia (the editorial board).

Lenin Countrymen Worldwide

[Page 217]

Reb Avrom-Yitskhok Slutsky

by Mordechai Rubenstein (Migdalovich)

Translated by Sara Mages

R' Avraham Yitzchak and his wife Chava Slutsky

R' Avraham Yitzchak Slutsky, one of the greatest and most prominent figures among the former residents of our town, immigrated to the United States decades ago at a young age. He's a gifted man with a beautiful spirit and beautiful soul. He was one of the first founders of Lenin's "Landsmanshaft" in America. The main functions of the organizations were: to submit material and spiritual aid

[Page 218]

to the needy of our town and to the "green" immigrant who arrived to America, by obtaining him a job and a warm corner until he settled.

His hearty attitude to his birthplace in faraway Polesia didn't dim his longing and his love to the Land of Israel, and his soul was full of concerns and anxiety to the country during the War of Independence. It's difficult to describe his joy when the country of Israel was established (unfortunately he wasn't able to visit Israel for family reasons, and I hope that one day we'll be able to see him here among us).

Needless to say, how much energy and initiative he devoted to the realization of the idea to publishing a "Yizkor" book for the souls of our loved ones, who were destroyed and slaughtered like sheep by the Nazi beast. He showed great enthusiasm to the plan when it was just an abstract concept, before the material was in our hands and without the pictures of our loved ones, whose form has been preserved in our hearts and our thoughts. He was the first to provide lists of personalities and figures from our town. Skillfully, and with all the warmth and love in his heart, he included in this book every soul that he had remembered. He was the first to provide us with a collection of photos, with public and social value, that were preserved by relatives and former residents of the town. He made every effort to collect the money needed for the purchase of the printing paper and the fabric for the binding and also obtained the permit to ship them to Israel. There was no shortage of opponents to this project also there, but thanks to his hard work and the aid of his many loyal friends, like the scholar Kalman son of R' David Temkin HaCohen and others, he fought them and won.

His beloved wife, Chava, who accompanies him in his way of life, has done her best to help the needy residents of Lenin, and to the love of her birthplace. She especially devoted herself to help the Holocaust survivors in Europe. Her house is wide open for parties and receptions for the benefit of the community, and she also helps her husband with his blessed work.

The affection and appreciation of the former residents of Lenin will accompany them in their devoted work, and we wish them that they will be able to continue it for many more years.

[Page 219]

The town's elders and the committee activists in Israel

With the participation of the guest Y. Skalier z"l from the
United States, on the memorial day for Lenin's martyrs, 5713 -
1952/3

The Book Committee

Sitting (from the right): Menashe Yulevich, Chaim Shalev (Nakritz),
Sara Fogelman (Kolpanitsky), Ben-Zion Forman,
Standing (from the right): Mordechai Zaichik, Yitchak Slutsky,
Mordechai Rubenstein (Migdalovich)

[Pages 223-235]

Lenin – the Community Register

Notes

The Community Register is a three parts listing of victims of the Holocaust.

Part A. is a listing of 521 individuals plus at least 201 unnamed children from Lenin and a few surrounding communities murdered on August 14, 1942 in the extermination of the Jews of Lenin by German execution squads and on various other dates during the German occupation. . This part is entitled "A. The Martyrs of Lenin, who were murdered by the Germans on the 2nd day of Elul - August 14, 1942 (pages 223-232). This list was prepared by: M. Zaichik, Lipa Mishelov, Masha Slutsky"

Part B. is a listing of 79 residents of Lenin who were killed in battle or perished elsewhere (pages 232-233). List prepared by M. Zaichik.

Part C. is a listing of 102 Partisan fighters who were killed fighting the Nazis in the forests (pages 234-235). List prepared by M. Zaichik. Approximately 903 individuals are listed including unnamed children.

Listed separately are:

The names of 141 relatives in part A

The names of 51 relatives in part B

The names of 50 relatives in part C

These names are used in the Lenin Yizkor Book List to identify the martyrs and those presumed to have survived. Names of surviving relatives may be duplicated in parts A., B., and C. Relatives listed as survivors may also be listed as martyrs.

This translation consists of two parts:

1. Translation and transliteration of The Community Register from the Hebrew original in the Yizkor Book by Rachel Ben-Chaim (Rochelle Moss Kaplan) January 8, 2004.
2. Six lists (not included in the original Lenin Yizkor Book) provide a cross-reference of all individuals named in the translation. The first three spreadsheets, entitled "Lenin Community Register Necrology Part A, Part B, Part C," respectively, list those named in the Yizkor Book as martyrs. The last three spreadsheets, Part A., Part B., and Part C., list relatives of the martyrs used in the Yizkor Book to identify the martyrs. The martyrs lists are sorted alphabetically first by Family Name then by First Name. The relatives lists are sorted first by relationship Code, then by Family Name, then by First Name. The list was prepared by Sanford A. Kaplan (Translation Coordinator) on January 8, 2004.

Notes For Column Headings:

1. Code – M=Martyr; H=Husband, W=Wife, F=Father, Mo=Mother, S=Son, D=Daughter, Presumed Survivors.
2. Family Name – Married Name (last name of husband) for women if known, otherwise maiden name. In cases where only the woman's name is given, I have assumed it is her married name and the children carry that family name. In some cases the text of the original Martyrs List is unclear as to an individual's relationships. I have made a best guess based on context contained in the text. (For instance: B daughter of A and C her son. Is he A's or B's son?). If the text states "X, wife of Y", I have assumed X was martyred and Y survived. If family name is not given it is listed as Unknown Or Unknown.
3. First name – First name + female maiden name if known.
4. Children's Names – Children listed by first name. If names are unknown they are listed as "four sons," etc.
5. Children, spouses, fathers also listed separately by their first name. Presumed survivors are also listed separately for cross referencing purposes using their Code – H,W,F,Mo,S,D.
6. Page # – Page number of listing in translation of the original Lenin Yizkor Book. For instance: 223L = Page 223 left column; 226R = Page 226 right column. Note: Translation left column = original Hebrew right column.
7. Comments – Other information in original text or cross-reference information.
8. Other Abreviations – (Unknown or Unknown) Unknown First or Family name.

9. Please communicate to the Yizkor Book Project any corrections to the assumptions of relationships or survival.

Sanford A. Kaplan

[Pages 223-232]

Lenin – the Community Register

Part A. The Martyrs of Lenin, who were murdered by the Germans on the 2nd day of Elul - August 14, 1942

Prepared by: M. Zaichik, Lipa Mishelov, Masha Slutsky

Code	Family name	First name	S E x	Spouse name	Father	Children's names	Page ref. #	Comments
M	AFMAN (FRIZIER)	Efraim	M		Yakov		224L	Mother is Tzira
M	AFMAN (FRIZIER)	Faygel	F		Yakov		224L	Mother is Tzira
M	AFMAN (FRIZIER)	Pesha	F		Yakov		224L	Mother is Tzira
M	AFMAN (FRIZIER)	Tzira	F	Yakov		Efraim (M), Pesha (F), Faygel (F)	224L	
M	AFMAN (FRIZIER)	Yakov	M	Tzira		Efraim (M), Pesha (F), Faygel (F)	224L	
M	AKA	Masha	F	Shlomo (Tatel)			226L	
M	AKA	Shlomo (Tatel)	M	Masha			226L	
M	BARUCHIN	Alta	F	Mordechai		Ephraim	228L	
M	BAVKIN	Dvora	F	Nosson		Basya(F),	223L	Basya, wife of Yakov KAPLAN
M	BAVKIN	Faigel	F		Kalman		223L	
M	BAVKIN	Mina Rochel	F			Bayla (F)	223R	
M	BAVKIN	Nosson	M	Dvora			223L	
M	BAVKIN	Vichna	F	Kalman		Fagel(F), Bracha(F), Kalman(M),	223L	Bracha married to Avrom ZAVIN
M	BEHON	Eshka	F		Eizel		227R	
M	BEHON	Mendel	M		Eizel		227R	

M	BEHON	Sara	F		Eizel		227R	
M	BEHON	Shmuel	M		Eizel		227R	
M	BEHON	Shprintza	F		Eizel		227R	
M	BEHON	Velvel	M		Eizel		227R	
M	BEHON	Zissel	F	Eizel		Eshka(F), Shprintza(F), Sara(F), Velvel(M), Mendel(M), Shmuel(M), Two more children	227R	
M	BERGMAN	Brocha	F		Nissen		225L	
M	BERGMAN	Chinka	F		Nissen		225L	
M	BODNITZ	Chana	F			Infant	230L	
M	BOIMAN	Esther	F	Unknown	Aron Shkliar	One Child	232L	
M	BRESLER	Etel	F	Zalman		Shayna (F), Meyer (M), Yitzhok (M)	224R	Shayna wife of Boma Rappaport
M	BRESLER	Meyer	M		Zalman BRESLER		224R	Mother was Etel
M	BRESLER	Yitzhok	M		Zalman BRESLER		224R	Mother was Etel
M	BRODATSKI	Alter	M	Riva		Isaac(M), Gittel(F), Chaya(F), Faygel(F), Basha(F)	229R	
M	BRODATSKI	Basha	F		Alter		229R	
M	BRODATSKI	Chaya	F		Alter		229R	
M	BRODATSKI	Faygel	F		Alter		229R	
M	BRODATSKI	Gittel	F		Alter	Two Children	229R	
M	BRODATSKI	Isaac	M		Alter		229R	
M	BRODATSKI	Riva	F	Alter		Isaac(M), Gittel(F)	229R	
M	CHINITCH	Adel	F				232R	From Chvorostow
M	CHINITCH	Chana	F		Shmuel		226L	
M	CHINITCH	Esther Dvora	F		Shimshon		224L	
M	CHINITCH	Leib	M	Necha			231L	
M	CHINITCH	Miriam (Mara)	F	Shimshon		Esther Dvora (F), Risha (F)	224L	
M	CHINITCH	Necha	F	Leib			231L	
M	CHINITCH	Sender	M				231L	

M	CHINITCH	Shaynka	F	Fayvel	Chaim Dovid	One Child	230L	
M	CHINITCH	Shmuel	M	Tzira		Chana (F)	226L	
M	CHINITCH	Tcharna	F		Yisroel		228L	
M	CHINITCH	Tema	F			Freydel Slutsky(F), Yenta Slutsky(F), another Daughter	231L	
M	CHINITCH	Tzira	F	Shmuel		Chana (F)	226L	
M	CHINITCH	Yocheved (Yocha)	F	Yisroel		Tcharna	228L	
M	ELEYNIK	Chaya Krayna	F	Nachman		Dvora(F)	229R	
M	ELEYNIK	Dvora	F		Nachman		229R	
M	ELEYNIK	Nachman	M	Chaya Krayna		Dvora(F)	229R	
M	EPSTEIN	Chanan	M	Hinda		Sonya Tziglig	230L	
M	EPSTEIN	Eva	F				224R	From Warsaw
M	EPSTEIN	Hinda	F	Chanan		Sonya Tziglig	230L	
M	FELDMAN	Dr.	M	Esther			228L	
M	FELDMAN	Esther	F	Dr. Feldman	Yacov LAZAVNIK		228L	
M	FIXMAN	Krayna	F	Unknown	Mordechai	Four Children	225R	
M	GACHMAN	Masha	F	Unknown		Daughter	231L	
M	GELANSON	Aharon	M	Simka	Yisroel	Three Daughters and One Son	228L	
M	GELANSON	Chaya Sara	F	Hershl Kusha		Rochel (F)	228L	
M	GELANSON	Faygel	F	Moshe'ke		Two Little Girls	230L	
M	GELANSON	Hershl Kusha	M	Chaya Sara		Rochel (F)	228L	
M	GELANSON	Rochel	F		Hershl Kusha		228L	
M	GELANSON	Sara	F	Shlomo		Two Children	228R	
M	GELANSON	Simka	F	Aharon		Three Daughters and One Son	228L	
M	GELANSON	Yekutiel	M				229L	Grandson of Zelig
M	GELANSON	Zelig	M			Fraydel Tzukrovitz(F)	229L	Grandfather of Yekutiel
M	GINSBERG	Asher	M		Yosef		228R	
M	GINSBERG	Bayla	F	Eliyahu		Busha Kandelstein(F)	232L	
M	GINSBERG	Eliyahu	M	Bayla	Asher	Busha Kandelstein(F)	232L	

M	GINSBERG	Eshka	F	Yitzkhok	Layzer Golob	One Child	231R	
M	GINSBERG	Khisha	F		Asher		228R	
M	GINSBERG	Riva	F		Yosef	One Child	228R	
M	GINSBERG	Shayndel	F	Yosef		Riva(F), Asher, Yitzkhok	228R	
M	GINSBERG	Wife	F	Yitzkhok		Four Children	228R	
M	GINSBERG	Yitzkhok	M	Eshka		One Child	231R	
M	GINSBERG	Yosef	M	Shayndel	Asher	Riva(F), Asher, Yitzkhok	228R	
M	GLEIBERMAN	Bayla	F	Asher		Miriam(F), Chama(F), Beba(F)	223R	Daughter of Mina Rochel BAVKIN
M	GLEIBERMAN	Beba	F		Asher		223R	Daughter of Bayla
M	GLEIBERMAN	Chama	F		Asher		223R	Daughter of Bayla
M	GLEIBERMAN	Miriam	F		Asher		223R	Daughter of Bayla
M	GOLDBERG	Efraim	M	Finkel		Esther	224L	
M	GOLDBERG	Esther	F			Golda'le (F), Isser'ka (M)	224R	Daughter of Efraim and Finkel
M	GOLDBERG	Finkel	F	Efraim		Esther	224L	
M	GOLDMAN	Chaimke	M		Hershl		225L	Mother was Yokheved Rasamakha
M	GOLDMAN	Dvora	F	Yisroel	Yakov Kravetz		229L	
M	GOLDMAN	Yokheved Rasamakha	F	Hershl		Chaimke	225L	
M	GOLOB	Channa	F	Yehuda		Four Children	226R	
M	GOLOB	Esther	F	Avraham		Luba Shapira	231L	
M	GOLOB	Esther Rochel	F			Two Children	232R	From Chvorostow
M	GOLOB	Henya	F	Layzer		Malka(F), Meir(M), Eshke(F)	231R	
M	GOLOB	Layzer	M	Henya			231R	
M	GOLOB	Lena	F	Moshe		Two Children	225L	
M	GOLOB	Malka	F		Layzer		231R	
M	GOLOB	Meir	M		Layzer		231R	
M	GOLOB	Michla	F			One Child	232R	From Chvorostow

M	GOLOB	Miriam (Mera)	F		Chaim	Two Children	232R	
M	GOLOB	Rochel Vitzerbin	F	Asher			231L	
M	GOLOB	Yehuda	M	Channa	Chaim	Four Children	226R	
M	GORODETSKI	Avrom'l	M		Hirshl Leib (?)		226L	Ethel's Son
M	GORODETSKI	Basha	F	Duda	Yosef SHKLIAR	One Child	225R	
M	GORODETSKI	Ethel	F	Hirshl Leib		Avrom"l (Her Son), Chaia (her Daughter)	226L	
M	GORODETSKI	Shimon	M	Wife	Hershl Leib	Five Children	226R	
M	GORODETSKI	Wife	F	Shimon		Five Children	226R	
M	GUREVICH	Alter	M	Gittel		Gronia(F), Sonia(F)	227L	
M	GUREVICH	Faigel	F	Leivick		Henya(F), Michlia(F)	227L	
M	GUREVICH	Gronia	F		Alter		227L	
M	GUREVICH	Henya	F		Leivick		227L	
M	GUREVICH	Leivick	M	Faigel	Michla	Henya(F), Michlia(F)	227L	
M	GUREVICH	Mordechai	M		Moshe		227L	
M	GUREVICH	Sonia	F		Alter		227L	
M	GUREVICH	Chaya	F	Yakov		Four Children	232R	
M	HABERMAN	Wife	F	Unknown Haberman		Infant Son	223L	HABERMAN from Poland
M	HOLTZMAN	Tziril	F	Shmuel		Two Children	230L	
M	HARFON	Avrom-Yitzkhok	M		Meir		226L	Son of Itka
M	HARFON	Hershl	M		Eliyahu		227R	
M	HARFON	Itka	F	Meir		Luba (F), Avrom-Yitzkhok (M), Two more children	226L	
M	HARFON	Laybel	M		Eliyahu		227R	
M	HARFON	Luba	F		Meir		226L	Daughter of Itka
M	HARFON	Meir	M	Itka		Luba (F), Avrom-Yitzkhok (M), Two more children	226L	
M	HARFON	Moshe	M		Eliyahu		227R	
M	HARFON	Necha	F	Eliyahu		Laybel(M), Moshe(M),	227R	

						Hershl(M), one more child	
M	HARFON	Sonia	F	Sender		One Son, Four Daughters	226L	
M	ISERS	Chaya	F		Yisroel-Aron		230R	
M	ISERS	Nechama Sara	F	Yisroel-Aron		Nishka(F), Chaya(F), Yitzkhok(M)	230R	
M	ISERS	Nishka	F		Yisroel-Aron		230R	
M	ISERS	Yisroel-Aron	M	Nechama Sara		Nishka(F), Chaya(F), Yitzkhok(M)	230R	
M	ISERS	Yitzkhok	M		Yisroel-Aron		230R	
M	KAHAN	Chaya	F	Unknown		Moshe(M)	231R	
M	KAHAN	Moshe	M		Unknown		231R	
M	KAMINSKY	Mordechai	M	Riva		Two Daughters	229L	
M	KAMINSKY	Riva	F	Mordechai		Two Daughters	229L	
M	KANDELSTEIN	Busha	F	Unknown	Eliyahu Ginsberg	One Child	232L	
M	KANIK	Basha	F		Daniel	one child	226R	
M	KANITZ	Itka	F	Sholem		Four Children	223R	
M	KAPLAN	Basya (BAVKIN)	F	Yakov		Yosef(M), One Daughter	223L	Daughter of Nosson
M	KAPLAN	Chana Basha	F	Gedalya		Esther(F), Nesha(F)	230L	
M	KAPLAN	Esther	F		Gedalya		230L	
M	KAPLAN	Golda (BAVKIN)	F	Asher		Tsila(F)	223R	Daughter of Mina Rochel BAVKIN
M	KAPLAN	Nesha	F		Gedalya	Two Daughters	230L	
M	KAPLAN	Tsila	F		Asher		223R	Daughter of Golda
M	KAPLAN	Yosef	M		Yakov		223L	Son of Basya
M	KATZMAN	Chashka	F	Unknown		Two Children	229L	
M	KATZMAN	Unknown	M	Chashka	Pesach Lamdin	Two Children	229L	
M	KIRSCHENZWEIG	Necha	F	Unknown	Gronem MIGDALOVICH	One Child	225R	Daughter of Sara Tziril MIGDALOVICH
M	KIRSHNER	Eva	F				224R	From Warsaw
M	KIRZNER	Bayla	F	Nachman		Three Children	225L	
M	KIRZNER	Beinish	M	Tema			225L	
M	KIRZNER	Chaya	F		Dovid (?)		226R	

M	KIRZNER	Esther	F	Dovid		Chaya(Her Daughter), One son	226R	
M	KIRZNER	Rochel	F		Yakov		231R	
M	KIRZNER	Tema	F	Beinish			225L	
M	KIRZNER	Tzirka	F	Mordechai		Three Children	228R	
M	KLIGER	Unknown	M				231L	Refugee
M	KOLPANITSKY	Bashka	F		Yitzkhok		228R	
M	KOLPANITSKY	Bayla	F	Yitzkhok		Esther(F), Bashka(F)	228R	
M	KOLPANITSKY	Betzalel	M	Dina			228R	
M	KOLPANITSKY	Breindel	F				228R	Leah Kolpanitsky's Daughter
M	KOLPANITSKY	Dina	F	Betzalel			228R	
M	KOLPANITSKY	Esther	F		Yitzkhok		228R	
M	KOLPANITSKY	Leah	F			Breindel(F), Faygel	228R	
M	KOLPANITSKY	Liba	F	Velvel		Two Daughters	230L	
M	KOLPANITSKY	Velvel	M	Liba		Two Daughters	230L	
M	KOLPANITSKY	Yitzkhok	M	Bayla		Esther(F), Bashka(F)	228R	
M	KONICK	Chaya Elka	F	Leib			230R	
M	KOROVOCHKA	Chisha	F		Nossen Yitzkhok		225R	Daughter of Nossen Yitzkhok
M	KOROVOCHKA	Masha	F	Unknown		One Son	225R	Simka KOROVOCHKA's Daughter
M	KOROVOCHKA	Simka	F	Nossen Yitzkhok		Masha	225R	Simka's Daughter
M	KRAVETZ	Channa	F				229L	
M	KRAVETZ	Eshka Rayzel	F	Mordechai		Yehudis(F), Henya(F), Shimon(M)	228L	
M	KRAVETZ	Fayvel	M				229L	
M	KRAVETZ	Golda	F		Yehuda	Two Children	227L	
M	KRAVETZ	Hasha (HARFON)	F	Chaim		Three Children	226L	
M	KRAVETZ	Henya	F		Mordechai		228L	
M	KRAVETZ	Michlia	F	Yehuda	Leivick	Golda	227L	Maiden Name GUREVICH

M	KRAVETZ	Rayzel	F	Yakov		Channa(F), Tzvia(F), Fayvel(M),Shayndel(F), Yeshaya(M), Dvora Goldman(F), One Child	229L	
M	KRAVETZ	Shayndel	F				229L	
M	KRAVETZ	Shimon	M	Mordechai			228L	
M	KRAVETZ	Tzvia	F				229L	
M	KRAVETZ	Yehudis	F	Mordechai			228L	
M	KRAVETZ	Yeshaya	M				229L	
M	KRAVETZ	Luba	F	Hershele		Three Children	223R	
M	KRIBITZKY	Faygel	F		Yitzkhok		224R	Mother was Nechama
M	KRIBITZKY	Nechama	F	Yitzkhok	Aryeh	Faygel (F)	224R	
M	KUNITCH	Ita	F		the sexton		225L	Mother was Malka
M	KUNITCH	Malka	F			Ita(F), Sara(F)	225L	Wife of the sexton
M	KUNITCH	Sara	F		the sexton		225L	Mother was Malka
M	LAMDIN	Pesach	M		Eliyahu	Chashka Katzman(F)	229L	
M	LAPCHICK	Basya	F		Beinish KIRZNER	Three Children	225L	
M	LATOCHA	Akiva	M	Khysha		Three daughters	228L	
M	LATOCHA	Baruch	M	Golda		Two Daughters	231R	
M	LATOCHA	Basha	F	Zev			228L	
M	LATOCHA	Chava	F	Yeshaya		Gittel(F), Masha(F), Tzirel	227L	
M	LATOCHA	Gittel	F		Yeshaya		227L	
M	LATOCHA	Golda	F	Moshe		Chaya Kahan(F)	231R	
M	LATOCHA	Golda	F	Baruch		Two Daughters	231R	
M	LATOCHA	Khysha	F	Akiva		Three daughters	228L	
M	LATOCHA	Masha	F		Yeshaya		227L	
M	LATOCHA	Tzirel	F		Yeshaya		227L	
M	LATOCHA	Zev	M	Basha			228L	
M	LAZAVNICK	Baruch	M		Yacov		228L	
M	LAZAVNICK	Michlia	F	Moshe'ka		One Child	228L	
M	LAZAVNICK	Rayzel	F	Yacov		Sonya	228L	

M	LAZAVNICK	Sonya	F		Yacov	Two Children	228L	
M	LAZAVNICK	Yacov	M	Rayzel		Sonya(F), Esther Feldman(F), Baruch(M), Moshe'ka	228L	
M	LEVIN	Faygel	F		Yehuda		231R	
M	LEVIN	Sara Henya	F	Yehuda		Faygel	231R	
M	LEVIN	Yehuda	M	Sara Henya			231R	
M	LIFSHITZ	Fruma	F	Yakov	Moshe Reuven ZARETZKI	Laizer'ka (M)	225R	
M	LIFSHITZ	Laizer'ka	M		Yakov		225R	
M	LILENBERG	Baylka	F		Eliezer Chaim		224R	Mother is Nechama
M	LILENBERG	Nechama	F	Eliezer Chaim		Baylka (F)	224R	
M	LILENBERG	Sara Chana	F	Kalman			225L	
M	LUTZKY	Sara	F				232R	From Volka; Lived by Chanan Epstein
M	MACON	Alta	F	Mordechai		Basya(F), Fanya(F), Marisha(F)	231L	
M	MACON	Basya	F		Mordechai		231L	
M	MACON	Fanya	F		Mordechai		231L	
M	MACON	Marisha	F		Mordechai	One Child	231L	
M	MACON	Mordechai	M	Alta		Basya(F), Fanya(F), Marisha(F)	231L	
M	MARGOLIN	Berl	M				224R	Mother was Yentel MARGOLIN
M	MARGOLIN	Ber'la	M				224R	Mother was Liba MARGOLIN
M	MARGOLIN	Esther	F	Zelig	Gronem MIGDALOVICH	Three Children	225R	Daughter of Sara Tziril MIGDALOVICH
M	MARGOLIN	Liba	F			Aydel (F), Ber'la (M)	224R	
M	MARGOLIN	Lipa	M				224R	Mother was Yentel MARGOLIN
M	MARGOLIN	Yentel	F			Berl (M), Lipa (M)	224R	
M	MASLOV	Chaim	M		Yakov		231L	
M	MASLOV	Yakov	M	Yentl		Chaim	231L	

M	MASLOV	Yentl	F	Yakov		Chaim	231L	
M	MAYKIN	Khysha	F				223R	Mother is Osna MAYKIN
M	MAYKIN	Osna	F			Khysha(F)	223R	
M	MIGDALOVICH	Chana	F		Shmuel Yitzkhok		224R	Mother was Leah MIGDALOVICH
M	MIGDALOVICH	Chishka	F	Nachman		Four Daughters	224L	Her mother is Golda SCHNEIDMAN
M	MIGDALOVICH	Elyakim	M	Miriam (Mara)		Shachka (F), Shayndel (F)	224R	
M	MIGDALOVICH	Esther	F		Aharon		225L	Mother was Sara
M	MIGDALOVICH	Faygel	F		Gronem MIGDALOVICH		225R	
M	MIGDALOVICH	Leah	F	Shmuel Yitzkhok		Chana (F), Riva (F)	224R	Daughter of Lipa and Shayndel TEMKIN
M	MIGDALOVICH	Leah	F		Moshe Nissel		227R	
M	MIGDALOVICH	Manya	F	Moshe Nissel		Leah(F), Yentel(F)	227R	
M	MIGDALOVICH	Miriam (Mara)	F	Elyakim		Shachka (F), Shayndel (F)	224R	
M	MIGDALOVICH	Risha	F	Gronem		Berl	226R	
M	MIGDALOVICH	Riva	F		Shmuel Yitzkhok		224R	Mother was Leah MIGDALOVICH
M	MIGDALOVICH	Sara	F	Aharon		Esther	225L	
M	MIGDALOVICH	Sara Tziril	F	Gronem		Faygel (F), Necha (F),Esther (F)	225R	
M	MIGDALOVICH	Shachka	F		Elyakim		224R	Mother is Miriam
M	MIGDALOVICH	Shayndel	F		Elyakim	One child	224R	Other children survived?
M	MIGDALOVICH	Simka	F	Chaim-Yakov			225L	
M	MIGDALOVICH	Wife of Berl	F	Berl		Two Children	227L	
M	MIGDALOVICH	Yentel	F		Moshe Nissel		227R	
M	MIGDALOVICH	Avraham	M	Shayna		Ovadyahu(M), Rochel(F), Yenta(F)	229L	From Haritchinovitz
M	MIGDALOVICH	Ovadyahu	M		Avraham		229L	
M	MIGDALOVICH	Rochel	F		Avraham		229R	

M	MIGDALOVICH	Shayna	F	Avraham		Ovadyahu(M), Rochel(F), Yenta(F)	229L	
M	MIGDALOVICH	Yenta	F		Avraham		229R	
M	MIGDALOVICH	Duba	F	Moshe		Herzl(M), Sara(F), Velvel(M), Yossi(M), Somch(M)	230R	
M	MIGDALOVICH	Herzl	M		Moshe		230R	
M	MIGDALOVICH	Sara	F		Moshe		230R	
M	MIGDALOVICH	Somch	M		Moshe		230R	
M	MIGDALOVICH	Velvel	M		Moshe		230R	
M	MIGDALOVICH	Yossi	M		Moshe		230R	
M	MILLNER	Aharon	M	Channa		Dovid(M), Moshe(M)	229L	
M	MILLNER	Channa	F	Aharon		Dovid(M), Moshe(M)	229L	
M	MILLNER	Dovid	M		Aharon		229L	
M	MILLNER	Moshe	M		Aharon		229L	
M	MILLSTEIN	Fruma	F		Rabbi Moshe		225L	
M	MILLSTEIN	Hadassa	F		Rabbi Moshe		225L	
M	MILLSTEIN	Ita	F		Rabbi Moshe		225L	
M	MILLSTEIN	Rabbi Moshe	M	Rochel		Hadassa (F), Fruma (F), Yakov (M), Ita (F), Yitzkhok Hershele (M)	225L	
M	MILLSTEIN	Rochel	F	Rabbi Moshe		Hadassa (F), Fruma (F), Yakov (M), Ita (F), Yitzkhok Hershele (M)	225L	
M	MILLSTEIN	Yakov	M		Rabbi Moshe		225L	
M	MILLSTEIN	Yitzkhok Hershele	M		Rabbi Moshe		225L	
M	MINKAS	Unknown	M	Wife		Children	230L	Refugees
M	MINKAS	Wife	F	Unknown		Children	230L	Refugees
M	MISHELOV	Chisha	F	Moshe			232L	
M	MISHELOV	Esther	F	Mordechai		Malka(F)	228R	
M	MISHELOV	Malka	F		Mordechai		228R	
M	NOVICK	Alta	F	Moshe (The Cantor)		Golda (F), Sonia (F)	226L	Alta's Daughters

M	NOVICK	Golda	F		Unknown		226L	Alta's Daughter
M	NOVICK	Sonia	F		Unknown		226L	Alta's Daughter
M	PADARESKY	Basha	F	Unknown		Yosef(M), Yacov(M), Pesha(F), Ehska Rubenstein	229R	
M	PADARESKY	Faygel	F				229R	
M	PADARESKY	Pesha	F				229R	
M	PADARESKY	Riva	F	Chaim		Yosef(M)	229R	
M	PADARESKY	Yacov	M				229R	
M	PADARESKY	Yosef	M				229R	
M	PADARESKY	Yosef	M		Chaim		229R	
M	PAKAY	Unknown	M				231L	Refugee
M	PASETZKY	Chaya	F	Gershon		Daughter	230L	
M	PLAT	Chaya (GORODETSKI)	F	Nachman	Hirshl Leib (?)	Twin Sons	226L	
M	PLISFEDER	Yeva (Yokheved)	F				223L	Escaped From Warsaw
M	RABINOVITCH	Hinda	F	Berl		Two Children	227L	
M	RAPPAPORT	Shayna	F	Boma	Zalman BRESLER		224R	Mother was Etel
M	REICHMAN	Chayka (REINGOLD)	F	Hershl	Yitzkhok	Two Children	226R	
M	REINGOLD	Esther	F		Yitzkhok		226R	Mother was Golda
M	REINGOLD	Golda	F	Yitzkhok		Esther(F), Henya(F) (Her Daughters)	226R	
M	REINGOLD	Henya	F		Yitzkhok		226R	Mother was Golda
M	RIKLIN	Fraydel	F	Leib		Golda(F)	227L	
M	RIKLIN	Golda	F		Leib		227L	
M	ROVNITZ	Bashka	F	Shaul		Two Children	229R	
M	ROVNITZ	Shaul	M	Bashka		Two Children	229R	
M	RUBENSTEIN	Bashka	F	Mattityahu		Sima	230L	
M	RUBENSTEIN	Bella	F		Lipa		231R	From Mikishevitz
M	RUBENSTEIN	Chana	F	Shlomo		Shayndel (F)	224L	
M	RUBENSTEIN	Chana	F		Hershl		226R	
M	RUBENSTEIN	Eshka	F	Boaz			229R	

M	RUBENSTEIN	Esther	F	Hershl		Chana(F), Laybel(M), Lena (SHULLMAN)(F), another child	226R	
M	RUBENSTEIN	Itka	F		Noach		231R	
M	RUBENSTEIN	Khysha	F	Yosef			223L	
M	RUBENSTEIN	Laybel	M		Hershl		226R	
M	RUBENSTEIN	Leah	F	Lipa		Bella(F)	231R	
M	RUBENSTEIN	Lipa	M	Leah	Shamai	Bella(F)	231R	
M	RUBENSTEIN	Noach	M			Itka(F)	231R	
M	RUBENSTEIN	Rivka	F	Yehuda		Tilya (F)	224L	
M	RUBENSTEIN	Shamai	M			Lipa(M)	231R	
M	RUBENSTEIN	Shayndel	F		Shlomo	Eshka STAROBINSKI	224L	Daughter of Chana
M	RUBENSTEIN	Sima	F		Mattityahu		230L	
M	RUBENSTEIN	Tilya	F		Yehuda		224L	Mother is Rivka
M	RUBENSTEIN	Yosef	M	Khysha	Noach		223L	
M	ROVNITZ	Alter	M		Chaim Simcha		231R	
M	ROVNITZ	Chaim Simcha	M	Chana		Chaya Itya(F), Alter(M), Henya(F)	231R	
M	ROVNITZ	Chana	F	Chaim Simcha		Chaya Itya(F), Alter(M), Henya(F)	231R	
M	ROVNITZ	Chaya Itya	F		Chaim Simcha		231R	
M	ROVNITZ	Henya	F		Chaim Simcha		231R	
M	SADOVSKI	Chaya	F				225R	Daughter of Rochel
M	SADOVSKI	Esther	F	Eliyahu		Rochel (F)	225R	
M	SADOVSKI	Rochel	F	Unknown	Eliyahu	Chaya	225R	
M	SCHWARTZMAN	Breindel	F	Hershl	Alter Yulevich	Three Children	229R	
M	SEGALOVITCH	Bunya	F		Moshe'ka		230R	
M	SEGALOVITCH	Dvora	F	Moshe'ka		Henach	230R	
M	SEGALOVITCH	Henach	M				230R	
M	SEGALOVITCH	Moshe'ka	M	Dvora		Bunya	230R	
M	SHAPIRA	Avraham'l	M		Moshe		231L	
M	SHAPIRA	Luba	F	Moshe	Avraham Golob	Avraham'l	231L	
M	SHKLIAR	Aron	M	Chaya Rochel		Chiska(F), Esther Boiman(F)	232L	

M	SHKLIAR	Chaya Rochel	F	Aron		Chiska(F), Esther Boiman(F)	232L	
M	SHKLIAR	Chaya Sara	F	Yosef		Basha	225R	Basha wife of Duda GORODETSKI
M	SHKLIAR	Chiska	F		Aron	Two Children	232L	
M	SHKLIAR	Yosef	M	Chaya Sara	Aharon	Basha	225R	Basha wife of Duda GORODETSKI
M	SCHNEIDMAN	Chayka	F		Avraham	Two Children	224L	
M	SCHNEIDMAN	Golda	F		Avraham		224L	
M	SCHNEIDMAN	Sara Faygel	F	Avraham		Golda (F), Chayka (F)	224L	
M	SCHNEIDMAN	Wife	F	Simcha		Two Children	224L	
M	SHULLMAN	Adina	F		Moshe		226R	
M	SHULLMAN	Lena (RUBENSTEIN)	F	Moshe	Hershl	Adina	226R	
M	SHUSTER	Chaya Shayndel	F	Meir Ber			230R	
M	SHUSTER	Faygel	F		Sender	One Child	232L	
M	SHUSTER	Meir Ber	M	Chaya Shayndel			230R	
M	SHUSTER	Rivka-Rochel	F	Sender		Faygel	232L	
M	SCHUSTERMAN	Bayla	F	Yitzkhok	Mordechai	Five Children	228R	Also Bayla's Sister
M	SCHUSTERMAN	Dovid	M	Rochele			229L	
M	SCHUSTERMAN	Faygel	F	Dovid	Mordechai Schusterman	Three Children	230R	
M	SCHUSTERMAN	Hodel	F	Yitzkhok		Sonya	229L	
M	SCHUSTERMAN	Masha	F		Dovid		229L	
M	SCHUSTERMAN	Mordechai	M			Faygel Schusterman	230R	
M	SCHUSTERMAN	Rochel	F	Dovid			229L	
M	SCHUSTERMAN	Shimon	M		Dovid		229L	
M	SCHUSTERMAN	Shimon	M		Moshe Aharon		229L	
M	SCHUSTERMAN	Sonya	F		Yitzkhok		229L	
M	SCHUSTERMAN	Wife of Moshe	F	Moshe		Two Children	230R	

M	SCHUSTERMAN	Zlata	F	Moshe Aharon		Shimon(M)	229L	
M	SHUB	Channa	F		Yosef		228L	
M	SHUB	Faygel	F	Yosef		Channa(F), Hershle	228L	
M	SHUB	Hershle	M		Yosef		228L	
M	SHVERIN	Elka	F	Chaim		Faygel(F), Sara(F), Rochel(F) (Her Daughters)	226R	
M	SHVERIN	Faygel	F		Chaim		226R	
M	SHVERIN	Rochel	F		Chaim		226R	
M	SHVERIN	Sara	F		Chaim		226R	
M	SLUCHAK	Chashe	F			One Girl, One Boy	231R	
M	SLUTSKY	Chaim	M	Chaya	Aharon	Chisha	227R	
M	SLUTSKY	Chana	F	Hershele			223R	
M	SLUTSKY	Chaya	F	Boruch	Zelig	Daughter	223R	
M	SLUTSKY	Chaya	F	Chaim		Chisa	227R	
M	SLUTSKY	Chayka	F		Yeshaya	Two Children	224R	Other children survived? Mother was Faygel
M	SLUTSKY	Chisa	F		Chaim		227R	
M	SLUTSKY	Dvosha	F		Meyer		224R	Mother was Nechama
M	SLUTSKY	Elka	F		Yeshaya		224R	Mother was Faygel
M	SLUTSKY	Faygel	F	Yeshaya		Chayka (F), Elka (F), Yenta (F)	224R	
M	SLUTSKY	Fraidel (Franya)	F				223R	
M	SLUTSKY	Fruma	F	Gronem			227R	
M	SLUTSKY	Gershon	M	Rochel	Nachum	Yenta	225R	
M	SLUTSKY	Nechama	F	Meyer		Riva (F), Dvosha (F)	224R	
M	SLUTSKY	Riva	F		Meyer		224R	Mother was Nechama
M	SLUTSKY	Rochel	F	Gershon		Yenta	225R	
M	SLUTSKY	Sara Faigel	F				225R	
M	SLUTSKY	Wife	F	Yitzkhok (Itchka)			225L	

M	SLUTSKY	Yenta	F		Yeshaya		224R	Mother was Faygel
M	SLUTSKY	Yenta	F	Unknown	Gershon	Two Children	225R	
M	SLUTSKY	Yeshaya	M	Faygel	Aharon	Chayka (F), Elka (F), Yenta (F)	224R	
M	SLUTSKY	Freydel	F		Yisroel Slutsky		231L	Daughter of Tema Chinitch
M	SLUTSKY	Second Wife	F	Asher		One Child	230R	Second Wife of Asher
M	SLUTSKY	Yenta	F		Yisroel Slutsky		231L	Daughter of Tema Chinitch
M	STAROBINSKI	Betzalel	M	Yenta			230R	
M	STAROBINSKI	Eshka	F	Binyamin		Shulamis (F), Avram'l (M)	224L	Daughter of Shayndel RUBENSTEIN
M	STAROBINSKI	Yenta	F	Betzalel			230R	
M	STRIGATCH	Basha	F		Baruch		230R	
M	STRIGATCH	Chaya	F	Feivel		Gittel(F)	227L	
M	STRIGATCH	Feivel	M	Chaya		Gittel(F), Mirel(F), Nechama(F)	227L	
M	STRIGATCH	Gittel	F		Feivel	Two Children	227L	
M	STRIGATCH	Leibel	M		Baruch		230R	
M	STRIGATCH	Mirel	F		Feivel	One Child	227L	
M	STRIGATCH	Nechama	F		Feivel		227L	
M	STRIGATCH	Rayzel	F	Baruch		Leibel(M), Zalman(M), Basha(F)	230R	
M	STRIGATCH	Zalman	M		Baruch		230R	
M	TANIS	Nachum	M	Sonia			226L	
M	TANIS	Sonia	F	Nachum			226L	
M	TEMKIN	Hershele	M		Chaim-David		226L	Hinda's son
M	TEMKIN	Hinda	F	Chaim-David		Hershele (Her Son)	226L	
M	TEMKIN	Wife	F	Izel		One child	226L	
M	TEMKIN	Doba	F		Nechemia	One Child	225L	
M	TEMKIN	Faygel	F	Hershele		Two Children	228R	Leah Kolpanitsky's Daughter
M	TEMKIN	Feygel	F	Dovid			231L	
M	TEMKIN	Lipa	M	Shayndel		Leah (F)	224R	Riva married to Shmuel Yitzkhok MIGDALOVICH

M	TEMKIN	Shayndel	F	Lipa		Leah (F)	224R	Riva married to Shmuel Yitzkhok MIGDALOVICH
M	TOPCHIK	Baruch	M		Yakov		230L	
M	TOPCHIK	Eliyahu	M		Yakov		230L	
M	TOPCHIK	Esther	F		Benya		225L	Mother was Itka
M	TOPCHIK	Itka	F	Benya	Nissen	Esther	225L	
M	TOPCHIK	Miriam	F		Yakov		230L	
M	TOPCHIK	Miriam	F		Lipa		230L	
M	TOPCHIK	Riva	F	Yakov		Shlomo, Zelig, Baruch, Eliyahu, Miriam	230L	
M	TOPCHIK	Sara	F	Lipa	Dov	Miriam	230L	
M	TOPCHIK	Shlomo	M		Yakov		230L	
M	TOPCHIK	Zelig	M		Yakov		230L	
M	TZIGLIG	Adel	F		Eliyahu	Two Girls	229R	
M	TZIGLIG	Baruch	M	Sonya		One Child	230L	
M	TZIGLIG	Chaya Leah	F	Eliyahu			229R	
M	TZIGLIG	Sonya	F	Baruch	Chanan Eptsein	One Child	230L	
M	TZIGLIG	Basya	F		Mordechai		223L	Daughter of Rochel
M	TZIGLIG	Brocho	F		Yakov		226L	
M	TZIGLIG	Eliyahu	M	Gittel	Yosef		223L	
M	TZIGLIG	Elka	F		Leib		223L	
M	TZIGLIG	Gettele	F		Gedalyahu (?)		226R	Daughter of Rochel
M	TZIGLIG	Gittel	F	Eliyahu			223L	
M	TZIGLIG	Itka	F	David		Zelig(M)	227L	
M	TZIGLIG	Leib	M		Yosef	Sheindl(F), Elka(F)	223L	
M	TZIGLIG	Moishele	M		Gedalyahu (?)		226R	Son of Rochel
M	TZIGLIG	Mordechai	M	Rochel	Yosef	Basya (F)	223L	
M	TZIGLIG	Mordechai Leib	M				226R	
M	TZIGLIG	Risha	F	Yeshaya	Shimshon CHINITCH		224L	Mother is Miriam
M	TZIGLIG	Rochel	F	Mordechai		Basya (F)	223L	
M	TZIGLIG	Rochel	F	Gedalyahu	Yakov	Moishele (Her Son), Gittele (Her Daughter)	226R	
M	TZIGLIG	Sheindl	F		Leib		223L	

M	TZIGLIG	Wife	F	Yehuda		Two Children	223L	Yehuda, Son of Leib
M	TZIGLIG	Yakov	M		Boruch	Brocho (F), Rochel (F)	226L	
M	TZIGLIG	Yenta Rochel	F	Zelig			226R	
M	TZIGLIG	Zelig	M		David		227L	
M	TZUKROVITZ	Fraydel	F	Moshe	Zelig Gelanson	Two Daughters	229L	
M	TZUKROVITZ	Chisha	F	Leib	Alter Yulevich	One Child	229R	
M	TZUKROVITZ	Feigel	F				227R	
M	TZUKROVITZ	Itka Tzirel	F				227R	
M	TZUKROVITZ	Lifsha	F	Dovid			228R	
M	TZUKROVITZ	Sara	F			Itka Tzirel(F), Feigel(F), Feivel	227R	
M	TZUKROVITZ	Wife of Feivel	F	Feivel		One Child	227R	
M	UNKNOWN	Masha	F			One Child	227L	Wife of German, Sister of Sabina. Both From Warsaw
M	UNKNOWN	Pesha	F				227R	Mother of Necha Harfon
M	UNKNOWN	Sabina	F				227L	Sister of Masha. Both From Warsaw
M	UNKNOWN	Sister	F				228R	Sister of Bayla Schusterman
M	UNKNOWN	Chanche	F				231L	Sister of Galya
M	VILK (BLECHER)	Frayda	F	Yitzkhok		Two Children	226R	
M	VILK (BLECHER)	Yitzkhok	M	Frayda		Two Children	226R	
M	WINIK	Feyvel	M		Masha's Son		231L	
M	WINIK	Galya	F				231L	
M	WINIK	Itka	F			Masha	231L	
M	WINIK	Masha	F	Tuvya		Sonya, Feyvel	231L	
M	WINIK	Ovadyahu	M	Galya		Yentl Maslov	231L	
M	WINIK	Sonya	F		Tuvya		231L	
M	WINIK	Tuvya	M	Masha		Sonya	231L	
M	WANDEROV	Faygel	F	Berel		Moshe(M), Hinde(F)	228R	
M	WANDEROV	Hinde	F		Berel		228R	
M	WANDEROV	Moshe	M		Berel		228R	

M	WARSHAL	Dvora	F		Shlomo Nisson	Three Children	230L	
M	WARSHAL	Freidka	F	Yitzkhok			232L	
M	WARSHAL	Miriam	F	Yitzkhok		Shulamis	230L	
M	WARSHAL	Rochel Leah	F	Shlomo Nisson			230L	
M	WARSHAL	Shulamis	F		Yitzkhok		230L	
M	YOSELEVSKY	Nesha	F	Unknown	Dovid Schusterman	Teibele	229L	
M	YOSELEVSKY	Teibele	F		Unknown		229L	
M	YULEVICH	Alter	M	Simka		Shaynka(F), Breindel Schwartzman(F), Chisha Tzukrovitz(F)	229R	
M	YULEVICH	Faygel	F	Dovid		Four Children	231R	
M	YULEVICH	Noach	M	Riva			231R	
M	YULEVICH	Riva	F	Noach			231R	
M	YULEVICH	Shaynka	F		Alter	Two Children	229R	
M	YULEVICH	Simka	F	Alter		Shaynka(F), Breindel Schwartzman(F), Chisha rTzrukovich(F)	229R	
M	YULEVICH	Golda	F	Nachum Nossen		Minya	224L	
M	YULEVICH	Minya	F		Nachum Nossen	Three Children	224L	
M	YULEVICH	Nachum Nossen	M	Golda		Minya	224L	
M	ZARETZKI	Hasha	F	Eliyahu-Aron			227R	
M	ZARETZKI	Lipka	F	Moshe Reuven		Fruma LIFSHITZ (F)	225R	
M	ZARETZKI	Moshe Reuven	M	Lipka		Fruma LIFSHITZ (F)	225R	
M	ZARETZKI	Necha	F	Yosef			228R	
M	ZARETZKI	Yosef	M	Necha			228R	
M	ZAICHIK	Aharon Leib	M	Rishka		Bayla (F), Batya (F)	224L	
M	ZAICHIK	Batya	F		Aharon Leib		224L	
M	ZAICHIK	Bayla	F		Aharon Leib		224L	
M	ZAICHIK	Elka	F		Betzalel		223R	
M	ZAICHIK	Guta	F		Laybel		227R	
M	ZAICHIK	Hillel	M				227R	

M	ZAICHIK	Hindl	F		Betzalel		223R	
M	ZAICHIK	Laybel	M			Guta(F), Lipka(F), Osna(F), Shifra(F)	227R	
M	ZAYTTCHIK	Lipka	F		Laybel		227R	
M	ZAICHIK	Osna	F		Laybel		227R	
M	ZAICHIK	Rishka	F	Aharon Leib	Isaac (Unknown)	Bayla (F), Batya (F)	224L	
M	ZAICHIK	Sara	F		Lipa		226L	Daughter of Lipa
M	ZAICHIK	Shaindel	F	Lipa			226L	
M	ZAICHIK	Shayndel	F	Moshe			227L	
M	ZAICHIK	Shifra	F		Laybel		227R	
M	ZAVIN	Aydel	F	Velvel			224R	Mother was Liba MARGOLIN
M	ZAVIN	Bracha (BAVKIN)	F	Avrom	Kalman		223L	Daughter of Vichna BAVKIN
M	ZAVIN	Kalman	M		Avrom		223L	Son of Bracha
M	ZAVIN	Laibel	M		Manus		225R	
M	ZAVIN	Manus	M	Riva		Laibel (M), Sonia (F)	225R	
M	ZAVIN	Riva	F	Manus		Laibel (M), Sonia (F)	225R	
M	ZAVIN	Sonia	F	Unknown	Manus ZAVIN	Three Children	225R	
M	TZUKROVITZ	Fayvel	M	Tzyrka	Dov	Three Sons	223R	
M	TZUKROVITZ	Hinde	F	Dovid Sholom		Four Daughters	223R	
M	TZUKROVITZ	Tzyrka	F	Fayvel		Three Sons	223R	
S	TZUKROVITZ	Feivel	M	Wife		One Child	227R	
W	SLUTSKY	Dina	F	Asher		Two Children	230R	First Wife of Asher

[Pages 232-233]

Lenin – the Community Register

Notes For Column Headings:

1. Code – M=Martyr; H=Husband, W=Wife, F=Father, Mo=Mother, S=Son, D=Daughter, Presumed Survivors.

2. Family Name – Married Name (last name of husband) for women if known, otherwise maiden name. In cases where only the woman's name is given, I have assumed it is her married name and the children carry that family name. In some cases the text of the original Martyrs List is unclear as to an individual's relationships. I have made a best guess based on context contained in the text. (For instance: B daughter of A and C her son. Is he A's or B's son?). If the text states "X, wife of Y", I have assumed X was martyred and Y survived. If family name is not given it is listed as Unknown Or Unknown.

3. First name – First name + female maiden name if known.

4. Children's Names – Children listed by first name. If names are unknown they are listed as "four sons," etc.

5. Children, spouses, fathers also listed separately by their first name. Presumed survivors are also listed separately for cross referencing purposes using their Code – H,W,F,Mo,S,D.

6. Page # – Page number of listing in translation of the original Lenin Yizkor Book. For instance: 223L = Page 223 left column; 226R = Page 226 right column. Note: Translation left column = original Hebrew right column.

7. Comments – Other information in original text or cross-reference information.

8. Other Abreviations – (Unknown or Unknown) Unknown First or Family name.

9. Please communicate to the Yizkor Book Project any corrections to the assumptions of relationships or survival.

Sanford A. Kaplan

Lenin – the Community Register

Part B. Jewish Partisans from Lenin who fell in battle, perished in the Ghettos and in locations outside of Lenin

Prepared by: Mordechai Zaichik

Code	Family name	First name	Gender	Spouse name	Father	Children's names	Page ref. #	Comments (Place where Killed)
M	ABRAMOWITZ	Esther	F	(Abramowitz)	Mordechai		233L	Mikishewitz
M	BAVKIN	Moishe'le	M		Nossin		232L	in battle
M	BERGMAN	Avrom'l	M		Nissen		232R	with the withdrawal of the Russian troops
M	BRESLER	Dovid	M		Zalman		232R	Koranitch
M	CHINITCH	Tema	F		Leibah (mother)		233R	Pinsk?
M	GELANSON	Yeshayhu	M		Zelig		233R	Baranovich
M	GINSBERG	Boruch	M		Eliyahu		233R	Baranovich
M	GINSBERG	Channa	F		Yosef		233R	Brisk
M	GINSBERG	Michal	M		Yosef		233R	Brisk

M	GOLOB	Bayla	F			Avrom		233R	Baranovich
M	GUREVICH	Yitzkhok	M			Yakov		233R	in battle
M	HARFON	Eliyahu	M			Moshe Nissen		233L	in battle
M	KAMINSKY	Shmuel	M					233R	
M	KAPLAN	Yakov	M			Nossin Bavkin, father-in-law		232L	in battle
M	KIRZNER	Aron	M			Dovid		233L	in battle
M	KIRZNER	Avrem'l	M			Dovid		233L	in battle
M	KOLPANITSKY	Yitzkhok	M			Leah (mother)		233R	In German Captivity
M	KRAVETZ	Hershele	M			Yehuda		233L	in battle
M	MANDELBAUM	Yitzkhok	M			Mordechai		233L	Pinsk
M	MIGDALOVICH	Aron'ke	M	Malka		Rozhka		233R	Mikishewitz
M	MIGDALOVICH	Ben Zion	M			Rozhka		233R	Pinsk
M	MIGDALOVICH	Chaim	M			Hirshl		233L	Lachwa mother Liba
M	MIGDALOVICH	Feivel	M			Aron		232R	Yanov near Sokolky
M	MIGDALOVICH	Gittel	F			Rozhka		233R	Rovna
M	MIGDALOVICH	Hershka	M			Moshe Nissen		232L	with withdrawal of the Russian troops
M	MIGDALOVICH	Hirshl	M			Chaim Beryl	Tuvya, Chaim	233L	in battle
M	MIGDALOVICH	Liba (Shub)	F	Hirshl			Tuvya, Chaim	233L	Lachwa
M	MIGDALOVICH	Malka	F	Aron'ka				233R	Mikishewitz
M	MIGDALOVICH	Tuvya	M			Hirshl		233L	Lachwa mother Liba
M	MIGDALOVICH	Yisrolik	M					233R	Pinsk
M	MIGDALOVICH	Yitzkhok	M			Elyakim		232R	in battle
M	MISHELOV	Pesil	F			Mordechai		233R	
M	PADARESKY	Chaim	M			Yosef		233R	with the withdrawel of the Russians
M	REINGOLD	Eliyahu Aron	M			Yitzkhok		233L	in battle
M	RIVLIN	Sonya (Mandelbaum)	F	(Rivlin)		Mordechai		233L	Mikishewitz

M	RUBENSTEIN	Isaac	M		Noach		233R	Starobin
M	RUBENSTEIN	Lipa	M		Shayma		233L	Mikishewitz
M	ROVNITZ	Yisroel	M		Shaul		233R	in battle
M	SCHNEIDMAN	Fayvel	M		Avrom		232L	in battle
M	SCHNEIDMAN	Zhama	M		Avrom		232R	In German Captivity
M	SHUSTER	Zelig	M		Sender		233R	In German Captivity
M	SCHUSTERMAN	Moshe	M		Mordechai		233R	in battle
M	SLUTSKY	Eliyahu	M		Chaim		232R	in battle
M	SLUTSKY	Feivel	M		Nachum		233L	Mikishewitz
M	SLUTSKY	Gronem	M		Nachum		233L	Khvorostov
M	SLUTSKY	Khaya	F		Chaim		233L	Warsaw
M	SLUTSKY	Vitsha	M		Chaim		233L	Pinsk
M	STAROBINSKI	Ephraim	M				233R	Davidhorodok
M	STAROBINSKI	Gronem	M				233R	Lachwa
M	STRIGATCH	Manya	F		Feivel		233L	Pinsk
M	TEMKIN	Hershl	M		Sarah, Mother		232L	in battle
M	TEMKIN	Yitzkhok	M		Lipa		232R	in battle
M	TZIGLIG	Ben-Zion	M		Mordechai		232L	Horodisht
M	TZIGLIG	Betzalel	M		Leibeh, Mother		232L	in battle
M	TZIGLIG	Boruch	M		Mordechai Leib		233R	Hantzevich
M	TZIGLIG	Faygel (Weisblat)	M	Yeshaya			233L	Mikishewitz
M	TZIGLIG	Shlomo	M		Mordechai		233R	in battle
M	TZIGLIG	Yakov (Yatsha)	M		Mordechai		233R	in battle
M	TZIGLIG	Yeshaya	M		Eliyahu		232L	in battle
M	TZIGLIG	Yeshaya	M	Faygel	Zelig		233L	Mikishewitz
M	TZIGLIG	Yisroelik	M		Mordechai		232L	in battle
M	TZIGLIG	Yoel	M		Mordechai		233R	in battle
M	TZUKROVITZ	Leibel	M		Dov		232L	In German Captivity
M	TZUKROVITZ	Feivel	M		Sara, mother		233L	Khvorostov
M	WEISBLAT	Alte	F	Aron Moshe		Sender, Berl	232R	Mikishewitz
M	WEISBLAT	Berl	M		Aron Moshe		233L	Mikishewitz

M	WEISBLAT	Sẹnder	M		Aron Moshe		233L	in battle
M	WINIK	Laybel	M		Itka		233R	Luninyetz
M	WINIK	Leivick	M	Shayndel	Ovadyahu		233R	Mikishewitz
M	WINIK	Nachman	M		Ovadyahu		233R	in battle
M	WINIK	Shayndel(Tziglig)	M	Leivick			233R	Mikishewitz
M	WINIK	Tuvyah	M		Itka		233R	Davidhorodok
M	YULEVICH	Shmuel	M		Nachum Nossen		232R	Lachwa
M	ZARETZKI	Children			Vitsha (mother)	Unknown	233L	Pinsk
M	ZARETZKI	Vitsha	F		Moshe Reuven		233L	Kvotiok-Pinsk
M	ZARETZKI	Eliezer	M		Yosef		233L	Busko Zadroy
M	ZAVIN	Avrem'l	M		Manos		233L	in battle
M	ZAICHIK	Moshe	M		Aharon Leib		232L	Kremnitz
M	ZAICHIK	Moshe Dovid	M		Leibel		233L	in battle

[Pages 234-235]

Lenin – the Community Register

Part C. Jewish Partisans from Lenin who fell in battle with the Nazis in the forests of White Russi

Prepared by: Mordechai Zaichik

Code	Family name	First name	Gender	Spouse name	Father	Children's names	Page ref. #	Comments
M	BEHON	Eisel (Isaac)	M		Chaim		234R	
M	BARUCHIN	Mottel (Mordechai)	M		Dov		234R	
M	DRUGGIST, THE	Son of	M		The Druggist		235L	
M	DVORIN	Yerachmiel	M				234R	
M	EPSTEIN	Chanan	M				235L	
M	FIXMAN	Gedalyahu	M				234R	
M	GELANSON	Chaim	M		Kusha		235L	
M	GELANSON	Laizer	M		Kusha		235L	
M	GELANSON	Leyba	M		Kusha		235L	

M	GELANSON	Mendel	M		Kusha		235L	
M	GELANSON	Moshe	M		Zelig		234R	
M	GELANSON	Shlomo	M		Kusha		235L	
M	GLEIBERMAN	Asher	M				234L	
M	GOLDMAN	Hershel	M	Yocha			234L	
M	GOLDMAN	Yisroel	M				234R	Naphtali Kravetz father-in-law
M	GOLOB	Laizer (Eliezer)	M			Yitzkhok, Pinya (Pinchas)	235L	
M	GOLOB	Pinya (Pinchas)	M		Laizer (Eliezer)		235L	
M	GOLOB	Yitzkhok	M		Laizer (Eliezer)		235L	
M	GORODETSKI	Yisroel	M		Moshinke		235L	
M	GRUSHKE	Chanan	M		Son-in-law of Sender		235R	
M	GUREVICH	Binya	M		Yakov		235R	
M	GUREVICH	Yakov	M			Binya	235R	
M	HUBERMAN	Unknown	M				235R	Refugee
M	ISERS	Ephraim	M		Yisroel Aron		235L	
M	ISERS	Gilek	F	Nishka			235R	
M	KAPLAN	Gedalyahu	M				235L	
M	KATZMAN	Yisroel	M		Oesach Lamdin's son-in-law		235R	
M	KENDELMAN	Unknown	M				235R	Refugee
M	KIRSCHENZWEIG	Eliezer	M				234R	
M	KLIGER	Unknown	M				234L	Refugee from Warsaw
M	KOLPANITSKY	Eliezer Aron	M		Yitzkhok		235R	
M	KRAVETZ	Avrom'l	M		Leivik		235L	
M	KRAVETZ	Chaim	M		Yehuda		235R	
M	KRAVETZ	Kushe (Yekutiel)	M		Leivik		235L	
M	KRAVETZ	Yakov	M		Naphtali		234R	
M	KRIBITZKY	Yakov	M		Yitzkhok		234L	
M	KRIBITZKY	Yitzkhok	M			Yakov	234L	
M	KURZNER	Mordechai	M				235R	

M	LAPCHICK	Hershel	M				234R	
M	LATOCHA	Yeshayahu	M				234R	
M	LATOCHA	Dovid	M				235R	Fell in battle in Berlin, after being released from the Partisans
M	LILENBERG	Eliezer Chaim	M				234L	
M	MACON	Yitzkhok	M		Esna		234L	
M	MARGOLIN	Zelig	M		Liba		234R	
M	MIGDALOVICH	Mendele	M				235R	
M	MIGDALOVICH	Shmuel Yitzkhok	M		Gronem		234R	
M	MISHELOV	Lipa	M		Moshe		235L	
M	MISHELOV	Shakhne	M		Mordechai		235L	
M	MISHELOV	Shmulik	M		Mordechai		235L	
M	NOVICK	Dovid	M		Moshe		234R	Fell in battle after leaving the partisans
M	PARETSKY	Laizer	M		Gershon		235L	
M	PARPLIUCHIK	Nachum	M				235R	Fell in battle after being released from the Partisans
M	RABINOVITCH	Nissel	M		Eliezer		234R	
M	RUBENSTEIN	Boaz	M		Noach		234R	
M	RUBENSTEIN	Laizer (Eliezer)	M		Matityahu		235L	
M	RUBENSTEIN	Matityahu	M			Laizer (Eliezer)	234R	
M	RUBENSTEIN	Yehuda	M		Shlomo		234L	
M	RUBENSTEIN	Isaac	M		Hershel		234R	
M	RUBENSTEIN	Moshe	M		Hershel		234R	
M	ROVNITZ	Eliyahu	M		Shaul		235R	
M	SADOVSKI	Hershel	M		Eliyahu		234L	
M	SCHWARTZMAN	Hershel	M				235L	
M	SCHWARTZMAN	Leibel	M		Yosef		235R	Fell in battle after being released from the Partisans

M	SEGALOVITCH	Eliyahu	M		Moshe		235L	
M	SHAPIRA	Moshe'le	M	Luba Golob			235L	
M	SCHNEIDMAN	Simcha	M		Avraham		234L	
M	SHUSTER	Avrom'l	M		Sender		235R	
M	SHUSTER	Baruch	M		Meir Beryl		234L	
M	SHUSTER	Baruch	M		Yehuda		234R	
M	SHUSTER	Mottel (Mordechai)	M		Meir Beryl		234L	
M	SHUSTER	Sender	M		Chaim	Avrom'l, Chanan Grushke (Son-in-law)	235R	
M	SHUSTER	Shmuel	M		Meir Beryl		234L	
M	SCHUSTERMAN	Dovid	M		Mordechai		234R	
M	SLUCHAK	Yitzkhok	M				234L	
M	SLUTSKY	Ahar'tche	M		Elyakim		234L	
M	SLUTSKY	Baruch	M		Aharon	Moshe, Zelig	234L	
M	SLUTSKY	Elyakim	M		Aharon		234L	
M	SLUTSKY	Hershel	M		Elyakim		234L	
M	SLUTSKY	Lipa	M		Elyakim		234L	
M	SLUTSKY	Moshe	M		Baruch		234L	
M	SLUTSKY	Yehiel	M		Chaim		234L	
M	SLUTSKY	Yeshayahu	M		Elyakim		234L	
M	SLUTSKY	Yitzkhok	M		Yeshayahu		234L	
M	SLUTSKY	Zelig	M		Baruch		234L	
M	STAROBINSKI	Benyamin	M				234L	
M	STRIGATCH	Bonya (Baruch)	M		Feivel		234R	
M	TEDELIS	Chaim	M				234L	Leib Tziglig father-in-law
M	TOMCHIN	Isaac	M		Chaim Dovid		234R	
M	TZIGLIG	Bonya (Baruch)	M		Dovid		234R	
M	TZIGLIG	Eliyahu	M			Yeshaya	235L	
M	TZIGLIG	Yakov	M		Leib		234L	
M	TZIGLIG	Yeshaya	M		Eliyahu		235L	
M	TZIGLIG	Gedalyahu	M		Yakov		235R	Fell in battle after being released

								from the Partisans
M	TZUKROVITZ	Moshe	M		Dov		234L	
M	VARSHEL	Yitzkhok	M		Shlomo Nisson		235L	
M	VILK	Ephraim	M		Yitzkhok		234R	
M	VILK	Hanekh	M		Yitzkhok		234R	
M	YULEVICH	"Rikas" Rika	F	Leizerke			235R	
M	YULEVICH	Leizerke	M	"Rikas" Rika			235R	
M	YULEVICH	Shmuel	M		Mother Dvora		235R	9 months old
M	ZARETZKI	Shmuel	M		Moshe-Reuven		234R	
M	ZARETZKI	Zaber	M	Bracha			235R	
M	ZAVIN	Velvel (Zev)	M		Manos		234R	

Lenin – the Community Register

Presumed Surviving Relatives

Notes For Column Headings:

1. Code – M=Martyr; H=Husband, W=Wife, F=Father, Mo=Mother, S=Son, D=Daughter, Presumed Survivors.
2. Family Name – Married Name (last name of husband) for women if known, otherwise maiden name. In cases where only the woman's name is given, I have assumed it is her married name and the children carry that family name. In some cases the text of the original Martyrs List is unclear as to an individual's relationships. I have made a best guess based on context contained in the text. (For instance: B daughter of A and C her son. Is he A's or B's son?). If the text states "X, wife of Y", I have assumed X was martyred and Y survived. If family name is not given it is listed as Unknown Or Unknown.
3. First name – First name + female maiden name if known.
4. Children's Names – Children listed by first name. If names are unknown they are listed as "four sons," etc.
5. Children, spouses, fathers also listed separately by their first name. Presumed survivors are also listed separately for cross referencing purposes using their Code – H,W,F,Mo,S,D.
6. Page # – Page number of listing in translation of the original Lenin Yizkor Book. For instance: 223L = Page 223 left column; 226R = Page 226 right column. Note: Translation left column = original Hebrew right column.
7. Comments – Other information in original text or cross-reference information.
8. Other Abreviations – (Unknown or Unknown) Unknown First or Family name.

9. Please communicate to the Yizkor Book Project any corrections to the assumptions of relationships or survival.

Sanford A. Kaplan

[Pages 223-232]

Lenin – the Community Register

Part A. The Martyrs of Lenin, who were murdered by the Germans on the 2nd day of Elul - August 14, 1942

Listed below are names of presumed surviving relatives used to identify martyrs

Prepared by: M. Zaichik, Lipa Mishelov, Masha Slutsky

Code	Family name	First name	Gender	Spouse name	Father	Children's names	Page ref. #	Comments
D	YULEVICH	Macha	F			Minya(F)	229R	
D	YULEVICH	Minya	F			Daughter	229R	
F	BERGMAN	Nissen	M			Brocha(F), Chinka(F)	225L	
F	GINSBERG	Asher	M			Khisha(F),	228R	
F	GINSBERG	Asher	M			Eliyahu	232L	
F	GOLOB	Avram Yitzkhok	M			Moshe	225L	
F	GOLOB	Chaim	M				226R	
F	GOLOB	Chaim	M			Miriam (Mera)	232R	
F	GORODETSKI	Yisroel	M			Two Children	231R	
F	GUREVICH	Moshe	M			Mordechai	227L	
F	KANIK	Daniol	M			Basha	226R	
F	KIRZNER	Yakov	M			Rochel(F)	231R	
F	LAMDIN	Eliyahu	M			Pesach(M)	229L	
F	RUBENSTEIN	Noach	M			Yosef (M)	223L	
F	SCHUSTERMAN	Mordechai	M				228R	
F	SLUTSKY	Aharon	M			Chaim	227R	
F	SLUTSKY	Nachum	M			Gershon	225R	
F	SLUTSKY	Nachum	M			Gronem	227R	

F	SLUTSKY	Yeshaya	M			Yitzkhok (Itchka)	225L	Yeshaya from Hariznovitz
F	TEMKIN	Nechemia	M			Doba (F)	225L	
F	TEMKIN	Nechemia	M			Two Children	228L	
F	TZIGLIG	Yosef	M			Mordechai (M), Leib (M), Eliyahu (M)	223L	
F	UNKNOWN	Chaim Dovid	M			Shaynka Chinitch(F)	230L	
F	UNKNOWN	Dov	M			Sara	230L	
F	UNKNOWN	Isaac	M			Rishka Zaichik (F)	224L	
F	UNKNOWN	Zelig	M			Chaya Slutsky (F)	223R	
F	ZAICHIK	Betzalel	M			Elka (F), Hindl (F)	223R	
F	TZUKROVITZ	Dov	M			Fayvel (M)	223R	
H	BARUCHIN	Mordechai	M	Alta		Ephraim	228L	
H	BAVKIN	Kalman	M			Vichna (F)	223L	
H	BEHON	Eizel	M	Zissel		Eshka(F), Shprintza(F), Sara(F), Velvel(M), Mendel(M), Shmuel(M), Two more children	227R	
H	BOIMAN	Unknown	M	Esther		One Child	232L	
H	BRESLER	Zalmon	M	Etel		Shayna (F), Meyer (M), Yitzkhok (M)	224R	
H	CHINITCH	Fayvel	M	Shaynka		One Child	230L	
H	CHINITCH	Shimshon	M	Miriam (Mara)		Esther Dvora (F), Risha (F)	224L	
H	CHINITCH	Yisroel	M	Yocheved (Yocha)		Tcharna	228L	
H	GACHMAN	Unknown	M	Masha			231L	
H	GELANSON	Moshe'ke	M	Faygel		Two Little Girls	230L	
H	GELANSON	Shlomo	M	Sara		Two Children	228R	
H	GINSBERG	Yitzkhok	M	Wife	Yosef	Four Children	228R	
H	GLEIBERMAN	Asher	M	Bayla		Miriam(F), Chama(F), Beba(F)	223R	
H	GOLDMAN	Hershl	M	Yokheved Rasamakha		Chaimke	225L	
H	GOLDMAN	Yisroel	M	Dvora			229L	
H	GOLOB	Asher	M	Rochel Vitzerbin			231L	
H	GOLOB	Avraham	M	Masha		Luba Shapira	231L	
H	GOLOB	Moshe	M	Lena	Avram Yitzkhok	Two Children	225L	

H	GORODETSKI	Duda	M	Basha		One Child	225R	
H	GORODETSKI	Hirshl Leib	M	Ethel		Avrom"l (Her Son), Chaia (her Daughter)	226L	
H	GUREVICH	Yakov	M	Chaya		Four Children	232R	
H	HABERMAN	Unknown		Wife			223L	From Poland
H	HOLTZMAN	Shmuel	M	Tziril		Two Children	230L	
H	HARFON	Eliyahu	M	Necha		Laybel(M), Moshe(M), Hershl(M), one more child	227R	
H	HARFON	Sender	M	Sonia		One Son, Four Daughters	226L	
H	KAHAN	Unknown	M	Chaya		Moshe(M)	231R	
H	KANDELSTEIN	Unknown	M	Busha		One Child	232L	
H	KANITZ	Sholem	M	Itka		Four Children	223R	
H	KAPLAN	Asher	M	Golda		Tsila(F)	223R	
H	KAPLAN	Gedalya	M	Chana Basha		Esther(F), Nesha(F)	230L	
H	KIRZNER	Dovid	M	Esther		Chaya(Her Daughter), One son	226R	
H	KIRZNER	Mordechai	M	Tzirka		Three Children	228R	
H	KIRZNER	Nachman	M	Bayla		Three Children	225L	
H	KONICK	Leib	M	Chaya Elka			230R	
H	KOROVOCHKA	Nossen Yitzkhok	M	Simka		Chisha	225R	Nossen Yitzkhok's Daughter
H	KRAVETZ	Chaim	M	Hasha (HARFON)		Three Children	226L	
H	KRAVETZ	Mordechai	M	Eshka Rayzel		Yehudis(F), Henya(F), Shimon(M)	228L	
H	KRAVETZ	Yakov	M	Rayzel		Channa(F), Tzvia(F), Fayvel(M),Shayndel(F), Yeshaya(M), Dvora Goldman(F), One Child	229L	
H	KRAVETZ	Hershele	M	Luba		Three Children	223R	
H	KRIBITZKY	Yitzkhok	M	Nechama		Faygel (F)	224R	
H	LATOCHA	Moshe	M	Golda		Chaya Kahan(F)	231R	
H	LATOCHA	Yeshaya	M	Chava		Gittel(F), Masha(F), Tzirel	227L	
H	LIFSHITZ	Yakov	M	Fruma (ZARETZKI)		Laizer'ka (M)	225R	
H	LILENBERG	Eliezer Chaim	M	Nechama		Baylka (F)	224R	

H	LILENBERG	Kalman	M	Sara Chana			225L	
H	MARGOLIN	Zelig	M	Esther		Three Children	225R	
H	MIGDALOVICH	Aharon	M	Sara		Esther	225L	
H	MIGDALOVICH	Berl	M	Wife	Gronem	Two Children	227L	
H	MIGDALOVICH	Chaim-Yakov	M	Simka			225L	
H	MIGDALOVICH	Gronem	M	SaraTziril		Faygel (F), Necha (F),Esther (F)	225R	
H	MIGDALOVICH	Gronem	M	Risha		Berl	226R	
H	MIGDALOVICH	Moshe Nissel	M	Manya		Leah(F), Yentel(F)	227R	
H	MIGDALOVICH	Nachman	M	Chishka		Four Daughters	224L	
H	MIGDALOVICH	Moshe	M	Duba	Moshe	Herzl(M), Sara(F), Velvel(M), Yossi(M), Somch(M)	230R	
H	MISHELOV	Mordechai	M	Esther		Malka(F)	228R	
H	MISHELOV	Moshe	M	Chisha			232L	
H	NOVICK	Moshe	M	Alta		Golda (F), Sonia (F)	226L	He Was the Cantor; Her Daughters
H	PADARESKY	Chaim	M	Riva		Yosef(M)	229R	
H	PASETZKY	Gershon	M	Chaya		Daughter	230L	
H	PLAT	Nachman	M	Chaya (GORODETSKI)		Twin Sons	226L	
H	RABINOVITCH	Berl	M	Hinda		Two Children	227L	
H	REICHMAN	Hershl	M	Chayka (REINGOLD)		Two Children	226R	
H	REINGOLD	Yitzkhok	M	Golda		Esther(F), Henya(F), Chayka(F), (Her Daughters)	226R	
H	RIKLIN	Leib	M	Fraydel		Golda(F)	227L	
H	RUBENSTEIN	Boaz	M	Eshka			229R	
H	RUBENSTEIN	Hershl	M	Esther		Chana(F), Laybel(M), Lena (SHULLMAN)(F), another child	226R	
H	RUBENSTEIN	Mattityahu	M	Bashka		Sima	230L	
H	RUBENSTEIN	Shlomo	M	Chana		Shayndel (F)	224L	
H	SADOVSKI	Eliyahu	M	Esther		Rochel (F)	225R	
H	SCHWARTZMAN	Hershl	M	Breindel		Three Children	229R	
H	SHAPIRA	Moshe	M	Luba		Avraham'l	231L	

H	SCHNEIDMAN	Avraham	M	Sara Faygel		Golda (F), Chayka (F)	224L	
H	SCHNEIDMAN	Simcha	M	Wife		Two Children	224L	
H	SHULLMAN	Moshe	M	Lena (RUBENSTEIN)		Adina	226R	
H	SHUSTER	Sender	M	Rivka-Rochel		Faygel	232L	
H	SCHUSTERMAN	Dovid	M	Faygel		Three Children	230R	
H	SCHUSTERMAN	Moshe	M	Wife		Two Children	230R	
H	SCHUSTERMAN	Moshe Aharon	M	Zlata		Shimon(M)	229L	
H	SCHUSTERMAN	Yitzkhok	M	Bayla		Five Children	228R	
H	SCHUSTERMAN	Yitzkhok	M	Hodel		Sonya	229L	
H	SHUB	Yosef	M	Faygel		Channa(F), Hershle	228L	
H	SHVERIN	Chaim	M	Elka		Faygel(F), Sara(F), Rochel(F) (Her Daughters)	226R	
H	SLUTSKY	Gronem	M	Fruma	Nachum		227R	
H	SLUTSKY	Hershele	M	Chana			223R	
H	SLUTSKY	Yitzkhok (Itchka)	M	Wife	Yeshaya		225L	Yeshaya from Hariznovitz
H	SLUTSKY	Asher	M	Dina: Second wife		Two Children; One Child	230R	
H	STAROBINSKI	Binyamin	M	Eshka		Shulamis (F), Avram'l (M)	224L	
H	STRIGATCH	Baruch	M	Rayzel		Leibel(M), Zalman(M), Basha(F)	230R	
H	TEMKIN	Chaim-David	M	Hinda		Hershele (Her Son)	226L	
H	TEMKIN	Izel	M	Wife		One Child	226L	
H	TEMKIN	Dovid	M	Feygel			231L	
H	TEMKIN	Hershel	M	Faygel		Two Children	228R	
H	TOPCHIK	Benya	M	Itka		Esther	225L	
H	TOPCHIK	Lipa	M	Sara		Miriam	230L	
H	TOPCHIK	Yakov	M	Riva		Shlomo, Zelig, Baruch, Eliyahu, Miriam	230L	
H	TZIGLIG	Eliyahu	M	Chaya Leah			229R	
H	TZIGLIG	David	M	Itka		Zelig(M)	227L	

Code	Family name	First name	Gender	Spouse name	Children's names	Page ref. #	
H	TZIGLIG	Gedalyahu	M	Rochel (TZIGLIG)	Moishele (Her Son), Gittele (Her Daughter)	226R	
H	RTZRUKOVICH	Moshe	M	Fraydel	Two Daughters	229L	
H	TZUKROVITZ	Dov	M	Lifsha		228R	
H	TZUKROVITZ	Leib	M	Chisha	One Child	229R	
H	WANDEROV	Berel	M	Faygel	Moshe(M), Hinde(F)	228R	
H	WARSHAL	Shlomo Nisson	M	Rochel Leah		230L	
H	WARSHAL	Yitzkhok	M	Miriam	Shulamis	230L	
H	WARSHAL	Yitzkhok	M	Freidka		232L	
H	YOSELEVSKY	Unknown	M	Nesha (Schusterman)	Teibele	229L	
H	YULEVICH	Dovid	M	Faygel	Four Children	231R	
H	ZARETZKI	Eliyahu-Aron	M	Hasha		227R	
H	ZAICHIK	Lipa	M	Shaindel	Sara, his daughter	226L	
H	ZAICHIK	Moshe	M	Shayndel		227L	
H	TZUKROVITZ	Dovid Sholom	M	Hinde	Four Daughters	223R	
S	TZUKROVITZ	Feivel	M	Wife	One Child	227R	
W	SLUTSKY	Dina	F	Asher	Two Children	230R	First Wife of Asher

[Pages 232-233]

Lenin – the Community Register

Part B. Jewish Partisans from Lenin who fell in battle, perished in the Ghettos and in locations outside of Lenin

Listed below are names of presumed surviving relatives used to identify martyrs

Prepared by: Mordechai Zaichik

Code	Family name	First name	Gender	Spouse name	Children's names	Page ref. #
F	BAVKIN	Nossen	M		Moishe'le, father-in-law of Yakov Kaplan	232L

F	BERGMAN	Nissen	M		Avrom'l	232R
F	BRESLER	Zalman	M		Dovid	232R
F	GELANSON	Zelig	M		Yeshayhu	233R
F	GINSBERG	Eliyahu	M		Boruch	233R
F	GINSBERG	Yosef	M		Michal, Channa(F)	233R
F	GOLOB	Avrom	M		Bayla (F)	233R
F	GUREVICH	Yakov	M		Yitzkhok	233R
F	HARFON	Moshe	M		Eliyahu	233L
F	KIRZNER	Dovid	M		Avrem'l, Aron	233L
F	KRAVETZ	Yehuda	M		Hershele	233L
F	MANDELBAUM	Mordechai	F		Sonya (Rivlin), Esther (Abramowitz), Yitzkhok	233L
F	MIGDALOVICH	Aron	M		Feivel	232R
F	MIGDALOVICH	Chaim Beryl	M		Hirshl	233L
F	MIGDALOVICH	Elyakim	M		Yitzkhok	232R
F	MIGDALOVICH	Moshe Nissen	M		Hershka	232L
F	MIGDALOVICH	Rozhka	M		Ben Zion, Gittel(F), Aron'ke	233R
F	MISHELOV	Mordechai	M		Pesil(F)	233R
F	PADARESKY	Yosef	M		Chaim	233R
F	REINGOLD	Yitzkhok	M		Eliyahu Aron	233L
F	RUBENSTEIN	Noach	M		Isaac	233R
F	RUBENSTEIN	Shayma	M		Lipa	233L
F	ROVNITZ	Shaul	M		Yisroel	233R
F	SCHNEIDMAN	Avrom	M		Fayvel, Zhama	232L
F	SHUSTER	Sender	M		Zelig	233R
F	SCHUSTERMAN	Mordechai	M		Moshe	233R

F	SLUTSKY	Chaim	M		Eliyahu	232R
F	SLUTSKY	Chaim	M		Khaya, Vitsha	233L
F	SLUTSKY	Nachum	M		Gronem, Feivel	233L
F	STRIGATCH	Feivel	M		Manya	233L
F	TEMKIN	Lipa	M		Yitzkhok	232R
F	TZIGLIG	Eliyahu	M		Yeshaya	232L
F	TZIGLIG	Mordechai	M		Benzion, Tisroelik	232L
F	TZIGLIG	Mordechai	M		Yakov (Yatsha), Yoel, Shlomo	233R
F	TZIGLIG	Mordechai Leib	M		Boruch	233R
F	TZIGLIG	Zelig	M		Yeshaya	233L
F	TZUKROVITZ	Dov	M		Leibel	232L
F	WINIK	Itka	M		Laybel, Tuvyah	233R
F	WINIK	Ovadyahu	M		Leivick, Nachman	233R
F	YULEVICH	Nachum Nossen	M		Shmuel	232R
F	ZARETZKI	Moshe Reuven	M		Vitsha	233L
F	ZARETZKI	Yosef	M		Eliezer	233L
F	ZAVIN	Manos	M		Avrem'l	233L
F	ZAICHIK	Aharon Leib	M		Moshe	232L
F	ZAICHIK	Leibel	M		Moshe Dovid	233L
H	WEISBLAT	Aron Moshe	M	Alte	Sender, Berl	232R
Mo	CHINITCH	Leibeh	F		Tema (F)	233R
Mo	KOLPANITSKY	Leah	F		Yitzkhok	233R
Mo	TEMKIN	Sarah	F		Hershl	232L
Mo	TZIGLIG	Leibeh	F		Betzalel	232L
Mo	TZUKROVITZ	Sara	F		Feivel	233L

[Pages 234-235]

Lenin – the Community Register

Part C. Jewish Partisans from Lenin who fell in battle with the Nazis in the forests of White Russia

Listed below are names of presumed surviving relatives used to identify martyrs

Prepared by: Mordechai Zaichik

Code	Family name	First name	Gender	Spouse name	Father	Children's names	Page ref. #
F	BEHON	Chaim	M			Eisel (Isaac)	234R
F	BARUCHIN	Dov	M			Mottel (Mordechai)	234R
F	GELANSON	Kusha	M			Leyba, Chaim, Shlomo, Laizer, Mendel	235L
F	GELANSON	Zelig	M			Moshe	234R
F	GORODETSKI	Moshinke	M			Yisroel	235L
F	ISERS	Yisroel Aron	M			Ephraim	235L
F	KOLPANITSKY	Yitzkhok	M			Eliezer Aron	235R
F	KRAVETZ	Leivik	M			Avrom'l, Kushe (Yekutiel)	235L
F	KRAVETZ	Naphtali	M			Yakov, Yisroel Goldman (Son-in-law)	234R
F	KRAVETZ	Yehuda	M			Chaim	235R
F	LAMDIN	Oesach	M			Father-in-law of Yisroel	235R
F	LATOCHA	Baruch	M				235R
F	MACON	Esna	M			Yitzkhok	234L
F	MARGOLIN	Liba	M			Zelig	234R

F	MIGDALOVICH	Gronem	M			Shmuel Yitzkhok	234R
F	MISHELOV	Mordechai	M			Shmulik, Shakhne	235L
F	MISHELOV	Moshe	M			Lipa	235L
F	NOVICK	Moshe	M			Dovid	234R
F	PARETSKY	Gershon	M			Laizer	235L
F	RABINOVITCH	Eliezer	M			Nissel	234R
F	RUBENSTEIN	Noach	M			Boaz	234R
F	RUBENSTEIN	Shlomo	M			Yehuda	234L
F	RUBENSTEIN	Hershel	M			Isaac, Moshe	234R
F	ROVNITZ	Shaul	M			Eliyha	235R
F	SADOVSKI	Eliyahu	M			Hershel	234L
F	SCHWARTZMAN	Yosef	M			Leibel	235R
F	SEGALOVITCH	Moshe	M		Eliyahu		235L
F	SCHNEIDMAN	Avraham	M			Simcha	234L
F	SHUSTER	Chaim	M			Sender	235R
F	SHUSTER	Meir Beryl	M			Baruch, Mottel (Mordechai), Shmuel	234L
F	SHUSTER	Yehuda	M			Baruch	234R
F	SCHUSTERMAN	Mordechai	M			Dovid	234R
F	SLUTSKY	Aharon	M			Baruch, Elyakim	234L
F	SLUTSKY	Chaim	M			Yehiel	234L
F	SLUTSKY	Yeshayahu	M			Yitzkhok	234L
F	STRIGATCH	Feivel	M			Bonya (Baruch)	234R
F	TOMCHIN	Chaim Dovid	M			Isaac	234R
F	TZIGLIG	Dovid	M			Bonya (Baruch)	234R
F	TZIGLIG	Leib	M			Yakov, Chaim	234L

						Tedelis (Son-in-law)	
F	TZIGLIG	Yakov	M			Gedalyahu	235R
F	TZUKROVITZ	Dov	M			Moshe	234L
F	VARSHEL	Shlomo Nisson	M			Yitzkhok	235L
F	VILK	Yitzkhok	M			Ephraim, Hanekh	234R
F	ZARETZKI	Moshe-Reuven	M			Shmuel	234R
F	ZAVIN	Manos	M			Velvel (Zev)	234R
H	ISERS	Nishka	M	Gilek			235R
Mo	YULEVICH	Dvora	M				235R
W	GOLDMAN	Yocha	F	Hershel			234L
W	GOLOB	Luba	M	Moshe'le Shapira			235L
W	ZARETZKI	Bracha	F	Zaber			235R

Yiddish

The Rise of the Shtetl Lenin

Our Shtetl (Village) Lenin
A Yizkor (Memorial) Book

Mordechai Zaichik

Translated by Sanford A. Kaplan

Published by The Committee of Lenin Landsleit (home-town people) in Israel
With the Participation of Lenin Landsleit in America
Tel Aviv, 1957

[Page 237]

[Page 243]

The Founding of Lenin

by Eng. Mordechai Zaichik

Translation by Yocheved Klausner

A.

The main difficulty in the research of the shtetl Lenin is to establish the exact, or at least the approximate date when it was founded, considering the fact that there are no real historical documents on which we can confidently rely.

Seeking to establish the beginnings of Lenin I used: 1. inscriptions on old gravestones in the old cemetery; 2. the register of the *Hevra Kadisha* [Jewish burial society] and other sources, for example stories told by the oldest residents of the town, who remembered well what their grandfathers had told them about the former generations, etc.

Relying on these data and calculations, we can state almost with certainty that the shtetl was founded around the years 1640-1650. An error of 10 to 15 years is possible; however, considering the above-mentioned sources we can state that the date is correct.

According to general knowledge, the name Lenin originates from the fact that in all the neighboring fields the plant Linum was grown, from which they made flax. According to what we have found out, however, the name Lenin could derive from the name Lena, a baroness living in the area, who was honored by calling a town on her name.

B.

The first years of its development

The first house, around which more houses were built as time passed, was a tavern, or inn; the inn stood on the road that years later was to become the main street of the town, several hundred meters from the river Slutch. The inn was built by a nobleman, who used to travel in the region for his business.

The nobleman was the owner of very large fields and woods

[Page 244]

in Russia, part of them in the Pinsk region. There were some – very few – settlements in the mud covered valleys and between them were large stretches of uninhabited land. Such "taverns-inns" were built on the roads, and travelers could get there a glass of hot tea, a drink of brandy, something to eat and a place to sleep. Most of the inn owners were Jews, who were called "the Nobleman's Jews."

The Location of the shtetl

The location found for the shtetl was appropriate: very close to the river Slutch. Since the communication means were scarce at that time, the main travel was by water.

The river Slutch, quite deep, was an ideal way for the transport of great masses of wood of all kinds – natural and manufactured – and the logs were left to move with the current until they reached the Pripet, into which the Slutch flowed, and from there even further to the Dnieper and the Black sea.

It is interesting, that even in later years, the shtetl was built and developed near and around the tavern, although the ground was very low and muddy, and pouring sand on it did not help, and although at a distance of 1-2 kilometers to the north, also near the river, there was a good area, high and dry, with pine trees, much more suitable for the needs of the population.

The Jews settled in the place gradually, as did the Christian population, the "white Russians." The first Jews that appeared were from Slutsk (90 Km. north of Lenin) and from the region of Pinsk. Later, some came from the shtetl Lachve (30 Km. west of Lenin), which was older than Lenin.

The development of the shtetl during the first hundred years was very slow, and the general number of residents did not exceed one hundred.

C.

The Growth of the Shtetl in the Second Century of its existence

During the second century, the development and growth of the shtetl increased. We know, that in the first half of the second century

[Page 245]

of the shtetl, there were several *minyanim* [*minyan* = prayer-quorum of ten male adults] of Jews, who could afford to hire their own *shochet* [ritual slaughterer], R'Leibke Zaichik from Minsk, who came to Lenin around 1770 and remained there.

The number of the Christian residents increased as well; they worked in the fields, lived in small houses with straw roofs and traded with the Jews, buying from them the elementary necessities.

D.

The large families in the shtetl

The largest families in those early times were: the Tzigligs, the Slutskys, the "Dovid's," and following them the Galovs and Zaichiks.

The Tzigligs originated in Lachve. At first, two brothers, Mendel and David came to Lenin. Mendel's children, Yashke and Mordechai had large families and occupied a corner at the very end of the street, in the direction of the river.

David's son, Baruch, had a large family as well. They were called the "Broches." They lived on the other end of the street on the Christian side, and they occupied an entire block.

The Slutsk family, who originated, as their name shows, in the Slutsk region, was one of the oldest and most numerous families in Lenin. They were notable in their good health and simplicity.

The third large family, the "Dovid's" were named after old David, who had many daughters and all were married to fine sons-in-law, knowledgeable in Torah and general science; most of them came from Slutsk.

The other large families, like the Rubensteins, Migdalovich and others arrived later, from the neighboring and more distant villages.

E.

The Cultural Life in Those Years

The chief place for meetings and social life was the synagogue, where almost always one could listen to the learning of a "page of the Talmud" [*daf gemara*] a portion of the Pentateuch [*chumash*] with Rashi commentary or just have a chat and hear news from the wide world.

[Page 246]

Main Sources of Livelihood and Existence

The main occupation of the Jewish population was crafts: there were cobblers, tailors, carpenters, ironsmiths – and later there were also some shopkeepers, mostly grocers. The first grocery shop was opened by Chaim Papyerna.

The forest and lumber occupations also had an honored place among the local Jews. Since the shtetl was surrounded by woods, all connected occupations were common.

The woods belonged to Graf [nobleman] Wittgenstein, who owned entire Gubernias. In later years, part of the woods, in the Pinsk region, was bought by Agarkov and the wood business grew and ramified.

The lumber was prepared for export. Several professions were needed for this task: brokers, "secretaries" or scribes to keep the necessary registers etc.

These professionals were Jews. On the other hand, hard work, like cutting the logs, transporting by water on the rafts or barges and other such work remained in the hands of the peasants, who would stay for many weeks – even months sometimes – on the river with the lumber. Everything – eating, sleeping etc. – was done on the barges.

Many Jews and Christians made their living by this work. It is also worth mentioning, that many first-class types of wood was grown in these forests: oak, fir, birch, elm, linden and others.

[Page 247]

The Estate and the "Office Quarter"

Yehoshua Greenberg (Argentina)

Translated by Yocheved Klausner

In a remote corner, somewhere among woods and marshes our little shtetl Lenin (Lyelin) was located. When I remember its good-hearted people, who are very dear to me, I am proud that it was the place where I was born and brought up.

In my time Lenin numbered not more than 120 Jewish families, approximately 700-800 persons – laborers, craftsmen, wagon drivers, some merchants, very few lumber traders and three or four shopkeepers.

Until 1891, the land of the shtetl belonged to the baroness Hohenlohe, who was part of the German imperial family. In 1890, the Russian government published a law, which forced all foreign residents who owned land to adopt Russian citizenship. The baroness had no interest to change her citizenship, so she sold her large estate – more than 35,000 square kilometers – to the Russian citizen Stefan Fiodorovitch Agarkov.

Agarkov came to Lenin, to take over the management of the estate. He was accompanied by a staff of clerks and laborers, among them two Jews, high-level employees, Semion and Greenberg.

The office complex (the "Office Quarter" or, as it was called: the "Quarter") was located at the edge of town and included the apartments of the clerks and workers, the management offices of the estate as well as two large beautiful houses for the estate owner and his family. As all this was still occupied by the workers and employees of the former owner, Agarkov and his people lived temporarily in big houses that belonged to the rich lumber merchant Ben-Zion Tziglig. They remained there 15 months, during which time the old buildings were rebuilt and renewed to the taste of their new residents.

Agarkov bought the large estate for one million and hundred thousand Rubles. Part of the sum he paid by signed promissory notes; each month an officer of the court would come to collect payment. They also imposed mortgages on various parts of the estate – the buildings and whatever else that was possible.

They began looking for means to cover the debts. Semion Perelovitch

[Page 248]

called on his brother Yakov Perelovitch, a known lumber merchant, who had established a Shares-Society of merchants: Yakov Ragovin from Minsk, Moshe Lev, Pinchas Kaplan from Lachve and others.

In cooperation with the group of lumber traders, Yakov Perelovitch began cutting the trees and sending the logs through the waterways to export them – and with the profits they covered Agarkov's debts.

Lenin began to bloom economically. Not only local people were able to make a living; people came from neighboring towns and villages, and some pf them even settled in our shtetl. Forest-management employees came as well. A time of prosperity began, and the neighboring villages actually envied Lenin.

One summer-day in 1897, the office clerk Mordechai Tziglig (or, as he was called: Motel Yoshkes) brought the news that Stefan Fiodorovitch died, and as an expression of mourning the offices closed for one month.

Stefanleft one son, Fiodor Stefanovitch, and three daughters. The large estate was divided into three parts: Lenin, Tchotchwitz and Diakovitch. The son Fiodor inherited the two important parts: Lenin and Tchotchwitz; the third part, Diakovitch, was divided between the three sisters.

After the 30 mourning days passed, the young Agarkov came to our town, accompanied by one of his managers. He appointed as the head manager of the estate one by the name of Fangalos. The new manager began to institute his own regulations. He stopped the connection and relationship with the Jewish lumber merchants, his plan being that his management would conduct all commercial operations as well as the commercial connections with foreign countries. However, Fangalos failed badly. Nothing came out of all his planning. He was forced to resign from his high position, and the management was entrusted into the hands of one by the name of Chruschtschow, a brother of Agarkov's brother-in-law who, however, was no better than his predecessor. Fiodor Agarkov became convinced finally that both of them were of no use and that he could not expect anything from any of them. He hired as manager a Jew, Lazar eLevine.

Everything became refreshed and revitalized; the great lumber merchants arrived and reestablished the

[Page 249]

connection with the main offices. Among them were Lavzinski, Chaim Weizman's brother-in-law, and the well-known merchant from Krementchug, Gur-Arie.

Lazar Pavlowitz Levine was a man with a Jewish heart. He did all he could to establish a brotherly relationship with the Jews in the shtetl. Often he came to shul. He lived for a time in Ben-Zion Tziglig's house. Later he brought his family and took residence in one of the buildings in the Quarter.

He introduced many suitable and beneficial administrative changes in the estate management and the Quarter. He brought professionals and specialists in the lumber business – people of various nationalities: Germans, French, Jews and Latvians, who were famous woodcutters. Levine also divided the entire area of the estate into precisely measured parts.

He began drying the swamps; this enterprise gave work to many laborers, who dug canals to drain the swamp waters.

Thanks to L. P. Levine, an atmosphere of liberalism was created in the Quarter. He sent Avraham, the cantor-shochet's son, to study music in the Conservatoire, and a talented Russian to study agriculture – both at the expense of the Quarter.

This liberal atmosphere that began in the time of L. P. Levine and thanks to him, continued in the Quarter after him as well; The Russian managers who arrived later treated the non-Russians the same way as they treated the Russians.

Levine also brought to the Quarter a Jewish employee, who settled in the shtetl with his family and had a very good influence on the population. His name was Zelig Singalovski and his family – his wife, one daughter, Sara (now in Israel) and five sons: Yehoshua, Yakov, Nachum, Shechna and Aharon.

The Singalovski children learned in secondary and high schools in the great cities. But on vacation and holidays they would come home – and the young people in town would be stimulated and enlivened. They would gather around the young students, hear news and learn from them – and from the Singalovski children one could really learn a great deal.

[Page 250]

The single two-story house in Lenin
(Herzl Paperna's house, in the center of town)

Culture and Education

[Page 253]

The Cultural Situation in our Shtetl

by Avraham Yitzhak Slutsky

Translated by Yocheved Klausner

About fifty or sixty years ago, the cultural situation in our Shtetl was deplorable. There was no public library – the need for it was not felt and a person who would take the initiative and establish a library was not to be found.

There were, however, in the shtetl several intelligent and well-to-do families who owned private libraries. Some of them would lend a book occasionally, but we, the children of poor parents did not feel comfortable to ask from the rich aristocrats. So we read what we could find.

From time to time, a travelling book-seller would pass through our town and we would buy a novel, a book of wise sayings or a book of jokes about Hershele Ostropoler. These pieces of literature were read occasionally at an assembly of young people.

The same happened concerning newspapers. The rich and intelligent received Yiddish, Hebrew and even Russian newspapers, some individually and some in partnership with a neighbor or a friend. According to the postal arrangements at that time, the newspapers would arrive twice a week. The Wednesday, Thursday and Friday newspapers would arrive on Sunday, and the Sunday, Monday and Tuesday newspapers on Wednesday.

As mentioned before, the newspapers were the privilege of the very few and chosen. All the other people had to be satisfied with hearing the news of the entire great world in the synagogue, in the evening between the *mincha* and *maariv* prayers, from the newspaper readers Motel (Mordechai) Tziglig or Aharon-Leib Zaichik. Around them a circle of people would form, who "swallowed" every word.

We, the young people, children of the simple folk, wanted to have a newspaper for ourselves. Three of us – Shlomo Dalgin (was murdered by village bandits on the Starobin-Slutzk road), Mordechai the son of Yehoshua Tziglig and I, jointly subscribed to the BUND newspaper "Folks-Zeitung." Who could compare with us? We would read the newspaper through and through, from beginning to end. In the middle of a circle of listeners one of us would read and we all listened eagerly.

I think it is necessary to relate a few interesting episodes, which had a certain effect upon the cultural development in our shtetl.

[Page 254]

The *gabai* [chief attendant and treasurer] of the Old Shul – Motel Mandelbaum or Leizer Vladovski (I am not sure) – had brought from Pinsk a bookbinder, to bind and renew the books in the synagogue. The bookbinder was an intelligent and lively young man, and also had some dramatic talent. He met Tzviyu and Dvor'ke, the daughters of Israel-Chaim the cantor, and suggested to create a young group and study drama, and then produce a Yiddish play. We liked the idea very much and it was decided to learn and produce the operetta "The Witch" [*Hamechasheifa*] by Avraham Goldfaden. Since at the time I was a member of the cantor's choir, I was attracted to this enterprise together with another member of the choir, Aba-Moshe Elias and also Avraham'ke, the cantor's son. I remember that Mania Migdalovich played Mire'le. The young bookbinder chose the cast, and the rehearsals took place three times a week, in the cantor's house. All winter we were busy with Goldfaden's play and each of us studied diligently his and her part.

We performed the operetta before a small audience and we were ready to play in a bigger hall. This, however, we could unfortunately not accomplish, because our director left us after Passover and went home, and the famous "drama group" fell apart, leaving us with only a sweet dream.

The second episode was a result of our own initiative, without any help from outside. We decided to play the traditional "Purim-Spiel" *Hochmat Shlomo* [Shlomo's wisdom]. During the entire winter, we had rehearsals every Sabbath at the house of Zelig Yulevich Itche Neche's. His son Zalman also participated in the play. I played two parts – "Bat-Sheva" and little David. With a little pebble I killed the big Philistine Goliath.

When Purim came, the players walked through the streets with golden crowns on their heads and swords in their hands – every one full of pride… We wore royal attire with golden buttons, and were accompanied by a music band – Efraim the klezmer and Efraim on the drum. The entire shtetl followed us: young people, girls, women and men. Even Christians accompanied us – boys and girls – you can imagine the procession…

We were not allowed into the houses, however, for fear that we would break the windows. Our first performance took place at the house of the synagogue attendant, the *shames* Chaim Berl. The house was full – we barely escaped after the performance, our royal clothes torn.

[Page 255]

I remember that Noah Rubenstein, afraid of more damage, helped us out and when we were safely outside he gave us five Rubles, asking us to come next year… The income from the performance was devoted to the Talmud Tora.

In short, it was not a great success financially, but culturally it was a very important achievement.

Several days after Purim, the Pristav summoned Ben-Zion Tziglig and interrogated him about the festivities, wanting to know whether the procession with the crowns and swords had anything to do with the revolutionary events in the country at that time. The Pristav accepted the calm explanation, that the Purim-Spiel was an old tradition without any political significance. Yet he asked not to repeat such processions through the streets of the town. Thus ended the cultural activity in Lenin.

[Page 255]

The Cultural Life

by Eng. Mordechai Zaichik

Translated by Yocheved Klausner

Schools

Since the first few years after WWI a *Tarbut* School was active in Lenin, as part of the *Tarbut* chain, with its central administration in Warsaw.

The average number of pupils was about 150 children yearly. There were 4 or 5 grades and a preparatory class. There was no kindergarten; the children began first grade at the age of 5.

The teachers were mostly from other towns or cities, sent by the *Tarbut* Center. They would teach in our shtetl between 1 and 3-4 years.

An exception was the teacher A. L. Zaichik, who served in the shtetl nearly 5 decades…

During the 18 years of the school's existence in Lenin a varied "collection" of teachers, men and women, of all sizes and colors, worked at the school.

In truth, a school existed in Lenin before, since about 1900. It was a regular school, situated in a special building, with discipline, with grades and a syllabus, with "recess" and even with a bell…

[Page 256]

This school was on Lachov Street, among the big houses, and it had a large yard where the children could play during recess.

There were four teachers. The program consisted of *Chumash* [the Five Books of Moses], *TANACH* [the Bible] and secular studies: grammar, arithmetic, geography, history (mostly Jewish history), language, etc.

Understandably, the *Tarbut* School was more modern and suited the new times; the school hours were a little shorter, but new subjects were added, as music, sports etc.

One must confess that the discipline was not as strict as before, yet on the average, the children learned diligently and behaved well.

After graduating from this elementary school, some of the young students – especially those who possessed the means and desired to continue their studies – went to Pinsk and enrolled in the Hebrew High School, or to the Vilna Teachers College. Some went to the vocational school ORT in Brisk.

The shtetl had also a Polish elementary school, of 7 grades. Some of the Jewish children learned there, especially in the higher grades.

The *Tarbut* Library

The young people in town would meet at the *Tarbut* Club. There they would spend the evening reading various newspapers and journals in several languages.

Meetings were also held there: at the meetings various reports were presented, mostly from the *Shlihim* [messengers] to Eretz Israel, and discussions took place on various subjects.

The place contained also a quite rich and well-organized library, which in time developed and grew, and lately possessed a great number of books in several languages, and periodicals as for example *Hatekufa* and others. The library became very popular and had a great number of registered readers.

One of the important aspects of the Club was that people from all social layers would meet there – children of laborers and other professions – and through the constant contact they became close and learned to live together.

All political parties were of course represented in Lenin: BEITAR, the General Zionists, *Hashomer Hatza'ir* etc. There were disputes and conflicts between the parties, as usual,

[Page 257]

but it never led to serious incidents. Sometimes, on a holiday like Chanuka or Purim a conflict would flare off, but soon the parties would make peace…

Theater and Music

The history of the theater in Lenin is quite old, beginning from the time a performance was called a "spectacle" and was staged in a "pozharne."

What was a "pozharne?" usually a long and narrow building, about 20 meters long and 8 meters wide, which contained the "town pozharne" that is, the fire fighter's equipment, consisting of several barrels on wagons, each equipped with a water pump with two handles, one on each side, a few ladders and some shining helmets…

When a "spectacle" was scheduled, all these things were taken out. It was done about two days before the show; during that time we arranged seats – chairs, benches and armchairs – collected from the Jewish population of the town, and then we decorated the stage. When all was ready we put on the show… All the Jews in town prepared themselves a long time in advance, for the day of the "spectacle," which became a true holiday.

The first plays were "historic" or biblical – not modern: "The selling of Joseph," "David and Goliath" and so forth. Later we presented newer, more modern plays, among them even "L'Avare" [The Miser] by Molière.

After we left the pozharne building, we played in the building of the Russian "Narodnaya Utchilitche" [Russian elementary school], which possessed many large halls.

Later yet, during Polish rule, when the "Dom Ludowi" was built, all theatrical performances as well as movies were presented there. The hall, the stage, and the service rooms were built for that purpose.

Various plays were staged at that time, for example: "God, Man and Devil," "Chasye the Orphan," "Motke Thief" and even such famous plays as "The Dibbuk," "Tevye the Milkman" [*Teyvye der Milchiker*] and others. We performed even operettas… The players were, of course, local people, people of our own, some of them quite talented.

[Page 258]

The performance of "Tevye the Milkman"

From right to left: Yoche Rosomacha, Moshe Rabinovitch, Beile Golob, Tzalke Starobinski's daughter, Bashe Mordche's Tziglig, Grones Starobinski, Neshe Schusterman

The successful director was Meir Buckstein, who was also a teacher and a talented artist (painter).

As to moving pictures – the shtetl was privileged to see its first movie in 1923. The spectators were overcome with marvelous wonder: people, horses, were moving on the screen, moving their hands, running, fighting, etc…

During the last several years, a film was shown in Lenin almost every week. But a movie-house has not been built yet.

The shtetl was also rich in musical performances. It had an orchestra, which accompanied the theatrical performances; after the performance ended the music continued to play and people began to dance, sometimes until early in the morning…

[Page 259]

The people would enjoy the opportunity that when a performance took place they were allowed to remain outside all evening and came by masses. All the time that Lenin was under Polish rule, a curfew was imposed on the population from dark until morning – the reason being that the town was situated near the Russian border, in the so-called border-zone.

Because of this special position of the town, the population, especially the youth, suffered from the harassment of the police and patrols, whose main purpose was to guard the town and keep everybody in their houses during the night. Almost every resident passed at least one night either at the police or in jail, because he was found in the street a few minutes after the curfew time. The punishment was to spend the night in jail or to pay a fine. If a person broke the law several times he was taken to Luninetz and the punishment would be more severe.

Interesting and strange curiosities would happen when people who stayed outside too late were caught.

For young people, naturally, it was not easy to lock themselves up in the houses too early in the evening, in particular during the long winter evenings. We used to gather in one of the houses and spend the time together, reading, playing cards etc. – but going home later was indeed a problem!

We had to be very attentive and maneuver with great care, sneak from courtyard to courtyard, climb over fences and with fear arrive finally home. It often happened that right by your house a policeman would be positioned… Often we managed to get to the door and be inside in a second, then slam the door in the policeman's face – to come in he didn't dare, or maybe he was not allowed to do that.

The cold winter, with frost all around and snow under our feet, was a blessing and a disadvantage at the same time. The advantage was, that we heard from a distance the policeman's steps on the snow and could hide; the disadvantage was the same: the policeman could wait in ambush for a victim, and when you were quite close he would shout: "Halt! Who is walking?"

One way or another – for young people it was an interesting challenge.

[Page 260]

Sports

The development of sports in Lenin began in 1923. The sports group was quite small, consisting of a number of students who, during vacation came home from Pinsk and Vilna where they studied and were joined by a few local youths.

The main sports activity was the game of football (soccer), then volleyball and basketball etc. During the first years the level of the games was quite low. The player would hit the ball with his shoe, his boot or his bare feet (and, by the way, the ball would sometimes tear and the play had to be stopped…).

Only several years later a football association was formed, and in the meantime the players learned to play according to the accepted rules.

At first the members of the football team were all Jewish. Later a mixed team was formed, together with Russians, and they would play against strong Polish military teams; they lost often, but at the same time they learned from experts how to play.

The mixed team was at its best during the years 1930 – 1933. They played against strong teams from Mishkewitz and Lachwe, sometimes with good results (once they won 2:0 against Lachwe).

As to other sports – there was swimming and skating.

Walks and entertainment places

Lenin was rich in places where one could "take a walk." Long ago, before WWI, before Lenin became a border-town, the place to take walks, in particular on Shabat and Holidays, was on the other side of the bridge; we would go to "the Green Mountain" or farther to the "Zavod" (the mill, or factory) or the "Mayak" (a tall tower in the forest).

The Green Mountain was the closest. It was not a mountain really, just a low hill, but for Lenin it was considered a mountain, because it was surrounded by low valleys and marshes.

On the way to the Green Mountain we would catch snakes – the place was full of them – and carry them with their heads down all the way to the "mountain" that was full of ants. There we would throw the snakes into the large anthills, among the million ants, which would cover each snake instantly. The snake

[Page 261]

would twist and struggle with the ants but to no avail. In a few minutes nothing would remain except the empty skin.

On the way to the "mayak" we passed the "zavod." As a matter of fact, a long time there was no factory, only a remnant of a burned up building.

The "mayak," built at the beginning of the First World War, was about 100 meters tall, standing on a little mound not far from the river, about 3 kilometers from town.

Only the most courageous of the young people dared to climb up to the very top. On the top there was a little platform with a little table placed on it. One could crawl up, or going by ladders from level to level. People looked very small and funny when seen from the ground. Some would take with them a small log when climbing up and then throw it down from the height of the tower, to see how it would sink in the marsh below.

It is worth mentioning, that a large pine-tree forest has grown around the tower, and the air had a wonderful scent.

After the war, the road has become overgrown with grass, and people began taking their walks in another direction – the infirmary on the road to Yawitch. Pine-trees grew there as well, and the air was dry and pleasant. But mostly we walked to the Makewitch Road, on the way to Makewitch, about 3 kilometers from our town. This was a "romantic" road, in particular in autumn, when it was all covered with the fallen oak leaves.

An important place to go for long walks was the "Kantarski plantation." This was a large piece of land, which belonged to the rich Agarkov. He and his family spent most of the time outside the country and came home for very short times. The plantation contained various fruit-trees, famous in the entire region. The fruit was exported, not before the needs of the town were met.

[Page 262]

In addition to all that, there was the flour-mill, the famous "white house" with the beautiful ornate windows and other decorations, where guests would always stop during their short visits; then "The Red Wall" built entirely of red bricks, and many more structures, a granary and others, beside the living quarters and apartments of the laborers and employees.

There were two beautiful boulevards: the Beryozov and the Yadlow Streets.

Many shrubs grew everywhere, carrying all kinds of berries, nuts etc. and between the thick trees one could sometimes see wild goats running around.

Lately, several bears appeared in the area, and the people of the town took care of them; when young bears were born they built for them a large iron cage.

The entrance to the plantation was through the end of the Lachow Street. During the summer we would go there to buy fresh fruit. The plantation was rented every year, mainly to Lenin Jews, who hired guardians to protect the place.

The seasonal fruits were sent to various towns to be sold. Special fruits, which could be stored for a longer time, were saved for local use.

[Page 265]

Living Conditions

Education and Sanitary-Medical Situation in Lenin

by Avraham-Yitzhak Slutsky (New-York)

Translated by Yocheved Klausner

Interrupted Education...

The name of our *shtetele* will not be found on a regular map. Lenin was situated in the Polesia woodland, at the gate of the well-known "Pinsk Marshes," and on the bank of the "Slutch" river, an affluent of the big and rich Pripyat River, which cut through the right side of the "Pinsk Marshes." The shtetl was one of hundreds of shtetlach in the "Jewish Pale of Settlement" – the area where the Russian Czar governments allowed the Jews to live... In this area there was almost no industry, in particular not in the small towns. For the Jews, other sources of livelihood were closed as well, by the strict limits that the governments imposed. They were not allowed to own land in the villages and work the land. No wonder that poverty and need were always present in the shtetlach.

In our shtetl Lenin, some of the inhabitants made their meager living with the help of a cart and a horse – they were the "wagon-owners" [the *balegules*]. During the winter they carried wood from the forests to the ice-covered rivers, preparing for the springtime when the logs would float down the thawed river, to the lumber mills.

In the beginning of the winter, the wagon-owner would buy a working horse and begin working as soon as the first snow fell and the rivers and marshes froze. Work usually ended at the beginning of spring, after the snow melted; then the wagon-owner would sell his horse and be out-of-work during the entire summer.

The living conditions of the craftsmen – tailors, cobblers, tanners and others – were not much better. Neither were to be envied the small businessmen, and the other so-called "merchants" or plain peddlers.

In short: The Lenin Jews – with very few exceptions – lived a difficult life. The material state affected, naturally, the general cultural state of the shtetl residents. In my childhood years, Lenin had no decent educational institutions. The shtetl lacked the means, as well as people who would be able to take care of cultural needs. However, the situation greatly improved in the later years: a "Modern Heder" [*heder metukan*] was opened, and in a short time it developed into a regular advanced school, which could serve as a model for the neighboring shtetlach.

[Page 266]

The initiators and founders of the Modern Heder were the teachers Yehuda Rubenstein, Nissan Bergman and Aharon-Leib Zaichik.

I was not lucky enough to be one of the pupils of the school, because my parents preferred the old *Heder*, where we learned the prayers and a little writing. There were other *Hadarim* [plural of *Heder*] with very capable teachers [*melamdim*], but the pupils were mostly from well-to-do families. My fate, as the fate of other poor children, was to complete their "education" at the age of eleven-twelve years, and to be taken to the marshy forests to help their parents haul the logs, or to learn a craft as a tailor, a cobbler or a carpenter.

This happened to me as well. My *melamdim* praised my qualities and my diligence, but nothing came out of it. When I was thirteen, my parents took me out of the *heder* and "gave" me to Avner Golob (now in Israel) to learn to be a carpenter.

The Sanitary Situation

Understandably, due to the poverty and troubles, the sanitary situation in our shtetl was far from brilliant. Epidemic illnesses and fires were common guests in the place. The shtetl was

"The Great Street" in the spring

[Page 267]

clustered in a small place, surrounded by water and swamps, and many houses did not have the necessary sanitary facilities. All this caused diseases, especially children's infectious diseases, which often cost the lives of tens of young children… We had no decent medical care; we could say, with very small exceptions, that "there was not a house where there was not one dead." (Ex. 12:30). There were families, where the angel of death took two or three children.

Another curse of the shtetl was the frequent fires, the common reason being overcrowding. In the last fire that I remember most of the town burned down; an interesting fact about that fire was that the government suggested that the houses should be rebuilt in a less crowded way and with better sanitary equipment. This plan, however, demanded that some of the houses would be left out, and the residents opposed that, naturally. An assembly was called, and it was decided to send a delegation to Minsk, to the

Governor. Elyakim the tavern-owner was one of the delegates, and the plan was called off: the houses were rebuilt in the same crowded way as before.

Medical Help

The supervisors of the health situation – and sometimes over life itself – in the shtetl were Hershke the doctor and Israel the doctor. Both were interesting people, but their medical knowledge was limited indeed. They would prescribe medicines, or "powders," that were prepared in a primitive way. In many cases the sick person recovered only because of the psychological effect. Such "miracles" happened only in the light illnesses, but when somebody suffered from a serious illness the end was unfortunately sad. There was also an old lady who lived in the Jewish Street, by the name of Sheine Rochel, who cared for a special type of sick people and gave them self-produced primitive "grandmother" medications. The sick were mostly from among the wagon owners, who tore their guts by hauling the heavy logs in the forest. She would massage their bellies and hope for the best. As a remedy for a blow she would apply a honey cake, for a wound – a baked onion; she had also remedies against the "evil eye" and many other troubles.

So, this was the way our Lenin Jews lived – and died…

[Page 271]

Destruction and Revenge

The Years 1939 – 1941

by Mordechai Zaichik

Translated by Yocheved Klausner

The German attack on Poland happened, as is well known, on Friday the 1st of September 1939, at dawn. Since Western Ukraine and Belarus were occupied by Russian army, Lenin, which was located right on the border, was under Soviet rule. This way, the residents of our shtetl and in particular the Jews had the privilege to live almost 2 more years as human beings. The towns and shtetlach located at the West of the Bug River, suffered immediately the bitter taste of the Nazi rule.

Although Lenin was situated on the border and it was thought that the Soviets would march in right away, several days passed until the Soviets actually took over, and during that time the shtetl remained sort of a no man's land.

The Polish official forces did not exist anymore – part of them disappeared and part went in hiding, trembling with fear.

During that period of a few days of transition the shtetl was disturbed and tense: the Jewish population was afraid that the farmers in the neighborhood would invade and attack the shtetl (there were rumors to that effect).

The Jewish youth organized and stood guard constantly, particularly during nights. They did not have arms, but they patrolled and watched all the time. Fortunately, nothing happened.

As soon as the Soviet forces entered by crossing the river (there were no victims during the occupation) they established a temporary administration and the military forces continued their advance to the West. In only a few days it was not even felt that the town was for 20 years under Polish rule: no Poles, no police, no border guards…

When all this happened, it was considered a great tragedy, but later it was realized that it had been their good luck, since all the inhabitants were saved, survived the war and came back home.

[Page 272]

Some of the Jews who had been sent away to the distant camps are now in Israel, some in America and other countries. Who knows, what their fate would have been, had they fallen, like other Lenin Jews, in the hands of the Germans…

Concerning the cultural life – it was strengthened to a certain measure. The Drama Club was restored and theater performances and moving pictures were often presented. Also a rich library was established, with a large reading hall.

The shtetl became important in general, since it was made a county seat, where all governmental offices were located. People came from remote corners of the region to arrange their official affairs.

Even the near–by shtetl Mikoshewitz belonged to the Lenin District and all its local affairs were taken care of in the Lenin Offices.

Partisans

By Yehuda Tziglig

Translation by Yocheved Klausner

A short time after the occupation of Lenin the Germans sent all the Jews able to work to the forced labor camp in Hantzewitch. Since we could not stand the indescribable conditions in the camp, we all fled to the near–by forest. Many of us perished. I and Zev Zavin tried to escape; we went through the mud and arrived in the village Heritzinowitz. At nightfall, we found a group of Partisans, among whom we knew several Christians – Rehar Romankes and the Commander Pavel Katowitz from the village Zalyotitz, who had known my father z"l. He received me and Zev and soon we left with them to blow up the railroad in the neighborhood. The commander told us, that we should not be afraid and that the operation must be carried out. If we did it, we would earn the right to remain in the Partisan unit. If not – we will be sent to join our brothers… loud and clear…

Zev and I swore that we shall die for *Kidush Hashem* [sanctification of God's Name] and take revenge on the Germans. The commander showed me how to handle explosives and what I was supposed to do. He called a few more fighters, but we, the two Jews, were the ones chosen to be the first victims [lit. "the sacrificial hen"], we, the troubled and hungry,

[Page 273]

who had made it through the mud in Gritzin and walked on the animal trails.

When we approached the railroad at the village of Bastin, where the explosion had to take place, the commander made a speech and then ordered us to go. We had only vengeance in mind, and we did the work: a train of 43 wagons full of ammunition was thrown into the air. Then we returned to the point where the commander waited for us, and he announced that we can remain in his unit.

I could not rest, and the thought of revenge on the German murderers did not leave me. I spoke to the Commander Pavel and promised him heaven and earth – at that time the fighters were without good clothes or shoes. I promised to procure clothing and shoes for all and suggested to the Commander to go to our shtetl Lenin, to kill the murderous dogs, who spilled so much clean and innocent blood and to take away from them all that they had robbed. My plan was accepted. The commander connected with several other Partisan groups and they established a unit of about 120 fighters. A few days passed until we acquired the necessary ammunition. Then they called me and Zev to help with the final plan of action. I hadn't known before the commander who headed the operation. He personally appointed me as responsible for the success of the action, and sent me to do the preliminary investigation, to find out where exactly the Germans lived in Lenin. We were a small group. We found a Christian woman, who pointed at the houses where the Germans lived, starting from Baruchi's apartment near Israel Gelanson. There was the nest of the murderers – they were a strong power in Lenin.

I reported to the Head Commander and he ordered me to lead the fighters to the right places, and if not, "he will shoot me like a dog." This was his keyword: shoot you like a dog. I answered him that he can do with me what he wanted, but as far as I know my shtetl and am familiar with its streets, I think that the attack will be successful. He stretched out his hand and wished me well, and gave me 10 armed fighters to lead the way and after us will come the rest of the partisans. We kept in contact until we arrived close to Lenin. My task was to bring the fighters

[Page 274]

to the previously determined places. The attack was set to begin at 4 o'clock in the morning, after seeing a red rocket in the sky. Everything was carried out in silence and even the dogs did not sense it. At 3 o'clock all stations were staffed and we waited impatiently for the signal, the red rocket. Finally we began the attack, which lasted without interruption until 8 o'clock in the morning. We received two hand grenades and threw them in through the window into Rodnitzki's apartment, where the German economy–commander lived now. After the explosion of the grenades we moved in, and found the treasures of our shtetl: gold, diamonds and so on. I was not particularly interested in all that; only the wish for revenge burned in my heart. I found a machine–gun and armed myself.

I could not rest. I thought that some people were still in the ghetto. I told my commandant that I have filled all his orders. Meanwhile bullets flew from all sides, because the murderers defended themselves fiercely. Finally we set all their houses on fire and all the German murderers perished.

I received permission to move freely, and I left the fire and walked toward the ghetto. Near the wall I met a policeman from the Palustewitz village. When he saw me he froze, out of fear. My blood boiled and my machine–gun moved him out of my way. Now – over the bridge and into the ghetto. Nobody was in our house. But I spotted the priest's wife, who lived near our house. She told me, that over twenty Jews are in itsky's house. I went there right away and all surrounded me, glad to see me.

I found Yehuda Schuster with his family, and Nashke's daughter with her little twins in her lap. She cried, not knowing what to do with her children. I gave her my last piece of bread and showed them all in what direction to go. Then Moishe Rabinovitch with his family appeared and began to kiss me, asking me what he should do. I mentioned a place where we could later meet, and soon he left. I helped all of them to pass among the fighters. Then we received an order to burn down all the large apartments.

[Page 275]

We burned Hillel Epstein's house, which served as a storehouse for all the robbed Jewish property in Lenin. On my way I met Herman Henkes' brother, a great murderer. I took revenge on him.

Finally, Zev and I went to the graves where our dearest slaughtered relatives rested.

The Partisans' Operation in Sinkewitz

By I. Beigelman

Translation by Yocheved Klausner

On 12th October 1942 the Lenin German police arranged an ambush on the road leading to the Timoshewitz village. Three members of the Girasimowitz Partisan group were caught by German policemen and shot on the spot.

Our leaders decided to take revenge. One hundred armed partisans were organized, headed by our commander Misha. We prepared a plan to blow up the iron bridge and the railroad on the way from Sinkewitz to Mikoshewitz and kill the Germans and the policemen who were there.

When we arrived at the place, we found that special fighters had already cut the telephone wires, and at dawn we were in our places and ready for the attack.

First was the bridge. Our sniper shot the guard, and then several partisans ran and placed 40 kilograms of explosives and the bridge flew in the air.

Our main force awaited this signal and attacked the Police Station and all the nearby buildings. The Germans had not expected that. A difficult battle developed and finally the Police Station and the buildings around it were set on fire. Some of the policemen surrendered, but they received their punishment.

A short time after the blow–up of the bridge a train full of ammunition arrived and stopped at a short distance. We received the order to set the train on fire.

[Page 276]

Soon the train was in flames and a series of explosions began, which destroyed the burning cars. The terrible explosions of the ammunition continued several hours until they reached the last car. Not even one window pane remained unbroken in Sinkewitz and the nearby Makrawa. The explosions were heard to a distance of 40 km.

Three Jews took part in this operation – the writer of these lines, Berl Ginsberg and Boris Kaplan, a young man who died heroically in that battle.

The operation was a great success and we felt we had taken some revenge on the Germans.

Bad News

By Masha Slutsky

Translation by Yocheved Klausner

Dear Friend![1]

You are asking about every one. The men between 14 and 60 years were assembled and sent to a labor camp in Hantzewitz. Only sick people and women with children remained in town, as well as old people like Mordechai Leib, Hillel the Sokowitzer and the rabbi with his 5 little children and pregnant wife. Aharon Neches was the president of the Judenrat; such a "dear" man like him – would he allow the Germans to send him to work?? So he remained home together with Yitzhak Kolpanitsky. There were some 15 such Jews in town and all of them were taken to Hantzewitz, where the Lenin Oblast (district) was established. Elyakum was not taken, because he was very weak, and I had to send my 4 grown sons.

Well, so the Pesach Holiday passed until we reached the month of *Elul* – and all the time they had demands; every hour there was another complaint. Two or three times a day they would come to the Judenrat and demand goods: ten blankets, twenty pillows and so on. Meanwhile they would take the members of the committee – the rabbi Aharon, Lazavnick and Yitzhak Kolpanitsky and ordered that everything should be ready in two hours; if not, they will be shot. Well, you can imagine the sorrow and crying in the streets. Once they demanded ten packs of tobacco, so they called Aharon and asked him to give them the tobacco and they did not release him.

[Page 277]

Neche ran through the streets crying, and we all thought that it was our end, but somehow we gathered what we needed and we thought that we will be left in peace. But nothing helped – and in the month of *Elul* the entire community of Lenin was slaughtered.

How did I survive? I shall tell you, but I don't know whether you will understand me. It was like this: Friday at dawn, the second day of *Rosh Chodesh* [beginning of the month] *Elul* I was sleeping (woe to our sleep!) and suddenly I heard loud cries from the house of Chana and Baruch–Yankel. I said: "There are lowd cries from Chana's house, they are probably murdering them." I left the house quickly, and I saw your Nechem'ke, wearing a coat, running in the street and shouting: "Jews, get up, disaster is here!" Everybody ran out of their houses in tears, asking themselves "Why do we deserve this?" The street was full of people and they began to shout: "Women and children first!" and everybody began to march in line, and I was among them, with my child and Elyakum. First the murderers chose persons who were able to work and had small families, and they wanted to take David, Chaye–Sore's brother. But he had a family, a daughter and a grandchild, so he said "No, I will not let them kill my daughter" so I caught the mother by her hand and I took Elyakum and the child. Then they tore the mother from my hand saying "she is an old woman and she can die". So they took us, 28 Jews, to the New Synagogue – I and Chaia and Yudel with our families and the rest were children. We were kept in the synagogue until 4 in the afternoon. Two patrols were on watch near the synagogue, to see that we will not escape. Through the windows we managed to see, over Zalman's fence, how they led everybody to the automobiles and we didn't know what happened there. We didn't hear shots or shouts, and we only sat in the synagogue not knowing what was going on.

[Page 278]

probably kill us, so why should we go out in the street? The Christians would come to look at us as to some wonder, so when we went to work I would cover my eyes. We lived this way four weeks, until the eve of *Rosh Hashana* [the Jewish New Year]. It was Friday. At about 3:30 in the afternoon we heard shots in the shtetl. What shall we do? We should certainly not go out in the street, but we had already heard from the Christians that in the nearby forest there are partisans so we figured that there was an attack there. What shall we do? I looked through the window and saw Leibe Yoshke's son, Yehuda'ke, running in the street and as he saw me he shouted: "Come with us!" They had already killed seven Germans, and the rest ran away. They were setting the shtetl on fire, so we all came out and ran to the woods.

Elyakum lived in the forest one year and two months and died, and some of the Jews were killed, and others, like myself, survived finding shelter in the houses of good Christians. Don't think that all people are the same. We were their slaves, but they risked their lives by keeping us. Hundreds of Jews were saved by partisans as well.

Well, my friends, it is impossible to describe how I survived the fear in the forest. I don't know, if you will be able to read my letter – because my eyes run with 4 years of a sea of tears, and I don't really see what I am writing. Perhaps someday I will tell you the end of the forest story. – –

Footnote:

1. From a letter to Itka Chinitch in America

[Page 281]

Parties and Institutions

The Zionist Movement

by Avraham Yitzhak Slutsky

Translated by Yocheved Klausner

The Zionist Movement in Lenin began right after the First Zionist Congress. As far as I can remember, the Zionist idea and ideal was brought to Lenin by the young people, who at that time were students in the *Yeshiva*, at the universities or elsewhere. These were Yehoshua Mordechai Tziglig, Yakov Chaim Greenberg, Zalman Bresler, Avraham Meir Paperna and others. I remember that they held their meetings in the attic of Moshe-David's house, as well as in Ben-Zion Tziglig's house. They organized and enlarged the movement. They also organized a children's reading circle. The children's periodical *Olam Katan* [Small World] was received from Warsaw and I would read aloud from it, for my friends, and they liked that very much. I also remember that we sold shares of the Bank Anglo-Palestina, 10 Rubles per share. Very few were able to buy a share for themselves so they bought with a partner. They also bought lottery tickets for 50 Kopekas each. When the sum reached 10 Rubles we would put in a hat the names of all the buyers and drew lots. The winner would receive the money.

In connection with that I remember an interesting event. Among the buyers there was a Christian young man by the name of Albert. His father Martin was an employee of the administration. The young man was befriended with Jewish boys and girls. Once, it happened that he was the winner of the lottery. We suggested that we pay him 10 Rubles for the share he had won, but he refused and kept it as a charm that he hoped would bring him luck.

The movement was strengthened and ramified thanks to new people who appeared in town. In the neighborhood of the administration offices the family Singalovski lived: R'Zelig Singalovski, his wife, their five sons and a daughter. All the sons were handsome, talented and educated. They have studied in the big cities in the country and abroad. They would come home on vacation or for the Holidays and the young people in town would seek their friendship. One of the brothers, Aharon, was a very talented speaker. Once, on the Shabat after the fast of Tish'a BeAv [*Shabat Nachmu*] it was announced that Aharon Singalovski will speak at three o'clock in the afternoon at the New Synagogue. People came, and the synagogue was packed. The speech aroused

[Page 282]

the tempers and people came close to ecstasy. I remember, when he finished his speech people simply surrounded him and kissed him. Yankel Latishka lifted him on his arms and cried with emotion.

An unfortunate incident should also be mentioned, however, which mirrored the feelings of certain circles of the Jewish population and their attitude toward the Zionist ideal. After the speech, when the public calmed down, one of the most respected personalities that lived in town at that time – R'Isser Nakritz, ascended the podium. He began speaking about the Zionist ideals, and suddenly his father-in-law David Graeib, a respected person, rose and immediately caused an uproar. And the meeting, which certainly had been a historic one in our shtetl, broke up. Of the Singalovski brothers I remember that one of them – I think Nachum – went to Eretz Israel and Aharon became one of the main leaders of the ORT organization in Berlin.

Singalovski often visited the United States concerning the ORT affairs. As the president of the Lenin Landsmanshaft in New York, I would invite him to our meetings and, no matter how busy he was, he would gladly come to the meeting. He felt at home and amazed us with his wonderful speaking talent.

The "General-Zionist" *Hechalutz* in Lenin

by Henia Schusterman

Translation by Yocheved Klausner

The General-Zionist *Hechalutz* in our town was founded in 1930-1931. The founders were, as far as I remember:

1. Hershke Singalowitz
2. Shimon Schusterman z"l
3. Shlomo Gelanson
4. Shmuel Schusterman z"l.

Naturally, the main reason for establishing the organization was national, but for our shtetl it was also a specific need, considering the cultural, economic and educational situation of our youth at that time.

[Page 283]

For us, former Lenin residents, it is naturally not necessary to describe the special local conditions of the town; they were felt by every one of us. But since I am trying to write a page of history, I simply cannot skip such an important moment.

Lenin, being a border town, lived constantly under evening curfew. In the summer we could move freely in the streets until 10 and in the winter until 8 in the evening.

It was very difficult for the young people to adapt to the limited evening-hours and there was a constant strive to escape from the confinement and restraint [lit. Sodom-bed] called Lenin. The most important factor was the national feeling, which burned in the young people's hearts. As soon as the organization was formed, the members were ready to go on *Hakhshara* [training].

The writer of these lines was among the first to go on *Hakhshara*. We were sent to several places in Poland. It is difficult to forget the happy moment when one received the authorization to go on *Hakhshara* and later the authorization to make Aliya. Who could equal us! We couldn't imagine a greater happiness. We didn't realize how important we were. As soon as we arrived we were recognized as excellent pioneer elements in all areas; whether in the love of work or in an unlimited devotion to the national ideal. Thanks to that attitude, in a short time all Lenin trainees were admitted to the Aliya group – even before completing the training period.

Apart from very few, who for personal reasons could not make Aliya, all of us went out into the wide world and achieved recognition in its fullest sense. We opened our eyes and saw ourselves in the right light. We found in ourselves hidden and dormant strength, a creational spirit and a healthy world-view. The majority of the Lenin pioneers managed well in Eretz Israel, and were of use to the nation and the land in every respect.

But the heart is bleeding for all those who did not make it.

[Page 284]

Lenin Daughters

Recollections

[Page 287]

Once There Was a Shtetl

Mordechai Zaichik

Translation by Paula F. Parsky

Once there was a shtetl Lenin, a shtetl like all other little shtetlekh in the former Poland. This shtetl was located on the right bank of the river Slutsk[1] which runs into the river Pripets. Since the year 1939, Lenin belonged to Poland. The shtetl, which existed for about 300 years (according to the inscriptions on the oldest gravestones and according to the pinkes [record book] of the Khevre Kadishe [ritual burial society] and other similar sources), was always called Lenin.

It was a great wonder that-the Polish powers tolerated the name of the shtetl for so long and did not change it immediately in the first days of Poland's liberation. Only in 1939, 6 weeks before the Red Army marched into Western Byelorussia and into Western Ukraine, the Polish goverment remembered and changed the name from Lenin to Sosnkovice. But the inhabitants could not get used to the new name and very soon, as soon as the Red Army entered, again called the shtetl by its old name, Lenin.

By and large, Lenin was a very beautiful, clean and happy shtetl. After the end of the schools there, many young people continued their studies in Pinsk or in Vilne. The Jewish youth was 'cnlightened' and intelligent. The shtetl possessed a beautiful public assemply place [folkshoyz], library, electric station, mill, etc. Everything existed until… the German animals in human form entered Lenin. Everything was quickly extinguished, and the destruction of the shtetl began.

In the beginning the Germans drove all the Jews, men and women, to different kinds of labor every day. Often, therefore, they were beaten without justification. The Jews were sent out ahead to repair the roads, so that if a mine lay somewhere, it would blow up on a Jew…

The first victim in Lenin was Nachum Aleynik, who was shot in the neck by an S. S. man as he lay sick in bed. He was shot because he did not give the officer vodka and tobacco quickly enough…

That same evening this same bandit and another of his friends, commanded 8 Jewish youth to be brought into the courtyard of the "Gymne" [gymnasium-a high level high school] and there shot every one of them. One of the young men, Isaac Brodatski, fled, but they pursued him, and seeing that they would very soon capture him, he jumped from the bridge in to the deep lake and never surfaced again. He chose death in the water rather than falling into their murderous hands alive.

After a brief time every day the murderers ransacked and searched, sure that he had surfaced somewhere and was in hiding.

[Page 288]

In a matter of days, the murderers had killed another 15 people. Among them, the Gorodetski family of five, who were killed because of the betrayal of the Burgermeister's [mayor's] wife, a Gentile who had quarreled with the young wife Khaye Gorodetski over a petty thing. Khaye shouted at her, "Don't think your power has come!" And that was enough. That same evening she and her mother were led to "the little mountain" outside the shtetl and on the way, in the street, both were shot in the neck. They lay there in the street for an entire day. Her brother and two small sons (twins) were shot in their homes and the twins were then thrown outside. The next morning, nothing more that remained of them but their heads, gnawed by pigs.

Chaya Gorodetski and her husband, with their twins, Asher'ka and Yudela

In a short time, the 10th of May 1942, they made a ghetto in Lenin and drove all the Jews from the shtetl into one street, fenced in on all sides. Each house held between 20-30 people. Going out was forbidden, except with special work permits. The situation worsened daily, though in truth, it must be written that some members of the Gentile population helped greatly and by various means made efforts to smuggle bread, flour, milk, potatoes, etc. into the ghetto. Yet there was not a day when all sorts of things were not confiscated from the Jewish population: once shoes, another time, clothing, laundry, watches, sugar, cocoa, soap, perfume, musical instruments, etc., etc.

[Page 289]

Misery and fear of the unknown future were in everyone's face. Very often we used to speak among ourseles to strengthen each other, saying that this government would not last long, and ultimately, they would suffer a defeat, regardless of the temporary entry of the Red Army. We had no contact with the neighboring shtetlakh, but we knew that ghettos existed everywhere.

One evening all the Jews of the ghetto were rounded up and those able to work were selected. In the morning of the 22nd of May 1942, they were sent by train to a work camp in Hantsevitsh (near Baranovitsh). There were already 120 Jews from the shtetl Pagost (near Pinsk) there; altogether, including us, there were 350 men between the ages of 14 and 60 years old. Fathers and sons were there, and often some sets of brothers. We were quartered in a far corner of the shtetl in a small dirty alleyway, in some little houses, 30-40 men in a house, sleeping on 3-tiered bunks. In such close quarters we had to be concerned about sanitation. In a sanitary inspection, if a louse was found, the "infested one" could be shot. Also for becoming sick or getting mange (or scabies), etc., – a bullet. Therefore, though we had to work hard, nobody dared to fall ill. We got 200 grams of bread a day and 20 grams of barley-that was all.

Groups of people immediately began to think about running away. But to where and with what? We had very dark news about locating partisans anywhere,. We were guarded at work during the day; at night, we were watched-by the police. Very often there would be a sudden inspection to verify that we were all in our places. If a person were missing, it was said, that the entire camp would be shot.

Every day, the decision to escape became stronger. But we had to arrange it that everyone would run at the same time, not individually. If we had organized merely the pile of people who were all the while chomping at the bit to escape, all those who remained in the camp and those remaining in our shtetl Lenin would have been murdered.

One evening in late summer, all as one, we abandoned everything, and without even a bit of bread, began to run in the direction of the woods, about 2 kilometers from the city. This happened so spontaneously and unexpectedly that by the time the Germans and the police realized it, we had already overcome all the obstacles on the way, like deep ditches of water, barbed wire fences, etc. and were entering the woods.

[Page 290]

It had become very dark. The whole group got scattered and lost. Not knowing well enough where to run, we divided up into groups and spread out in different directions. In my group were 23 men. The shooting around us seemed to be growing closer in every direction, but thanks to the deep woods and our own carefulness, we succeeded in part to break through, and in a while many of us reached various partisan camps that took 3 or 4 of us in. A great many of us were killed along the way; some by the bullets of the Germans and the police; some were captured and brought back and hanged. Among those hanged were the five Gelanson brothers, two fathers and their sons, and others; all together 20 men. In total, those of us who remained alive joined partisan groups, perhaps 80-90 men of 230 who fled. I personally wandered around for eight weeks until I was taken in by partisans. Almost the entire time I ate only berries and raw mushrooms.

At that time, a punishment force of S. S. men arrived in Lenin, and with the police of Lenin and the surrounding villages, they cruelly slaughtered the entire Jewish population, leaving only 28 "specialists," who a month later, joined the partisans who had entered Lenin. All the remaining people, over 900 souls, were surrounded on all sides by the Germans and led in cars in groups to the "little mountain" outside the shtetl. On the way, the young women sang songs and shouted "Down with the bandits! Long live the Red Army which will avenge our young blood!"

Tanis the pharmacist and his wife poisoned themselves on the way in the car. Someone jumped in the lake. Near the little mountain everyone removed their clothes and was shot by automatic weapons and thrown, most still alive, in mass graves, bodies laid on top of each other. The blood of the elderly mixed with the blood of women and small children. In one hour's time, everything was finished. Lenin was judenrein.

In a few days, three young women who had hidden themselves were found by the local police and shot. One woman who was found and locked up overnight hanged herself there.

No better fate befell the remaining Gentile population of the shtetl. A few months later the 800 people were driven into a foundry which was set afire, and they were burned alive. After setting fire to the entire shtetl, the Germans and the police of the area left for Mikashevitsh, where they remained until the arrival of the Red Army.

[Page 291]

Not one house remained in Lenin; the streets became overgrown by tall, wild grasses; it was simply difficult even to recognize whose home once stood in which place. Only by the hills of bricks and charred remains of trees could you stumble upon it.

This is the tragic summary of the three year reign of the Nazi murderers in Lenin. It is a bit of consolation that a small number of the German murderers were paid back in kind, and that among those who took vengeance upon the barbarians were many young people from Lenin, either as partisans or as solders of the Red and Polish armies.

Many of our youth sacrificed their lives to exterminate the Nazi pest.

[1]   NB: The names of places in this document have been transliterated from Yiddish; I have not researched their Polish language equivalents.

Types and Customs

Mordechai Zaichik

Translation by Paula F. Parsky

With a bit of pride, it can be recalled that, in contrast to many of the nearby shtetlekh, even the artisans of Lenin were not ignorant. Many of the wagon drivers and artisans liked to embellish their words with the sayings of the Sages and Biblical passages and ruminate over a chapter of Isaiah. They were also well acquainted, some of them even versed in the Talmud.

Yisroel the Blacksmith

Yisroel Gelanson, or Yisroel the Blacksmith, as he was called, worked all his life at his forge. But always in his free hours after work he would sit with his Gemorrah and actually understood what he studied.

Baynish the Shoemaker

Baynish the shoemaker, a quiet, tall Jew, who walked erect with a cane, his hands on his back, would sit more often in shul with a page of Gemorrah than he would sit at work. And he could study.

Khayim Khaykl

Khayim Khaykl, a simple but very pious Jew, worked hard, always dragging a "Utshinke" or a skin of a calf with his big, heavy boots covered in mud... But Shabbos! He threw off all his dirt and cares!

The entire day he would enjoy himself in shul at the pulpit, saying Psalms, the congregation after him- that was his "franchise"… he was more gifted than anyone else in Psalms. It ran through him like a psalm.

Wagon Drivers

Even traveling with the wagon drivers in the long, always muddy ditches to the station in Mikashevitsh, you were not bored, because of the various sayings, passages, legends and stories that you would hear from them the entire time.

They would even speak to their horses with a special "Hebrew" [Holy language] lexicon taken from Tevye the Milkman.

Betzalel Zaichik and his sons, Binyamin and Yehuda and a grandson

Betzalel "the Greek"

Here I will recall a very special type of the years gone by, that was Betzalel Zaichik, or Betzalel 'the Greek," as he was called.

They called him "the Greek" because he was one of the cantonists of the time of Nikolai the First when young boys would be seized and sent away to study in the military, where they had to serve for an entire 25 years…

Betzalel was one of those, who, as an eleven year old boy, was captured and loyally served the entire 25 years.

Although he had spent so many years among the Gentiles, he used to say he almost never profaned the Sabbath and also did not eat "treyf."

Physically, he was well-developed-- in gait and appearance, a true military man. He rose to the rank of sergeant-major, in those days, a great accomplishment.

Specific Russian curses which he would use when he became angry remained with him.

He lived a very long time, and until the end, was healthy and in full control of his faculties.

In the year 1928, during the visit of Polish General Skladowski to Lenin, among other delegates, Betzalel Zaichik presented himself, asking the General to recognize his right to a pension, which he deserved, in his opinion, because of his long years of service to the Russian Czar. Besides, he bragged of his distinguished service-- among other things, in his participation in the suppression of the famous Polish uprising of 1863. The General, hearing these words, angrily replied, "What?! You fought against us and want us to be grateful for you and grant you a pension for this?!" Of course, he received none.

"Snagging" a Cow

In his old age, people would go to him to snag a cow (it was called that because he was an expert in this), this means, when a cow didn't return from the fields with the herd and wandered off somewhere. In such circumstances the owner of the cow would come to Betzalel "the Greek," to have him "snag" it. That meant that the cow would remain in one place, where it had strayed and not go off to another place. This made it easier to find the cow and bring it back home.

He did not do this willingly, complaining that he couldn't do it, that he was mere flesh and blood. But he would nevertheless let himself be convinced to "snag" the cow.

People would also go to him to undo an "evil eye."

He died at the age of 94 in 1933.

[Page 294]

My Mother

Sarah Fogelman

Translation by Paula F. Parsky

In a street of our shtetl that was inhabited mainly by Gentiles and only a few Jews, lived a Jewish family with a lot of small children. The father of the family, a weak man, was not able to fully care for his children. And the household often went hungry and never had enough to eat. The father would go away on Sunday for the entire week to the neighboring villages to earn his living. The daily burden and care of the entire family fell chiefly to the mother, a small, exhausted woman, her hands always busy with work and her head always full of worries about how to get a bit of food for her children. In addition, there was also an old father, who together with the entire family, ten souls all together, lived-in the same little one room house.

From time to time the family, like other families who lived in difficult social conditions, were helped for the Sabbath with various products, like Shabbos candles, challah, etc., as was the custom in the little shtetlekh. But, given the poverty of the family, this support was like a drop of water in the sea.

Nevertheless, the cleanliness and order of the little house was something to marvel at. Right at the door, you could see the yellow sand that had been scattered so that no one would track inside the mud for which our shtetl, located in the middle of several swamps, was noted. Opening the door, you always would encounter the mother, her hands occupied with washing, darning, dusting or preparing food-a few spoiling potatoes and barley. That was generally their lunch.

Because there were children of my age to play with, I was a frequent guest in that house. I would observe how the little children would sit around the table and wait impatiently until the mother cut off a bit of the black, rounded bread for each outstretched hand. Many times, a child would not be content with his portion, and would complain that his brother's piece was a little bigger, until the mother would shout for quiet, and with a sigh, burst into tears, quietly resume her work. I remember that in my house, we didn't lack for food, and yet suddenly, such an appetite would come upon me that it seemed to me that if the woman had offered me such a bit of bread, I would have eaten it gladly!

On Friday evenings, the children would look out into the distance for their guest-their father-with great happiness. Seeing him approaching, they would run to meet him and help him carry his sack that he carried on his shoulders, with the bit of products he earned for his week's work. Often his wife would pour the pain and bitterness of the entire week onto the head of her husband. And yet she didn't complain too terribly about her fate and hoped patiently that when the children would grow up, they would lighten their heavy burden.

And so it happened. In time, the two older sons each taught themselves a trade, and in that same room which served as the lodging for the entire family, there was also a place for their workshops. It is hard to imagine, but even this did not disrupt the cleanliness of this living space, with the two beds, always--made up with white sheets, taut pillows, and brightly embroidered covers which remained from her girlhood. The two only beds near the oven served the entire family. Each night before going to sleep the mother did not forget to change the pretty covers of the pillows to simple ones, to preserve the decorated ones. She knew that she would not be able to buy new pretty pillowcases very easily.

So this family lived, like many other families, unpretentiously, in poverty, suffering, hope and faith. They raised a generation of quiet, honest children, artisans who later lived, worked, and earned a living for themselves and their families. This continued until the Holocaust that made an end to everything and everyone, and equalizing everyone in one mass grave: no more cares, no more worries, no more earnings, no more life; one mass grave for everyone, for the hungry and for the well-fed, for the contented, for the suffering.

The filthy Nazi hands destroyed everything and left only a mass grave to commemorate our little shtetl Lenin.

[Page 295]

Berele the Bookseller [*Mokher Sefarim*]

Yitzhak Slutsky

Translation by Yocheved Klausner

Berele the Bookseller came to our shtetl when I was still a young boy. It was said that he came to town from "somewhere" and remained. He had no family, lived alone and was in general a great mystery. He never said a word about himself and told us nothing.

There was a rumor, that he came from Vilna, that he had committed a terrible sin,

[Page 296]

and, to atone for his sin he was ordered by the rabbis to go on exile and to wander all his life, rejected by his home and family. Our shtetl has been his place of exile.

I never knew how much of this was true. As you can see by his name, he sold books. His books were: a prayer book, a collection of sayings and commentaries, a book of prayers for women, a booklet of the blessing after meals, *mezuzahs*, *tzitzit*, a Book of Psalms, a novel, Hershele Ostropoler's stories, a *Chabad* booklet and the like. He held all this under lock and key in the synagogue, where he kept several boxes. From this book–trade, however, he could not support himself, even though he lived alone, so he became assistant to the beadle in the new synagogue. He worked also as a water–carrier: the poor man would carry two buckets full of water from the river, hanging from a wooden bar on his shoulders, for the people in town.

In addition to all that, he became a watchman. As you know, in our town we had night–watchmen, who would take turns to walk through the town during the night, to watch for fires or thieves. When someone was too lazy to go, or couldn't do his turn for other reasons, he would engage Berele the bookseller who, for three Kopeks would walk at night around town with a large "clapper" to let know the thieves that he was there…

There were rumors in town, that Berele had saved money, since he worked day and night, slept in the synagogue and ate almost nothing. Some day his exile punishment would end and he will return to his family with a treasure. – – – –

Chaim Grone–Yentes

Avraham Yitzhak Slutsky

Translation by Yocheved Klausner

Chaim "the crazy one," as I remember him, was not crazy at all. He was a very handsome young man, tall, slim, with a clear face and a small, beautiful blonde beard.

He was a great learner. He would sit in the old shul and study together with Itche (Yitzhak), the son of the old rabbi. People used to call him Chaim Grone–Yentes, after the name of his wife. He had a daughter, her name was Mirl. She lives now in America.

His mental illness, as I remember, was expressed only by his long walks on the outskirts of town, alone and absorbed in thought. He was always a loner, isolated and abandoned by his family. The children in town liked him. They followed him and he told them beautiful stories, fables and legends.

[Page 297]

But not only the little children; the lumber merchants greatly enjoyed a chat with R'Chaim and loved to listen to his good jokes. As soon as he was seen, he was encircled by listeners – every one of them trying to "catch a word" with him. He always had some small change, and was never in want of a meal. However, he never stretched out his hand to ask for charity; on the contrary, it was considered an honor when R'Chaim agreed to accept a few coins or a meal. On Sabbath he was always the guest of R'Zecharia Koptzes.

Many of the lodgers in Baruch–Yankel Baruchin's guest–house were workers in the lumber business. It was told that Pessel, Baruch–Yankel's wife, asked R'Chaim to "say a good word" – and Chaim, without thinking much, said:

"I wonder about your father: I remember him as a good and righteous Jew – how come such a Jew transgressed and violated an explicit prohibition of the Torah?!"

"What prohibition did he violate?" asked Pessel.

"It says very clearly in the Ten Commandments: 'You shall not make any Pessel' [carved idol] – and your father has made a 'Pessel' …."

Chaim was popular not only among the Jewish population. Many of the Christians knew that one can always hear from Chaim a witty saying or a clever answer. Peasants from a neighboring village once told us, that on Sunday, going to church, they met Chaim and said to him: "Chaim'ke, you ought to be killed."

"Why?" asked Chaim.

"Because your Jews have killed our god."

"No – said Chaim – the Lenin Jews wouldn't do such a thing. Maybe it was the Starobin Jews." (Starobin was a neighboring village).

The lumber merchant Pinchas Kaplan liked to tell stories and anecdotes, and also liked to listen to them. One day at twilight, he sat with other merchants near the beautiful entrance of Ben–Zion Tziglig's house. Chaim passed by, deep in thought. Pinchas said to him: Chaim, tell us something, and you receive a Ruble.

Chaim stopped and said: "Well, if you answer my question, you get all my possessions" – and he took out of his pocket twenty Kopeks and said "this is all that I possess."

"OK, ask" they said to him.

"Listen – said Chaim – I am coming now from the river. I was standing on the bridge, looking at the water. I was looking hard, and what did I see?

[Page 298]

another Chaim: exactly as you see me here in front of you – Chaim with the unbuttoned shirt, with a leather belt on his pants, just like the belt on my own pants. In one word – the same Chaim as the one in front of you. Only the other Chaim, God help me, was standing on his head – his head down and his feet up on the air. Now I am asking you: That other Chaim, who is standing with his head down, what does he need the belt on his pants for?…

Several answers were given, but not one of them was satisfactory. So Pinchas Kaplan finally asked: "Well, Chaim, you tell us, what is the answer?"

"Don't you understand – said Chaim – that if that other Chaim in the river would not have a belt on his pants, this Chaim's pants – the Chaim who is standing before you – would fall down?"

Chaim was strangely attracted to the river. He was often seen on the bank of the river, looking thoughtfully to the water, observing the little fish swimming around and saying: How good would it be, if I were also a little fish with all the other fish. I wouldn't have to suffer my terrible headaches.

Chaim was a very good swimmer. In the summer, the bathing season, he saved children from drowning, many times.

Aharon Singalovski said: in the streets of Lenin, a living encyclopedia is walking around – the crazy Chaim. He knew Talmud, *Poskim* [deciders in religious Law], and the entire Rabbinic literature. He knew the Jewish history – not from the history books but from reading the Rabbinic Responsa.

And this wonderful scholar, whom we all – children and adults – loved and admired, well knew that he was mentally ill. Sometimes he would talk and complain about it. In my time he was calm, but one of the elders in our community, who now lives in Israel, relates that at the beginning of his illness Chaim was very disturbed. Moshe Yakov Temkin, Yechiel's son, once saw him running wild in the streets. Moshe Yakov wanted to calm him down, but Chaim raised his strong hand and slapped him. Later, when the attack was over, Chaim went to Moshe Yakov and asked forgiveness. When the acute phase of his illness was over, he gave his wife a divorce. Since then he slept in Yechiel Temkin's home and ate his Sabbath and holiday meals at the home of Zecharia Slutsky (Koptzes), the father of Eliyahu–Aharon the slaughterer.

[Page 299]

My Parents

Henia Schusterman

Translation by Yocheved Klausner

Our dear Shtetele and our beloved home, which we have lost and were uprooted from it so soon!

My holy parents, sisters and brothers z"l, how can I diminish your pain and suffering? I shall, at least, remember your holy names with a few words.

I remember the glowing holidays, how beautifully my father recited the prayers, with his sweet voice! His handsome face, his stature and his proud walk commanded respect. I would wait for the Sabbath morning walk to shul. Early in the morning, when all were still in bed, my father would read the *Tehillim* [Psalms] Book or study the weekly Torah Portion. I thought that this would last forever, as would his beautiful beard (we were a very religious family).

People would come to us and say to my father: Reb Dovid! See, we must do something, our young people, even your own children, shave on Sabbath day, smoke on Sabbath – they are not Jews anymore! To you they will listen, if you talk to them! And my good and wise father would reply: We should be good Jews ourselves. As to our dear sons and daughters – of course it would be good if they were following the path of their parents. But I tell you, dear Jews, we should not sever the good relations with our dear young men and women, they are going to build Eretz Israel... we must understand them...

My father perished and soon my mother perished too, and my sisters and brothers. All have worked for the community, but did not live to see and hear what we have accomplished.

May God avenge their blood!

The Lenin Hard Workers

Menashe Yulevich (Latocha)

Translation by Yocheved Klausner

I am certain, that many of those who deserve to be mentioned in a Yizkor Book will, for various reasons, not be included.

As a matter of fact, every person who has lived in the shtetl should be remembered, because

[Page 300]

every single one is so dear and unforgettable – all of them, old and young, all the good and honest Lenin Jews. Our merchant was not fully a merchant, not in the full sense of the word; a considerable part of his time he spent reading a book or learning a "page" of the Talmud. For many, commerce was a kind of side–occupation.

What remained unforgotten in my mind from my childhood years in Lenin were the craftsmen, the hard workers, the heavy toilers, who worked from dawn until late at night to earn the piece of bread for their families, never complained, and lived a righteous, honest Jewish life.

They were truly religious, got up at dawn for the morning prayer, ran late afternoon to the synagogue for the *Mincha* prayer, remained in the synagogue for some study and finished their day with the evening prayer, *Maariv*. This was their only free time, since afterward, coming home, they went back to work and before going to bed they never forgot to recite the *Keri'at Shema*.

Yet, they were not always entirely immersed in their work. Their strength of character helped them create a way of life that was filled with spiritual power as well as worldly culture. Many were talented in song, music and art, but not always did they have the means to develop their talents, which were therefore lost sometimes. Some had beautiful voices: from the tailor's, cobbler's or carpenter's workshops heartwarming pieces of *Hazanut* [cantor's prayers] would be heard, as well as the cantor's own compositions, especially before the High Holidays.

I remember that Gedalia Kaplan, R'Menuse's son–in–law, had a fine tenor voice; he would sing the prayers beautifully; I remember also the prayer of R'Nachum Nathan, or, as he was called by all Nushke – an honest hard–working Jew with a beautiful Jewish face. This was for him a source of joy in his hard life. His melodies are ringing in my ears to this day.

Other craftsmen excelled in Talmud study, and through the years some reached a high level of knowledge so that they could learn by themselves or even teach – like R'Beinush Kirzner the shoemaker and R'Israel Gelanson the smith.

A special meaning for the workers had the Sabbath, the real Day of Rest. On this day the toiling man turned into a prince, and he welcomed the Queen of Sabbath with due respect and honor.

The craftsmen could truly savor the Sabbath, after a week of hard work. Friday night, when all was shining, the wooden floor scrubbed clean and covered with sawdust and the room filled with the fine smell of the Sabbath dishes – was for them the true holiday, as the *Shechina* [Divine Presence] was all around.

[Page 301]

The man comes home from shul, greets his wife with a hearty "*Gut Shabes*" and begins to recite the "*Shalom Aleichem*" Sabbath song. The wife, weary with toil, who all week baked bread for the entire family, carried wood for the stove, brought water, fed the children – and all this without help – is now feeling good and satisfied. She had spread her hands over the candles in the brass candlesticks and said a silent prayer, thanking God for everything, not complaining about her hard life, asking for just one thing for her husband and family – health and peace…

The bloody storm that erupted over hundreds of cities and towns has not spared our shtetele, and all our workers, their mothers and their lives – all perished. The human mind cannot grasp and the heart cannot bear the great disaster.

Your memory will remain with us forever.

A Guest in our Town
(The visit of Chaia Sara Lifshitz, summer 1933)

M. Jaffe

Translation by Yocheved Klausner

A feeling of well–being prevailed among the Lenin Jews. They were like one wide family, with mutual devotion and care.

When a happy event occurred in a family – when someone's daughter married or a child was born and the family celebrated his *Brit* [circumcision], it was a happy occasion for the entire town; everybody, old and young, took part in the festivity, feeling involved and happy together with the family.

Also when, God forbid, a sad event occurred, mourning in a home, the entire shtetl felt sad and mourned with the bereaved family.

And when a rumor spread that someone had difficulties in earning his livelihood, that a family did not have enough for the marriage of their daughter or that a family had a sick person at home and couldn't afford to call the doctor – many were immediately prepared to help. Quietly, almost secretly, the needed money was collected. Not one refused to contribute something, naturally according to their means – the Lenin Jews were never very rich people.

There were times in the shtetl, when some of the Jews – individuals or entire families – began imitating the people of neighboring villages or shtetlach and wandered out of the old home to

[Page 302]

far lands over the ocean, some to rich America, some to Argentina, in later years to Eretz Israel as well. Difficult, very difficult was the separation from their beloved and warm home, from the dear Jewish Shtetele where all the dear and beloved Jews grew up together, were happy together and mourned together. All of them missed very much their abandoned shtetele. Those who left as well as those who remained felt the longing.

During many long years and to this day a permanent correspondence is maintained between the Lenin Jews. Will you ever find a Lenin Jew, wherever he might live, who wouldn't have a relative "abroad?" But who needs a blood relative? Every Jew, if he comes from Lenin, is considered one's own, just like a member of the family. All Leniner are keeping in close contact, correspond with each other, share happy – and sad – events and try, as much as they can, to help each other when needed.

* * *

Can one imagine the joy and delight of all Jews in town when, after a long separation of 25 years a visitor came from America – one of our own, a former Leniner? Such was the feeling when Chaia Sarah Lifshitz, the daughter of Avraham Schusterman from Anantchitz, came in 1933 from America on a visit. She made that long trip to take part in the happy occasion of the marriage of her niece Bashe (Ashman), the daughter of her sister Gitl Gurevich. It was a great joy all around. The impressions of those happy days are to this day engraved in the memory of many Leniner.

Chaia Sarah is still living in Brooklyn and is well–known as a devoted communal worker. In her younger days, she was the living spirit and the most outspoken member of the American committee of the Lenin Landsleit. During her visit in Lenin she acted the same way: she gave the many gifts she had brought with her, and she didn't rest before she organized a Women's Relief Committee (see photo on page 303), whose stated aim was to help the needy in town.

Not always does God shed His Grace on the good and righteous people; sometimes they are the ones who are painfully punished. After her return from Lenin, Chaia Sarah became ill and her right leg and left hand became paralyzed and she suffers great pain to this day.

[Page 303]

This picture shows a gathering of the Lenin Women's Relief Committee with its organizer, Chaya Sarah Lifshitz (holding flowers)

Top row, standing (from right to left): Rochel Schusterman (perished), Zisha Epstein (lives in America), Freidka Vagshal, Sarah Henya Levin (perished), Basha Ashman (lives in Tel Aviv), Henya Latocha (lives in Tel Aviv), Yentl Starobinski (perished), Esther Slutsky (lives in Tel Aviv), Chana Tziglig (lives in Tel Aviv), Risha Yehoshuas (perished).
Middle row, seated (from right to left): Chana Kravetz (lives in Tel Aviv), Golda Mandelbaum (died), Chasha Riva Zavin (perished), Ethel Bresler (perished), Rochel Millstein - The Rebbitzen (perished), Chaya Sarah Lifshitz - the guest (lives in America), Gitel Gurevich (perished), Necha Zaretzki (perished), Chaya Leah Chinitch - the wife of the Cantor (perished), Raizel Lazavnick (perished).
Bottom row, seated (from right to left): Breindl Migdalovich, Sarah Rubenstein (lives in Israel), Faigel Schmelkin (died in Russia), Yehudit Kolpanitsky (lives in Tel Aviv)

[Page 304]

Jews of Lenin bid farewell to Chaya Sarah Lifshitz upon her return
to America

[Page 305]

The Rabbi R'Yehuda Turetski z"l
(The articles by Mordechai Zaichik and Avraham-
Yitzhak Slutsky, pp. 309, 312)

[Page 307]

Synagogues and Religious Personnel

Mordechai Zaichik

Translation by Yocheved Klausner

The Old Synagogue

The Old Synagogue was built around 1870. Before that, a small synagogue stood on the same plot of land.

The new shul [synagogue] was built around the old one, on all four sides, without touching it, and the prayers were held regularly until the new building was completed. Only then was the old little shul torn down.

The new building (still called, of course, "The old Shul") was tall and was built from the best wood, acquired at a reasonable price from the owner of the forests, the Graf Witgenstein.

Most of the expenses of the work and the additional material needed, until completion, were met by the *Gevir* [rich man] of the town at that time, R' Mordechai Tziglig, son of Mendel.

The synagogue had many seats, a large *Bimah* with additional seats around it, a beautifully carved Ark for the Torah Scrolls, etc.

The women's section was situated on the second floor, with a view to the men's section. There was also a small room for an extra *minyan* [prayer service, lit. prayer quorum of 10 men], mostly for those who came in late.

The people who prayed in the synagogue itself were of the old and well–situated families in town. The rabbi and the cantor had their own permanent seats in the South–Eastern, honored corner of the synagogue.

Most of the other people who prayed in the shul were plain laborers of the lower classes, *amcha* – "Simple Jews."

As mentioned, the synagogue was large, especially in relation to the town itself, and occupied an area of 400 square meters.

In later years, the long beams that supported the ceiling began to bend, and they were strengthened by four wide columns.

The Bimah and the Ark were quite beautiful, but not too luxurious.

The synagogue also served as the place where various disputes and quarrels between members were resolved, not excluding even fights and slaps on the face – and to make it worse, even on Shabat… and when? during the reading of the Torah. The reasons of the fights were often petty and trivial, even foolish.

[Page 308]

Various festivities, in honor of the Russian, and later the Polish holidays were held in the synagogue as well.

Clearly, the various preachers delivered their sermons in the Shul. Also, only here could one say his prayers with all his heart and soul. Only in the Old Shul could one feel the meaning of truly "pouring out one's soul."

No one was ashamed to pray from the depth of his heart and burst into tears for as long as he wanted.

Always, at any hour of the day one could find here a man sitting with his *Talit* and *Tefilin* [in prayer, lit. with prayer–shawl and phylacteries], or learning a "page of the Talmud" [*daf Gemara*], or simply read from a book.

The New Shul

The New Shul was much younger than the Old one – was built later, in 1900–1904. It was located at the beginning of the Parlipie Street, on the left side.

It was much smaller than the Old Shul, but much more beautiful. It can be truthfully said that it was a very beautiful Shul. The walls and the ceiling were artfully painted and the Torah Ark was a masterpiece of carved branches and fruits, which stared at us as if they were real.

This was where the Lenin intelligentsia prayed, the well–to–do house owners [*Balebatim*] and the sons–in–law who had come from other towns and shtetlach.

Old, established Lenin families were few in that shul. Here, one felt a little more free. In the near-by *shtiebel*, actual politics was analyzed and discussed constantly…

On Friday nights, especially in the winter, when the evenings were long, outside was cold and inside the shul pleasant warmth was spreading from the little stoves around the *bimah*, people would gather after the Shabat dinner to listen to the Weekly Portion of the Torah.

The rabbi was the teacher, and all kinds of people would sit around the table and listen: learned Jews and simple Jews, who loved to listen to the beautiful stories, in particular from the books of Genesis and Exodus.

This was not simple and superficial learning of the Torah Portion; it comprised profound discussions about the various commentators, legends, wise sayings of the great scholars through the generations, etc.

The members of the congregation loved to come to these lessons and really enjoyed them.

[Page 309]

At the same time, the younger boys and some of the 14–15 year-old boys would sit together around the warm stoves, in half darkness, and listen to various mystery and miracle stories, told by the older lads: about devils, robbers, jokers, heroes from Russian tales, as Ilya Murametz, Elyosha Popovici and others.

The young listeners would sit close to one another, fearing to make a move and listen breathlessly to the stories that the older boys told.

And, at times of distress, people would come running to the old or the new synagogue. The Holy Ark with its Torah Scrolls, more than once listened and absorbed the anguish and weeping of the women, who came the "cry out" for illness, suffering or persecution…

The Rabbi R'Yehuda Turetski z"l

Mordechai Zaichik

Translation by Yocheved Klausner

A

We do not have any information about the first rabbi in our shtetl. It is only known, that a rabbi was officiating in Lenin during the years 1830–1860. He was probably one of the first, since before that the number of Jews was too small to afford a rabbi. The slaughterer in town performed the functions of a Rabbi as well.

The history of the rabbis in Lenin begins with the arrival of the rabbi R'Yehuda Turetski, about 1860. A detailed discussion should be devoted to this rabbi, for several reasons: first, he served as rabbi in the shtetl for over 66 years; second, because of his personality and exceptional qualities as a person.

Rabbi Yehuda devoted all his time – day and night, at the shul and at his home – to studying Torah, make Halakhic decisions, resolving arguments, marrying bride–and–groom, etc. He distanced himself from worldly affairs, did not know even one word of the Russian language.

He was a wise Jew, sometimes left the impression of being a strict, even angry person.

He was the student of famous great scholars from the old generation and a friend of the "Chafetz Chayim" and several other great rabbis.

Almost all his years he lived in poverty, only during the last few years his situation improved a little. The reason was not that the town could not afford to support him; in those times it was taken for granted that a

[Page 310]

Rabbi should lead a modest life, as it is written [in *Pirkei Avot* – Wisdom of the Fathers]: "Bread and salt should you eat"…

The rabbi made his living "from the 'karabke'" ["from the tax–box"], that is, from the "concession" to sell candles for Shabat, sell yeast, recite the Yizkor prayer [memorial prayer for the dead], sell the *Hametz* [leavened food] before Passover, as well as from various small payments and gifts from the rich and well–to–do.

The rabbi was much loved not only by Jews, but by the municipal authorities and by the surrounding Christians as well. In particular was he loved by the priest, who would visit him often, especially when he was ill; they would sit for hours and talk, with the help of an interpreter.

The Christians had great respect for the rabbi, although he was very seldom seen in the street. They regarded him as a holy man.

As mentioned, he was almost always sitting by the open *Gemara* [Talmud] or another book; his custom was also to pace through the room back and forth, with small quick steps, thinking of what he was studying at the time.

When a Jew would bother him too long with trivial questions or discussion, he would say to him: "Well, a good night to you" and gave him his hand, as if saying: "Go home in good health, R'Jew"…

His room was never empty – with every small matter the Jew would go to the rabbi; all the disputes and worries he would bring to the rabbi; no court of justice was held in greater respect.

He lived in town, as mentioned, 66 years, and died at the age of 96 years.

Perhaps he would have lived even longer, had he not broken a leg. One day the rabbi stumbled and fell, and his leg broke. They brought for him the famous surgeon from Minsk, Dr. Yevseyenka, who operated on the leg and did what he could regardless of the age of the rabbi, and the leg began to heal. But as fate would have it, he soon broke the same leg again, and this time it was necessary to amputate. This difficult surgery was too much for him and he passed away.

It is hard to describe the mourning of the entire town after the death of the old and beloved rabbi. The Lenin Jews mourned for a long, long time and could not forget their great *Tzadik*.

Famous rabbis from the surrounding towns and shtetlach came to the funeral, with eulogies by R'Itchele, the Lachover rabbi, R'Valkin the rabbi from Pinsk and others.

R'Yehuda Turetski had 4 sons and 3 daughters – all talented and learned: R'Itche, R'Aba, R'Shmuel–Mechl, R'Moshe, Sheindl, Ete and Bashe.

R'Itche died young, of a snake bite in the forest;

[Page 311]

R'Moshe was rabbi in London; R'Shmuel–Mechl was rabbi in Pinsk and was called "the Karliner *dayan*" [dayan = judge in the religious court]. He was a Jew with a silken soul, a great learner and very erudite. He published a book dedicated to his father, which contained a collection of sermons, commentaries and "good words" [sayings, explanations]. The daughter Eta lived in Pyotrikov; Bashe and her husband R'Yakov the slaughterer lived at first in Lenin where they had a grocery, and later in Minsk; Sheindl and her husband R'Hillel lived in Kazhanhorodek.

* * * *

After the rabbi's death, R'Nachman Wasserman was appointed rabbi. He was a wise and worldly Jew, good looking and friendly. His home was always full of people, who came mostly to ask for advice. He was a gifted speaker. The shul was full when he delivered his Shabat sermon. He was a Zionist. But he did not stay long in Lenin, for he was appointed as rabbi in the shtetl Stavisk, near Lomzhe.

* * * *

After R'Nachman Wasserman left it was not easy to choose a new rabbi. More than six months passed, and the shtetl could not find a suitable rabbi. There were two "camps" that couldn't come to an agreement: when one candidate was accepted by one camp, the other camp was against, and vice–versa…

Still there was one thing that the entire shtetl enjoyed during all that time: The congregation heard speeches and sermons from all types of rabbis: young and old, with black, yellow and red beards, and some even without a beard at all. Every member of the community could almost become a rabbi himself…

Fridays and Saturdays, sometimes even during week-days, the synagogues were full of men, women and children, who came to hear the sermons. It looked as if everybody left their work only to come and see the rabbis, how they looked and how they spoke, in order to decide who would be the best candidate and should stay in town. Obviously, each candidate made every effort to show his best side, until the people became utterly confused… Finally, they chose as rabbi R'Moishele Millstein, or R'Moishele "Warshaver" – a young rabbi, a known *Illuy* [genius] and good looking; he was also a *maskil* [enlightened], that is he knew several languages and was involved in general issues. He had 5 children, all of them beautiful. Had a pleasant voice for learning and prayer… He had lived for some time under German rule; they harassed him and he suffered much, as is described in the previous

[Page 312]

chapter. He served as rabbi in our shtetl for about 12 – 13 years. During the worst times and the critical moments of the Nazi occupation, he would say that that he was certain that the Germans will lose the war and Hitlerism will succumb. He would say that he has proof. He was knowledgeable in world politics; he was interested in all subjects. He was the last rabbi in Lenin. He perished by the bestial Nazi murderers, together with the other Jews, on 14 August 1942.

Avraham–Yitzhak Slutsky (The United States)

B

This rabbi was of the old type of small–town rabbis, a wise Jew, very modest. Not a big entrepreneur and not a brilliant speaker. He was, however, a great learner and not a fanatic. But he did not have the qualities necessary to lead the life of the community. His apartment as well as the room where he conducted his court were in a house that belonged to the community, located in back of the Old Shul. He was very poor, and I remember a wedding in a rich family, where all the important people of the town were invited. At such a wedding the cantor would come, with his choir, and sing for the guests and the prominent family. At the time of the dinner, when all were sitting at the tables, the rabbi rose and addressed himself to the important *balebatim*, telling them that he was so poor that he couldn't afford to buy a wagon of firewood to keep his house warm during the winter. At the time he made his living by selling yeast for two Kopeks to the housewives, to make Challa for Shabat. Obviously this could not be called "to make a living."

From then on, discussions in the matter began in the community, and after several meetings it was decided that the rabbi shall receive a raise, and instead of 2 Kopeks they will pay him 3. In addition, it was decided that the groceries will not be allowed to sell candles for Shabat, and the entire candle business shall be handled by the rabbi. After many unpleasant discussions with the grocers, the candle business was given to the rabbi, and more light and warmth spread in his home.

[Page 313]

Cantors

Mordechai Zaichik

Translation by Yocheved Klausner

A cantor, in a shtetl like Lenin, had to be a slaughterer and a *Mohel* [circumciser] as well. But the main function was that of the cantor, and it concerned, obviously, music. The cantor was required to be knowledgeable in music, even if he did not have a very beautiful voice. It was very important that he be able to recite his part of the prayers accompanied by a choir, so that the congregation could enjoy a "good piece" that would really touch the hearts…

The cantor was not necessarily required to be able to reach "the high C", but he needed to have a pleasant voice and pray from the heart.

He was helped by the choir on regular holidays, on the High Holidays [*Rosh Hashana* and *Yom Kippur*] as well as on the first days of *Selichot* ["prayers of forgiveness" on the week before the Jewish New Year] – one day in the Old Shul and the next day in the New Shul.

On Yom Kippur the arrangement was: *Kol Nidrei* in the New Shul, next day in the old Shul. Every year he would bring some new melody.

We, in Lenin, could hardly imagine that in other shtetlach the prayers were held without a choir. How could that be?? How would that feel?

The cantor was paid a salary. For the prayers on holidays, when he had a choir, he received an extra bonus. He was in charge of assembling the choir every year. The choir was a great help: the cantor could rest while they were singing or when they held "a long note." On Yom Kippur, at the time of the "kneeling" [*kor'im*] the cantor was already so weak that two of the choir members had to help him stand up…

The congregation in the Old Shul was most eager to hear the singing of the cantor and his choir. They were even more attached to the music than the people in the New Shul, and many would go to the New Shul, to hear again the "concert"….

And now some history:

The first cantor and slaughterer in Lenin, years ago, was R'Leibke; later came R'Hershel Hoskowitz, who was a *melamed* [Torah teacher of young children] as well, because in those times it was not possible to earn a living as a cantor and slaughterer alone.

Later still, the cantor was R'Israel Chaim. After him there was no "professional" cantor for a stretch of time, but there were several good *Baalei Tefila* [performing the function of cantors, lit. "prayer–people"] in Lenin, for example R'Chaim Berl Migdalovich. For some time the prayers were conducted by the cantor Yakov Shmuel, who considered himself a Lenin man. He prayed very pleasantly.

From him we remember the special melody of *Ki hem chayenu* in the evening prayer [*ma'ariv*],

[Page 314]

R'Israel-Chaim Hacohen

a very beautiful melody, which was adopted for many years by other cantors as well.

The cantor Leibl Gershon caused a real sensation. He came for a trial period with a choir, which included a limping baritone, an alto, a handsome soloist, who always wore a scarf around his neck and others.

The cantor and his choir were a great success; it was a real choir, and they sang using a real musical score, like in the big city. The trial period was successful and he remained in the shtetl as cantor and slaughterer. From the choir he kept only the alto.

The cantor, a tenor with a blond-yellow little beard, was fat and strong (at the slaughtering house, he would throw down the heaviest ox with one move). He came from Minsk at the beginning of WWI and served in town 5–6 years. From his famous prayers, which were continuously repeated in town, it is worth mentioning: *Kevakarat ro'eh edro, Vayehi Vayom Hashlishi* and others.

After him, the community hired as cantor and slaughterer R'Feivel Chinitch, who came from Starabin – Slutzk.

He was a "beautiful Jew" [*a Sheiner Yid*], with a dignified look and a thick black beard. He was also a scholar, and liked to learn. He was a good musician, although without a musically educated cantor–voice, but his prayers came from the depth of his heart. He also had a choir. The prayer that was remembered from him was, in particular, the Kadeshsaid after the *Ne'ila* prayer [the prayer that concludes the Yom Kippur service] – a special, joyful melody, which erased in one stroke the difficult

R'Feivel Chinitch

[Page 315]

day of fasting, together with the sins… The entire congregation would join the singing…

After him the cantor and slaughterer was R'Moshe Novick, who came from the small shtetl Snow near Baranovitch. With all the others he was sent by the Germans to the concentration camp in Hantzewitch, later fought with the partisans and lives now in Eretz Israel.

Sextons [shamash] and Assistant–Sextons

Since a shamash in a shul, especially in Lenin, received a very low salary, never enough to feed his wife and children – he was forced to take on additional work, as learning Gemara [Talmud] with the older boys etc. In addition, the functions of a shamash included such minor seasonal work as the customary "flagellation" on the eve of Yom Kippur and others. All in all, the sexton could never become a rich man…

Lenin had various types of sextons. Below we shall tell the story of the most interesting among them.

In the Old Shul, there was an assistant–sexton by the name of Tolye Kanik, who was always busy, either sweeping the floor of the big shul, or carrying water, or chopping firewood to heat the shul.

He was a short man. When he was hired for his post he was quite young, and he didn't know Yiddish, that is, he did know the language but he pronounced only half of each word and one had to make an effort to understand what he meant. Later, as people got used to his speech, they almost understood him. He would say that he "got this from the war"; he was a "soldier" and was still suffering from the wounds…

He was a good worker: even in the greatest frost he would cut the thick, heavy pine logs to prepare them for firewood.

Children were always looking at him, how he was dragging the heavy firewood into the cellar of the shul, to place them in the stove in order to keep the fire going and the entire shul pleasantly warm. He was a quiet man, but when the children would tease him and take one of his tools, it was terrible.

His wife was even shorter than he, a fat Jewess, almost round, with black shiny hair… They were a strange couple. It was interesting to see how they would sit and talk, on the stone bench in front of the house. They were like a pair of loving doves… but when she spoke, her voice was heard as far as two streets away… Those serious discussions would take place mostly on Sabbath eve, and they concerned the

[Page 316]

fact that soon the Holy Sabbath is beginning and they still had nothing: Challah [Sabbath bread], fish, meat…

Once, on a frosty winter day, the wife of the sexton, Alte (that was her name), while going to the well to get water, slipped on the heavy ice that formed every winter around the well. She fell and rolled down into the well, which was about 8–10 meters deep.

By a miracle she was not hurt much, but as she was round and plump she filled exactly the size of the well and was stuck, sitting in the cold water… Finally, after great efforts, they pulled her out of there.

In his older years, Tolye complained of pain in the ears and the head, and several years later he died.

A funeral in Lenin
We can see the Ohel (lit. tent: a structure built over
the grave of a Tzadik or another prominent person) over
the grave of the rabbi R'Yehuda Turetski

[Page 319]

Personalities

R'Avraham-Yitzhak Chinitch

by Avraham Yitzhak Slutsky (New-York)

Translated by Yocheved Klausner

He was tall, thin and very handsome. Any one who saw him for the first time would stop and admire his stature again and again: "Has Dr. Herzl raised from his grave?!"… Because R'Avraham-Yitzhak looked exactly like Dr. Herzl: the same tall stature, the same excellence and splendor, the same black beard and the same beautifully shaped lips.

He was one of the six sons-in-law of R'David Graeib and was always worrying about getting enough "*parnose*" [livelihood, making a living]. His large house, in the center of the Shtetl served as a guest-house (hotel) and he was devoted to serve the community.

Thanks to his initiative the New Synagogue was built, and for many years he was the *gabbay*.

He was blessed with a pleasant voice, and our people enjoyed having him pray as cantor, and even more so on the High Holydays – *Rosh-Hashana* and *Yom Kipur*.

His children immigrated to America, and in 1921 R'Avraham-Yitzhak left Lenin as well and joined his children. He served as Rabbi in one of the synagogues in Brooklyn.

After the First World War, when the economic situation in Lenin became worse and the number of the needy people grew every day, R'Avraham-Yitzhak devoted himself, with soul and life, to organizing an aid-campaign among our Landsmanshaft in America for their impoverished brothers at home.

No obstacle could have prevented R'Avraham-Yitzhak Chinitch from making the effort and come to the meetings of the Landsleit – not bad weather nor his advanced age... His house was always the center of activity... Together with his daughter Itka, they carried the heaviest burden, more than their strength could endure. And now, when R'Chinitch died, she continues his work, may God give her strength.

His funeral was one of the biggest in Brooklyn. Great rabbis eulogized him, and thanks to him our Landsmashaft is active to this day.

[Page 320]

Uncle R'Moshe

by Aharon (Arke) son of Avraham-Yitzhak Chinitch

Translated by Yocheved Klausner

He was my grandmother Henye's brother. We called him Uncle Moshe; in town he was known as "R'Moishe."

He made his meager living by being a *melamed* [Torah teacher of young children]. What did he need? A cup of tea and a pack of tobacco was all he needed in this world, he never felt the need of cash in his pocket. The tuition he was paid was managed by his wife aunt Bashe. He never asked for anything, the most important thing for him was study. All day long he was busy with his *Cheder*, and at four o'clock before dawn he would begin his own study, after he had studied until late at night.

Uncle Moshe's life consisted of learning without end. When he needed to visit his sick mother in Bobruisk, he took with him the necessary books and studied while on the wagon or the train. Many, many pages of the Talmud he knew by heart.

On the Sabbath he would entirely remove himself from this world, as if a thick wall would be raised as a border between him and everything else. All week he did not speak words that were not connected with Torah study, but on the Sabbath he did not speak at all. All day he prayed and studied passionately, almost angrily, as if he wanted to chase "bad thoughts" out of his mind. His utterance of the word EHAD in the prayer of *Shema Israel* was recognized in the entire town: long and loud, with much truthfulness, dedication and zeal. In the Bet Midrash, he did not seek the *Mizrach* seat [the honored seat in the East side of the synagogue]; he sat in the corner, in the West side, among the "simple people," at the long table where he would give a *Mishna* lesson after prayer. On Sabbath he was the last to leave the synagogue, and walked not seeing the street; he would recite all the time verses from the Bible. When someone greeted him "Gut Shabes" [A good Sabbath] he would reply "Sabbath," "Sabbath," without the word "good" because the word "good" was a weekday word, a secular, not holy word.

I liked more the weekday uncle Moshe, because on the Sabbath he was too strict, too far away. On Shabbath afternoon, when I

[Page 321]

would come to him to learn "*Perek*" [*Pirkei Avot* = The Wisdom of the Fathers], he was strict, not the weekday Uncle Moshe with the childish smile on his beautiful shining face. He loved people and people loved him. He saw everything and everyone on the side of merit. I remember, once somebody came to him and told him that the dentist Noah, Berl Baruchin's son, does not participate in prayer. –"At least he puts on the *Tefillin*?" – "No, Rabbi." – "Impossible, impossible" – he cried with pain. He could not believe that a Jew would not put on his *Tefillin*. Such a thing was unthinkable.

When one came to him with a *Shale* [question, religious problem] when the Rabbi of the shtetl was not at home, he would work very hard and make every effort to give a verdict of "Kasher" – everything to the side of merit.

Hos modesty was unlimited. I was a witness once, when somebody brought him a present, a chicken for the Holiday of *Shavuot*. He smiled with satisfaction that he was not forgotten and sighed with pleasure: "Why did I deserve this?" – it was too good for him, to enjoy something of this world. His wife, aunt Bashe, would complain against him, why he was so distanced from this world. Even in front of me, a boy of 12 years, she complained that uncle Moshe neglects her as a wife. "Only Talmud and TANACH, Talmud and TANACH. This is all he knows" – she grumbled. To calm her a little, uncle Moshe promised her that he will give her half of his *Olam Haba* [the World to come]…

I shall never forget how easy it was for me to obtain from him the copper *dreidl* as a Chanuka gift (Chanuka money). As soon as the door opened he carried it to me with joy. It was the only time in the year when he had his own little money, to use as Chanuka money for the children who came to claim it.

I remember: one summer afternoon, uncle Moshe studied with us a page of the Talmud. He moved his body back and forth and spoke loudly from the depths of his heart. Suddenly my sister ran in shouting: "Uncle, uncle, a *Paritz* is calling you, right in our house!" And when the *Paritz* is calling, one asks no questions. Our uncle, scared, got up from his chair, entered the other room and put on his Sabbath *Kapote*, and walked to our house, with me running right after him. My father met him outside, and told him the good news, that the "*Paritz*" was no other than his own brother, Zalman from Baku, whom he had not seen over thirty years.

One has to have a sharp pen, in order to describe the meeting between the two brothers. First of all, uncle Moshe recited a blessing, then they embraced each other and cried like little children. All present, and I among them, helped them cry.

[Page 322]

The weeping could be heard in the entire house. It was like the story of Yosef and his brothers in the Book of Genesis. After they cried out their hearts, they served drinks and the atmosphere became joyful – a real holiday. The festivity continued three days – eating, drinking and having a good time. The whole shtetl was excited and happy. This was the first time that uncle Moshe has spent time dealing with secular matters. For three days he didn't hold his lessons regularly, and we, his pupils, did not go to the *cheder*. However he did compensate for that after uncle Zalman left. Uncle Zalman, who had become rich in Baku through the sugar commerce, left a few nice rubles for uncle Moshe.

I remember: uncle Moshe received a letter from his other brother, Hillel from Odessa, from whom he hadn't heard for many years. Hillel became rich from the grain trade. The letter was signed: Grenadi Zundelevitch; it means Hillel son of Zundel. Uncle Moshe looked at the signature and became angry: "Well, you want to be Grenadi, let it be; but what do you have against our father?"

The last time that I saw my uncle was before I went into service, when I came to say good-bye to him. He accompanied me to the door and said to me, angrily: "I am telling you, a soldier you will never be, this is what I'm telling you!" – he repeated this several times.

He died while I was in the Russian army. I was not at his funeral. I was told, that while in his sick bed, he was very sad that he had to skip several times "putting on the *Tefillin*."

His study was also interrupted many times during the First World War, because of lack of petrol to light the lamp. He studied "by heart" as much as he could. By the end of his life he had a small "collision" with the sergeant. It was Friday evening, during the war, when it was not permitted to use lights at night because of the airplanes. Uncle Moshe was studying by the light of his small lamp. The sergeant ran in shouting angrily: "Turn it off, turn it off!" But my uncle – would he possibly desecrate the Holy Sabbath? – nonsense. The sergeant was yelling "off!" and uncle Moshe was running around murmuring to himself "off off." Naturally, at the end the sergeant was the one who extinguished the lamp, not uncle Moshe.

[Page 323]

Autobiography of Avrohom-Yitskhok Slutsky

by Mordechai Zaichik

Translated by Stephen M. Cohen, Ph.D.

I was born in the month of Kislev, in the year 5648 (December 1888). I was the third son. The two children before me (boys) did not survive their third birthday, and before I entered the world, my mother, as she used to say, remained with "empty hands". The cause of their early death was the crowdedness, poverty, and want, and, above all, the epidemic childhood diseases that rampaged wildly and untamed in those days. They therefore could say, *"eyn beys, asher eyn sham meys"* [no house without death therein]. Very rarely were there parents who raised all their children to adulthood.

When my mother came to the time to bring me into the world, she decided to change residence and tried to give birth in Lakhva, whence she originated, and where she had her whole family. And actually in Lakhva, on a frosty night, my mother (upon her be peace), at her uncle's home, behind the oven, brought me into the world. And there, behind the oven, I noticed for the first time the bright shine of—an oil lamp....

Thereafter, they brought me into the covenant of *Avraham Avinu* [Abraham our Ancestor], gave me the name "Avrohom Yitskhok", and blessed me, "*zeh hakotn godol yihyeh*" [This little one will be great], and I was already a youth of 4 weeks old, when my mother had to return home to Lenin. Burdened with fear for the life of her child, she took me to the old Lakhva rabbi, the esteemed sage *R' Dov Ber Zts"l*, who blessed me, that I should extend my days and my parents should live to see me raised to Torah, to the marriage canopy, and to good deeds. Because of this, the rabbi laid upon me a third name, *Alter* [the old one]. So I still call myself "Alter Avrohom Yitskhok". If all the attempted methods caused me to be able to write this in my sixty-fourth year—I don't know, perhaps yes....Because in the house into which my mother brought me and where her elder two children died, it is really a great miracle that I survived. Even greater is the miracle and wonder that after me were born five more children in that alleged "house", of which only one, a boy aged three, died of diphtheria. That is *amshteygns* said was no house, but a grave. A little room with one window, without a bit of sunshine. And so in the "house", a family of seven souls crammed itself in. Until today, when I think of that time, I get a chill, that grave with many other similar living corpses are gone with the fire in the great conflagration that came about in the year 1904.

My education

The only education that Jewish children received during that time was the *kheyder* [Hebrew school]. Among parents of the better teachers, they taught beyond that Chumash with Rashi, Tanakh and Gemara, and also writing Yiddish a little, with arithmetic. Russian I learned almost by myself. I was always fluent and had a good head for learning. Four semesters I learned in the Lakhva Talmud-Torah, which had at that time was famous in our area. Many Lenin youths traveled to study in Lakhva. The teachers in Lakhva were straight from Lenin; one, Moyshe the *stiblevitsher*, the second, Avrohom Bregman, Nisn Bregman's father. Both of them were great Talmudists. The ladder of the Talmud-Torah was at that time Hershl Mendl, Pinye Kaplan's son.

After the four semesters of studying in Lakhva, I could already read a page of Gemara with Tosafot. To my good head for learning I added a good little voice, and I sang for four years with the old cantor, *R' Yisroel Khayim* (upon him be peace), and used to gain pleasure from my singing the prayers in synagogue. And certainly, with all my abilities, I was no rabbi, as many have suggested, but also no famous cantor. I was a tradesman—a carpenter. In the conditions and circumstances in which I found myself, it was impossible—regardless of my will and diligence—that I could reach something higher. Being a fourteen-year-old youth, I came to Avner Golob in Kantor to learn carpentry. Also, the arrival in Avner's in Kantor was a big thing, to which not all of my equals could attain. In the Kantor carpentry-shop, one worked according to one's own hours, with a two-hour break for lunch. In the other town workshops, they slaved the whole day, including Saturday night. At age 18, I went away to Ekaterinoslav. There, in the big city, I opened up a new world for myself. I joined a reading group, read and learned a lot, and acquired a certain amount of knowledge in Yiddish and Russian literature. I also learned to play a musical instrument (guitar). Politically, I belonged to the "S.S." (Zionist-Socialists), today's *Po'alei-Tsiyon*. In general, my three years in Ekaterinoslav were the best years of my life. Attaining 21 years of age, I came home to military conscription. That was at the end of 1909, I was freed from service as a first *legotnik*, i.e., provider for the family. Six months later, in March 1910, I married my cousin Khave, the daughter of my mother's sister, and in October of the same year we left for America.

Hard, very hard it was for me to separate from my poor, unlucky parents, whose only consolation in their dark life I was. Very dear also were my relatives and friends, and also my dear pals. In America, in the golden land, at the beginning we were just like all greenhorns, going not birdlike. In March of 1911, towards the anniversary of our marriage, my wife gave birth to our first and only son (after him came our three daughters), and life began to flow its normal course.

Landslayt [home-town people]

At that time in America, we already found a quite a few *landslayt* from Lenin. Some were already here since before the end of the previous century, such as the brothers Benyomin and Mordkhe Zaichik, the sons of Leybe Feykun. Also, Yenkl Medvedyev, who returned to Mikashevitsh, and many others, who came with the immigrant stream at the beginning of the new century. In 1910 I already found here quite a nice *fareyn* [society]. The goal of the *fareyn* was at that time to get together twice a month, in order to drive out the feeling of loneliness and pining for the old hometown. Thereby also to help out each other in need, or, God forbid, sickness. The *landsmanshaft* [home-town society] was founded in October, *Khol Ha-Moed* Sukkot, 1906, and already owned its own cemetery plot (that is the first thing that *landsmanshaftn* worry about).

The first week after coming to America, I was immediately attached to my brother *landslayt*. I came to their get-together, and that was the initiation of my lifelong activities in America. I provided my whole energy, all my abilities for my brother and sister *landslayt* in all domains, both in joy, and, God forbid, in sorrow. In brief, I took part in all activities of our *landslayt* organization: philanthropic activities, communal and national ones, such as the "United Jewish Appeal", etc.

Our *landsmanshaft* has nothing to be ashamed of, with its work in all domains. Just the opposite, in fact: it brings itself closer to the moment when our *landsmanshaft* will celebrate its fiftieth anniversary. We will have much to explain, as a small bunch of immigrants showed so much accomplishment.

I am proud that I and my wife Khave have a big share in all the good deeds.

[N.B.: Lakhva and Mikashevitsh are nearby shtetls; Kantor is a town whose non-Yiddish name I have not researched. All words and names are transliterated according to YIVO conventions. The abbreviation *R'* stands for "*Reb*", a respectful honorific for Jews similar to "Mr.", and is left untranslated.]

[Page 329]

Landslayt (countrymen) in America

The Activity and Aid of the American Landsmanshaft

Translated by Yocheved Klausner

The history of the Lenyin Association in America begins with its foundation on 6th October 1906, *Hol–Hamoed* (intermediate days) of the holiday of Sukkot, in New–York.

❖❖❖❖❖❖❖❖❖❖❖❖❖❖❖❖

LENYIN-LACHWER
Benevolent Association

— 1942 —

ORGANIZED OCTOBER 6 1906

Meets Every Second and Fourth
Thursday Evening of the Month

A T
15 SECOND AVENUE
NEW YORK

❖❖❖❖❖❖❖❖❖❖❖❖❖❖❖❖

לעניִן-לאַחװער
בענעװאָלענט אַסאָסיאיישאָן

←→

1942

←→

אָרגאַניזירט דעם 6טען אָקטאָבער, 1906

מיטעט יעדן 2טען און 4טען דאָנערשטאָג אָבענד
אין מאָנאַט

אין

15 סעקאָנד עװעניו
ניו יאָרק

Announcement of meetings of the Society

Of the first 12 founders of the Society, today 3 are alive: David ben [son of] Yehuda Shullman, Yitzhak ben Chaim Yakov Ginsberg and Itche ben Yosef Noah Rabinovitch; the others are deceased:

[Page 330]

Name	Died on	At the age of
Chaim Dov Hashkowitz	21.9. 1937	82 years
Binyamin Siklik (Zaichik)	16.4.1922	58
Akiva Neiman	15.5.1933	59
Nathan Rovnitz	22.11.1934	58
Avraham Yitzhak Kravetz	31.12.1934	62
Makhe, granddaughter of Israel Harofe	30.5.1939	62
Grunem Migdalovich	19.10.1949	72
Menachem Mendel Zaichik	17.8.1949	72
Itche Unterman (Greenberg)	18.6.1948	73

Until WWI there was in fact almost no special aid activity for the benefit of the old home. The real work began only during the world war. The European Continent was still locked for us and we had almost no information or news from there. We were very worried since we felt that terrible things were happening.

Akiva Neiman z"l

Chaim Dov Hashkowitz z"l

We started to establish and prepare a fund which should enable, as soon as we could make contact, to help and support the needy there. We called special meetings; we elected a committee and we managed to collect a sizeable sum of money.

[Page 331]

Right after the war ended, although not everything had returned to normal, we contacted the Lenin leaders, A.I. Chinitch, Zalman Bresler and others and we began sending aid in the form of food, clothing and money.

In order to improve the aid–activity of the organization we sent – after the example of other organizations – a special delegate to the localities that needed our help, to get acquainted with the local people and the situation and organize the work. The delegate was our esteemed landsman Yakov Golob; we sent with him a considerable amount of money. Unfortunately, however, his mission did not succeed, since he arrived in Warsaw at the time of the Polish–Bolshevik war and the shtetl Lenin was at that time on the Russian side of the border and it was impossible to reach it. After waiting 8 months in Warsaw, he had to return to New–York, regrettably.

In time, when our shtetl Lenin was back, finally, under Polish rule, the contact improved and we began receiving bad news: the population was very impoverished, the taxes were high and people couldn't make a living etc. They wanted to emigrate, but America introduced the "quota."

At that time, many former Lenin residents traveled to Lenin to meet their relatives and acquaintances, and to see the situation with their own eyes. Among them was Dr. Tilya Schmelkin, who stayed in Lenin during 1929. Upon her return to America she described to the members the true situation in Lenin, and began, with full enthusiasm and devotion, together with others, to organize a Women's Association, which should devote its time solely to create aid and send it to the needy in Lenin.

On 4 June 1929, a meeting was held in the home of Dr. Tilya, with the participation of the following women: Dr. Tilya Schmelkin Waltman, Khishe Kahan, the sisters Itke Pitkin and Sara Levinson (daughters of Yehuda Schusterman), the sisters Sara Carmen and Pashe Etke Kadesh(daughters of Nisan Bregman) and Masha Rovnitz.

These women organized a committee with the purpose of establishing a Women's Association. Mrs. Khishe Kahan asked the president of the Landsmanshaft to help her in this matter, and on 30 June 1929

[Page 332]

the Women's Association was founded. Dr. Singalovski also participated in the meeting. The following women were elected to the various functions: Sara Carmen – president; Khishe Kahan – vice–president; Itke Chinitch – secretary of finance; Dr. Tilye Waltman (Schmelkin) – treasurer.

The purpose of the Association was entirely different from that of our men's association. While the men's association dealt with mutual help for our Landsleit here in America, the women's association's purpose was to help the Landsleit in the old home. Little–by–little more landswomen joined, and soon a lively group formed, which devoted itself with heart and soul to creating means of aid for the old home.

It is difficult to describe here the various forms of help that the ladies association organized during its long years of existence. The results of that great and devoted work were noted by all.

Those who were saved and are still alive certainly remember *Erev Rosh Hashana* [the eve of the Jewish New Year] and the eve of Passover in town, when aid of all sorts would arrive from America, in the form of money, food packages and clothing.

As testimony stand the many thank–you letters that we received from Lenin, for the aid that saved many, in particular the poor, who simply did not have the possibility to prepare for Passover or other holidays.

We would receive from Lenin a list of the needs and the needy, and we would prepare the materials accordingly, adding things for good measure. The money was sent to the address of Graeibs, and Itke Chinitch would add a note that in case that there were in town needy people who were not on the list – they should give them the needed sums and they will be reimbursed.

Some of the people, about whom we knew that they were ashamed to ask openly for help, we would bring the packages to their homes, secretly.

Once, on Passover eve, it happened that we were late in sending out the help, and the committee distributed among the needy "coupons" with which they could buy what they needed in the local shops.

[Page 333]

Later the bills would be sent to America and be paid promptly.

The Women's Association did a tremendous amount of work after WWII as well, by establishing contact with Europe and sending help to the survivors in the various camps, in the form of money and food packages. This aid activity is continued to this day in various forms, according to the example and tradition of the many social and aid–institutions, with which we, the Jews of America, are blessed.

Writing about the important meaning of the women's organization, we must stop and mention a very important person, who was strongly connected with the Association and played an important role in its activity, from the first days of its founding to the last days of its existence. This is the very well–known and esteemed Avraham Yitzhak Chinitch z"l. He was entirely devoted to the aid–activity, participated in every meeting of the ladies despite his advanced age, despite cold, snow or rain. They called him, with respect, "our father."

His passing was a great loss for the association and for the leading members. Work became more difficult, and most of it fell on the shoulders of the daughter Itke, who continued the great tradition of her father.

We shall mention shortly the few leading persons of the Association and some of the members as well, who, by their devoted work and efforts helped bring the great aid–activity to full success during the long years of its existence.

Sara Carmen – the first president of the association – an intelligent and talented activist and speaker and her husband Mr. Carmen, since few years secretary of protocol.

Khishe Kahan – first vice–president – a very able organizer and leader, she organized the "Khassye" Club of the pioneer women – a very important Zionist Women organization for the benefit of Israel.

Dr. Tilye Waltman (Schmelkin) – the first organizer and treasurer of the women's association.

Itke Chinitch – finance secretary – one of the most loyal and devoted doers; about her a separate article is written.

Hellen (Chaia) Bushler (Nathan Rovnitz' daughter) – the second president of the association.

[Page 334]

Her father Nathan was the first president of the men's association and finance secretary.

The following were vice–presidents and occupied important places in leading work of the association: Ethel Rubin and Bessy (Beyzie) Rivkin with her husband – daughters of Chaim Yakov from Gritchinowitz; Khine Dubitzki – Avraham Mordechai KHarfon's daughter; Riva Goldberg – granddaughter of Israel Harofe; Geigel Yaz and Masha Greenwald – Yakov Yeshaya Lifshitz' daughters; Chaia Sara Feder – Chaim Dov Khashkowitz' daughter; Mally (Menucha) Kaplan – granddaughter of Yechiel HaCohen; Asne Weiner – wife of Moshe Chaim Weiner z"l; the sisters Chava Muziker and Razy (Rashke) Levin; Chana Merke Marmer – Berl Khlapiners' daughter; Dobe Blum – Makhe's wife; Yitzhak (Ike) Ginsberg and his wife – son of Yakov from Gritchinowitz; Bessie (Bashe Etke) Kadesh and her husband – daughter of Nisan Bergman; Yakov Yeshaya and Chaia Sara Lifshitz – devoted members, of the most active in the association; Chaia Sara (Seidy) Levinson – daughter of Yehuda Shullman – one of the main founders and leaders, together with her sister Itka Pitkin; Khishe Faley and her husband Yeshaya – daughter of the widow Osne; Ette Temkin, wife of Chaim Temkin z"l; Mania Sokolov – daughter of Yechiel Hacohen z"l; Khishe Slutsky; the two sisters: Frume Weiner – wife of Hillel Weiner z"l and Sara Feigel – wife of Sender KHarfon.

The new arrivals, survivors of the last war and camps, as well as partisans are also very active and of great help for the general success of the undertaking. Naturally, almost all local Landsleit, in the various cities, have done great work in help and support. Without them, the leaders could not have succeeded in carrying out the work.

To all these, we express our best and deepest thanks. May all blessings, sent by those who have felt the helping hand of their sisters and brothers in Ameriva, by fulfilled.

Written by M. Zaichik
(According to letters from America)

[Page 335]

Itke Chinitch – "the Mother of Lenin"

by Mordechai Rubenstein (Migdalovich)

Translated by Yocheved Klausner

A

Itke Chinitch

A normal phenomenon: stars are shining in the sky, and sometimes it seems to us that one star is torn out of its place, falls and is extinguished. This natural phenomenon is also characteristic of us, dwellers of this world. We meet persons, talents, blessed public workers during certain periods of their lives and suddenly we notice that their source, for various reasons, has dried out and they retire to a quiet corner. To our great satisfaction, this has not happened to the rare woman, whose portrait I shall try to depict shortly here.

Since tens of years, Itke is, literally, the living spirit, the recognized authority among our American Landsleit. For tens of years she is the address where anyone who needs help in one form or another is being listened to, with the greatest attention. For years, Itke is the direct "address" to obtain, read and reply to uncounted letters and to organize help: collect clothing and money and send out food packages.

I had the privilege to follow with great attention her blessed activity during the years after the destruction of our most beloved families, when the few survivors were lost in the various camps in bleeding Germany, Austria, Italy and Cyprus on their way to Eretz Israel. Later I have seen her activity for the benefit of those who came to our shores. She was always ready to welcome and help all needy, especially those who did not trust themselves to ask for help directly.

Understandably, everything was done with the active help of the entire Women's Committee – R'Nissan Bergman's daughters, Mrs. Khisya Cohen, Mrs. Chava Slutsky and many

[Page 336]

others, whose names I unfortunately do not know, and with this opportunity I wish to express – to the known and to the unknown – a heartfelt "well done!" and thanks.

But what was the source from which the physically weak lady drew so much strength and energy? This is a question that is not easy to answer. It is clear and certain, that Itke is a flowing spring of human love in general and Jewish love in particular, of devotion and feeling for any sufferer.

We all wish her – and us – that she continue for many, many years, with the same courage and good health, her blessed activity, and continue to carry with pride the name "the Mother of Lenin," for the benefit of all those who mention her name with respect and greatest honor.

Kalman Temkin

B

As we remember our dear martyrs from our shtetl, we should also remember and mention those, who helped the *she'erit hapleita* [the surviving remnants].

Quietly and modestly, without noise and promotion, Itke Chinitch devoted most of her life to others, especially those whom the bitter fate has thrown into concentration camps and then, if they survived, into homeless barracks.

All these know very well who Itke Chinitch is, because she was and remained a loving mother and a devoted sister to all who needed help. Whoever needed an address of relatives, a package of food or clothing, or a little money so he could stand on his own feet – would turn to Itke Chinitch and no one was sent back.

Not taking into account her frail health, this noble lady never stopped calling and waking, and organizing the holy help activity – since helping others is her life–ideal.

May you be blessed, our dear Itke. We are proud of you and of your life's work. You gave us courage and renewed our belief in humankind. We all wish you good health and long, long years of fruitful work.

[Page 337]

Helen (Chaia) Bushler

(Daughter of Nathan
Rovnitz). Second president
of the Lenin Women's
Association

Ethe Temkin (with her husband Chaim Z"l)

They brought from Lenin to America the spirit
of *Tzedaka* (charity), hospitality and religious life.
Ethe's devotion is almost impossible to evaluate…

[Page 338]

Khishe Cohen

Translated by Yocheved Klausner

Khishe Cohen
First vice-president of the Lenin Women's Association

I had the good luck to meet our Khishe Cohen, Welvel Latocha's daughter from our shtetele, when she visited us during the summer.

When I saw her the first time, I thought that she was another tourist from our shtetl, like all those who have visited us. But soon I realized that Khishe Cohen was a hard–working public activist, a daughter of the Jewish people who sacrifices her strength and life in order to help build our State. I listened with joy to every word, which was full with taste and reason. My respect for her increased, when I heard that she has raised a daughter, who also took part in the effort to build our State, following in the steps of her mother. I remember the evening when we all, the Lenin family, sat together: her face shone with joy, and we all were happy with her visit.

We wish her many long years with her family, may she be active for the building of our country.

Menashe Yulevich

[Page 339]

Nathan and Masha Rovnitz

[Page 340]

R'Yehuda Shullman z"l

He was devoted wholeheartedly to all Landsleit and
relatives; always ready to help the needy. His children
are behaving the same way.
He is remembered with respect by all his friends and
acquaintances, to this day.

Avraham Smit z"l

R'Akiva Neiman's son-in-law. An
important active member of the Lenin
Landsmashaft.

David ben-Yehuda Shullman

One of the first 12 founders of the Lenin Aid-
Association

[Page 341]

Yehoshua and Hishe Paley

Good people, all heart. Great charity givers. They
help the poor and needy with a full hand and also
by *matan baseter* [charity in secret]. They raise their
children in the same spirit.

[Page 342]

20th anniversary of the Lenin Landsmanshaft

Sitting from right: Yakov-Zalman Shkliar, Zev Goldberg, Avraham-Yitzhak Slutsky (president), Avraham-Yitzhak Kravetz z"l, Shlomo Chaim HaCohen
Standing from right: Menachem-Mendel Zaichik, Shmuel Korn, Arie-Leib Cheifetz z"l, Hillel Weiner z"l, Akiva Neiman z"l, Monye Lehrman

[Page 343]

Lenin Landsleit in America

[Page 344]

Yakov (Jacob) Yulevich

Jacob Yulevich, the immigrant from a small Belarus Shtetl, Lenin, is one of our great and wonderful heroes on the home-front. A former carpenter, who came to America as a young man of 21 years, he has done for America much more than many locally born important and esteemed people, rich men, who made here their wealth.

Jacob Yulevich attained, on his own, 12 million dollar worth war-bonds, which – at first himself and later with the help of his family – he collected by going from house to house, waking and encouraging the American population to fulfil their duty to their homeland, to the world, to humanity, which we must free from under the claws of the destroyer Hitler and the imperialistic desires of the Japanese war-mongers.

Soon, the name of the interesting Bonds seller reached Washington, and he was named a "One dollar-a-year man," that is, he received a salary of one dollar a year, and this meant that he became part of the American administration-machine. His name became very popular, and the way that he succeeded in selling war-bonds for millions of dollars made a great impression in Washington. The Federal Bank issued about him a brochure, "The Story of Jake Yulevich." The brochure was distributed in the country in a great number of copies, as an inspiration for others in the area of selling bonds. Later it was reprinted by tens of banks that sold bonds. Several finance newspapers published articles praising the interesting immigrant Jake Yulevich, the champion seller of war-bonds. Mr. Yulevich, however, did not rest on his laurel crown. On the eve of Yom Kippur, when all Jews gather in the synagogues and the sentiments are intense – Mr.

Yulevich went from synagogue to synagogue and persuaded the members to fulfil the holy duty of buying bonds; later this custom was adopted by the rabbis and spiritual leaders of the synagogues.

Der Americaner [The American], 11.2. 1944 **S. Hirshson**

[Page 345]

Fallen in the Defense of the Homeland

Translated by Yocheved Klausner

[Page 346]

Moshe Dolgin

He was born to his parents Mordechai and Fanya Dolgin on 5 Shevat 5690 (1930) and fell by the hands of the Arab Legion on 1 Tevet 5708, as he came to help the people under siege in Ben Shemen. His way shall serve as a model for the youth in our country, for which he fought and sacrificed his young life.

Moshe Dolgin graduated from the elementary school Tel-Nordau. After he graduated "Cum Laude" from the vocational school Max Fein he worked as a locksmith and became independent. He was a member of the *Gadna* [Youth Unit] and participated in all exercises and training. Since 1946 he participated in guarding and security activities and fulfilled his missions with punctuality and responsibility, until his last day. He was a model soldier, trusting his power. He would calm his mother by the words "Even against a tank I can fight by myself."

When rushing to the aid of his friends in Ben-Shemen he was killed by the Arab Legion in Bet Naballa. He was buried in the Nahalat Yitzhak cemetery. A page in his memory is found in the book *Eikh Naflu Giborim* ["How are the Mighty Fallen"].

(From the book "Yizkor" publ. by the Ministry of Defense)

[Page 347]

Avraham Topchik

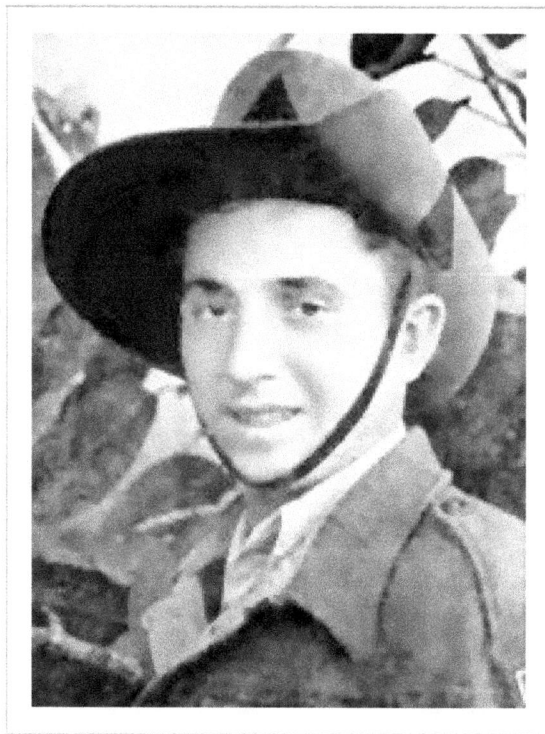

Son of Arie and Lea. Was born on 18 Elul 5690 (930) in Poland and made Aliya in 1935. Graduated from the "Takhkemoni" school in Tel Aviv and worked in a weaving factory. He was a devoted member of the "Etzel" Organization in the "underground period" until his parents found out and implored him to leave the Organization. He refused for a long time, but in the end he gave up and joined the "Jewish settlements police force" [*Mishteret HayiShubim Ha'ivrim*].

With the outbreak of the War of Independence he participated in the defense of the kibbutz Tirat-Zvi, and in securing the road from Sede-Nachum, as well as in several other battles in the area, managing a machine-gun and encouraging his friends in battle. During the cease-fire he was sent to a course of section-commanders, and as the fights resumed he was sent to the Negev area. When the convoy stopped for a while, he descended from his command car and gathered in his hands a handful of the Negev soil. He took part in the "Assaf" Operation in the Negev, near Kibbutz Nirim. He fell on 7 December 1948 during the enemy counter-attack and was buried on the same day in the Nahalat-Yitzhak cemetery.

(From the book "Yizkor" publ. by the Ministry of Defense)

[Page 350]

Memorial Candles

Translated by Yocheved Klausner

[Page 351]

In Memory of our Grandfather and Grandmother z"l

R'David son of R'Chaim Graeib z"l
Died in Lenin, 5 Marcheshvan 5680, at the age of 88

Mrs. Shprintza daughter of R'Efraim Brakerman z"l
Died in Lenin, 10 Av 5681, at the age of 86

May their memory be for a blessing

[Page 352]

**Yehoshua, Mordechai, Beile (nee Graeib), Chaim, Esther, Sara -
Tchetchik**

In memory of my mother Beile and my sister Sara,

Who died in the Russian exile
And did not have the merit to make Aliya to Eretz Israel -
The yearning of their hearts

Shifra Chinitch, New-York

[Page 353]

R'Avraham-Yitzhak Chinitch,
died in New-York,
Elul 5607 (1947), aged 84

Rivka Chinitch,
died in New-York, Lag
Ba'omer
(18 Iyar) 5704 (1944),
aged 83

**R'Israel Isser HaLevi
Nakritz,**
born 21 Kislev 5626,
died in Tel-Aviv, 20 Tevet
5697

Chana Nakritz,
daughter of **R'David Graeib,**
died in Tel-Aviv, 21 Cheshvan 5714

[Page 354]

**Itka, daughter of R'David
Graeib Rabinovitch**
died in America, 12 Cheshvan
5696 (1935), aged 70

R'Yosef Noah Rabinovitch,
died in Lenin, 12 Iyar 5689
(1929), aged 54

[Page 355]

Yosef son of R'Eliezer Zaretzki, died 4 Marcheshvan 5696; Neche daughter of R'David,
their daughter Chana and her son David, her husband Aharon son of the Rav Zev Miller,
their son Eliezer - perished by the hands of the Nazi oppressor,
First day of Rosh Hodesh Elul [30 Av] 5702

[Page 356]

In memory of our father
Arie son of R'David Graeib,
born 5622 (1861),
died in Tel Aviv, 15 Adar
5706 (1946)

In memory of our mother
Devora Feigel,
daughter of R'Yosef,
)rn 5633 (1873), died in Lenin,
28 Kislev 5691 (1930)

In memory of my parents:

Batya
daughter of R'Arie Graeib,
was killed by murderers in
Otbotzk

Avraham-Eliezer
son of Israel Belezhovski,
died in Otbotzk,
26 Av 5677 (1917)

[Page 357]

In memory of our sister and our brother-in-law and their children

Yitzhak Kribitzky
Nehama Kribitzky
Yakov Kribitzky
Feigele Kribitzky

Murdered by the Nazis
In the year 5702 (1942)

May G-d Avenge their Blood!

[Page 358]

Efraim son of Reuven
Goldberg z"l

Finkel daughter of David
Graeib z"l

In Memory of our Dear Parents

Killed by murderers, 1 Elul 5702 - May God avenge their blood

Our **father**, a scholar and a practical person, a merchant and
a learner who set time for study Spoke the truth and gave
charity, never a spot on his clothes and never a fault in his
deeds; And our **mother**, carried the burden of keeping the
house, helped him in earning a livelihood and supported his
deeds

May their Memory be Blessed

Their children David and Chaia, in Australia

In memory of our sister Esther daughter of Efraim and Finkel,
with her husband David Minski and their daughter Zahava,
who were murdered by the oppressor, may his name be erased

Their brother David Goldberg

His sister Chaia Lassy

[Page 359]

Elka Baruchin,
daughter of Yehuda Tziglig,
died 3 Tevet 5697

R'Dov
son of R' Noah Baruchin,
died 5 Tishrei 5680

Golda
daughter of R'Yehuda,
died in Lenin, 9 Kislev
5694 (1934)

Mordechai
son of R'Yakov Mandelbaum z"l

[Page 360]

In memory of our dear parents Zalman and Sara-Lea Schmelkin

In memory of our mother Hindl Bresler,
who died in New-York **Finia Bresler, Dr. Israel Schmelkin,**
(and –may she have a long life – **Dr. Tehila Schmelkin**)

Eliezer and Eliyahu Bresler

[Page 361]

**In memory of our brother Zalman Bresler, his wife Ethel,
their son David and their daughter Sheina**
May God avenge their blood and may their soul be bound in
the bond of the living
Perished by the Nazis, may their name be erased.

Eliezer and Eliyahu Bresler

[Page 362]

In memory of Aharon-Yakov Bodnitz and his wife Stisha,
their son Yitzhak and his wife Rivka,
their daughter Chana Fisetzka, who perished by the hand of
murderers.

May God avenge their blood.

Their daughter Gitl

Their son Zvi Bodnitz

Oizer Gellman, son-in-law of R'Yakov z"l

In memory of our dear father who perished in his young
years by murderers

His daughter Frida, his son Eliahu

[Page 363]

In memory of our father, our teacher
R'David son of R'Avraham Schusterman
and our mother our teacher Rachel, Nasha daughter of
David,
Mashka daughter of David and Shimon son of David, his
wife Chana and their son Eliezer,
Fell prey to wild murderers.
Their memory will never be forgotten from our hearts.
May this book be also a monument on their unknown
graves.

Yakov and Henia Schusterman Chmelnitzi

In memory of our father **R'Eliahu son of R'Asher, our mother,**
our sister and our brother who fell by the hands of murderers
on Rosh Chodesh Elul 5702

May their memory be blessed

Yitzhak, Masha, Yakov Ginsberg

[Page 364]

[Caption follows]

[Page 365]

In deep sorrow we are mourning the death of our parents,
our sisters and our nephew,
Who were murdered by the murderers of our people, may their
names be erased:
Our father **R'Eliyahu-Yosef**, son of R' Moshe Gurevich, an
honest and God-fearing man;
Our modest and righteous mother Mrs. **Gitl** daughter of
R'Avraham;
Our pure-of-heart sisters **Grunia** and **Sonia**;
Our nephew **Mordche'le** son of Moshe and his mother **Gutka**,
Perished in the mass-slaughter in Lenin, on the first day
of Rosh Hodesh Elul 5702.
May God avenge their blood.

Our brother **Moshe** was killed in the prime of his life

May their memory be blessed

The mourners:

Dvoshka, Batya, Aliza, Chaia-Risha and their families

* * *

In memory of my brother and my sister-in-law
Aharon and Sima Glenson
And their families
Killed by murderers, may their name be erased

His brother Shlomo

[Page 366]

In memory of my parents **Zvi-Yekutiel and Chaia-Sara Glenson;**
My brothers: **Leiba, Chaim, Shlomo, Eliezer, Mendel;**
My sister **Rachel**
Who were killed and hanged by murderers
May God avenge their blood
May their souls be bound in the bond of the living

Their son and brother **Aharon**

[Page 367]

In memory of the dear members of our family
Who were murdered by the Nazis

Our father **R'Aharon-Leib Zaichik** – during almost 50 years
teacher in our town;
Our mother Mrs. **Rishka** (nee Shvedyuk) – a modest and righteous
woman of a respected family;
Our brother **Moshe** and his wife **Minka** (nee Pudels) and our two
sisters **Beile** and **Batya**

May their memory be blessed
May God avenge their blood

Their sons and brothers **Mordechai** and **Dov**

[Page 368]

In memory of Gitl, Masha, Miriam (Mere) and Fetch
Eliyahu Sadovski

In memory of my son Hirshel who perished among the partisans
in the forest and my daughter Rachel who was murdered in
Lenin

Their father **Elyahu Sadovski**

[Page 369]

In memory of our father, our teacher R'Shlomo-Nisan
son of R'Yechiel Moshe Varshel and our mother,
our teacher Rachel-Lea daughter of Eliyahu-Pesach, murdered by
the Nazis

In memory of our sister Dvora daughter of R'Shlomo-Nisan
and her husband Shimshon son of R'Aharon Rubenstein,
and their children Sonia, Yona and Moshe who were murdered by the
Nazis

Their daughters and sisters

Frida Dolgin and her husband Mordechai

Masha Avineri and her husband Avner

[Page 370]

In memory of our brother

**Yitzhak son of R'Shlomo-Nisan Varshel,
his wife Miriam and their daughter**
who were murdered by the Nazis

Their mourners
**His sisters
Frida Dolgin and her husband Mordechai**

Masha Avineri and her husband   Avner

[Page 371]

Eidel daughter of **Zvi-Mordechai Domenitz**
Fell by the hands of murderers in the month of Elul

Avraham son of **Eliyahu Chinitch**
Died in Khvorostov, 6 Nissan 5681

In memory of Father and Mother z"l

Father, a practical man of a clear mind, trusted by his fellows and
speaker of truth; Mother, a charity giver, helping her husband,
wise and industrious with her daughters Michal and Esther-Rachel and
their children.

Murdered by the Nazis, the wild people.
May this be a Memorial on their graves and may their memories be
blessed.

Tzipora daughter of Idel and **Yakov** Dolgin
Their children and grandchildren

[Page 372]

In memory of our parents

R'Aharon and Sara Migdalovich

Mourning them:
Their sons **Moshe** and **Dov**

And their daughters **Zahava** (Golda)
and **Hasida** (Fruma) **and their families**

Chaim-David son of R"Aharon Migdalovich

Fallen in battle during the Second World War in Russia

His daughter Frida, his son Eliahu

[Page 373]

In memory of **R'Feivel** son of **R'Aharon Migdalovich** and
his family

Killed by the Nazis in the shtetl Yanova

Esther daughter of **R'Aharon Migdalovich**

Killed in Lenin with all the martyrs

[Page 374]

In memory of grandfather **R'Zev Migdalovich**

In memory of our beloved who were murdered by the Nazis:

Our father **R'Moshe-Reuven Zaretzki**,
our mother **Libka** daughter of **R'Zev Migdalovich**,

My sisters **Vitya** and **Fruma**, my brother **Shmuel**,
my brother-in-law **Avner Khutyuk** and his son **Hillel**

May God avenge their blood

Pinchas Zaretzki
Devora Frenkel

[Page 375]

R'Yeshaya and Mrs. Freidl Latocha

R'Yeshaya, aged sixty, ill and weak, worked from dawn until late at night, and helped many families in Mikshewitch which was under siege. His wife **Freidl** endangered her life at the time of the curfew and went to collect food and distribute it among the needy.

Seven of their children escaped to Russia, six of them made it to Israel. Their son Yakov was taken prisoner by the Germans and probably perished.

R'Yeshaya became ill with cancer and couldn't talk; his wife took him, at a time of mortal danger, to Pinsk, there he was operated on and a month later she went and brought him back. He was not permitted to work, but he started working several hours a day to help the needy.

May their memory be honored.

Shmuel Zaichik, from Mikshewitch

[Page 376]

Sheindel daughter of R'Shmuel Chaim
(wife of R'Mordechai son of R'Simcha Yulevich)
Died in Tel Aviv 5708 (1948)

R'Mordechai son of R'Simcha Yulevich

He was one of the last elders of our town. He lived by the toil of his hands, until he moved to a Home for the Aged, together with his wife. There too, he continued to help, as much as he could, the lonely old people. Even after he lost his sight, he would get up in the middle of the night to help, while reciting every hour chapters of the Book of Psalms. When his friends tried to prevent him from making this effort, he would reply: "Every Jew who is in need of Heavenly mercy – the Psalms can help him and bring him comfort…"

He gave charity all the time (after his death his family found hundreds of invoices and notes from social institutions and Yeshivas).

The day he arrived on Aliya to Eretz Israel was the happiest day of his life.

He left a great family, involved in the life of the country, a son and a daughter, grandchildren, great-grandchildren - gg-grandchildren and ggg-grandchildren.

Died in Tel Aviv, Kislev 5715

Menashe Yulevich (Latocha)

[Page 377]

Mina daughter of **R"Mordechai (Yulevich) Lachs,** her husband and their four daughters.

Perished in Stolin on 29 Elul 5702

[Page 378]

Yakov son of R'Mordechai Yulevich z"l

Always ready to help, as if he lived for his fellow man, not for himself.

Of an extra-ordinary good heart, full of mercy, he would say: "How else could one act? It is the duty of every man to act this way!"

Every person from our town who made Aliya, will always remember how he helped them as they came, with all his heart and all his soul.

He was an honest and work-loving man. In the later years of his life he left his work as a tailor and went to work in a factory in Haifa. There tragedy struck, when a steam boiler exploded and he lost his young life. He could have done a great deal of more good - and he was killed in the prime of his life.

We mourn our loss and we shall not forget him. May his memory be blessed.

May his Soul be Bound in the Bond of Life

[Page 379]

R'Nathan son of R'Mordechai Yulevich

During the difficult years in Eretz Israel, he applied for a "Certificate of Aliya" for himself and his family. This was a daring step, but the burning desire for Eretz Israel was strong. In 1925 he made Aliya with his family.

A quiet and modest man, he accepted lovingly the "pains of adaptation," even when he was out of work. He strongly opposed those who spoke ill of the country. He was a God-fearing man and kept our tradition but at the same time he understood the spirit of the young generation and always found a way to defend them. He raised his sons and daughters in the spirit of love of the country and love of work.

He followed closely the political events and expressed his hope that we shall, sooner or later, reach independence. However, he did not have the merit to see the establishment of our State. He died a painless death [lit. "died by a kiss"] – in the prime of his life, aged 52.

May his Soul be Bound in the Bond of Life

Chaia-Kreina (daughter of R'Mordechai Yulevich) Oleynik and her daughter Devora
(perished in the Holocaust)

[Page 380]

Dov (Berl) son of R'Zev Latocha

The news that Dov fell in battle during WWI - in 1915 - struck us like thunder on a clear day.

He was the hope of the family and a great future was expected: he was God-fearing, sharp of mind, studious and diligent, gentle and modest.

R'Yakov Winik would tell, that he saw in the synagogue remarks and new interpretations on the margins of the Talmud pages - and they testified to sharpness and depth. He mentioned it to the rabbi R'Moshe Millstein z"l, who revealed to him that the author of the remarks was R'Dov son of R'Zev. The remarks were the fruit of the mind of a genius; Dov was immersed [lit. swam] in the "Sea of the Talmud" and collected pearls. He was considered a wonder in the eyes of the Tora scholars in our town.

When the bitter news arrived - his father almost lost his mind and his mother suffered indescribable pains of the soul, and the entire family and town mourned him.

May his memory be blessed

Menashe Yulevich

[Page 381]

In memory of my mother, my teacher **Chana Rubenstein**, my
brother **Yehuda**, his wife **Rivka** and their daughter **Tehilla**, my
sister **Eshka** and her husband **Binyamin Starobinski** with their
children **Shulamit** and **Avraham**, and my sister **Sheindl** - who
perished in the Holocaust with all the holy martyrs of the Jewish
people.

   May their Souls be Bound in the Bond of Life

                    Sara Rubenstein-Buchhalter
                              Avihail

[Page 382]

In memory of our parents **Chaim-Bezalel** and **Dina Kolpanitsky**, our brother **Yitzhak** and his wife **Bella nee Tchetchik** and their children **Esther, Eliezer-Aharon** and **Batia** – victims of the terrible Holocaust

A Monument to their Memory

Shlomo, Lea, Elka, Sara, Yehudit and Yehuda
and their families in Israel and in the United States

[Page 383]

In memory of our aunt **Batia (Basha) Pederaski (nee Rubenstein) and the members of her family:**

Feigel, Chaim, Eshka, her husband **Boaz** and their children **Yosef, Yakov** and **Pesia** – victims of the Holocaust. They were uprooted, and no remnant was left.

Their names will never be forgotten

Members of the Family

[Page 384]

R'Noah son of R'Avraham Rubenstein (born in the village of Poritz) and his wife, Yehudit. Their home was open to any traveler. Mrs. Yehudit died in 1926. R'Noah made Aliya to Eretz Israel in 1934. Died in Tel Aviv in 1946. His son Yosef and his wife Khasia were murdered in Lenin. His son Aizik-Michael, his wife and their five children were murdered by the Nazis in Starobin.

Mourning them:

Their daughter Sara and her husband Ben-Zion Forman

Their daughter Tzipora and her husband Yosef Halperin

[Page 385]

Leeba (nee Kabak) Rubenstein

Noah son of R'Yehuda Rubenstein
Died 17 Kislev 5712 (1951)

Noah was born in Lenin, was an educated man and a famous timber merchant. When his children grew up and he wanted to give them a good education, he moved with his family to Pinsk and later to Warsaw.

Their home in Lenin was a meeting place for Zionists and Culture lovers.

Their daughters **Rachel** and **Hadassa** made Aliya with the "Third Aliya" [*Ha'aliya Hashlishit*] and were among the founders of the kibbutz *Mishmar Ha'emek*.

Before WWII broke out he made Aliya with his wife and their son **Naftali**, and after living some time in Tel Aviv, they built a home for themselves in *Mishmar Ha'emek*.

Noah and Leeba died in *Mishmar Ha'emek* and were put there to eternal rest.

May their memory be blessed

[Page 386]

The Reibach Family

In memory of my beloved who died untimely:

My father **R'Moshe** son of **Avraham** – died 22 Adar 5685 (1925).

My mother **Feigel**, my sister **Lyuba**, her son **Moshe**, her daughter **Miriam** and her husband **Pinchas Galetzki** – who were shot by the Hitlerism murderers in 1942, in Mikshewitch

My brother Shlomo, died in Moscow in 5711 (1951)

May their memory be blessed

Their son and brother
Dov Reibach

[Page 387]

In memory of our father, our teacher **R'Shamay** son of **R'Yakov Rubenstein** and our mother, our teacher **Chana-Miriam**.

Their memory will remain in our hearts forever…

Mourning them, their children:
Esther, Sara, Lea and Dov

In memory of our brother **Lipa** son of **Shamay Rubenstein**, his wife **Liza** and their daughter **Baba**, who fell prey to the wild Nazi murderers.

May this book be a monument on their unknown graves.

                              Esther, Sara, Lea and Dov

[Page 388]

In memory of our dear beloved

Our father, our teacher **R'Elyakim** son of **R'Ovadyahu**

Our mother, our teacher **Miriam** daughter of **R'Yitzhak (nee Rubenstein)**

Migdalovich

Who perished with the entire Community of Lenin on 1 Elul 5702 (1942)

May their memory be blessed

                    Mordechai and Vitya and their families

[Page 389]

In memory of our beloved: Our sister **Sara**, our
sister **Sheindl** and her baby

Who perished in Lenin on 1 Elul 5702 (1942)

And our brother **Yitzhak**, who was declared missing in action
in WWII in the Russian Army.

May their memory be blessed

Mordechai and Vitya and their families

[Page 390]

In memory of our parents **R'Mordechai** and **Esther Mishelov** and our brothers and sisters **Shmuel, Shekhna, Pesia** and **Malka** who were murdered by the Nazis, and, may they be inscribed for a long life: **Lea and Shoshana** in **Israel** and **Lipa** in the USA, who mourn their memory.

In memory of my father **R'Yitzhak Danenberg** and my mother **Esther**, who perished by the hands of the Nazis.

Mourning their memory - their only daughter **Chava**

[Page 391]

R'Chaim Slutsky   Yosef, son of R'Chaim Slutsky

Perished in Mikshewitch and with them - **Fanny, Michael and Yehudit Slutsky**

Aharon Migdalovich and his wife **Malka** - perished in Mikshewitch and with them: Israel, **Yehudit and Sheindl Migdalovich**

Mourning them:
their son Herzl and his family

[Page 392]

Frada Singalovski   **R'Avraham-Zelig Singalovski**

In memory of our dear parents and sister

My father **Eliezer-Chaim** son of **R'Kalman Lilenberg**
My mother **Nechama** daughter of **R'Baruch (nee Zhorbalov)**
My sister **Beile** daughter of **Eliezer-Chaim**

Perished by the hands of the murderers in 1942 in Lenin and in
Hantzewitz

Their son and her brother
Avraham Lilenberg

[Page 393]

The memory of our parents and our sisters will remain in our hearts forever

Masha daughter of **R'Shekhna nee Feinstein** from Slutzk, died in Lenin on Thursday, 16 Menachem-Av 5688 (2.8.1928)

R'Chaim son of **R'Elyakim Slutsky**, died in Lenin, on Tuesday 2nd day of Rosh Chodesh Tamuz, 5695 (2.7.1935)

Vitya Tennenbaum, daughter
of **R'Chaim Slutsky**, perished
in the Pinsk Ghetto, 1942

Chaia-Feiga Segal, daughter
of **R'Chaim Slutsky**, died in
Warsaw, the 3rd day of
Chanuka, 27 Kislev 5694

Families:
S. Slutsky - Moscow
I. Slutsky - Tel Aviv

[Page 394]

Dr. Yitzhak (Isac) Gitler, born in Kamenetz-Podolsk, graduate of the faculty of Natural Sciences and School of Medicine at the University of Kiev. Over thirty years served as doctor in Lenin.

His wife Chana (Anna), born in Muzir, a pharmacist, beautiful and gentle. Devotedly supported the needy of the town.

Aged sixty when they fell by the hands of the murderers

Their eldest son Dr. Tuvia-Tima, graduate of the School of Medicine at Warsaw University. He worked in the Jewish Hospital "Tchista" as assistant to prof. Dr. Filisok, worked on his post until he fell.

May their memories be for a blessing

Their son
Dr. Nachum Gitler, Tel Aviv

[Page 395]

R'Yakov Shkliar

Former resident of Lakhva. A friend of A. I. Slutsky and his
family. One of the leaders of the joint organization Lenin-
Lakhva. Was very active - and activated others - in helping the
needy. Had a warm heart and was always willing to listen.

Twice visited Israel and in 1954 took part in a memorial assembly
in honor of the martyrs of our town; on this occasion our
townspeople had the opportunity to get to know him and appreciate
him.

His life ended on 6 June 1955. It was a great loss.

His memory will remain with us forever and his soul is bound in
the bonds of our lives

[Page 396]

In memory of my parents **Israel-Aharon** and **Nechama-Sara**,
my brother **Yitzhak**, my brother **Efraim**, my
sisters **Nishka** and **Chaia**, who fell by the hands of
murderers, may their name be erased.

May God avenge their blood.

When our father fell by the hands of the murderers, we
remained seven young orphans, and my mother z"l raised
us with devotion and great efforts and was mother and
father for us.

Mourning them

Their daughter and sister **Devora Isseres**
(Kisselowitz)

[Page 397]

The family of **R'Yitzhak Reingold**, perished in the Lenin
Ghetto,
except **R'Yitzhak** who is living in Israel and his son who is
living in Russia.

R'Hirsh-Leib Gorodetski (deceased) and his three children
(perished in the Holocaust)

[Page 398]

In memory of my uncle **Yeshaya Slutsky** and his wife **Lea** z"l - at
the tombstone of my father,
may he rest in peace, in the cemetery of the Lenin
Community, **Avraham Yitzhak Slutsky**

The inscription on the tombstone:
Here is buried
A righteous and honest man

Moshe Yakov

Son of R'Yitzhak
Died 29 Adar I, 5687

May his soul be bound in the bond of life

[Page 399]

R'Dov ber Winik and his wife **Doba (Dobka)**, died
in Lenin

In memory of
Nechama daughter of **Shlomo Tzukrovitz** z"l

[Page 400]

R'Avraham Ozer and his wife **Itka z"l**

R'Moshe Valitzkin and his wife **Devora z"l**
("Moshe the Shteblewitzer")

[Page 401]

Risha, wife of **R'Yeshaya Tziglig**

Perished in the Holocaust
Second day of *Rosh Hodesh* Elul 5702

Mordechai son of **Yosef Tziglig**

He was known in our tows by the name "Motl Yoshke's." He was careful in keeping all *mitzvoth* [comandments], one of the first to get up early in the morning and go to the synagogue to pray. He was one of the esteemed people in town, and his place in the Old Synagogue was at the Eastern Wall. He prayed with enthusiasm and devotion. For many years, he was the one to blow the Shofar during the High Holy Days.

He was a scholar. He always found time to look into a book. Since his childhood he was a friend of my father z'l. He was the only Jew in our town who worked for many years as an employee in the Agarkov Estate, and thus enjoyed special privileges.

His home was a meeting place for culture lovers. He gave his sons a good education - his son and his daughter are medical doctors, they live in Moscow.

May his memory be blessed

M. Zaichik

[Page 402]

Mordechai son of R'Yosef Zaichik

Mordechai was born in 1919 in Lenin to Yosef and Yachna Zaichik. His father worked in a plywood factory in Mikshewitz and before WWI he moved there.

Mordechai was given a Jewish and Zionist education; when he grew up he learned carpentry and began to help his father in the sustenance of the family.

When the Russians occupied the town, he began to work in the factory in Mikshewitz and in 1940 he was drafted to the Russian army and was sent to serve at the Finland border. When the Russian-German war broke out, he served in the Red Army and was one of the first to fight the German invaders. He excelled in his service and reached the rank of First Sergeant and received medals as a tank commander.

His family was murdered in Mikshewitz, with the local Jewish population. Mordechai was spared during the entire war, but one month before the end of the war the fate caught up with him; in 1945 his death was reported to the family.

His cousin
Yehosua Lichtenstein,

from Lakhva

NAME INDEX

www.ingramcontent.com/pod-product-compliance
Lightning Source LLC
Chambersburg PA
CBHW062017090426

42811CB00005B/884